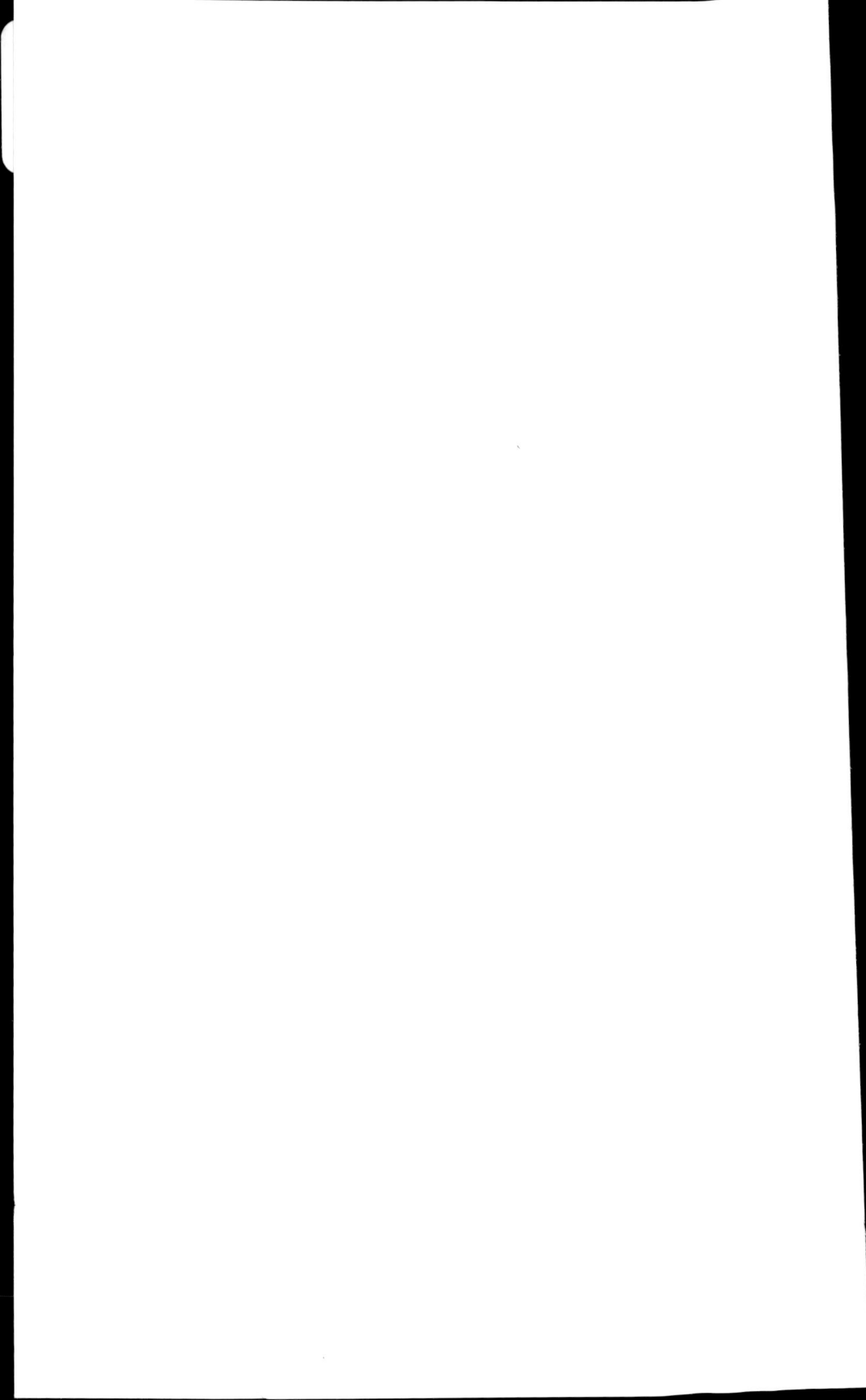

JEAN BETHKE ELSHTAIN

CATHOLIC IDEAS FOR A SECULAR WORLD

O. Carter Snead, series editor

The purpose of this interdisciplinary series is to feature authors from around the world who will expand the influence of Catholic thought on the most important conversations in academia and the public square. The series is "Catholic" in the sense that the books will emphasize and engage the enduring themes of human dignity and flourishing, the common good, truth, beauty, justice, and free-dom in ways that reflect and deepen principles affirmed by the Catholic Church for millennia. It is not limited to Catholic authors or even works that explicitly take Catholic principles as a point of departure. Its books are intended to demonstrate the diversity and enhance the relevance of these enduring themes and principles in numerous subjects, ranging from the arts and humanities to the sciences.

JEAN BETHKE ELSHTAIN

Politics, Ethics, and Society

EDITED BY
Debra Erickson and Michael Le Chevallier

UNIVERSITY OF NOTRE DAME PRESS

NOTRE DAME, INDIANA

University of Notre Dame Press
Notre Dame, Indiana 46556
www.undpress.nd.edu

Library of Congress Cataloging-in-Publication Data

Names: Erickson, Debra, editor. | Le Chevallier, Michael Thomas, 1984– editor.
Title: Jean Bethke Elshtain : politics, ethics, and society / edited by Debra Erickson and
  Michael Le Chevallier.
Description: Notre Dame : University of Notre Dame Press, 2018. | Includes index. |
Identifiers: LCCN 2017055859 (print) | LCCN 2018000915 (ebook) |
  ISBN 9780268103071 (pdf) | ISBN 9780268103088 (epub) |
  ISBN 9780268103057 (hardcover : alk. paper) | ISBN 0268103054 (hardcover : alk.
  paper)
Subjects: LCSH: Elshtain, Jean Bethke, 1941–2013. | Ethics. | Political science—
  Philosophy. | Social philosophy.
Classification: LCC BJ354.E473 (ebook) | LCC BJ354.E473 J43 2018 (print) |
  DDC 191—dc23
LC record available at https://lccn.loc.gov/2017055859

CONTENTS

ACKNOWLEDGMENTS

This book results from the labor of many contributors over several years. First and foremost, the editors wish to thank the McDonald Agape Foundation for funding the Engaged Mind conference series, out of which these essays emerged, and for its support of the publication of this volume. Al McDonald in particular has been a tireless supporter in sustaining these ongoing conversations with Jean Bethke Elshtain and her work. Thanks are also due to the conference participants whose contributions shaped the conversation but are not directly represented here.

We are also grateful for the administrative and material support provided by the Martin Marty Center at the University of Chicago Divinity School, which provided a home for the project throughout its life. Here we recognize William Schweiker, past director of the Marty Center, for his insight and encouragement; Susie McGee, for her logistical capability and deft handling of details; and Terren Wein, director of communications, for guiding publicity and marketing. Michelle Harrington assisted with the first conference, and numerous other members of the Divinity School community contributed time and talents to make this effort a success.

In the process of shaping the original contributions into a single book, we received advice from John D. Carlson on publication, who also wrote an essay for this volume. We thank Steve Wrinn at the University of Notre Dame Press for his support and guidance, Scott Barker for his excellent copyediting, and all the staff at the press.

The group of contributors to this volume is without parallel. Their reputations speak for themselves. We are grateful for the opportunity to bring these thinkers into conversation with Elshtain's work and with each other, and for their patience in the process of bringing their essays to publication.

We also want to acknowledge the significant help we received from Jean Elshtain's family, including her husband, Errol Elshtain, and son, Eric Elshtain, in the writing of the introduction and the preparation of the manuscript. We look forward to the fruits of their effort to publish the remainder of her unpublished work.

The coeditors recognize the essential nature of each other's contribution to the project. Since we began working together on the conference planning, now more than five years ago, we discovered that our talents meshed well, and we both believe that without the other's work, the book likely would not have come to fruition.

Both of us were fortunate to have worked closely with Jean Elshtain in the years before her death. Her gifts to us are too numerous to recount, but we hope that our debts to her are at least partially discharged with the publication of this book.

Debra Erickson   Michael Le Chevallier
Bloomsburg University   University of Chicago

ABBREVIATIONS

ALP   *Augustine and the Limits of Politics.* Notre Dame, IN: University of Notre Dame Press, 1995.
 DT   *Democracy on Trial.* New York: Basic Books, 1995.
  JA   *Jane Addams and the Dream of American Democracy: A Life.* New York: Basic Books, 2002.
 JWT   *Just War against Terror: The Burden of American Power in a Violent World.* Second edition. New York: Basic Books, 2004.
  NW   *New Wine and Old Bottles: International Politics and Ethical Discourse.* Notre Dame, IN: University of Notre Dame Press, 1998.
   PT   *Power Trips and Other Journeys: Essays in Feminism as Civic Discourse.* Madison: University of Wisconsin Press, 1990.
PMPW   *Public Man, Private Woman: Women in Social and Political Thought.* 2nd ed., with a new afterword by the author. Princeton, NJ: Princeton University Press, 1993.
  RP   *Real Politics: At the Center of Everyday Life.* Baltimore: Johns Hopkins University Press, 2000.
   S   *Sovereignty: God, State, and Self.* New York: Basic Books, 2008.
 WAW   *Who Are We? Critical Reflections and Hopeful Possibilities.* Grand Rapids, MI: William B. Eerdmans, 2000.
  WW   *Women and War, with a New Epilogue.* 2nd ed. Chicago: University of Chicago Press, 1995.

Introduction

Jean Bethke Elshtain, Life and Work

Debra Erickson and Michael Le Chevallier

A DEMOCRATIC LIFE

Who is Jean Bethke Elshtain to the work she leaves behind? For certain ethical thinkers, their biography is interesting, but incidental to their work: Peter Lombard, John Calvin, or, at an extreme, Thomas Aquinas, whose anonymity as an author is heralded as a virtue. For others, their biography and their writings are inseparable: Augustine and Luther, Bonhoeffer and Havel. Elshtain never published a memoir, but she often peppered her essays and books with small anecdotes and stories. These are not stories of her travels or her many famous friends and acquaintances, including a pope, a cardinal, and a president; they are much more quotidian. As her grandson Bobby recounted at her funeral, he had shared late nights with her when she would discuss drinking vodka in the Soviet Union, but she also explained "why it was that she didn't dilate on such stories at the dinner table, since not everyone might have the chance she had to travel the world, and she did not want to trumpet her own opportunities."[1] The same principle seems to undergird the anecdotes found in her writing. Instead, she relates rather ordinary

1

stories: a childhood experience of going to a Home Economics class with her mother, a lecture she heard as an undergraduate, or her daughter's response to a book Elshtain had given her.

To what end did she include these stories? Amplifying the dedication to her "noisy children," Elshtain writes in the acknowledgments of her first book, "I owe to Sheri, Heidi, Jenny, and Eric, precisely *because* they were never hustled out of sight, earshot, or mind as I struggled with this text (they wouldn't have stood for interdictions of silence anyway), whatever deep, enriching connection *Public Man, Private Woman* retains to what people call *real life* in all its untidy concrete particularity" (*PMPW*, xviii). Through this appeal to her own life, Elshtain maintained a connection in her political and ethical writings to ordinary life and its mundane concerns. These stories are not added as mere rhetorical window dressing, but as a matter of principle. She writes in an essay entitled "My Mother, the Expert": "When we don't attend to local knowledge and lived experience, our politics grows eerily abstract and impositional. We begin to assume that because we have arrived at this position or that as a result of oh-so-careful argument, our views must in some sense come closer to the 'truth' than positions not similarly thought out or tested through argument."[2] Elshtain draws out the untidy particularity through her biography, giving voice and attention to the ordinary, modeling a challenge to the public/private distinction across her career.

Jean Paulette Bethke was born on January 6, 1941, to Paul Bethke and Hellen Lind, in the town of Windsor, in "the irrigated farm country of northern Colorado." Her grandfather had a piece of farm land there that he had acquired through "unrelenting effort on his part and the part of his family, and stern self-reliance, and just a bit of luck."[3] Her "Grandpa in the country," as they called him, had come over from "the Old Country," and often spoke out of his "deep-rooted ambivalence" for America, airing "his cynicism about the way power and money controlled things in his adopted homeland" and "to acknowledge his bitterness at having spent his first Christmas Eve in America shoveling a mountain of soggy, half-frozen manure for one of the big shots."[4] Although his wife would shush him by reminding him of what would have waited for them (Volga Germans) back in Russia, his reticence lasted only while his wife was in earshot. Elshtain later pieced together what she diagnosed as the source of his "dis-ease": a certain awareness of what "America did to families and communities," recalling "an earlier time of human solidarity when farm families gathered for picnics and polka dances, for baptisms and confirmations, for marriages and funerals."[5] Elshtain inherited from both her grandmother and her grandfather an appreciation of the virtues of America and a keen sense of its vices, along with a generous sympathy that did not temper her critique.

Elshtain grew up in the small settlement of Timnath, Colorado (population 185), a village by any standards. The appeal of the village runs through Elshtain's writings. In a 2011 public dialogue between Elshtain and Nicholas Wolterstorff, Wolterstorff drew a connection between his hometown ("a small farming village in Minnesota"), her village, and the type of community created at Hull-House, the settlement house in Chicago cofounded in 1889 by Jane Addams, the subject of Elshtain's 2002 biography. He described it as "a village in the city," saying that "the neighborliness of a small village was what characterized Hull-House," where you may not be friends with everybody, but you are neighbors with everybody.[6] Indeed, Elshtain's preface to *Augustine and the Limits of Politics* opens with such a village, but "a village of the mind" (*ALP*, xiii). Elshtain is not naïve about the dangers of small towns, where indeed everybody knows everybody and is in everybody's business. She is even more aware of the dangers of a blinding and "self-indulgent nostalgia" for a simpler, seemingly more wholesome past (*PMPW*, 347). Nevertheless, Elshtain points constantly towards the dignity of these ordinary small-town lives, where there are authentic examples of citizenship.

In an essay responding to literary authors writing about the weightiness and narrowness of small towns, Elshtain writes,

I appreciate the attacks on the small-mindedness of small places, but I am determined to lift up that which is good about small towns. For these were, and are, places where people are compelled to engage and cannot easily repudiate and spurn and ignore their neighbors. That ordinary people in our culture continue to pine for the idea of the small town means they are searching for a landscape that is not necessarily always warm and friendly, but rather, one that is recognizably human—that has discernible form and scale and invites us to inhabit and engage it. (*Real Politics*, 320)

Elshtain is not concerned with the perfect city, Plato's "city of words," but with a "human landscape" (*ALP*, xiii). In this appeal to the everyday, the small city where people are neighbors and they talk to each other, Elshtain finds the real stuff of political life.

It was also in Timnath's public school, small enough that grades one to twelve were all held in one building, where Elshtain's "democratic dreams" were nurtured. Students there were required to memorize the Declaration of Independence and the Gettysburg Address. In her combined seventh- and eighth-grade class, their teacher, Miss McCarthy, would signal the students to hum "The Battle Hymn of the Republic" as she recited the Gettysburg Address. The melodrama of it all left the "hummers in stitches." "But," Elshtain writes, "I never forgot the Gettysburg Address and its promise of democratic equality" (*Democracy on Trial*, 84).

There also, Jean Bethke became a budding feminist and a lover of pop culture, especially film. She recounts going alone at age eight to the movie theater to see Ingrid Bergman in *Joan of Arc*. She was so taken by Bergman's Joan that she marched directly afterward to the town's combined barber shop/beauty parlor and had her hair chopped to resemble Joan's by telling them it was her mother's wish that it should be cut short enough to be out of the way for doing her chores. Elshtain comments in *Women and War* that she cannot remember her mother's response, so bad it was. She writes,

> While I cannot conjure up any details of the family furor, I can recapture—as in an exemplary tale with me as dauntless heroine —my new sense of freedom, even though I had been quite vain about my hair. I did not care what the boys or the girls or the teachers said. One day I would be a leader of men, too. Maybe a warrior. Maybe a martyr—though there didn't seem to be much call for martyrs anymore. I could worry about that later. In the meantime, I dreamed of action, of Joan, of myself in male battle attire, fighting for morally worthy ends. Oh yes.[7] (*WW*, 17)

One wonders, is it mere coincidence that she shared a name with this childhood hero?

At ten, Elshtain experienced "the watershed event of her childhood": a polio diagnosis (*WW*, 19). When she returned home from the hospital, she was bedridden, unable to stand or walk. She recounts knowing the prognosis was bad. As she gained strength, her two childhood heroes, Joan of Arc and Abraham Lincoln, existed side by side as dreams in her head, "one of the warrior-soldier, a woman; the other of the war-hating, compassionate leader, a man" (*WW*, 19). These stood as two figures who did not give up, but carried forward in their lives with determination despite opposition and hardship. They helped her not to give up. Yet she also was a realist, and she was known to say throughout her life, "We must play the hand we are dealt."[8] Elshtain recounts, "After polio, Joan faded away. Warriors must be strong, able to run and leap and tear about. As I could no longer run, and was moreover soon caught up in the changes of adolescence, the story of Joan became a memory of childish romance and revolt; but that of Lincoln resonated through high school, into college, never deserting me, rekindled as I moved into adulthood and continued to struggle with what it means to be an American" (*WW*, 19).

Her hopes of becoming a warrior dashed, a new dream took hold. Reading *Life* magazine, Elshtain's attention was caught by the images of Marguerite Higgins, the female war correspondent. She decided that she too wanted to become a war correspondent. This dream led her to discover the writings of World War II journalist Ernie Pyle, who died at the end of the war. She checked out every volume of his collected reportage from the Bookmobile, Timnath's mobile library. Pyle's stories did not glorify war. Instead, he was a "chronicler of Everyman at War" (*WW*, 20). He demystified war, pointing once more to the human and mundane, even in the midst of something that can hardly be called quotidian. Elshtain writes, "War enlisted men in a common cause. Pyle brings such idealizations down to earth. And after a while, the ordinariness of everyday army life, dominated by boredom, sleeplessness, and fear took on an aura all their own, a kind of populist dignity very different from that evoked by George Washington rearing stiffly, all brocaded and bewigged, atop a monumental white stallion" (*WW*, 21).

For Elshtain, Pyle's writing invoked and involved his readers, reminding them that in a democracy, it was their war.

Despite what she was told by the doctor, Elshtain would relearn to walk. She pushed her body to its limits, an intransigent aspect of her character recognizable to all who knew her. From this time, she also pushed deeper into the life of the mind, and in the process exhausted the wares of the Bookmobile, exploring well beyond the limits of her now-disabled body and the small village of Timnath.

Elshtain attended public schools in Colorado and graduated from Colorado State University (AB, 1963). Like many women at the time, the questions raised by *Public Man, Private Woman* were not external and abstract, but real and intimate. Already married and a mother as a college student in the 1960s, she felt poignantly the split between the public and academic domain, where she was "taught the ways of the political world as the 'realist' . . . understood it," and the private realm, where she was the "the private dreamer, mother, novel reader, and Beatles buff" (*WW*, 31). It was a world split between "official, public *discourse*" and "unsystematic, private *understanding*" that she sometimes managed to reconcile in her own journal writing (a practice she picked up at age fourteen and kept up throughout her life).

Elshtain transgressed that boundary between private and public in practice long before she did in writing. She would later recount how she sometimes attended class with her children in tow, a practice no more routine then than it is today. In her late years of teaching, she designated Wednesdays as her day with her youngest granddaughter, Christie, whether they went to the Lincoln Park Zoo or to lectures and meetings at the University of Chicago. This arrangement was not due to a lack of childcare options (as in her student days), but from a commitment to family that pervaded her life and career. "I want to be sure that she remembers her grandma," Elshtain explained.[9] In her scholarship and in her life, Elshtain did not shy away from making the private world visible in the public realm.

After her first marriage to Norman Shaw ended in divorce, Jean married Errol Elshtain on September 3, 1965, and he would be her companion until her death. By this point, she had also earned a master's degree as a Woodrow Wilson Fellow from the University of Wisconsin.

Inspired by John F. Kennedy's call to public service, she received her PhD in 1973 from Brandeis University in politics with a focus on political theory. In a time when data-driven political science was ascendant, her dissertation was entitled (somewhat ironically, given her enduring emphasis on the concrete reality of everyday life) *Women and Politics: A Theoretical Analysis.*

This period marked another shift in Elshtain's life, as her intellectual and personal interests turned towards religion. Following the revision of her dissertation, published as *Public Man, Private Woman* in 1981, Elshtain received some unexpected critiques. She was suspected of being "covertly religious," accused (tenuously) of being "a believer,"[10] and of harboring "religious convictions."[11] These comments were surprising to Elshtain, because at the time she did not consider herself very religious, and certainly not a "believer" who wore her religious identity on her sleeve. Raised Lutheran, Elshtain remarked in an essay that she was a deist for two whole weeks in college before becoming an agnostic and then an "anguished agnostic."[12] Needless to say, she did not remain an agnostic. She returned first to the Lutheran faith of her youth and at the very end of her life, after a long engagement with the Catholic intellectual tradition, was received into full communion with the Roman Catholic Church on November 2, 2011, in the chapel of the archbishop of Chicago's residence by her intellectual and spiritual friend, Francis Cardinal George, then archbishop of Chicago.

Elshtain identified a few reasons that brought her to the question of religion: first, an engagement with the Western political canon in graduate school, where religion played an undeniable (though often excised) role in figures like Hobbes and Locke. We can see this influence in *Public Man, Private Woman*, where she drew upon classic religious figures of the Western tradition. Second, ever the contrarian, she felt compelled to offer a sympathetic defense on behalf of "all those unnamed men and women who were trying to live decent lives, to do right by their families and their communities, to live with some dignity, and who were sustained in that by their faith"[13] against a full frontal academic attack by a "radical separatist wing that engaged in vicious attacks on religious traditions and on people who had religious views."[14] Finally, those same reviews of *Public Man, Private Woman* pushed her to reconsider religion.

Indeed, though still a nontheological text, she retrospectively identifies the final chapter, which addresses the "search for an ethical polity," as the beginning of a moral quest that trails through all of her work (*Who Are We*, xvi). On that journey, she found intellectual kinship with Augustine, Luther, Reinhold Niebuhr, Martin Luther King, Jr., and John Paul II, among other religious and theological thinkers.

Elshtain's teaching career began at the University of Massachusetts at Amherst, where she taught from 1973 to 1988. Elshtain then joined the faculty of Vanderbilt University as the first woman to hold an endowed professorship in the history of that institution. As her reputation grew, she became widely sought after as a lecturer and speaker, keeping a grueling schedule of travel that spanned the globe. In 1995, she was appointed the Laura Spelman Rockefeller Professor of Social and Political Ethics in the Divinity School at the University of Chicago, and was jointly appointed in the Department of Political Science and the Committee on International Relations. Additionally, Elshtain held visiting professorships at Oberlin College, Yale University, and Harvard University; the Leavey Chair in the Foundations of American Freedom at Georgetown University; and was the Visiting Distinguished Professor of Religion and Public Life at Baylor University's Institute for Studies of Religion.

In the midst of her teaching career, Elshtain's research moved in multiple directions, unconstrained by tradition or disciplinary boundaries. Subsequent sections of this introduction will address the major themes in her work: feminism and the family; democracy and civil society; religion, theology, and politics; and international relations and just war. Yet even these broad themes do not completely cover Elshtain's career as an academic and as a public intellectual, which included forays into bioethics, political commentary, and pop culture.

For Elshtain, pop culture was another window into "what's going on," for good or ill. She loved movies, seeing most new releases in the theater. She used films like *Seven*, *Saving Private Ryan*, and *The Man Who Shot Liberty Valance* in her ethics courses and also wrote numerous movie reviews. She devoured mystery novels—"the last moral fiction," she called them. Literature also had a place in her classroom, once assigning P. D. James's *Children of Men* to a course on religion in public life. Elshtain was also a constant commenter on culture. She wrote a five-part series for *First Things* entitled the "Newtape Files," extending C. S. Lewis's *Screwtape Letters* for a new generation. In the persona of a demon trying to mislead the faithful, she commented on Madonna, Woody Allen, rap lyrics, and even misinterpretations of Freud, of whom she was a fan.

Although her life was marked by a prolonged engagement with the written word, Elshtain was also influenced by contemporary political events on both the national and global scales. She was both teased and criticized for an exhausting travel schedule that brought her face-to-face with some of the most significant political movements of her lifetime. In 1982, shortly after the publication of her first book, Elshtain was in Argentina at the invitation of a center for the study of women in culture and society. While wandering the streets of Buenos Aires, during a morning free from her sessions, she came across the Plaza de Mayo. She recounts,

> There, walking in a silent circle around a statue/monument in the heart of the Plaza, were hundreds of women wearing white scarves, some well-dressed and middle-class, others in rougher more rustic attire, their dark Indian faces a bold contrast to the whiteness of their covered heads. I noticed embroidered names and dates on the backs of the scarves and visible around the necks of these women were photographs of young men or women, some couples, some children. Beneath the photos were printed names and dates. Necklaces of despair: wearing grief as others might wear pearls or brooches.[15]

These were the "Mothers of the Disappeared," women whose children and grandchildren were abducted by the Junta during the military dictatorships starting in 1976, with no active confirmation of their death or survival. At the end of her brief stay, Elshtain was unsatisfied with what little she could find in writing about the Mothers.

Returning to Argentina in 1986 at the invitation of a former student and another woman who had served as a translator during that first trip, Elshtain requested the chance to meet with some of the Mothers.

Elshtain recounts the difficulty of doing justice to the Mothers on her return: "I had no desire to turn the Mothers into data. I was bearing witness. This, apparently, is an activity that has no home in our institutions of higher learning."[16] The success of *Public Man, Private Woman* may have led people to expect her to follow it with another book of theory, but Elshtain was drawn to the story of the Mothers and their struggle for truth and justice.

Although she would never complete the book she hoped to write on their struggle, the Mothers' voices and example remained with her and recurred in her writing on democracy. Driven by their private losses, these women found a collective voice and formed a public "we" despite the state terror that sought to erase protest and rend social relations. Elshtain writes, "By fusing a language of grief with a language of human rights, they not only kept alive the particular realities and identities of individuals, their sons and daughters, tormented and lost to state terror, but issued a call to nonviolent arms to their fellow Argentines and to the wider world: Protect mothers and families, but embrace and protect a democratic constitution as well" (*DT*, 130). Elshtain's attention to the Mothers highlights not only her care for the ideals they espoused, but also a methodological interest in the appeal to actual people— people who were in many ways ordinary but for the courage they had to demand accountability from their leaders. In her attention to the power of ordinary citizens, she recalls the lessons of her childhood.

During this same period, Elshtain's attention was also drawn to Eastern Europe, where the stirrings of a similar political dissent caught her eye. Elshtain first encountered Václav Havel, then a political dissident and premier playwright, and later the first president of Czechoslovakia (and after, the Czech Republic), through his writings from prison. In the face of totalitarian rule, Havel encouraged people to "live in truth," that is to say, to live as if they had a freedom they did not yet have, knowing that the consequences might be great, but that they would leave behind a powerful example for others. Indeed, Havel became an exemplar for her through her life. If Augustine was Elshtain's intellectual hero, Havel was her political hero. In her office at the University of Chicago, a political poster of him hung prominently on the wall, paired with a picture of them at a roundtable event together. They were the only such photos from a life filled with notable encounters.

Havel elicited Elshtain's admiration for the prospect of democracy abroad, and she ranked him with Reinhold Niebuhr and Jane Addams as a public intellectual for today.[17] In his writings, she found a kindred spirit, one who embodied a philosophy not unlike her own: he spoke out against the relativization of morals, identifying the need for political society to be founded on a transcendent anchor; he wrote of the need for a civil society robust enough to awaken citizens to their responsibility; and he identified politics not as the achievement of an election cycle but, as he would say in October 1992 to her and a group of others regarding Europe post-1989, as "the long tunnel at the end of the light,"[18] that is to say, the constant work of the everyday politics of a people.

The list of commendations that Elshtain received is long. Among many honors and awards, she was selected as a fellow of the American Academy of Arts and Sciences, a fellow at the Institute for Advanced Study at Princeton University, and a Guggenheim Fellow. She was a member of the boards of the National Humanities Center, the National Endowment for Democracy, and a member of the Council of the National Endowment for the Humanities. In 2006, she gave the prestigious Gifford Lectures, resulting in her final book *Sovereignty: God, State, and Self.* Adding to her lifelong influence on friends, peers, and dialogue partners, she mentored two generations of scholars.

Towards the end of her life, her health began to deteriorate due to postpolio complications, making it impossible to maintain the same vigorous schedule of lectures and teaching on top of her weekly commute between her home in Nashville, her teaching in Chicago, and whichever college or public institution had invited her to speak, lecture, or receive an award. On June 14, 2013, Elshtain was scheduled to give the Milton K. Wong Lecture in Vancouver, Canada. Given her health, flying was not a possibility. That same indomitable spirit that propelled her all her life took her on a 3,500-mile train journey from Nashville to Vancouver. It was to be her last speaking engagement. Returning by train, she suffered a heart attack in Minot, North Dakota. She died August 11, 2013, and was buried in Fort Collins, Colorado.

Jean Bethke Elshtain left behind her beloved family: her husband, Errol; her four children, Sheri, Heidi, Jenny, and Eric; and her four grandchildren, JoAnn, Bobby, Christopher, and Christie.

SEEKING THE ETHICAL POLITY

Elshtain also left behind a body of work rivaled by few of her peers. She brought 19 books to publication and wrote more than 600 essays for scholarly journals and journals of civic opinion, many of which later appeared in collected volumes. In addition to *Public Man, Private Woman*, *Augustine and the Limits of Politics*, and *Sovereignty*, her major books include *Women and War* (1987), an exploration of the traditional portrayal of women as noncombatants; *Democracy on Trial* (1995); and *Just War against Terror* (2003), a vigorous and widely debated moral argument for U.S. military engagement abroad.

As a scholar, she has been a controversial figure. As her University of Chicago colleague Susan Schreiner noted, following her death a trove of adjectives have been attributed to her: "controversial," "hard-nosed," "uncompromising," "a woman who stood her ground," "tough-minded," and, Schreiner's personal favorite, "against the grain." Schreiner adds her own adjective, perhaps one that is most fitting, because it captures how Elshtain might have seen herself. Calling to mind the Pauline exhortation to "be urgent in season and out of season," Schreiner writes that Elshtain was "intellectually out of season—and in a very real sense that was her calling, her vocation, her ministry."[19] This description alludes to a characteristically "Elshtainian" theme: she warned against the "rigidified categories" of the Left and the Right, liberal and conservative, which simply urged us to put on uniforms and to boo or cheer accordingly. She saw the terms as defunct, writing that "perhaps such recognitions [of unhelpful categories] will enable us to get off our increasingly unstable soapboxes and to 'put on our thinking caps,' as my first grade teacher, Mrs. Griffith, used to pipe cheerily each schoolday morning all those years ago."[20]

This description of an "off-season" thinker captures more than Elshtain's disdain for useless labels that prevent real thinking and genuine dialogue. Elshtain cut against the grain of culture as a matter of principle. She writes in *Who Are We*, "I take sloth to mean not simply inactivity but acquiescence in the conventions of one's day; a refusal to take up the burden of self-criticism; a falling into the zeitgeist unthinkingly, and in so doing, forgetting that we are made to 'serve God wittily, in the tangle of our minds'" (*WAW*, 83). Accordingly, she did not hesitate to critique reigning theories of the day. Elshtain's positions on controversial topics made her at times *persona non grata* among those who once considered her a vanguard and ally. She also habitually took on tasks of retrieval: of women in Western thought, of a near-forgotten democratic pioneer of the settlement-house movement, of Augustine for political thought, of just war doctrine in the post-Vietnam era, and of religious reflection on matters public.

In the sections below, we survey four distinct areas in which Elshtain both pushed new borders and cut against the grain. They follow her career in roughly chronological order.

WOMEN AND MEN IN PUBLIC AND PRIVATE

When it appeared in 1981, *Public Man, Private Woman* garnered wide attention and it has remained in print ever since. By this time, Elshtain had already been publishing for several years in journals such as *Dissent*, *Signs*, and *Salmagundi*. But *Public Man, Private Woman* cemented her reputation as an original thinker and a trenchant critic of both academic orthodoxy and extravagant experiments in political utopia. In this book, Elshtain brought the relationship of women to the polity onto center stage: what had been an afterthought for many of the key thinkers in the Western tradition became a central theme worthy of study on its own, and through it Elshtain turned a neglected topic into a coherent story.

At that time, asking about where women fit—as human beings with experiences distinct from men as the archetypical human—in political theory and public life was not yet routine. As Arlene Saxonhouse observes in this volume (chapter 2), what Elshtain accomplished in *Public Man, Private Woman* may seem commonplace now, but at the time, it was a pivotal intervention. The book also contained many of the hallmarks of Elshtain's later works. She insisted on two complementary claims: politics matters, but politics is not everything. Politics must attend to the common features of ordinary people's lives; it is bound by the fallible nature of the human beings who practice it. A politics that ignores, negates, or goes against the common features of human lives—which include men and women as distinct but sharing common (and morally equal) humanity; the desire for a family life that is separate from the public sphere; and the maintenance of local affiliations and loyalties that are not subsumed by an omniscient or omnipotent state—will be a distorted politics, severing rather than sustaining basic human bonds.

Though her later works turned to broader themes, Elshtain remained steadfastly feminist in the sense that she held that women's issues are human issues and that women share a civic equality with men. But she abjured a feminism that sought to eliminate all differences between men and women, to disenfranchise men, or to transform normal family life into a bureaucratic agency or juridical exercise in rights adjudication. Elshtain's conservative core held her back from some of the excesses of 1960s and 1970s radical feminism, and though the influence of a Shulamith Firestone or a Susan Brownmiller faded over time, Elshtain's reactions to that mode of thinking remained strong. She sought to conserve the institutions that sustained everyday life, and perhaps to reform them, but not to abolish them. Consequently, she believed the state had a responsibility to protect and support the institutions of family and community, making it possible for people to sustain particular attachments, rather than attempting to rationalize them through bureaucratic oversight (see "My Mother, the Expert"). Elshtain was always suspicious of totalitarian ideals, whether feminist or political. Elshtain's feminism was an attempt at redress, not revolution.

Elshtain's first single-authored book after *Public Man, Private Woman* introduces a second major theme, war, which would define her work for the next several decades. Difficult to classify, *Women and War* is not a history per se, though it dissects numerous historical examples. Neither is it traditional ethics or political theory. Instead, it argues for a particular relationship between women and warfare. In the same way as *Public Man, Private Woman* broke down the distinction between the public and the private (even as it in some ways reified it), *Women and War* redefined the archetypes that had assigned to men the role of active combatant and women the role of protector of hearth and home. Using the Spartan mother and Confederate woman as her paradigm cases, Elshtain showed that, as much as or more than men, women participated in the tradition of "armed civic virtue." Likewise, she mined war narratives to find examples of male responses to violence that participated more in the tradition of "beautiful soul" than did those Spartan or Confederate women.

As with *Public Man, Private Woman*, Elshtain confounded categories that consigned women to the private realm of personal morality and men to the arena of public virtue based on biological sex or gender perception alone. As John Carlson elucidates in this volume (chapter 12), in place of the Just Warrior/Beautiful Soul dichotomy, she offers instead the image of the chastened patriot, an idea she will defend until the end of her career, and a label that one can say with some level of confidence she would own to describe herself. In *Women and War*, Elshtain's methodological innovations are again on display: this book about war is not a book of strategy or the ethical argument she will later make in *Just War against Terror*. It is a kind of historical rhetorical analysis—Elshtain crafts her argument by paying attention to what people actually said, using their own words to challenge and build a theory about how we view gender in the context of war, and war in the context of gender. She resisted any simple identification of women with peace and virtue, and men with conflict and vainglory. Echoing her appeal to the Mothers of the Disappeared, she let women and men speak for themselves, so that her readers might listen and learn.

Politics, domesticity, and war are all brought together in the person of Jane Addams: a private citizen with public influence; a committed American but also an antiwar advocate; a writer but also an activist. Throughout the 1980s, Elshtain was drawn to Addams's life and writing, though Addams was dismissed by many feminists as a "maternalist," and others criticized residents of Hull-House as racist, criminally inclined, or oversexed.[21] This disregard spurred Elshtain to compile and publish a reader of Addams's essential writings,[22] along with an intellectual biography of Addams, *Jane Addams and the Dream of American*

Democracy (2002). As she wrote in the preface, "The reasons for Addams's posthumous eclipse are complex . . . although Addams's vision and action provided a basis for later social programs, her reputation and her contribution to American life have gone largely unrecognized. . . . Although Jane Addams has had her day, she has yet to receive her due" (*JA*, xxi–xxii).

Moreover, Addams exemplified much of what occupied Elshtain from her earliest works: women whose concern for the goods of the private realm (family, childrearing, ties of blood and affection) would lead them to become actors in the public sphere. In her work with immigrant women, Addams not only championed the dignity of the downtrodden, but also upheld basic American values of access to work, fairness, equality, and political participation. Much like Elshtain's, Addams's critique was cached within a firm belief in "the better angels of our nature." Though Addams herself was privileged and enjoyed the patronage of a circle of well-off women and men, a concern for the conditions of everyday life of regular people drove much of her work. Politics, then, truly was "at the center of everyday life."

DEMOCRACY AND CIVIL SOCIETY

Elshtain's books on Addams were produced during a period of sustained attention to democracy. Her short *Democracy on Trial* first appeared in 1995. In this book, a deceptively conversational tone belies the seriousness of her concerns. During an era when political correctness and identity politics arguably reached their zenith, Elshtain worried: Would the central promises of democracy—those of basic equality of persons, representative self-government, and limited government—hold? She worries not only about political fractures—political polarization and mistrust of political processes were already well entrenched—but also about social fragmentation: What of the poor, and of the promise that America had always extended that those who work hard will get ahead? What of the fraying of basic institutions, from families to civic organizations to churches, which had acted as schools for democracy? American democracy is a historical and political achievement, and its promise is unparalleled. That is why Elshtain is so worried: it is also fragile, and its disintegration would mean a loss as great as its achievement.

Throughout *Democracy on Trial*, she compares democracy with its thin counterfeits. Democracy is not merely a system, but a set of dispositions; it depends on certain virtues, including self-restraint, exercised for the common good. For each genuine virtue of democracy, there is a weak imposter: democratic debate is replaced by the plebiscite or juridical fiat; respect for individuals by individualism; social goods by aggregates of private goods; rights by entitlements. Themes Elshtain introduced in *Women and War* reemerge here, as democratic citizenship is contrasted not with armed civic virtue, but with various forms of corrosive individualism. She also brings ideas of public and private to bear on the American case, through the lenses of feminism, gay rights, and multicultural education.

Mirroring *Public Man, Private Woman*, she mines the history of political thought to illustrate democracy's checkered past, and she concludes *Democracy on Trial* with a set of guides for the future who are by now familiar to her readers: Arendt and Camus, King, the Mothers of the Disappeared, and Havel. Much like Elshtain, these thinkers' reflections arose not from abstract consideration of the ideal polity, but from a deep reflection on human nature and the possibilities and limitations that shared nature placed on the social order. These twentieth-century thinkers each survived times of severe threat to and even temporary eclipse of democracy, yet each bore witness to democracy's "enduring promise." Elshtain's eclectic group of fellow travelers is another hallmark of her intellectual style: despite indictments of her mature thought as "right-wing," Elshtain simply refused to align with an ideological camp. Like Luther, in whose religious tradition she was nurtured, Elshtain wrote as the times demanded.

Democracy on Trial is a tight, trenchant critique of the ills that plagued American democratic life at the end of the twentieth century. In making her case, Elshtain stiches together an astonishing range of contemporary phenomena, from gun violence to publicly funded health insurance. By the start of the twenty-first century, this theme was eclipsed in her work by a larger threat to the democratic project itself—the rise of illiberal, militant Islamic terror groups (at the time, primarily al-Qaeda). But at the close of what many people term "the American Century," the book was a call for Americans not to surrender their values, but to do the hard work—the hard *moral* work—that democracy requires. True democracy is more than voting, and certainly more than mere contestation of competing interest groups. Throughout her work on democracy, Elshtain argues that the ethical polity is not merely one that enacts ethical policies (though it is not less than that), it is one in which political and personal virtue is practiced.

By this time in her career, Elshtain's writing had established her as a major public intellectual. She served on the President's Council on Bioethics, contributing to consultations, working papers, and major reports.[23] On issues of bioethics, Elshtain often defended the most vulnerable members of society, particularly those who could not speak for themselves. She noted the paradox of modern American democracy seeking to become more inclusive of people with disabilities at the same time as it attempted to eliminate the disabled altogether through selective birth. As a person with a physical disability who was also the parent of a child with a developmental disability, Elshtain was keenly aware that the exclusion of the weak was a hallmark of totalitarian, not democratic, societies, and she vigorously defended a capacious definition of worthy human life. Yet bioethics, too, joins the ranks of issues about which Elshtain planned to write more. As Nancy Hirschmann indicates in this volume (chapter 5), there is still critical and constructive work to be done in drawing Elshtain's writing on democracy into closer conversation with disability studies.

RELIGION AND POLITICS

Elshtain's claims about the ethical polity naturally lead to a discussion of the role of religion in political theory and practice. Not all her exemplars were religious (chief among them Arendt and Camus), but all recognized what religion offers to human life and thought. "We are created to 'serve God wittily, in the tangle of our minds'" (*WAW*, 6). For Elshtain, this favorite line placed in the mouth of St. Thomas More by Robert Bolt in *A Man for All Seasons* captured the responsibility of a

Christian scholar and citizen. It is a call to relinquish fear, gloom, and sloth in the face of the moral and political problems of our society. Religion was never for Elshtain simply one contingency among others to be studied in the shifting political landscape. Neither was it to be relegated to the private sphere alone. Instead, from the moral revolution ushered in by early Christianity to her intellectual hero, Augustine, to contemporary martyrs and popes, across her career Elshtain actively drew upon Christianity's resources as she addressed political theory and pondered what it means to be a Christian seeking the ethical polity.

Elshtain's first explicitly theological foray into the intersection of religion and politics was with *Augustine and the Limits of Politics*, where she offers an alternative social vision to ground contemporary political thought. The closing chapter of *Public Man, Private Woman* had addressed the search for an ethical polity, and in the preface to *Augustine and the Limits of Politics*, Elshtain links this search and her theological turn. She draws again on the image of a village as the ideal democratic polity, with its landscape marked by the architecture and sounds of houses of worship, a local cinema playing Hollywood classics, and with people gathered in local pub, "arguing politics and religion—the important things" (*ALP*, xiii). This village scene sets the stage for a book about a man who also saw political life as centered on two imagined cities.

Elshtain's text is not primarily concerned with Augustine's historical context or even the myriad debates he entered into during his lifetime. Instead, she draws on an Augustine, who can help her better envision an ethical polity that is both human and limited. In an act of *ressourcement*, Elshtain's Augustine forms an alternative to the social contractarian classics of Western political thought—of Hobbes, Locke, and Mill—repudiating the "utopian possibilities" that lurked within them through his understanding of human finitude and the stubbornness of sin (*ALP*, 90). Augustine limits the extent of political possibility, but he also "creates a complex moral map that offers space for loyalty and love and care, as well as for a chastened form of civic virtue" (*ALP*, 91). As Nigel Biggar writes in this volume (chapter 7), Elshtain serves as an apologist for Augustine. She deftly draws Augustine into contemporary political conversations, underlining a foundation of human society in peace and cooperation and not in antagonism, while linking Augustine's conception of evil as privation with Arendt's more recent idea of the banality of evil. For Elshtain, the alternative imaginary offered through Augustine is not an outlier in the history of Christianity but a central occupation, since "Christianity ushered in a moral revolution into the world" (*PMPW*, 56), reenvisioning human persons as equal before God, thus challenging an image of the body politic reliant on "natural" dissymmetry.

It is not incidental that in Elshtain's village of the mind, the important conversations take place in a public house. Elshtain was interested in religion as a matter for the public square, not because of block voting or interest groups, but because it touched on the important things. In her intellectual travels, Elshtain did not limit herself to the path between Wittenberg and Rome, to strictly "religious" figures. Elshtain was drawn to writers and thinkers who stood against the *zeitgeist* of their times while defining something essential about their own era. She collected them and returned to them again and again.

She encountered Camus at eighteen, voraciously reading through his corpus after first discovering *The Stranger*, and was still teaching him more than fifty years later at the University of Chicago. Though a professed unbeliever, Camus is an exemplar for Elshtain of the dialectic of belief and unbelief: "Camus reminds us that the fruit of Western culture requires that we remember both Jerusalem and Athens, belief and unbelief, skepticism and faith" (*S*, 243). It is not by chance that Elshtain shares with him a love of Augustine, and from him she gains a further appreciation of the need for a politics of limits aware of our complex human nature. His work also indicates the dangers facing those who reject this dialectic: absolute sovereign selves, nihilism, the will to power, and totalitarianism.[24] Freud, another favorite, also rejected religion but nonetheless sought "moral grounds for human decency in a world of practical atheism."[25] Likewise Arendt, a secular Jew, nevertheless defended a robust understanding of politics as "one way human beings reveal themselves to one another."[26]

At the same time, Elshtain turned to key witnesses to the Christian tradition. Dietrich Bonhoeffer, moral exemplar and martyr in Nazi Germany, was also a rigorous thinker, standing almost alone among his intellectual peers in opposing the totalitarian state. He helps her to pose the questions: "What is to come? Where are the powerful tendencies and forces at century's end pushing us? What can we do about it?" (*WAW*, xv). Pope John Paul II, whom she called "the holy father of the intellect,"[27] was important in her writings as a constant defender and articulator of Christianity in modern society, and also in her own return to a more religious life.[28] Havel, a Christian playwright and politician, warned against modernity's loss of a transcendental anchor for human society. These thinkers provided resources and intellectual kinship as Elshtain sought to remain responsible and critical in her own time.

Elshtain's work on religion and politics moves from constructive *ressourcement* and theory to concrete application. As a discipline, political science tends to take a global, third-person perspective, describing religious affiliation through church attendance polls, baptismal records, and census documents. Elshtain argues, however, for a more substantive, first-person perspective, bringing Christian imagination into contemporary public discourse. In a 2004 op-ed in *Science and Theology News* entitled "Religion Crucial to Political Debates," Elshtain states, "Our government is secular; that does not mean that our society is thoroughly secularized. It isn't now. It never has been."[29] She goes on to say that religion addresses some of the most important questions of political life: "What kind of people are we? What sort of place is this? What do we hope for?"[30] These questions are not isolated within the private realm, but are convictions brought with the citizen into public debate.

Elshtain's 2000 book *Who Are We?* raises these central questions directly. Here, she leans on Havel, Bonhoeffer, and John Paul II to present a vision of freedom and an anthropology that provides an alternative to the impoverished landscape of political science. Throughout, however, one gets the impression her real audience is the interested and engaged Christian, as she does not shy away from such theological terms as "the fall" in diagnosing the besetting vices of contemporary American culture, namely, pride and sloth (read as uncritical acquiescence to cultural norms). She does not present a "Christian" ethical polity, but instead a vision of how one can be a Christian, with all of one's convictions, within a democratic polity.

Religion plays an altogether different role in the text resulting from her Gifford Lectures than in either *Augustine and the Limits of*

Politics or *Who Are We?* If the former offers an alternative social vision to the reigning theories of politics, and the latter embodies a Christian engagement with culture, then *Sovereignty* traces deeply the roots of one key idea within modern political discourse. In this last book, Elshtain returns to "good old-fashioned intellectual history"[31] to show how this idea migrates across several centuries and modes of discourse. Elshtain draws similar conclusions to some of her earlier texts, including her diagnosis of the modern self as confusing itself with Augustine's "selfsame," a fully independent and sovereign ruler, but the tenor of her argument is much different. Elshtain's prior texts appear to demonstrate the explanatory appeal of Christianity both to political theory and an engaged public. Here, through intellectual history, Elshtain identifies the roots of the political concepts of state sovereignty and self-sovereignty within ancient and medieval theological concepts. Nevertheless, *Sovereignty* is not the magnum opus she once thought it might be. Instead, the book is a marker—an important one, perhaps, but still just a stop—in an ongoing conversation. As Lisa Cahill notes in this volume (chapter 6), *Sovereignty* also betrays a tension between Augustinian and Thomistic perspectives on politics that is never fully worked out in her writings.

Across much of Elshtain's academic career, then, religion and theology play a central role in the search for an ethical polity. Christianity serves as a view from outside, enabling her better to critique politics and contemporary culture. It grounds her imagination, and its claims underlie some of the most important themes of contemporary political theory. Although never claiming to be a theologian herself, Elshtain writes as an apologist, a moralist, and an advocate, arguing for the critical importance of matters religious to the ethical polity.

INTERNATIONAL RELATIONS

The final period of Elshtain's scholarship, consisting of approximately the ten years prior to her death in 2013, marks a return to and expansion of the themes in her earliest work while also displaying the familiar hallmarks of her style. The first work in this period, essentially an extended occasional essay, was *Just War against Terror*. Written as a further argument in support of the statement "What We're Fighting For" (published in the *Washington Post* on February 12, 2002), that she had coauthored on behalf of sixty other scholars, clergy, and public intellectuals following the terror attacks of September 11, 2001, *Just War against Terror* is not her most polished work. And yet Elshtain had been thinking and teaching on terror since at least 1995, well before the specter of militant Islamic terrorism had risen to global prominence. In fact, her earliest reflections on terror were the result of sustained engagement with the work of Camus, Arendt, and other post–World War II thinkers. In that context, terror was linked to other forms of absolutism (fascism, communism), and as such constituted the anti-democracy. As with so much of her editorial writing, her occasional pieces (of which this was one) reflected a sustained engagement with history, philosophy, theology, and ethics. She could write *Just War against Terror* so quickly (the first edition was published in 2003, between the U.S.-led invasions of Afghanistan and Iraq) because she had written so much else before.

Against many others, Elshtain held several premises to be true: (1) state borders and sovereignty still mattered, and though international cooperation was essential, supra-national governments or agencies could neither replace state actors nor inevitably do better (and perhaps could only do worse); (2) as imperfect as its historical record was, the United States was still the best, even the only, entity capable of intervention in order to "interdict against" violence on the global stage, particularly genocidal violence; (3) Islamic terror posed a serious existential threat to the United States, and to the West more broadly. This was not quite the City of God versus the City of Man, but she did believe that the ideology of militant Islam was an assault against the idea of the secular as a place where the City of God and City of Man were "intermingled" during this temporal age. Militant Islam knows no secular and tolerates no dissent, particularly dissent framed as words and deeds forbidden by its rigid interpretation of the Qur'an.[32]

So democracy is tied quite centrally to Elshtain's understanding of international relations. Because democracy is many, not one, it is a preferable form of government for the secular world. Democracy opposes absolutism in all forms, political or religious. However, Elshtain was more than a procedural democrat. As we have seen in *Democracy on Trial* and *Who Are We?* democracy is not just following a process, it also entails a commitment to certain political virtues, to certain bedrock conceptions of human beings, and to the limited horizons of human government. Even so, democracy is not less than a process of coming to agreement (or compromise) through the sort of public debate that is characteristic of a healthy democracy. With Churchill, Elshtain believed that democracy was the form of government most appropriate to human beings, who are limited in powers but unlimited in appetites. The committed democrat must always be vigilant against the rise of the lust for domination—both within oneself and wherever it threatens the well-being of others.

In her thinking on just war, then, Elshtain began to formulate a version of the responsibility to protect. The tradition has always provided for self-defense as a legitimate reason to go to war against another sovereign state. In a world marked by overwhelming military capability on the part of the United States, significant vulnerability on the part of other states or minority peoples (sometimes from their own government), and super-empowered nonstate actors capable of inflicting significant casualties and creating significant instability, Elshtain believed that the United States had a moral responsibility to intervene militarily if a minority people faced extinction, particularly if their right to exist was being challenged by another, more powerful group. This responsibility to protect comes not from *realpolitik*—for it would not always be to the advantage of the major power—but, following Augustine, out of the Christian duty of neighbor-love and from a political duty to uphold a decent world order.

Some viewed her perspective as a continuation of a history of cowboy interventions abroad motivated by the *libido dominandi* of empire, a sign of hubris breeding only further conflict. But Elshtain defended the sovereign state, even as she challenged any totalitarian pretensions by the state. Elshtain did not view supranational bodies as capable of enforcing a moral political order, made up as they were of nations of all stripes, including those whose governments were not democratic, did not respect human rights, or did not look beyond parochial interests. Far from being an outmoded form of international organization, then, the sovereign state could challenge the legitimacy of other forms of authority. But, according to Elshtain, it also faced a challenge from the sovereign individual, who considered any state policy that infringed on the individual's goals, needs, or preferences as illegitimate. Being part of any larger group, whether that be a nation, a church, a civic organization, or a corporation, will mean that an individual will not always have free reign for his or her desires. The sovereign state can and does limit the rights of the individual, but an assertion of an individual's prerogative to create the self regardless of any limits—be they physical or mental, social or personal—can erode the basis of larger collectivities and threaten human sociality in general.

Much of Elshtain's life was lived during the Cold War era and its aftermath, and it was marked by fascism on one end and militant Islam on the other. Through each of these crises, Elshtain argued that the conflicts were over more than just interests—economic and otherwise—but were also over ethics: the driving moral centers of these political movements determined how states (and nonstate actors) behaved. She would always ask: What view of the human, and what view of God, lies behind a particular conception of the state? Does this entity's view of politics acknowledge any limits on its military activity? On its ability to manipulate its citizens' lives? On its ability to re-create the world after its own image and likeness? Does it allow for other views, other ethics, other societies to flourish, inside or outside of its borders? Does it recognize any obligation to the inhabitants of its territory, regardless of their religion, ethnicity, or economic status? Does it place the same value on each individual, regardless of ability? In this way, Elshtain argued that a polity could be morally judged; against the tradition of *realpolitik*, she argued that politics is inseparable from ethics.

There can be discerned, therefore, a continuity of thought across Elshtain's varied oeuvre. Although not a systematician, she worked from a set of anchoring principles that threaded through of her writing. Elshtain mined the Western philosophical tradition, but insisted on paying attention to the facts "on the ground." Her work was rooted in a view of the unassailable dignity of the human person, and following from that she defended the moral possibilities of ordinary life. She embraced a broadly Augustinian view of the aims and limits of politics, including the sometimes tragic necessity of violence. Throughout all of this, she remained a committed democrat and believer in the American experiment of one nation out of many, which she would defend as one example of the ethical polity.

AIM OF THIS VOLUME

To cover all aspects of Elshtain's published work would be a monumental task. This volume aims instead at the more modest goal of offering a comprehensive engagement with her primary works. As we have seen, over the course of five decades, Elshtain established herself as an original and sometimes controversial figure. Her scholarship defies easy categorization, and her place in modern scholarship is a subject of considerable debate. Consequently, this collection is composed of essays by prominent scholars and public intellectuals from across the spectrum of disciplines in which Elshtain wrote: political theory, international relations, democracy and civil society, feminist theory, religious studies, and law, many of whom were her longtime interlocutors. The essays have been carefully chosen for their interpretive and analytic scope. This volume is designed both to introduce readers to the work of a prominent contemporary thinker and to use Elshtain's writing as a lens through which to reflect on several major political and scholarly debates. The book has been constructed with three goals in mind: first, to expose new scholars to the wider corpus of one of the most original political thinkers and public intellectuals in the last half century; second, to highlight and evaluate Elshtain's contributions to public discourse; and third, to probe areas in which her scholarship should be questioned, extended, or revised.

ORGANIZATION OF ESSAYS

The volume is organized around four broad topics in four parts: (1) the political question; (2) politics and religion; (3) international relations and just war; and (4) the ends of political life, though each recur throughout the entire volume. Each part begins with a brief introduction that contextualizes its themes and describes, in brief, the essays therein.

In part I, essays focus on the nature of politics, the scope and limit of politics, why politics matters, and how to think and talk about politics. Contributions focus on the distinction of public and private with the family; Elshtain's method; a comparative analysis with Edmund Burke; and the stretching of the limits of political identity. It establishes Elshtain's basic framework for thinking and talking about political life, which was always grounded in lived experiences of real, specific people with bodies, families, jobs, homes, and dreams for their lives. Chapters in this part address how this stance located Elshtain as a scholar and help explain her originality as a thinker.

In part II, contributors consider the interaction between politics, religion, and theology. It addresses the mutual relation between theology and politics; the role that Augustine played in Elshtain's political analysis; the migration of the theme of sovereignty from the theological to the political; the implications of the doctrine of the Trinity on sovereignty; and the limits of sovereignty in light of the theological emphasis on the powerless and vulnerable.

Part III looks at these themes as they apply to war and international relations. This was some of Elshtain's most controversial and perhaps most misconstrued work. Consequently, the contributors here position Elshtain's work relative to her contemporaries, even as they evaluate both her methods and her conclusions. These chapters look at her use of history and historical thinkers, her responses to contemporary political events, and the ongoing applicability of her writing on terror.

Part IV returns to the question of the means and ends of political life by focusing on Elshtain's writing on democracy and civil society. In examining those topics, contributors in this part also look forward to consider the implications and continuing relevance of Elshtain's analysis to contemporary American political life. They address key questions: Will her analysis hold? What will be her enduring impact on the recurring questions that motivated her work and engaged her mind throughout her career?

It is not possible to address every aspect of Elshtain's thought in a single volume of this size, but we hope that this collection of essays does justice to the scope and significance of Elshtain's body of writing. By offering an overview of the major themes of her work, this book aims to identify the common threads that unified Elshtain's published record. In addition to advancing her central concern with the ethical polity, we hope that this volume will spark further scholarship on Elshtain's work and extend the many conversations to which she contributed during her long career.

NOTES

1. Margaret Mitchell, "Words of Welcome," *Criterion* 50, no. 2 (2014): 2.

2. Jean Bethke Elshtain, "My Mother, the Expert," *First Things*, October 1991, 12.

3. Jean Bethke Elshtain, "Generation without Forebears," *The Nation*, August 22, 1981, 153.

4. Ibid., 153–54.

5. Ibid., 154.

6. Jean Bethke Elshtain and Nicholas Wolterstorff, "Keynote Lecture: A Conversation," public dialogue held at the conference titled Democracy on Trial: Religion, Civil Society, and Democratic Theory, University of Chicago Divinity School, October 13, 2011.

7. Elshtain's early push against the proper societal gender boundaries extend beyond her coiffed hair. She recounts at the beginning of *Women and War* of her own desire for a gun as a child, in a country where the sport of hunting was often reserved for men (*WW*, 3). Her husband, Errol Elshtain, recounted that one Christmas, rather than the gun she desired, she received a wedding doll. Elshtain had her grandmother build a box for it with a glass front. Elshtain put a lock on it and set it out of reach. The family still has this heirloom (Interview with the author, November 3, 2015).

8. Susan Schreiner, "Memorial Eulogy for Jean Elshtain," *Criterion* 50, no. 2 (2014): 13.

9. Private communication with authors.

10. Jean Bethke Elshtain, "To Serve God Wittily in the Tangle of One's Mind," in Wittily *Christianity and the Soul of the University: Faith as a Foundation for Intellectual Community*, ed. Douglas V. Henry and Michael D. Beaty (Grand Rapids, MI: Baker Academic, 2006), 37–38.

11. Jean Bethke Elshtain, "How Should We Talk?" *Center Conversations*, no. 11 (June 2011): 2.

12. Ibid., 1.

13. Ibid.

14. Ibid.

15. Jean Bethke Elshtain, "Making Peace with Justice: The Story of Las Madres de Plaza de Mayo," *Revue Internationale de Sociologie* 2, no. 1 (1992): 53.

16. Ibid., 64.

17. Jean Bethke Elshtain, "Why Public Intellectual?" *Wilson Quarterly* 25, no. 4 (2001): 49.

18. Jean Bethke Elshtain, "Women and War: Ten Years On," *Review of International Studies* 24, no. 4 (1998): 447.

19. Schreiner, "Memorial Eulogy for Jean Elshtain," 13.

20. Jean Bethke Elshtain, "Critics and Crusaders on Neoconservatism," *Society*, February 1, 1989, 7.

21. Elshtain related this reception history in Elshtain and Wolterstorff, "Keynote Lecture: A Conversation," and in the introduction to *Jane Addams*.

22. Jean Bethke Elshtain, *The Jane Addams Reader* (New York: Basic Books, 2002).

23. Major reports produced during Elshtain's tenure include President's Council on Bioethics, *Controversies in the Determination of Death: A White Paper of the President's Council on Bioethics* (Washington, DC: President's Council on Bioethics, 2008), and *The Changing Moral Focus of Newborn Screening: An Ethical Analysis* (Washington, DC: President's Council on Bioethics, 2008).

24. Cf. Jean Bethke Elshtain, "Between Heaven and Hell: Politics before the End-Time," *Process Studies* 40, no. 2 (2011): 215–26.

25. Elshtain, "To Serve God Wittily," 45.

26. Ibid.

27. Ibid., 46.

28. Interview with Errol Elshtain, November 3, 2015.

29. Jean Bethke Elshtain, "Religion Crucial to Political Debates, Diversity," *Science & Theology News*, October 2004, 5.

30. Ibid.

31. The phrasing in quotations is the authors'. Elshtain describes her approach in the introduction to *Sovereignty* (xvi).

32. Her views should not be confused with a general critique of Islam as a whole. In fact, Elshtain was quite adamant about the possibility of an Islam compatible with democratic pluralism. She writes, "The testimony of brave Arab Muslim moderates promoting 'civic Islam' is abundant and clear: It is a form of cultural condescension to insist that Islam is, *per se*, incompatible with and hostile to democracy and basic human rights"; Jean Bethke Elshtain, "Democracy and Human Dignity," *Soundings: An Interdisciplinary Journal* 87 (2004): 23. During the last years of her life, Elshtain was engaged in talks with Jews, Christians, and Muslims in the Middle East, in an effort to promote a common democratic culture.

PART I

THE POLITICAL QUESTION

Introduction

Robin W. Lovin

Ours is a culture fascinated by human identity and aspirations. "Who are we?" is a question posed by evolutionary biologists, op-ed columnists, social psychologists, and cultural historians. Jean Elshtain believed that it is also the first question of politics. In her book with that title, published in 2000, she argued that human nature sets the limits for any effort to build an enduring system of government and society.

Asking basic questions about human nature is not an easy way to approach politics, nor is it particularly popular today. We prefer to think about who we are in terms of an almost infinite range of individual possibilities, or perhaps as a question to be answered by a group identity framed by ethnicity, gender, race, or class. We ask, "Who are we?," to set ourselves apart. We use the question to identify our claims, rather than to acknowledge our limits.

Yet the two ways of asking the question, personal and political, are closely connected. Jean Elshtain understood that, and her work as a whole may be seen as an effort to overcome the tension between self-interest and social commitment, between individual rights and natural limitations, between an assertion of identity and openness to communication. The chapters in this part view her work in that light, and each makes its own contribution to the broader understanding of politics that she developed in her work and encouraged among her colleagues and students.

In chapter 4, Peter Berkowitz locates Elshtain's political thought in the tradition of Edmund Burke, but he also interprets Burke in a way that reflects Elshtain's emphasis on the importance of restraint and balance in political claims, both between individuals and between citizens and their government. Burke as he appears here is not simply an apologist for tradition. No political system could survive on that alone. Tradition conserves a natural liberty, and liberty creates a space for reform. Elshtain would no doubt add that liberty is not the only thing that is natural, for all the attention that it received from the American revolutionaries, whom Burke supported, and from the French revolutionaries, whom he despised. The questions of democracy and rights that preoccupied the end of the eighteenth century, like the questions of human rights that were central to the twentieth, only make sense if we remember that the autonomous, individual subject of rights is also the product of a history and a family, a person with a gender and body.

Don Browning's life and work offered his own interpretation of this embodied selfhood, moving dialogically between theology and developmental psychology to establish a rich account of how we become persons and of how persons should be treated in the familial and social settings where they live. In chapter 3, written toward the end of his own long and distinguished career, Browning relates that developmental perspective to Elshtain's understanding of politics, a multidimensional, "thick" account of justice that relates to "concrete human needs in actual historical contexts." For Browning, it makes sense to locate this way of thinking in the natural law tradition that grows in Western law and Christian theology through the Augustinian account of human nature, which is also important to Elshtain's politics.

It is, of course, difficult to rely too much on human nature in contemporary political thought, and not just because the tradition on which Browning draws is closely connected with Christian theology. It is one of the leading ideas of recent political thought that "public reason" must proceed from premises that all participants can share. Although the idea may have originated in an earlier struggle for religious toleration, the contemporary formulations increasingly exclude all concepts drawn from a "thick" conception of human nature, giving the impression that questions about public security and economic efficiency are the primary issues open to discussion in any debate about public policy. Those who want to be taken seriously in the public forum will address the issues in terms of security and efficiency, whereas the use of other sorts of argument will be seen as questionable, or as a kind of rhetorical flourish.

This change affects all moral claims, not just those that might be put forward on specifically theological grounds. If security and efficiency set the terms for public reasoning, then "Who are we?" is not a public question. We are free to aspire to whatever we wish, but we should not expect it to make a difference in politics.

Paradoxically, however, this effort to open the field of public discussion by eliminating sectarian or particularistic appeals has had the effect of polarizing the discussion and alienating people from politics. We no longer see politics as an answer to the question, "Who are we?," because there is not enough of ourselves left in the discussion to make the answer interesting. In chapter 5, Nancy Hirschmann documents this disillusionment with our public life, drawing both on contemporary disability activism and on John Stuart Mill's "religion of humanity" for models in which an informed self-understanding can shape political claims and choices. Hirschmann in the end offers only a "slim sliver of hope" for our "democracy on trial," embodied in a set of very practical changes that might enable those who are currently excluded from public discussion to participate more fully. But she suggests that treating their participation as important might help us better understand why it is important, for everyone.

This leads us from the problems of human nature and public reason to more general questions about the relationship of public discussion and personal identity in a modern, pluralistic society. John Stuart Mill might have hoped for an educated elite whose "religion of humanity" would determine the common good, but our sensibilities and experience require more general political participation in which people speak for themselves. Browning points out that Elshtain's thought from the beginning related self-awareness to the experience of dialogue. Rather than being prepared for politics by an education that is prior to it, she suggested that we learn the skills of dialogue and the answers to our questions about ourselves in the political process. This is an idea developed in different ways by Paul Ricoeur's phenomenology and Hans-Georg Gadamer's hermeneutics, but, as Browning notes, Elshtain introduced it into North American political thinking before their theories were widely known.

It is appropriate, then, that two essays in this part focus specifically on Elshtain's interpretations of texts and her ideas about language. In chapter 1, William Galston poses the problem of how the loyalties and identities forged in family life can adapt to the more flexible relationships required in politics. He then provides an answer drawn from Elshtain's reading of *Antigone*. The result is a political pluralism that resists "any simple hierarchical ordering among spheres of human life." Human nature and political obligation as represented in the classic dialogue between Antigone and Creon interact to produce a situation in which loyalties are necessarily divided and tragic conflicts are always possible. But this dialogue is also the setting for human freedom and responsibility.

In chapter 2, Arlene Saxonhouse continues the hermeneutical study with a close reading of *Public Man, Private Woman*, a text that has become a classic of contemporary political thought. In Saxonhouse's essay, we have an interpretation of the argument that mirrors the interaction of nature and politics in Elshtain's thought. Our embodied selves limit our possibilities, but they also allow us to enter into dialogues that free us from our immediate environment and form communities in which we can become more than nature makes us. In the same way, Saxonhouse proposes, the theories that shape and constrain our thinking also make it possible for us to enter into dialogues that can change our thinking and ourselves. Saxonhouse writes, "Just as Elshtain insisted that we ourselves are not abstract individuals sprung to life like those Hobbesian mushrooms on the forest floor, she recognized that the theories with which we grapple and the conceptual frameworks within which we work must be set into the historical context of the traditions of Western political thought. She appreciated that we must grasp and draw on the theories of those who have informed our own thinking."

The dialogue of politics, the rich interaction between identity and otherness, thus makes possible a public discussion far wider in scope than the thin theories of public reason would suggest. It is important to recover this concept of the political question at a time when many people have concluded that politics is no concern of theirs and that the public forum simply cannot accommodate the goods that are most important to them. That is politically dangerous, because it implies that human goods are not part of an ordered reality to which we are all related, but are instead created by communities of like-minded people who define themselves and their goods in opposition to the others who cannot share our goods because they are not us. To lure such people back into arguments about a rich variety of public goods that reflects the range of their real aspirations risks conflict and tragedy, but it is a risk worth running, because it is the only way to find out who we are.

CHAPTER ONE

BECOMING JEAN ELSHTAIN

Exploring the Intersections of Social Feminism and Civic Life

William A. Galston

INTRODUCTION

Jean Elshtain's *Public Man, Private Woman* (*PMPW*) is painted on a grand canvass. It ranges over the entire Western tradition of political philosophy, and it fearlessly engages with the range of feminist theories that burst into public view in the 1970s. In this book, we see a thinker fighting to open a space for her own voice.

In many respects, Elshtain succeeded. But the critical dimension of her book was more fully realized than was her own affirmative stance. A sign of this: *Public Man, Private Woman* has an extensive index, but two names are conspicuous by their absence—Antigone and Jane Addams, figures central to the "social feminism" for which she was to become so well and controversially known.

Here I will integrate some themes from *Public Man, Private Woman* with key writings (see abbreviations list at the end of the chapter) that link its initial publication in 1981 to the afterword penned and appended a decade later. During this period, Elshtain propounded a distinctive style of doing political theory, fleshed out the substance of her own approach, and defended her understanding of the family while linking it to social feminism and to a revisionist account of the public/private distinction. These are the topics on which I will focus. My principal aim is descriptive-reconstructive; I want to do my best to get Elshtain's argument right and to state it clearly. Toward the end, however, I will raise a concern that might have impelled her to reflect a bit more on one of the major aspects of her thesis if time had permitted, which sadly it did not.

DOING POLITICAL THEORY

Elshtain's point of departure in *Public Man, Private Woman* is deceptively simple, though hardly uncontroversial. Critique, though essential, is not enough. Theorists who wish to make a legitimate claim on our attention must also offer a coherent vision of a livable future (*PMPW*, 298). The reason is this: critique untethered from affirmative proposals may generate discontent with what exists, but with no guarantee that anything better is feasible. At best this discontent is impotent, fostering cynicism and withdrawal. At worst, it breeds rage against the current order, and the spirit of abstract negation that disfigures so many revolutionary movements.[1]

In discharging this responsibility, it is not enough to give one's imagination (or fantasies) free rein. To offer serious alternatives, theorists must engage with reality, plumbing its possibilities and its limits. This engagement lies at the core of political theory as a vocation. Theory at its best is strongly reformist, but not utopian; Elshtain chides some first-wave feminists (she appears to have in mind writers such as Ti-Grace Atkinson, Susan Brownmiller, Mary Daly, and Shulamith Firestone) for burdening women with "implausible visions of a future perfect world, the realization of which would require a total disconnection between the world we live in and the world they fantasize about" (*PMPW*, 358).

Although political theory need not, and often should not, leave the world unchanged, it must take the everyday world as its point of departure. It must proceed bottom-up, using public language, rather than top-down, with philosophical abstractions. In this vein, Elshtain criticizes Simone de Beauvoir for deploying "Sartrian categories which have no meaning in ordinary discourse, terms that are unavailable to social participants themselves" (*PMPW*, 306, 314). While maintaining a clear-eyed awareness of the world's flaws, it must resist the temptation to exaggerate them into "hellish" evils (299). Elshtain seeks, not the abolition of ordinary life, but rather its "redemption" (335).

This perspective should shape the theorist's stance toward tradition. Two extremes are to be avoided—the modernist drive (traceable to Descartes) to wipe the slate clean and dismiss tradition as an irrational encumbrance, and the traditionalist temptation to embrace tradition nostalgically as the bearer of age-old wisdom and as evidence of a past preferable to the present day. We must neither discard nor venerate tradition, but rather interrogate it as a force that has shaped us and may furnish materials for shaping a better future (*PMPW*, 319). In this vein, Elshtain defends American leaders—Lincoln, Martin Luther King, Jr., and others —who have found in America's traditions resources for criticizing and ameliorating the injustices of American life. Theorists who genuinely wish to improve their community cannot stand wholly apart from it (345).

Finally, Elshtain insists, theory done right is theory done in the spirit of generosity and inclusion. She castigates Beauvoir for what she takes to be an elitist stance that denigrates everyday life (especially women's) and implicitly valorizes the heedlessness of the privileged (*PMPW*, 308). And she rejects the use of theory as a tool for ideologically silencing dissenting views, insisting that we must remain empathically open to people who see the world in ways very different from our own.[2] Feminist theorists who denounce right-to-life women as fascists cannot learn why these women think and feel the way the way they do, and feminist theory will be the poorer for it (312). (Elshtain mentions, but does not specifically cite, a feminist article that exemplifies this error).

THEORETICAL BASICS

In *Public Man, Private Woman* and subsequently, Elshtain develops the outline of a political theory based on her understanding of human beings, society, and the moral dimensions of politics. Consistent with a long theoretical tradition, she insists that humans are social and meaning-creating beings. To develop even minimal human characteristics, we must live with others, and when we do, our social relations and institutions encode meanings that go well beyond their utilitarian purposes. Culturally inflected burial rites, for example, appear to be coeval with human history.

Although humans are by nature social, not everything about us is socially determined. (Elshtain approvingly cites Dennis Wrong's famous article "The Over-Socialized Conception of Man in Modern Sociology."[3]) She denies that all human ills derive from "faulty and exploitative social forms that can, and therefore must, be changed"; the sad but inescapable truth is that "a large part of that unhappiness derives from the simple fact of being human, therefore limited, knowing that one is going to die" (*PMPW*, 301). It is in part because not all evils arise from the imperfections of society that Elshtain's theorizing is resolutely anti-utopian. Human beings are finite and flawed. We are bound to construct imperfect societies; our task is improvement, not perfection, and certainly not the construction of heaven on earth.

Nor, on Elshtain's view, can forms of human association be understood simply as social constructions. They also reflect aspects of our nature with which social forms must seek to cope but which society can neither deny nor abolish. Human beings are variable, but they are not infinitely malleable. The belief that they are can generate—has generated—regimes whose transformative aspirations end in oppression and cruelty.

Though Elshtain is critical of the excessive methodological individualism that she attributes to certain kinds of liberal theory (*PMPW*, 108, citing Hobbes), she emphasizes the moral significance of our separate individual existence. She invokes the Christian "social gospel," which sees individuals, "not as lost in some aggregate abstraction, but as unique, irreplaceable beings with inalienable human dignity" (345–46). (As developed by twentieth-century European thinkers, the late Pope John Paul II not least among them, this Christian personalism emerged as a significant theoretical counterweight to collectivism.) Unsurprisingly, the embrace of human dignity proves incompatible with any form of politics that sees individual human beings merely as means to larger collective ends.

Elshtain also rejects the temptation toward "totalism" in political theory, which she links to totalitarianism in political practice (*PMPW*, 300). She advocates instead a "politics of limits," which stands on three pillars: a core of unchanging human nature, which thwarts utopian aspirations; a conception of political means that are forbidden because they affront human dignity; and restraints on the scope and power of the public sphere (352).

Elshtain's politics of limits reflects the rejection of monistic approaches to morals and ideals. In a belated bow to Isaiah Berlin, whom her generation mocked in graduate school, she acknowledges and celebrates pluralism, diversity, and competing human values (*PMPW*, 320–21, 362). And she embraces political pluralism, describing human communities as containing separate "spheres" that differ qualitatively and that are not related in any simple hierarchy (AD, 58). Indeed, these two kinds of pluralism help define her vision of an ethical polity: "My ideal is the preservation of a tension between diverse spheres and [among] competing ideals and purposes. . . . Within an ethical polity the individual would, or could, have many irons in the fire. . . . Such persons could tolerate the ineradicable tension between public and private imperatives, thought and action, aesthetic standards and ethical principles" (*PMPW*, 351–52).

The risk, of course, is that pluralism can degenerate into a flabby live-and-let-live ethos that either makes no distinctions or lacks the courage of its convictions. Elshtain is alert to this danger. She rejects any Archimedean point from which the whole of human life can be assessed, but she acknowledges the need for a core of secure standards. "Each succeeding generation," she writes, "must respect some moral necessities, must have some 'taken for granteds,' rules without which even the minimal aspects of a human existence . . . will be jeopardized" (*PMPW*, 321). Some of these rules will rest on "an historically specific basic grammar of and for ethical and political life" (A, 360). Other norms are even more concrete. For example, the children of our species have certain "essential needs" that must be met in specific ways and in specific contexts. To have the right to pursue, and disagree about, competing ideals, we must begin by agreeing on, and doing our best to meet, basic necessities—for children and for all members of our community (*PMPW*, 331).

FAMILIES

It is in this multidimensional context—meeting the needs of children, and also reinforcing the politics of limits—that Elshtain considers the nature and role of families. She argues that the family is and always has been a prerequisite for any form of social life (*PMPW*, 323, 326–29; FFC, 447). At the same time, she insists, the family is not properly understood as simply instrumental to our social, or economic, or civic life (although it affects all those concerns, and more). Relations within families have an integrity all their own and generate human goods that are ends in themselves (*PMPW*, 322, 334, 351). Indeed, family relationships—cooperation, mutual care, intimacy, particularity—offer alternatives to relationships in the political sphere, which are driven by power, and to the self-interested striving of the economic sphere. This is not to deny the truth that has animated feminism from the beginning: relations within families can violate their constitutive norms and degenerate into what John Stuart Mill called a "school of despotism." Nor is it to say that politics is nothing but crude power relations. Elshtain is warning, rather, against the kind of valorization of the public world that can unwittingly impose its worst excesses on the private sphere (333).

To see families at their best as arenas of distinctive human goods is not to say that family life parallels, without intersecting, the sphere of politics. Families affect politics in two ways: by generating specific needs that the political system is challenged to meet, and by safeguarding a sphere that enjoys, or should enjoy, substantial immunity from the direct exercise of political power.

THE POSITIVE POLITICS OF SOCIAL FEMINISM: HUMAN NEEDS, VULNERABILITY, AND DIGNITY

Elshtain proposes "social" feminism as an alternative to radical, liberal, Marxist, and psychoanalytic feminisms, each of which she scrutinizes and finds wanting. Social feminism is based on the concrete lived reality of women (AD, 52). It places children and families at the center of its concern and demands that the public sphere respect and serve their needs—for example, by insisting that jobs pay a living or "family" wage, regardless of how the market may value them. In so doing, feminism necessarily challenges both irresponsible corporate power and an interest-group politics that ignores the unorganized, weak, and voiceless segments of society (*PMPW*, 336; FFC, 448). Jane Addams, who was "neither grandly public nor narrowly private," exemplifies this distinctive feminist social activism (AD, 57).

Women's lived reality leads beyond the family to what Elshtain bravely calls the historic mission of women—namely, "the protection of vulnerable human life" (FFC, 447). I say "bravely" because she knowingly risks strengthening the stereotypically gendered distinction between a politics of power and a politics of compassion. Indeed, she counsels against a feminism that simply accepts the dominant male conception of the public sphere as normative.[4] The male-dominated public sphere is more flawed, and private sphere more dignified, than this feminism acknowledges. As reshaped by women, Elshtain says, the public sphere will become more fully human, and humane (ADR, 225).

The protection of human life requires women to enter the public sphere and on occasion to display extraordinary courage. Elshtain writes movingly of the time she spent with the mothers of the Argentine "disappeared"—the thousands of people, mostly young, tortured and murdered by the military dictatorship. One mother she quotes described the path that led her from private grief to the public world: "At the beginning, we only wanted our children. But as time passed, we got a different comprehension of what was going on in the world. Today I was listening to the radio and there was somebody . . . singing about children, about babies starving. This is also a violation of human rights. Perhaps it is not much that we can do, but people [fighting] for human dignity and human rights must realize justice where they can" (ADR, 232).

Social feminism, Elshtain claims, comprises not only a distinctive agenda but also a unique way of seeing, and acting in, the world. Social feminism focuses not on aggregates and generalities, but on the concrete specificity of each individual, and it calls for a "thick" conception of society as a dense weave of human attachments standing over against the unencumbered individuals of the liberal imagination and the soulless machinations of Weberian institutions. It points, therefore, toward a "transformed vision of the human community against the arid plain of bureaucratic statism" (ADR, 226; AD, 58–59). And because social feminism counsels a form of public action that, as the Argentine mothers put it, has a "clear moral purpose" and has always been "non-violent and carried out with dignity," it represents "a rejection of amoral statecraft and an affirmation of the dignity of the human person" (ADR, 232; AD, 59).

THE NEGATIVE POLITICS OF SOCIAL FEMINISM: LIMITING THE REACH OF THE STATE

In the course of fleshing out her vision of social feminism, Elshtain famously, and controversially, revives Antigone as an exemplar for our time. In Elshtain's interpretation, Antigone stands for the proposition that the public sphere is not the only source of normativity: religious obligations and family ties have an autonomous moral force that is not derived from, and sometimes clashes with, public laws and values. When Creon orders the citizens of Thebes not to bury Antigone's traitor-brother Polyneices, he invokes the norms and interests of the city. Antigone counters with the bonds and god-given laws of the family. The ensuing clash yields disaster for both, as it must if the demands of the state are seen as all-encompassing.

And that is Elshtain's point: it need not lead to disaster, if the state refrains from asserting comprehensive authority. Properly understood, she says, Antigone helps us reconstruct the public/private distinction: "To reaffirm the standpoint of Antigone for our own time is to portray women as being able to resist the imperious demands and overweening claims of state power when these run roughshod over deeply rooted values" (AD, 55).

The lessons of the twentieth century, Elshtain says, underscore the need for this reconstruction. Totalitarian excesses of both the Left and the Right have taught us that in modern circumstances, the alternative to a vigorous and respected private sphere can only be brutal tyranny. And even in nontotalitarian orders, modernity brings risks: the technological capacity for surveillance and control of intimate relations, and bureaucratic mechanisms that are at war with concrete particularity—the heart and soul of intimacy (AD, 49, 51).

Feminists must be alert to these dangers, Elshtain argues. As a critical principle, the slogan "The personal is the political" can illuminate the ubiquity of power and domination. But taken as a prescription, it threatens to obliterate a line that all citizens have a stake in preserving (A, 357). Although traditional liberal theory may have improperly excluded some aspects of family life from public scrutiny and correction, it does not follow that we should lurch to the other extreme by opening everything to the gaze and power of the state. We need a complex response to liberalism that takes on board the best of what it offers, including rights that help define human dignity and defend intimacy. To the extent that relations within families violate these rights, the public sphere has the right—and often the duty—to intervene (PMPW, 342). Still, the challenge is to rethink the relation between the public and private spheres, not to erase the line between them (PPUS, 26).

In so doing, Elshtain says, we will of necessity reconstruct our understanding of the public and the private. Even in relentlessly criticizing modern bureaucracy, she counsels against nostalgia for the Greek conception of public life and civic space, which can lead us to denigrate the very real possibilities of public life here and now (PMPW, 346). The public realm can recognize a robust realm of human activities beyond its purview while preserving its vitality. To sustain itself, the modern public sphere must defend the private sphere and empower all to enter the public sphere, and at the same time recognize tensions between "diverse spheres and competing values and purposes" (PPUS, 33). Indeed, it is just these tensions that a healthy liberal democracy requires (PPUS, 34).

Via this route, Elshtain, who began her scholarly career as a critic of liberalism, reconciles with and rejoins the liberal tradition. Without retreating from her criticism of what she sees as liberals' excessive individualism, she recognizes the merits of a social liberalism that is not narrowly individualist (PMPW, 359). Social liberalism encompasses a thick notion of society—including but hardly limited to families and intimate attachments—from which social feminists and others can draw. Antigone is impelled to affirm the public relevance of obligations to the gods (ADR, 228–29). Similarly, for modern monotheists, religion is not simply a matter of inner piety and cannot be confined to the private realm. Religion speaks to issues of poverty, oppression, and war, among others, and reformers throughout American history have drawn upon it for guidance and hope (PPUS, 32–33).

REREADING ANTIGONE:
THE LIMITS OF SOCIAL FEMINISM

Elshtain compellingly portrays a type of feminism that both celebrates family life and engages a civic agenda. But one must wonder whether social feminism offers an adequate account of civic life. As Elshtain observes, "The rules of conduct that flow out of private relationships —loyalty, intimacy, fidelity—are not altogether transferrable to public relationships where different criteria, including the capacity for pro-visional alliances—no permanent enemies; no permanent friends—are required."[5] Imperatives arising from the private sphere constitute at most a part of the demands of public life and often stand in tension with them.

This fact has implications for Elshtain's critique of contemporary politics. It is indeed true, for example, that bureaucracies typically oper-ate in accordance with general rules that are to some extent insensitive to the specificity of individuals and contexts, but it cannot be otherwise. Maintaining basic order and functioning in large collectivities requires a measure of abstraction from particularity. Even as refracted through the judicial system, the rule of law is, and must be, less sensitive to unique congeries and facts than are parents in dealing with children (or thera-pists with patients).

This is even more the case in matters of national defense and inter-national affairs. There is a reason why we don a "uniform" when we join the military. We are supposed to leave elements of our particular selves behind; we know that superior officers will deal with us in accordance with our rank and role—bureaucratically defined generalities rather than what distinguishes us from others.

In this vein, Mary Dietz argues that because mothering and citizen-ship are generically different, the former cannot be an adequate model for the latter. The mother/child dyad is a relation among unequals, but citizens should relate to one another as equals. Mothering is an "intimate, exclusive, and particular activity"; citizenship—especially democratic citizenship—is collective, inclusive, and generalized. And finally, "the bond among citizens is not like the love between a mother and child"; the family offers a misleading—and if taken literally, dangerous—image of civic attachments.[6]

But how far can we take this thought? Dietz accuses Elshtain of turning Aristotle on his head and locating the family above politics as the "most elevated and primary realm of human life."[7] Even though Elshtain's view of the family is certainly more affirmative than that of most other feminists, I don't read her as creating a counterhierarchy. She is rather a kind of political pluralist, and pluralists resist any simple hierarchical ordering among spheres of human life. Her point is that the family at its best is the site of distinctive goods that are not reducible to the imperatives of civic life, even at its best. But to repeat, this is not to say that families have no influence on the exercise of public power, or that power relations are nowhere present within families.

Dietz repairs to Aristotle as a counterweight to Elshtain. She argues that to claim, as Aristotle does, that the political community is the most sovereign and inclusive of all associations, is to say that politics is an "integrative experience" to whose outlook and requirements all other human activities are subject—and that everything is potentially subject to political decision-making. Whether we like it or not, all aspects of family life are subject to political control. Indeed, Dietz argues, "Even the decision to allow them to remain 'private'—that is, left in the hands of mothers, fathers, and individual citizens—is ultimately a political one." And thus, she concludes, "Who we are allowed to be and what rights we are allowed to exercise, even in the supposed sanctity of the family, have always been and will continue to be governed by political determinations."[8]

As a factual claim, it is hard to disagree. And to the extent that only concerted political action can oppose and reverse misguided political determinations, Dietz's brand of realism translates into commonsense prudential practice. But it is easy to leap from the fact of omnipresent politics to a dubious theory of political totalism. Elshtain's point—with which I entirely agree—is that rightly understood, the sphere of public authority wielding coercive power is not—should not be—coextensive with all of human life. There are spheres of activity and association—the family and religion, among others—making claims upon us that cannot be reduced to civic imperatives. To be sure, public authority always influences familial and religious ties, but it does not simply construct them, and it should not claim comprehensive authority over them. When politics goes right, it recognizes and respects those aspects of human society that should be allowed to function without coercive interference, or even without public exposure. And understanding public power as limited helps us better align our political practice with defensible norms.

Politics and the family, politics and faith—these relationships are complexly horizontal, not simply vertical. There are no "lexical" priority rules that tell us how to manage the inevitable tensions. Sometimes family ties will dominate: Elshtain argues that Creon goes too far when he deploys civic norms to block the burial of Polyneices. Sometimes political authorities will have to tell parents that there are limits to permissible modes of child-rearing . . . or that their beloved child must go off to war. The tension between public and private can only be managed; it cannot be abolished.

This is not to say that Elshtain offers the only way of reading *Antigone*. In a dense and richly textured analysis, Bonnie Honig interprets the play as a clash between two understandings of politics—the democratic and the Homeric—of which competing rites of mourning and burial are a "synecdoche." In the process, Honig subverts traditional interpretations—for example, by interpreting Creon as embodying—to excess—the emerging democratic ethos—and Antigone as the defender of aristocratic individuality against democratic homogenization. In the end, however, Honig returns to a position not unlike Elshtain's, discerning a fundamental tension between "private lament" and the effort of the *polis* to confine it. Creon's grief, she says, is "ruptural." It shows that "no amount of history, polis commemoration, sovereign reasoning, ritual feasting, juridical concession, tragic theater, worship, or codes of lamentation can erase via substitution (the democratic oration), memorialization (the Homeric laments), or exception (tragedy, cult, and the concession or family exception) our undeniable mortality, awareness of which erupts from time to time by way of a keening grief that interrupts all efforts to channel, contain, or displace it."[9]

In another impressive reading, Patchen Markell argues that both Antigone and Creon try to assert univocal identities, and both fail. Though Antigone "frames her action as an expression of pious devotion of sister to brother [and refuses] the language of politics, . . . her expression of family piety turns out *also* to be an act of political subversion." Conversely, Creon's single-minded focus on the needs of the *polis* turns out to have familial implications that he cannot recognize until it is too late: his "defense of political order also turns out to be an assault on his own family." Both monistic conceptions of identity turn out to distort the complexity and interdependence of the social world in which these contending individuals must act.[10]

One wonders, though, whether Markell's reading undermines Elshtain's. Yes, in the real world, the actions that we undertake on behalf of our kin often have political ramifications that we do not intend and cannot control, and vice versa, and it is naïve and self-defeating to pretend otherwise. But Elshtain's pluralism does not deny this complexity. Indeed, pluralism is more comfortable with multiple, albeit conflicting, sources of individual identity than with monistic accounts. Struggle between individuals is often struggle within individuals.

In this context, it is not surprising that Markell seeks to mediate between Dietz and Elshtain. Markell writes:

> In a classic essay, Jean Bethke Elshtain argues that Antigone is a representative of "primordial family morality"—an identity that, in the form of "maternal thinking," is still available to be taken up in acts of resistance to modern Creons. In a response to Elshtain, Mary Dietz claims instead that Antigone represents "the customs and traditions of a collective civil life, an entire political ethos." Rather than taking sides in this debate about what Antigone, *properly understood*, represents, I suggest that we try to account for the fact that Elshtain's and Dietz's seemingly incompatible accounts of Antigone's identity are both partly *persuasive*. . . . Antigone's deeds do not smoothly flow from and reinforce, but *exceed* and *disturb* our (and her) conception of her identity.[11]

This seems right to me, and I conjecture that Elshtain would not have found this suggestion entirely objectionable. For there is no contradiction between saying that Antigone sets out to assert what she takes to be "primordial family morality" and also recognizing that she ends up doing something else—something else that not only makes a political claim but that also to some extent subverts the family morality with which she begins.

NOTES

The bare parenthetical numbers in the text refer to the 1981 edition of *Public Man, Private Woman*. Textual references to other writings by Elshtain are abbreviated as follows:

A   Afterword to the 1993 edition of *Public Man, Private Woman*.
AD   "Antigone's Daughters," *Democracy* (April 1982): 46–59.
ADR   "Antigone's Daughters Reconsidered," in *Lifeworld and Politics: Between Modernity and Post-Modernity*, ed. Stephen K. White, 222–36 (Notre Dame, IN: University of Notre Dame, 1989).
FFC   "Feminism, Family, and Community," *Dissent* (Fall 1982): 442–49.
PPUS   "Public and Private in American Political Life and Thought," in *The Public and the Private in the United States*, ed. Hitoshe Abe, Hiroko Sato, and Chieko Kitigawa Otsuru, 23–34 (Osaka: Japan Center for Area Studies, 1999).

1. For those who think that Elshtain has constructed a straw man, consider the following: "There is a [view] that I do firmly reject. That is the view that a philosopher (or theorist) must be 'positive,' i.e., that one may criticize some doctrine or institution only if one has a positive alternative to it to propose. . . . To accept [this line of argument] is to allow the existing social formation to dictate the terms on which it can be criticized, and it allow it to impose a theoretically unwarranted burden of positive proof on any potential critic"; Raymond Geuss, *Philosophy and Real Politics* (Princeton, NJ: Princeton University Press, 2008), 95–96.

2. For a serious effort to do what Elshtain recommends, see Kristin Luker, *Abortion and the Politics of Motherhood* (Berkeley: University of California Press, 1985).

3. Dennis Wrong, "The Over-Socialized Conception of Man in Modern Sociology," *American Sociological Review* 26, no. 2 (1961): 183–93.

4. For example, she criticizes the National Organization for Women (NOW) for arguing that compulsory military service is central to democratic

citizenship. In so doing, NOW unreflectively appropriated a male-centered civic republican tradition (ADR, 235n8).

5. Jean Elshtain, "The Displacement of Politics," in *Public and Private in Thought and Practice: Perspectives on a Grand Dichotomy*, ed. Jeff Weintraub and Krishan Kumar (Chicago: University of Chicago Press, 1997), 180.

6. Mary Dietz, "Citizenship with a Feminist Face: The Problem with Maternal Thinking," *Political Theory* 13, no. 1 (1985): 31.

7. Ibid., 21.

8. Ibid., 27.

9. Bonnie Honig, "Antigone's Laments, Creon's Grief: Mourning, Membership, and the Politics of Exception," *Political Theory* 37, no. 1 (2009): 30, 31.

10. Patchen Markell, "Tragic Recognition: Action and Identity in *Antigone* and Aristotle," (paper presented at the Center for Law, Culture, and Social Thought, Northwestern University, March 9, 2001), 14, 16, 28.

11. Ibid., 35n17.

CHAPTER TWO

THE CONTEXT AND TEXTS OF *PUBLIC MAN,*
PRIVATE WOMAN

Jean Bethke Elshtain in the World of Ideas and Action

Arlene W. Saxonhouse

In a 1982 essay published in *Signs* entitled "Feminist Discourse and Its
Discontents: Language, Power, and Meaning," Jean Bethke Elshtain
addresses one of the many issues with which feminists of the time were
grappling: the potentially oppressive role that a language constituted by
those in power might continue to play as a tool of control over those
who had been silenced throughout history, leaving those who wished to
resist that control with the task of discovering new modes of communication. Elshtain's essay is a response to this challenge. Even in acknowledging that language has the potential to oppress, Elshtain was not so
ready to abandon the past, as many other feminists were, not so anxious
to urge her readers to imagine a world that could escape the history, languages, and earlier discourses that have been bequeathed to us over the
generations. As she says: "There are among us . . . those who seek solutions to our public and private dilemmas by depriving us of a grammar
of moral discourse and forcing all of life under a set of terms denuded of
a critical edge. In so doing, they would deprive the human object, female
and male, of the capacity to think, to judge, to question . . . for all these
activities are importantly constituted by an everyday, ordinary language

infused with moral terms."[1] Elshtain's refusal to deny the past, though, does not make her a slave to that past. In this piece she articulates a view that highlights the liberatory role of language, once we are ready to work with its relation to who we are as situated creatures with particular and shared histories.

She acknowledges the hold that the past has on us, but Elshtain does not simply say that "the past shapes us" in a deterministic and negative way. Rather, we need to recognize the past as a resource we can use and explore to develop the new historical world we want to create for ourselves and those who succeed us. Thus she wrote in that *Signs* article of the task that confronts us, namely, articulating a model of discourse that works from a variety of traditions in order to offer us a portrait of language that frees and does not oppress, that responds to our deepest longings and capacities, and builds on them rather than rejects them. She was not ready to abandon the ties to the past and the historical connections that make us who we are—whether she was discussing our general history or the personal histories we all experience in the cru- cibles of our families: "The 'I' that I am grows out of a past that I can perceive but dimly, a past that can anger, enlighten, illumine, or mystify my thinking about what it means to be a female, a human being, a citi- zen, and a political theorist in a post-Holocaust, post-Hiroshima age."[2] The structure and movement of this 1982 article capture some of what makes Elshtain's work so powerful and important, namely, its refusal to practice an amnesia about who we are as individuals or as members of the particular cultures and families of which we are a part—and, in particular for my argument here—it constitutes a refusal to forget the ideas of earlier writers and actors who have thought deeply about the human predicament. Just as important, the article illustrates that she drank heartily from those resources, but she also refused to be a slave to that past or those ideas, to put them on an unassailable pedestal. They are fundamental to who we are, but that does not make them immune to criticism, to the recognition of how the past can distort and also create, how the critical eye appreciates and investigates at the same time.

In the comments that follow, I want to consider Elshtain's first major work, *Public Man, Private Woman* (*PMPW*), the book that catapulted her into the public figure she was. First, I set the book into its historical context, reviewing in the broadest of terms the context for the debates that were swirling around in political and feminist thought at the time, and then I show how that book accomplished what she admonished us all to do in her 1982 piece on language, that is, to recognize how indebted we are to prior discourses and how those discourses are not to be dismissed as simply oppressive tools used by those in power, but how they can provide linguistic resources and theoretical frameworks that open up opportunities and understandings rather than restrict and control.

In doing this in her agenda-changing book, Elshtain sought to moderate the shrill discourse of the time and foster a fundamental rethinking of the accepted categories and oppositions of one of the social movements that profoundly changed all of our lives in the twentieth century. *Public Man, Private Woman* was published more than thirty years ago. It is not my intention to diminish the multitude of contributions that have followed, but rather to highlight the radical splash of that work when it appeared and to suggest how that book served as a prelude to Elshtain's far-ranging subsequent contributions. I do so from my own academic specialty: political science and political theory.

THE CONTEXT

The first edition of *Public Man, Private Woman* appeared in 1981, at the culmination of the turmoil of the 1960s and 1970s. That period, to oversimplify terribly (as I shall in what follows), was a deep reaction to the quietism of the post–World War II era. Part of the reaction to the horrendous events of World War II was a fear of politics and the frightful effects that a powerful political rhetoric had stirred up in support of the excesses of a politics practiced by fascist regimes. The fear was specifically of a politics that had engaged many in a politics of fear and of hatred, of the horrors of popular political action gone terribly wrong with the misuse of power for the most evil of purposes. It was a fear that gave birth to a quietism and praise for the withdrawal from the political world that had wreaked such havoc.

The 1950s spawned within the field of political science what could be called the birth of apathy theorists, while in political theory the legacy

and dominance of logical positivism and its derogation of value statements as simply (in A. J. Ayer's evocative language from his 1936 book
Language, Truth, and Logic) "ejaculations" sent a cold chill over political engagement.[3] Philosophers and political theorists worried about the
legitimacy of any moral claims, and political scientists portrayed a political world where democratic stability depended on a disengagement
from politics, a world that might be better served if we tended our private
gardens rather than letting ourselves be guided by totalitarian ideas and
totalistic ideals. The legacy of fascism taught that profound dangers lay
in trying to transform and improve the larger world in which we lived.
In 1954, an article in the journal *Political Studies* from England could
have the title "In Defense of Apathy," and include the following sentiment: "Many of the ideas connected with the general theme of a Duty to
Vote belong properly to the totalitarian camp and are out of place in the
vocabulary of liberal democracy." Instead, apathy is described as a "sign
of understanding and tolerance of human variety."[4]

    This sentiment, stated so boldly by the English writer, simply cap-
tured what many others had already articulated, others such as Schum-
peter (already in 1942), or S. M. Lipset, or the Robert Dahl of the 1960s,
who in his *Who Governs? Democracy and Power in an American City* (1961)
introduced a theory of polyarchy.[5] That extensive study of New Haven,
Connecticut, politics showed that the city of New Haven would function perfectly well if political action only became part of our lives when
we felt that our own personal interests might be threatened. If the junk-
yard was about be situated next to our property, then we might want to
contact City Hall, but otherwise we could let those in City Hall deal
with the matters of City Hall—while we would merrily engage in our
own private affairs. Or there was the work of Bernard Berelson and his
several coauthors, *Voting: A Study of Opinion Formation in a Presidential
Campaign* (1954). In that volume the authors presented their research
on the 1948 presidential election and reported on just how ignorant the
citizens of Elmira, New York, were about the foreign policy issues that
were at the heart of the presidential election, and how their votes tended
to go to groups with which the voters were affiliated, without much
attention to the things for which those groups really stood. Assessing
these findings, Berelson and his coauthors concluded that this was not

such a bad thing. At the end of their book, they ask: "How could a mass democracy work if all the people were deeply involved in politics?" And they conclude: "The apathetic segment of America probably has helped to hold the system together and cushioned the shock of disagreement, adjustment, and change." They admit that this "is not to say that we can stand apathy without limit," but the bottom line remains that apathy is good for the political system as a whole.[6]

I exaggerate the praise of apathy characteristic of those decades—but not by much. Engagement would bring on instability, and instability could bring on the ravages of a devastating war. The world had seen enough of that. The 1950s and early 1960s were a time to recover, to tend our own private worlds, and to find pleasures far from the noisy contests of the political realm. Claims to moral and political certainties had fostered fascism; better to resist those claims by affirming their impossibility.

Nevertheless, assorted social development and political events did not allow the "defense," indeed the glorification, of the apathy of the 1950s and early 1960s to last long, and the political and social explosion that followed those decades reasserted the demands for engagement, for political action, and for self-empowerment in the face of the wrongs that apathy might foster. We became aware that apathy and tending our own gardens left openings for just the sort of public energies we feared, and so political life, community control, and self-governance came to the fore again. Sociologists like Richard Sennett could write books that in their titles decried *The Fall of Public Man* (1977).[7] Hannah Arendt's *The Human Condition* (1958) took on a new urgency and gained an astonishing popularity in the 1970s. The call was on for public action, and the attack was launched against the retreat into the quiet world of suburban conformity. And with the newfound activism came the women's movement, as women demanded to be part of this resurrected awareness of the importance of engagement, of the reassertion of the value of public life against those who extolled the political apathy that they assumed would ensure stability and security.

As the language of justice reasserted its place in our theoretical and national debate, attention to the private world of one's own garden came to be viewed as a narcissistic retreat from the "real" issues: racism, the exploitation of the poor, the urban crisis, the oppression of women, and an unjust war. The barricades called forth those committed to social justice into the world of public action. A concern for the consequences of this clarion call for the private world of the family did not weigh heavily in the thoughts of those fighting oppression. Indeed, the seeds (or even the full flowering) of oppression were just as likely to be found in the structure of the family as in the political and academic institutions behind an unpopular war and the racist policies of exclusion.

At this point in our narrative, *Public Man, Private Woman* appeared and took a courageous stand against the prevailing inclinations towards community action and political participation in social thought, and most particularly in the women's movement, towards a life that would take women beyond the family, the bedroom, and the suburbs. Elshtain did this by refusing to accept the facile assumptions concerning the priority of political over personal engagement that had been born in the reaction to apathy and expressed in a denial of the satisfactions (false) and importance (also false) of a private world that stood at such a distance from the tools and language of power. Elshtain refused to be drawn along by the powerful rhetoric of the period that focused on the need for attention to the public realm and on the necessary place for women along with men in that particular realm of action.

Her book, though, was not by any means a retreat into the quietism of the apathy theorists, nor was it an escape from the turmoil of the political world. Elshtain came forward as a critic of the unthinking dogmas of the women's movement, taking her bearings from neither the Right nor the Left, but from a deep understanding of the complexities of the issues of contemporary life and of the dangers that totalistic theories and certainties pose for our lives, the tragedies and the violations that by their very simplicity they may provoke, from whatever political leaning they came. Drawing on her readings of Wittgenstein, Elshtain adhered to his injunction, which she made the grounding of her writings, to "think really honestly" (*PMPW*, xii; also *Power Trips and Other Journeys* [*PT*]). This perspective informed *Public Man, Private Woman* and fostered her willingness to acknowledge the tensions that so many others preferred to deny or pretend not to see. This stance made her work very significant—and very controversial. In the reactive acclamation of

public engagement, Elshtain recognized the loss of attention to that
for which the public world existed—the pleasures, loves, satisfactions
that mark a private world. To leave that private world behind constituted for her the loss of our humanity, and Elshtain was not ready to
abandon it in response to the similarly powerful pull of public commitments. Nor was she ready to abandon it to the certainties that surfaced
in public policies and feminist theories concerning what the "family"
ought to be. She acknowledged the tensions and especially the messi-
ness that those tensions fostered in our full lives as both public and
private creatures.

Public Man, Private Woman stood in 1981 as a warning to those
who had overreacted to apathy theorists in their struggle to revitalize
the public world and who in the process had lost a sense of the values
inherent in a world of care for the particular rather than the universal.
In his trenchant criticism of Socrates's Callipolis, Aristotle remarked
bluntly: "Yet which is superior—for each of two thousand (or ten thousand) individuals to say 'mine' and address the same thing, or rather
the way they say 'mine' in cities now? . . . It is better, indeed, to have
a cousin of one's own, than a son in the sense indicated."[8] That view
resonated with Elshtain, but at the same time that she did not dismiss
the demands a public life, of necessity, made on the individual. Her work
represents the effort to embrace both, and all the complications that
such an embrace entails.

As others were racing to grasp the public world of power and influence and as that world suddenly, through the efforts of feminists, was
beginning to open slightly, Elshtain basically said, wait a minute. Is this
what we really want? What are the terms of that access and that power
we are so eager to have for ourselves? What will we accomplish once we
move into the public world of male power? What will happen when we
invite the language of power into the family? She raised these questions
in the effort to help us focus on the gender dimensions of what was
happening, and some of what was happening was not very pretty in its
implications for men and the roles that it was asserting women should
pursue. Arendt's *The Human Condition* extolled the agonistic public
sphere where men would display who they really were through contest
and debate concerning the issues of public action, and whereas Arendt

dismissed the private world as a realm of biology and necessity, Elshtain came back and said, "Let's not diminish the private world so readily."

Foreshadowing themes that would perhaps inspire her later book on St. Augustine, Elshtain found religious grounds for the claims of the private world on our attention and our love. In devaluing that private world, as an author like Arendt appeared to do, we were losing an essential part of ourselves, of what we value most, in particular, the capacity to love, to care, to share. Elshtain was not appealing to a sentiment that wanted women back in the home because nature decreed it. As she noted in her vibrant and brilliant attack on Allan Bloom's *Closing of the American Mind*, where appeals to Nature with that capital "N" seemed to suggest such a retreat for the females of the human species, "nature" is one of those messy terms that "may serve either as a weapon to put pressure upon social practices and institutions in order to reform or reconstitute them or as part of the arsenal of defense against such pressures." And in following through on that point in her review she appropriately asked regarding Bloom's use of "Nature": "How is one to tell what really existed by nature and what emerged historically? Furthermore, what difference does the locating of an institution, practice, or tradition in nature, or as natural, make?" (*PT*, 111). Rather than rely on the ontologically suspect language of nature in her images of the family and in her explorations into who we are in our humanity, she insisted that we not lose those attachments to particular individuals that allow us the opportunities for love and caring and the appreciation of the particularities of those with whom we share our lives. The retreat to the private that marked the post–World War II years may have fostered the revolt that marked a return to the engagement with the public world, but there was too much of value in the abandoned private world simply to let it lie on the garbage heap of past dreams. So many of Elshtain's subsequent pieces insisted that we bring to our public actions an awareness of the underlying concerns and orientations that inform our private lives.

One of the famous and almost universal motivating slogans of the women's movement of the 1970s affirmed that "the personal is political," a slogan that translated all relations, even our most intimate relations, into power relations, a view captured perhaps most vividly in the writings of Catharine MacKinnon—though she certainly was not alone—for whom all sex is rape and all families sites of oppression. Marriage understood in the political language of power and oppression became a realm of disempowerment for women. Elshtain was prescient in her 1981 warnings about the dangers of not "thinking really hard" about the meaning and consequences of this popular phrase and overused battle cry of "the personal is the political." Drawing on an understanding of public and private life that came from a reading of both political theorists and the feminist authors of the time, she warned in *Public Man, Private Woman* about the dangers of such a slogan and such a vision. She wondered whether maybe it is the political that ought to become personal, not the personal political. Maybe the political diminishes us, as does the race to embrace it as women's own. To see it as a world that needed to be wrested from male control and in turn to bring the political into our private lives has meant the loss of the capacity to treasure what really needs treasuring, has meant the transformation of those qualities and aspects of our personalities and psyches that provide a depth and richness to our lives that cannot be achieved in the abstract world of public and government, where we necessarily generalize rather than particularize. Or as she wrote in a later piece about this frequent battle cry of "the personal is the political": "It replicates a central presupposition of the 'totalizing' (hence totalitarian) regimes that have haunted the twentieth century. . . . I am not arguing that feminists wanted totalitarian politics. I am insisting that they did not pay sufficient attention to the implications of what they were claiming and just might unleash."[9] The "totalizing" regimes—the fascism of Nazi Germany, the communism of the Soviet Union—had transformed individuals into uniform units and severed the relations particular individuals had with one another into relations with the state. Elshtain feared that those who wished to destroy the private failed to acknowledge that such destruction might leave them unprotected against the overwhelming power of the state to abrade the diversity that she treasured.

Elshtain's call for the resurrection and appreciation of the private life was not a call for a retreat within, as the apathy theorists of an earlier generation might have suggested, but instead for the acknowledgment that the values and virtues that were part of that private world be brought to and—most importantly—inform our public lives. Inherent in her appeal to the value of what is private was also the resistance to the feminist move to see the private world only as a realm of oppression of female victims by male victimizers, of the weak who suffer and the strong who cause suffering. A committed democrat and egalitarian, Elshtain rails against the too-frequent feminist claims to a knowledge of what others say our lives must be like—without any consideration of how we ourselves experience those lives. To affirm oppression where there is love is to take an Olympian stance that Elshtain rejects. Trusting in each individual's experience of herself, Elshtain was not prepared to condemn whatever satisfactions that individual may have found in her private life as the result of a false consciousness.

TEXTS

In the previous section, I suggested that we need to understand *Public Man, Private Woman* contextually, as important *because* it was written at a certain time and in a certain place. I make that claim also in part because that is how Elshtain sees us, as embedded in context, and it is a context that most emphatically includes the family and the private sphere. That context pervades our conception of social reality and raises questions about a liberal feminism that atomized us out of those relationships. It is a context that, for sure, may be limiting, but it is also liberating, for it may contain who we can become, but it also opens for us the opportunities to take ourselves beyond our narrow spheres and into the larger domain of public action. Elshtain's appeals to draw on our own experiences in the private realm and on the emotions that derive from that world have not been without their critics, and a certain romanticism may permeate the warm portraits of the private world that sprinkle Elshtain's books and essays in general.[10] But such criticisms pay inadequate attention to the deep theoretical foundations for these autobiographical appeals. One's standpoint, one's perspective, depends on the world from which one comes. And that context includes the intellectual tradition of Western thought, the texts themselves that form the basis of that tradition.

Just as Elshtain insisted that we ourselves are not abstract individuals sprung to life like those Hobbesian mushrooms on the forest floor, she recognized that the theories with which we grapple and the conceptual frameworks within which we work must be set into the historical context of the traditions of Western political thought. She appreciated that we must grasp and draw on the theories of those who have informed our own thinking. Thus, as we are children of our parents, so are we children of the theories that have emerged across the millennia. Elshtain took this past seriously, and in the major part of *Public Man, Private Woman* that attends to the readings of the authors from the tradition, she explores the context from which our conceptual frameworks come and the perspectives from which we must move forward.

That forward movement, though, does not emerge from the total dismissal of what has been. Rather, we must see those texts as the cradle from which we grow, as informing how we understand the world in which live and act. One may go through those passages in which she explores the texts from the tradition and find those places where one might disagree with her interpretations and specific readings of particular portions. I, for one, disagree strongly with her reading of Plato's *Republic*. I would argue that were she to have read Socrates as a character in the dialogue exploring alternative visions of political organizations, she would have seen him as proposing just as messy and complex a world as the one she valued. Callipolis may be a totalistic regime in which "it can be said that its creation would require such drastic social surgery, all manner of disruptions, wrenchings, and griefs that the vast majority of individuals, in his time or our own, would, if asked, prefer to remain in their unjust societies than to undergo Plato's cure" (*PMPW*, 30). Yet, here the questions raised by Leo Strauss and Bloom (contra Elshtain) about the seriousness of the proposals and whether the Socratic character is himself forcing us to consider the weird and complex implications of such a vision, rather than simply advocating it, seem right.

When she turns to the women in Callipolis, she does follow those who in the desperate search for just one "good guy" besides John Stuart Mill among the pantheon of chauvinistic canonical writers found it in Socrates and his inclusion of women in the guardian class of Callipolis. Elshtain sees in that inclusion (as other feminists reading with less clear eyes failed to do) "the unacceptable price those women Plato [it should be Socrates] admits to parity with male rulers must pay for the privilege" (*PMPW*, 37), but she does not question what Socrates and Plato actually communicate to their readers by themselves illuminating that "unacceptable price" for inclusion. Perhaps, indeed, it shows male readers what price they too must pay in pursuit of political power. For one who sees so much complexity and so much irony in the world she observes, she misses the profoundly ironic tone of Plato's Socratic works. Yet, one nevertheless cannot help but admire the range of works that come under her purview as resources for discovering how and why we conceptualize public and private in the ways that we do.

Though in *Public Man, Private Woman* St. Augustine is only a relatively minor player in the panoply of others from the classical period through Marx that provide the background for Elshtain's reflections on the concepts of public and private and the feminist misconstrual of the relationship between the two, his presence in the chapter on early Christianity is key to her understanding of the issues she addresses. She finds in St. Augustine a voice that speaks to incorporating diversity without destroying distinction and particularity. Quoting a poignant passage from Etienne Gilson, she delights in St. Augustine's ability to celebrate diversity: "God knew how to beautify the universe through the diversity of its parts," and in her own words she describes the celebration of "unity within the diversity of sentient humanity" as a "joyous piety for St. Augustine" (*PMPW*, 69). She grants that Augustine legitimates the rule of husbands over wives, but she also recognizes how this claim needs to be understood in the context of his writing about peace and the Augustinian language that "even those who rule serve those whom they seem to command, for they rule not from a love of power, but from a sense of the duty they owe to others" (*PMPW*, 71).

The text of St. Augustine gives Elshtain a grounding through which to respond later in her book to the attacks by feminists on the family and the relations within the family, but it is perhaps in the book that she devotes entirely to St. Augustine that we get a sense of the full depth of how his writings informed her own and gave her thought its contextual and textual force. It is in this later book, where she offers her paean to Augustine, that we find the roots of her validation of a private realm, a world that does not diverge from, resist, or stand in opposition to the public world, but rather informs it. *Augustine and the Limits of Politics* is a beautiful exposition of why the bishop of Hippo, who so seldom makes his way into the mainstream language and thought of political science, political theory, or feminism, offers us a deep understanding of the value of the private world without sacrificing our commitment to the improvement of the social world within which we live. From Augustine we learn how the intertwining of public and private commitments enabled Elshtain to translate her concerns to the messy world of public policies, with issues like family and parenting, surrogacy, and the feminist bugaboo of pornography legislation, all of which came under Elshtain's critical appraisal through the years. The variety and range of topics she touched on in her various writings is impressive, but in her handling of them one can see the Augustinian injunction to see the beauty in the diversity of the world and the need to see our engagement in the public world as drawing its strength from the particular attachments that make us human. She worried about the dangers of a feminism that brings into both the public and private world atomistic liberal creatures creating rights out of our wants, a feminism that does not find its intellectual roots in the thought and texts of the past. Augustine began to be her guide from *Public Man, Private Woman* in 1982, but his importance in her thought only becomes fully evident, to me at least, with the poignant 1995 volume on Augustine.

That part of *Public Man, Private Woman* where she addresses the most prominent feminist writers of the time was both daring and prescient, but Elshtain was also daring when she applied the categories of gender to the canonical texts that are the focus of attention for much of the book. These were texts revered by generations of male scholars who read them as works speaking to them of the public world of political activities and constructions, far away from the untidy and lowly world of the household. As Elshtain shows in her studies of the assorted authors she considers, those public worlds were not so protected from the intrusion of private concerns; the blinders of earlier generations of readers needed to be shattered so the full significance of those writings could inform our own understanding. This could lead to uncovering the remnants of patriarchal undercurrents in liberal theory, to exploring

Tocqueville's insights into the meshing of domestic and political order, to expanding Hegel's conception of the engagement in the public world by drawing on his insights concerning women and language.

Elshtain, of course, wrote her book well before the canon wars of the late 1980s and 1990s were in full swing, and thus there is a refreshing lack of self-consciousness about the turn to the classics in the field of political theory. She acknowledged that the field has its share of awful sexist writings from male theorists across the millennia. No one can ignore Aristotle's comments in the *History of Animals* that attribute to the male the qualities of completion and perfection and to women the qualities of jealousy, despondency, and the tendency towards being deceptive and querulous. Or, there is, of course, notoriously Rousseau's comment in *Emile* that woman is expressly formed to please the man. But Elshtain was prepared to go beyond such comments, to learn from these authors rather than simply rail against the all-too-offensive statements that seem to deny those of us who are female our full humanity. She could go beyond all that to study the ancient, medieval, early modern, and modern thinkers for what they taught specifically about the interdependence of public and private, and most especially she worked out for us, with reference to these texts, how the gender component wormed its way into the underlying theories that to the casual reader seemed so focused originally only on the public world. Elshtain uncovered their interdependence and how, for example, in the case of Aristotle, the thoughtless dismissal of an author because of what appeared to some as sexist assertions meant the loss of the theoretical concerns about political engagement that force us to address pressing contemporary issues concerning the nature and significance of political participation.

Undoubtedly, though, the most daring part of *Public Man, Private Woman* is in the last third or so of the book, when Elshtain leaves the canonical texts she has analyzed with such subtlety and takes on the feminist theorists of the previous decade—the ones who had sharply placed feminism on the political agenda with such force and provocation. Elshtain's book was written when it was still "hip" to claim radical credentials and to take stances that made one seem more radical than thou—more damning of the male than your female neighbors dared be, when, for example, Ti-Grace Atkinson could describe men qua men as "ontologically 'insecure and frustrated'" creatures who engage in "meta-physical cannibalism" whereby they "devour and dominate women." Or there was Susan Brownmiller, who described a universal male lust for power that created a rape ideology by which "*all* men keep *all* women in a state of fear" (*PMPW*, 206 [italics in the original]). The list and the extreme language cited by Elshtain goes on and on; with a retro-spective glance the passages seem absurd and almost laughable, but the extremism did not mean that such language and proclamations were not taken seriously as true statements of the real status of the female in the 1970s. Elshtain was as aware as any of us females living and trying to get ahead in the 1970s of the discrimination and challenges to such engagement in our lives, but Elshtain did not with her clear voice jump on the bandwagon of excoriation and most especially she did not let her feminist sympathies lull her into the casual acceptance of the calls among feminists to jettison the family as the poisoned realm of patriar-chal oppression.

Her study of the classics of political theory—especially the writings of St. Augustine—had made her analyses far richer than the blunt tools the feminists she criticized were wielding, and she was unwilling to dis-miss the world of the private family as beneath contempt because it had been inhabited by women, because it was the realm where women may have flourished. She saw that the views of radical feminism in fact deni-grated women and what they most often cared about most profoundly, and that they thereby diminished women's potential contributions to the welfare of all. They sought public monuments for themselves rather than appreciating the artistry of the quilt. By prefacing her responses to the radical feminist writings with the texts of the Western tradition, Elshtain was able to draw from those texts the capacity to understand the complexity of the relationship between, and interpenetration of, the public and private rather than assume an untextured division between those worlds that prioritized one at the expense of the other.

Though Elshtain is certainly critical of the feminist theorists she treats in the second half of *Public Man, Private Woman*, she nevertheless affirms the importance of adding their voices to the discussions of our political lives and of the need to address their views, whether we accept them or not. Later in her career she would add other voices to the texts that comprise the context from which we need to reflect on the nature of public and private, male and female, and the interactions that constitute our world. The voices of Elizabeth Cady Stanton and especially of Jane Addams appeared in her work, forcing the opening up of discourse rather than trying to close it off through the dismissal of those who may not say precisely what we may like to hear. Through this openness to the range of voices in a multitude of texts, Elshtain differed from many of her critics and now stands as an important lesson in the dangers of stifling rather than encouraging conversation.

Elshtain's goal was never to overcome conflict or smooth over difference; eager to include many different voices she worried that premature reconciliation among competing points of view would close off debate. And she was never one to stand back from contention. Her readings of wide-ranging texts, whether they be canonical political theory, literature, poetry, or polemical documents, served as the pool from which she learned and drew her insights. She was an advocate for openness to different voices, the voices of the family, of caring mothers in a way that has too often been stilled in feminist circles. We are in debt to Elshtain for her determined insistence that we recognize the centrality of conflict and accept the tensions that emerge from our differences, and for the demand that the discussions that work off from those differences be kept open.

CONCLUSION

I have herein expressed profound admiration for all Elshtain accomplished with this early book, *Public Man, Private Woman*, and how that accomplishment continued to inform the massive amount of work she completed thereafter. Let me now, however, admit my one significant problem with it, namely, the title—certainly catchy and memorable— which reaffirms and plays to the aesthetic appreciation of binary oppositions or dichotomies. In the book itself and in so much of Elshtain's other work, she manages to move us beyond dichotomies. She urges us to understand the intermingling of familiar categories and the profoundly different means of participation that are available to citizens when the old dichotomies are transcended, when we dismiss a masculinist view of the public and private oppositions. She is impatient in her work with dichotomies that imprison us and that through their linguistic power often become part of social policies. She regularly asks us to embrace and endorse contradictions. Only then, for example, can we understand how the grandmothers on the plaza in Argentina, about whom Elshtain spoke and wrote so eloquently, in bearing witness to their missing children and grandchildren became political actors in a fashion that Arendt, for instance, with her agonistic public presentation of self, cannot capture. Or conversely, how public actors are informed by the concerns that arise out of their lives in families. Yes, the book is an attack on the simplicity of the dichotomy she uses for its title, but the brevity and thus the power of the title shelters an old set of oppositions that her analysis is meant to undermine and reframe. By giving the dichotomy such linguistic force, I fear that it may work more to instantiate it than to explode it in the variety of ways Elshtain may have set as her goal.

Throughout her work Elshtain presents a model of optimism, despite the attacks she endured on occasion by those who thought she was not radical enough, by those who said she was too soft on the male sex, and by those who deny the wonders of maternal love. She in turn treasured our everyday, personal experiences, as St. Augustine did. Certainly, she recognizes their limitations and the potential for harm and for good, but she does not therefore ask us to reject them. Rather, she asks that we build on them as a grounding for the broad set of relations that compose our social and political life, that we understand and protect that world of privacy. Elshtain celebrates our lives as full human beings through her books and articles. By acknowledging the context— political, social, textual—in which she presents these views in *Public Man, Private Woman*, we pay homage to the way in which she asks us to learn and the way in which she asks us to live.

NOTES

A condensed version, in a different form, of this essay was published as "*Public Man/Private Woman* in Context," *Politics and Gender* 11 (2015): 561–69.

1. Jean Bethke Elshtain, "Feminist Discourse and Its Discontents," *Signs* 7 (1982): 605.

2. Ibid., 620.

3. A. J. Ayer, *Language, Truth, and Logic* (New York: Dover, 1952).

4. Morris Jones, quoted in M. I. Finley, *Democracy: Ancient and Modern* (New Brunswick, NJ: Rutgers University Press, 1973), 4.

5. Robert A. Dahl, *Who Governs? Democracy and Power in an American City* (New Haven, CT: Yale University Press, 1961).

6. Bernard R. Berelson, Paul F. Lazarfeld, and William N. McPhee, *Voting: A Study of Opinion Formation in a Presidential Campaign* (Chicago: University of Chicago Press, 1954), 314, 322.

7. Richard Sennett, *The Fall of Public Man* (New York: Knopf, 1977).

8. Aristotle, *The Politics*, trans. Carnes Lord (Chicago: University of Chicago Press, 1984), 2.3.

9. Jean Bethke Elshtain, "Public and Private in American Political Life and Thought," in *The Public and Private in the United States*, ed. Hitoshi Abe and Chieko Katagawa Otsuru (Osaka: Japan Center for Area Studies, 1999), 26.

10. See, for example, Elshtain, "Feminism, Family, and Community," in *Feminism and Community*, ed. Penny A. Weiss (Philadelphia: Temple University Press, 1995), where she writes of her grandmother "instructing her grandchildren in the crafts that create things of beauty and utility to provide envelopes for our bodies, warmth for our beds, and food for our tables" (259). Or Elshtain, "Suffer the Little Children," *New Republic*, March 4, 1996, a devastating review of Hillary Clinton's *It Takes a Village*, where, though acknowledging that not all families are perfect, she again extols family life in the small town in which she grew up in Colorado, and praises her grandmother, who, as Elshtain was leaving with her family, "came out to the car for a last goodbye, thrusting into my arms more homemade noodles, another loaf of rye bread, freshly gathered eggs, a new apron, another remarkable quilt" (38).

CHAPTER THREE

ELSHTAIN'S "REFLECTIVE" ETHICS OF FEMINISM
AND FAMILY

An Appreciation and Critique

Don Browning

The use of the word "engaged" in the title of the conference where
this essay first saw light was insightful. It gets to the heart of both Jean
Bethke Elshtain's methodology in political philosophy and her ethics. If
one fully understands what it means to be engaged, one can understand
why it is appropriate to call Elshtain both a political philosopher and, by
necessity, a Christian theological ethicist.

The concluding chapter in Elshtain's *Public Man, Private Woman*
(1981) and her essay "Toward a Reflective Feminist Theory" (1983)
make the following points about methodology in political and social
philosophy.[1] First, a political philosopher should avoid bringing a priori
theory into efforts to account for and critique political action.[2] When
political theory is correctly understood, it is according to the Greek
word *theorein*, a "way of seeing." In Elshtain's view, it is by necessity also
conditioned by the historical, local, and natural particularity of both the
political philosopher and her subjects of analysis.[3] The purpose of this
seeing is not first of all the exercise of abstract theory but "giving voice"
to the subjects of political theory so that they can "sing their own song."[4]

This, for instance, is especially important for the women whom feminist political theory attempts to understand and explain. Elshtain's methodology assumes that these women—of whatever class, race, nationality, or political persuasion—are purposive and reflective agents with their own histories and self-understandings, which are the political theorist's first task to comprehend.

But the political theorist is also a purposive, reflective, naturally and historically conditioned agent, and these conditions will influence what she or he sees and theorizes.[5] This, for Elshtain, is not a limitation but an actual account of the real situation of political philosophy. Part of what conditions the political philosopher is what Elshtain calls a "discursive inheritance"[6]—a history of political discourse that begins in fifth-century Athens and includes not only Plato and Aristotle but the Bible and figures as diverse as Cicero, Augustine, Aquinas, Luther, Grotius, Kant, and Marx. The idea of discursive inheritance is close to Gadamer's concept of "effective history"—the lingering influence at the horizon of consciousness of highly influential classics of the past even if we do not consciously know them today.[7] But in the case of the Western-trained political philosopher, this effective history has become explicit and is part of the individually appropriated history that she brings to her interpretive "seeing."

Hence, in the early 1980s, before Gadamer and Ricoeur were widely known on the North American scene, Elshtain was proposing a methodology in political philosophy close to their understanding of description and explanation as dialogue. She writes this about her method of description and theory building: "My discourse, remember, locates female self-awareness, because it entails a dialogue and purpose. It also sets up an interpretive dynamic in which a subject may attain greater self-awareness, because it entails a dialogue which she arbitrates."[8]

This does not mean that Elshtain rejects the role of abstraction in political description and theory. Clearly the social location, history, and particularity of philosopher and subject are not identical. By necessity, there will be some distance between them, and this distance creates tension—the stuff of critique. Because of the philosopher's "discursive inheritance" of the history of political theory in the West, she brings potentially wider frameworks of interpretation within which to place the subjectivity, reflective self-awareness, and purposes of her subjects.[9] Description as dialogue will entail some degree of abstractive reinterpretation by the philosopher of the subject's life-world.

Nor does the political philosopher resist the task of critique. Indeed, bringing criticism and transformation to the subject and the subject's situation is a central task of political theory. In this sense, political theory as a form of situated "seeing" is an expression of *phronesis*—a kind of politically motivated practical reason.[10] But in Elshtain's view, critique follows, and does not precede, engaged description and explanation. It does not precede or neglect description as it often does in abstract forms of practical reason found in various Kantian, Marxist, feminist, and critical-theoretical forms of critique.[11] To say it more simply, the political theorist must listen before he critiques.

Elshtain challenges feminist political philosophers to listen to and uncover the genuine human concerns behind some of the most disquieting forms of reaction to feminism, such as Mirabel Morgan's 1975 rejection of feminism in her astoundingly popular *Total Woman*.[12] The sensitive theorist brings critique as close as possible to the lived world and self-interpretation of her or his subjects, something like how the interpretations of a good psychotherapist are fine-tuned to be as internal as possible to the words and self-understanding of the client or patient.[13] The engaged interpretations of the political theorist, however, are not psychotherapy; individual transformation is not the goal of political philosophy. But transformation of the social situation is a goal.[14] In this sense, both political theorists and psychotherapists have practical transformative goals. And in both cases, description and explanation must precede and mediate critique.

Since theory in the sense of *seeing* arises out of the historically conditioned and reflective selves of scholar and subject, Elshtain must acknowledge her Christianity—the way it has conditioned her own selfhood and its moral and metaphysical entailments. And, as we will see, she does acknowledge her Christian theology as one source of critique. She does this when discussing the influence of her grandmother,[15] early Christianity's implicit critique of the idolatry of temporal power,[16] and Christianity's subtle undermining of ancient patriarchy.[17]

A MULTIDIMENSIONAL VIEW OF ACTION

If one considers Elshtain's view of theory as conditioned seeing and dialogue, one soon discovers embedded in it a multidimensional view of
human action. This leads me to assert that she does not so much reject
systematic thinking in her political philosophy as she rejects any thin or
monodimensional view of it, whether in an overreliance on some form
of the categorical imperative as one finds in Kant and his recent followers, such as John Rawls, Susan Okin, or Lawrence Kohlberg; some form
of utilitarianism as one finds in John Stuart Mill or the situation ethics
of Joseph Fletcher; or some expression of ethical egoism as one sees
in the rational choice theories of Gary Becker, Richard Posner, and a
number of psychotherapists, such as Carl Rogers, Abraham Maslow, and
Fritz Perls, of the 1960s and 1970s.

Elshtain's multidimensional theory of action is derived from her
analysis of reflective-practical action—action by self-aware agents in
their struggles to pursue their purposes, understand their situation, cope
with obstacles and conflicts, and improve and transform their lives. Such
action has several dimensions. When one sees how Elshtain articulates
these dimensions, one grasps the key to both her political theory and
her ethics. I may in what follows give her multidimensional view more
systematic form than she might feel comfortable with, but I hold that
she implicitly uses these dimensions for both descriptive and normative
purposes.

First, there is the dimension of concrete *practices*—the activities of
specific individuals and societies that pattern their everyday pursuits.
Second, there is the dimension of bodily *tendencies and needs* that at some
level motivate our purposes. These bodily needs are, Elshtain acknowledges, always historically and culturally conditioned, but they are nonetheless present and functioning in human experience. Third, there are
always certain social, economic, and ecological *constraints* on the realization of people's purposes; humans act within the real world, and not
everything is possible, or at least not immediately or fully possible, in
this world. These constraints must be faced, something that utopian
perspectives fail to take seriously enough. Then, fourth, there is always
a *narrative* dimension to practical action—stories we both inherit and

revise that interpret and give meaning to our practices, needs, and constraints. And fifth, there is a critical and strategic dimension to practical
action; this appears when one brings some evaluative principle to our
practices, critiques them, and imagines strategies for the future. This is
the moment of opportunity for genuine moral judgment to be exercised,
but this judgment does not always occur or occur well.

These dimensions apply to both the philosopher and the subjects
she is trying to describe and explain. They run through the dialogue
between them. But when carefully identified and considered, they also
reveal the systematic elements that go into every dialogue and the ethical purposes of dialogue.

ILLUSTRATIONS OF ELSHTAIN'S MULTIDIMENSIONALITY

Elshtain's analyses and dialogues are complex orchestrations of her multidimensional view of experience. For instance, interest in the concrete
practices of the traditions of her subjects and interlocutors is rooted in
memories of her grandmother and the care with which she passed to her
heirs the recipes and customs of her European tradition. We also see it
in Elshtain's fondness for an old Celtic saying that goes, "We warm ourselves at fires we did not build; and drink from wells we did not dig."[18]
Elshtain is interested in uncovering the good, both moral and premoral,
that such practices contain, even though they often also need criticism
and updating. And she is skeptical of modern theorists who ignore or
denigrate such practical expressions of "everyday life."

She is especially interested in those practices that minister to the
concrete needs of growing children. In fact, the biological and developmental needs of children anchor her attention to the second dimension I listed above—the organic needs and tendencies that humans bring
to their experiences. Most central for Elshtain are children's needs for
long-term and stable attachments with care-giving adults.[19] In *Public
Man, Private Woman*, Elshtain gets very specific about the range and
number of needs that humans project into experience and that culture
and social institutions should work to meet. In one way or another,

she invokes this list throughout her career. They are the need for love, recognition, intimacy, sex (or the sublimation of sex), mutual sharing, creativity, and curiosity.[20] These needs must first of all be met in the family, but with increasing family fragmentation in all societies, more and more they are not being met there. According to her, the satisfaction and shaping of these needs provide the psychological capacity for adult morality and responsible citizenship. Responsible citizenship, she argues, is the analogical extension outward to others beyond the family of virtues first consolidated in families.[21] Elshtain refutes the political liberalism of John Locke when he asserted that humans have similar perceptions of reality but very different human needs. She reverses this by contending that humans have very different social perceptions but share quite similar fundamental needs. In holding this view, Elshtain has appreciation for the psychobiology of Aristotle and Aquinas (but not in every detail), and also some aspects of psychoanalysis (especially the work of Erik Erikson), and parts of sociobiology and evolutionary psychology (especially when reinterpreted by Mary Midgley).

When theories of the family and expressions of feminism neglect these hard realities of human nature, met on average by mothers and fathers in intact families, Elshtain has for decades exposed these omissions. The passage of time and the advances in social psychology, sociology, evolutionary psychology, social neuroscience, and economics have only served to confirm positions on these matters that she first advanced more than thirty years ago.[22]

But we should be reminded that Elshtain holds that we partially come to know our needs by witnessing the many concrete practices that religious and cultural traditions have developed to meet them—the baby's need for food through watching mothers nurse their infants, its need for recognition through the constant exchange of smiles between parent and offspring, or the withering decline that afflicts the young when these needs are not met regularly and enthusiastically.

A third dimension of Elshtain's multidimensional view of experience is the *contextual*. Our practices are partially shaped by social, cultural, and ecological contexts. She is particularly critical of radical, liberal, and Marxist feminists who fail to interpret correctly the context of contemporary marriage, family, and child-rearing. Radical feminists

such as Shulamith Firestone and Mary Daly ignore contemporary contexts when they criticize nature itself—the biological facts of conception, pregnancy, motherhood, and the differential roles of women and
men in these dramas (the fact that women bear the children, and men
often attach to offspring more slowly)—as the leading causes of the
oppression of women.[23] On the other hand, she criticizes liberal feminists who claim that patriarchy in the West and throughout the world
was the source of women's oppression. These liberal feminists champion the work demands of modern industrial societies as a source of
women's liberation without fully understanding how these pressures are
themselves sources of women's domination.[24] And she chides Marxist
feminists, who are indeed more perceptive about the strains on families
of modern forms of capitalism, but who also overemphasize the inevitability of the family simply becoming the pawn of capitalist production.[25]

Elshtain acknowledges the role of patriarchy in oppressing women
but has a much more subtle interpretation of it than is typical of many
feminist critiques. However, she locates the unique strains on modern
families in the modernization process and the Industrial Revolution.
When large numbers of women were absorbed into the wage economy,
both men and women—fathers and mothers—became more dominated
by the work demands of the market.[26] The entire family began to worship at the "altar of work and career."[27] Adequate amounts of *time* to meet
the love, attachment, recognition, intimacy, sexual, and curiosity needs
of the individuals of modern families began to disappear. And as we will
soon see, Elshtain offers a variety of practical strategies for addressing
the strains of modernization without, it should be noticed, removing
women from the opportunities of employment in the wage economy.

The fourth dimension of Elshtain's multidimensional view of both
description and ethics is what I would call its *narrative* dimension.
Elshtain holds that every normative theory, whether explicitly philosophical or more popular and grassroots in origin, is wrapped in a story
or narrative about the meaning of life. This can be seen in radical feminism, which tells a story of the past domination of women by the necessities of nature versus the possible unconditioned freedom of the future.
It is present in liberal feminism, whose narrative contrasts the patriar-
chal tyranny of yesteryears with the agency and fulfillment promised by

women's full incorporation in modernity's paid economy. And it can be found in Marxist feminism's drama of the class and economic determinism of all prerevolutionary societies versus the free "sex love" of Friedrich Engel's vision of women, men, and families in the classless society liberated from the exploitations and distortions of capitalism.[28]

Elshtain exposes these narratives and contrasts them with the story of the Christian faith, which *she* embraces but that is rejected if not ridiculed by these other perspectives. Elshtain believes that the Christian story about the sovereignty of God and Lordship of Christ over all earthly powers freed Christians from submitting their bodies to the warrior values of ancient Sparta and Athens[29] as well as the emperor worship and addiction to power of imperial Rome.[30] In contrast to the values of the valiant warrior and crafty political ruler of Greece and Rome, early Christianity honored the feminine virtues of gentleness and nurture and developed an image of men as nurturing fathers and husbands who cherished their wives as they did their own bodies.

These images are not perfect reflections of the modern egalitarian or equal-regard family, but they contributed to their development. The Christian narrative about the goodness of creation undercuts all efforts to blame nature for the domination of women. And its narrative of peace and forgiveness—when contrasted to the narratives of war and political domination that surrounded early Christianity—provided people with a new and refreshing alternative vision. It was a narrative that applied to both Christian men and women; its presence upsets all efforts to place special blame on Christianity for the patriarchal dominations of the past. Elshtain uses her own appreciation for the Christian narrative in her dialogue with, description of, and critique of the narrative envelopes surrounding her various subjects and interlocutors.

The fifth dimension of her multidimensional view of description and ethics is that of *critique*. It also lapses over into strategic prescription. For Elshtain, critique should be situated within the multidimensional reflection of self-aware agents of the kind I have been describing in these paragraphs. She is skeptical of those political philosophers who allow ideology critique to "swamp reflection,"[31] that is, philosophers who critique before "seeing" and describing, as she thinks is the case with the existentialist critiques of Simone de Beauvoir.[32] For Elshtain, criticism does not simply flow from a single abstract moral principle that applies to all situations. As we have noticed, her evaluative and critical responses flow from several of the other dimensions of reflection, for example, inadequate accounts of human needs and tendencies, thin and mistaken descriptions of social and cultural contexts, and distorting cultural and religious narratives that misinterpret or ignore the other dimensions of experience, such as our human needs and our social contexts.

But there is a special place, too, for moral principles in her view of critique. Elshtain is interested in promoting equality and justice, but not the thin kind found in Kant's categorical imperative or variations of it in liberal feminism. Elshtain wants a justice that can actualize concrete human needs in actual historical contexts. I think it is, using the terminology of William Frankena,[33] a kind of mixed deontological principle based on the radical ontological egalitarianism of early Christianity, but one that also promotes "what supports men and women in their distinctiveness."[34] By "men and women in their distinctiveness" she means the analogical goods, that is, neither totally identical nor distinct, that they both require and respectively contribute to human flourishing.[35]

This ontological equality is based on a view of humans as created in *imago Dei*. It grants equal dignity to all humans, including all men and women, while simultaneously actualizing the different and relative needs and goods of different genders, of parents and children, and different spheres of society. Her critical principle does not remain in the abstract. As a kind of difference feminist who explains family fragmentation with reference to the devouring demands of modernity and its tendency to absorb all adults into the wage economy, Elshtain's practical solutions do not entail pulling wives and mothers out of the salaried workforce. Instead, she proposes a variety of systemic changes to modern economies designed to force them to accommodate the needs of parents and children. She is all for men picking up more of the childcare and domestic chores.[36] But more than that, she wants industry and government to give more abundant parental leaves, less inclination by government to send mothers of infants to war,[37] and more tax advantages for couples with children.[38] Elshtain should affirm, and I think that she would affirm, even more radical systemic reforms, such as industrial and governmental support for a full-benefits thirty-hour workweek for

single parents and a combined sixty-hour workweek with full benefits
for couples with children to be divided between them as they see fit.
This was a leading proposal of the Religion, Culture, and Family Project
at the University of Chicago Divinity School from 1991 to 2003.

ELSHTAIN AND RICOEUR

It is worth bringing Elshtain into conversation with the critical hermeneutics of Paul Ricoeur for the many ways they can both illuminate
and reinforce each other's work. First, they are both multidimensional
thinkers. In a seminal article titled "The Teleological and Deontological Structures of Action: Aristotle and/or Kant" (1987), Ricoeur sets
forth the following multidimensional view of experience and dialogue.[39]
He illustrates his perspective around the simple descriptive statement,
"The farmer is plowing his field." Ricoeur holds that a full analysis of
this statement can be subdivided into roughly five dimensions: (1) the
practice, in this case a technical means-end task designed to move dirt in
order to plant seeds; (2) the *goods* that meet needs pursued in the practice
of plowing, for example, food, health, and wealth for self and loved ones;
(3) the ideals and *narratives* about the purposes of life that make plowing
as the teleological pursuit of these goods a meaningful action; (4) some
normative *principle of critique*—what Ricoeur calls the "deontological
moment"—that helps solve conflict;[40] and (5) a hermeneutic-descriptive
and explanatory analysis of both the farmer's original context and a
return to it for more refined moral action after the first four dimensions
are submitted to critical reflection.

With these five dimensions of description and ethics similarly articulated in both Elshtain and Ricoeur, I want to highlight what Ricoeur
contributes to the dimension dealing with goods and needs. Ricoeur
would insist that these natural needs are indeed in us, but we know them
partially through the linguistically coded practices that our history and
culture convey to us. Nonetheless, he would also contend that science
and critical reflection can provide some "distance" on the cultural construal of these needs.[41] This "distance" from culturally patterned ways
of defining them is not the objectivity of a foundationalist philosophy or

natural science. But it does provide us with "diagnostic" insight into the regularities of our natural needs— something like how a doctor uses his stethoscope or EKG to explain our consciously experienced shortness of breath—to account for the more obscure natural depths of our socially conditioned experience.[42]

This insight gives Ricoeur the grounds for a historically situated theory of natural law—a view of natural human needs, as conditioned as they are, that humans must both realize and stay within in ethically ordering their lives toward human flourishing. This is a view that Ricoeur acknowledged as possible but did not himself fully develop.

Using this approach to natural law, legal historian John Witte and I have scanned the history of Western marriage law, both religious and secular. We have found a far more prevalent presence of natural law thinking than we first assumed, generally nestled within a narrative framework about the goodness of creation and the covenant nature of the marital relationship. This was especially true of Christian jurisprudence after the twelfth century—a jurisprudence that provided the dominant model of marriage in the West, even for secular law.

This natural law, as Elshtain would expect, was significantly shaped around Aristotelian and Thomistic understandings of the needs of highly dependent human infants and how they elicited built-in kin-altruistic impulses of care in both mothers and fathers.[43] Aquinas held that these tendencies contributed to pair-bonding and led to long-term marriage at the human level in contrast to the more transient male–female relations of other mammals. This Aristotelian-Thomistic formulation was amazingly influential, not only among later Catholics, such as Francisco Vitorio and Francisco Suárez, but also with a string of Protestant thinkers, such as Melanchthon, Grotius, Althusius, and a number of English and Scottish Protestant Enlightenment thinkers, such as John Locke, Henry Home, Francis Hutcheson, Adam Smith, and even the skeptical David Hume. Today, this line of thinking gains even further reinforcement from the evolutionary philosophy of Mary Midgley (whom Elshtain appreciates),[44] the evolutionary psychologists Martin Daly and Margo Wilson,[45] the sociologists Pierre van den Berghe and David Popenoe,[46] the political scientist Larry Arnhart,[47] and the stunning revival of kinship studies in the synthesis of social anthropology and primatology in the recent very favorably reviewed work of Bernard Chapais.[48] Witte and I call this cluster of natural goods the "natural law configuration" of the Western legal tradition. We also acknowledge and explain how it informed, was stabilized by, and was idealized by the Western traditions that also saw marriage as a sacrament or covenant.

Elshtain writes eloquently about the natural needs of adults and children that lead to the legal and cultural institutionalization of marriage. She has resisted social and cultural efforts to undercut marriage as an institution, including several voices in feminist thought. Today, she would need to address trends in legal theory and its doctrine of "private ordering." This is the emerging legal assumption that adults should be legally free to form whatever intimate and procreative arrangements that they prefer and that civil law should confine itself to solving the financial, property, and custody conflicts that may result from these freely chosen arrangements. But she takes this stand without going far to develop a theory of natural law of her own, although she does mention, in a long footnote in *Public Man, Private Woman*, appreciation for the budding natural law views of Augustine.[49]

The outlines of such a dynamic, flexible, but stabilizing natural law theory are discernible in Elshtain's corpus. I am simply calling for a more explicit discussion of the idea. Something like Ricoeur's contextualized view of natural law and Witte and Browning's retrieval of the natural law configuration is both congenial to her sensibilities and potentially helpful in building on Elshtain's work in this area.

NOTES

1. Jean Bethke Elshtain, *Private Man, Public Woman* (Princeton, NJ: Princeton University Press, 1981), 298–354; Elshtain, "Toward Reflective Feminist Theory," *Women and Politics* 3, no. 4 (1983): 7–26.

2. Elshtain, "Toward Reflective Feminist Theory," 7, 11.

3. Ibid., 8.

4. Ibid., 10.

5. Ibid., 8.

6. Ibid.

7. Hans-Georg Gadamer, *Truth and Method* (New York: Crossroad, 1982), 267, 305.

8. Elshtain, "Toward Reflective Feminist Theory," 15.

9. Ibid., 13.

10. Ibid., 9.

11. Ibid.

12. Marabel Morgan, *Total Woman* (New York: Spire, 1975).

13. Elshtain, "Toward a Reflective Feminist Theory," 10.

14. Ibid., 13–14.

15. Jean Bethke Elshtain, "Families and Trust: Connecting Private Lives to Civic Goods," *Chicago Studies* 39, no. 1 (2000): 25–26; see also Elshtain, "Fingerprints on File: The Search for Missing Children," *Commonweal*, April 14, 1987, 229–30; Elshtain, "My Mother, the Expert," *First Things*, October 1991, 11.

16. Elshtain, *Public Man, Private Woman*, 60.

17. Ibid., 61.

18. Elshtain, "Families and Trust," 26.

19. Jean Bethke Elshtain, "Family Reconstruction," *Commonweal*, August 1, 1980, 431.

20. *Public Man, Private Woman*, 120.

21. Elshtain, "Families and Trust," 23.

22. For positions supporting Elshtain's early emphasis on the importance, *contra* much of early feminism, of natural mothers and fathers in intact families, see David Popenoe, *Life without Father* (New York: Free Press, 1996); Sara McLanahan and Gary Sandefur, *Growing Up with a Single Parent* (Cambridge, MA: Harvard University Press, 1994); Paul Amato and Alan Booth, *A Generation at Risk* (Cambridge, MA: Harvard University Press, 1997).

23. Jean Bethke Elshtain, "Feminism against the Family," *The Nation*, November 17, 1979, 497.

24. Ibid., 498.

25. *Public Man, Private Woman*, 260, 264, 270, 279.

26. Elshtain, "Families and Trust," 18–19.

27. Ibid., 19.

28. *Public Man, Private Woman*, 259–64.

29. Jean Bethke Elshtain, "Christianity and Patriarchy," *Modern Theology* 9, no. 2 (1993): 109–10.

30. Ibid., 111.

31. Elshtain, "Toward a Reflective Feminist Theory," 22.

32. Ibid., 20.

33. William Frankena, *Ethics* (Englewood Cliffs, NJ: Prentice Hall, 1961).

34. Elshtain, "Families and Trust," 21.

35. Jean Bethke Elshtain, "Women and the Dilemma of Equality," *Logos* 6, no. 4 (2003): 40–41.

36. Elshtain, "Families and Trust," 21.

37. Ibid.

38. Elshtain, "Marriage and Relationships," *American Experiment* (Summer 2001): 20.

39. Paul Ricoeur, "The Teleological and Deontological Structures of Action: Aristotle and/or Kant," in *Contemporary French Philosophy*, ed. A. Phillips Griffiths (New York: Cambridge University Press, 1987), 99–111.

40. Ibid., 107.

41. Paul Ricoeur, *Hermeneutics and the Human Sciences* (Cambridge: Cambridge University Press, 1981), 60.

42. Paul Ricoeur, *Freedom and Nature* (Evanston, IL: Northwestern University Press, 1966).

43. Thomas Aquinas, *Summa Theologica* (New York: Benziger, 1948), Supplement, 41.1.

44. Mary Midgley, *Beast and Man* (Ithaca, NY: Cornell University Press, 1978).

45. Martin Daly and Margo Wilson, "The Evolutionary Psychology of Marriage and Divorce," in *Perspectives on Marriage and Cohabitation*, ed. Linda Waite (New York: Aldine de Gruyter, 2000), 91–109.

46. Pierre van den Berghe, "The Family and the Biological Bases for Human Society," in *Biosocial Perspectives on the Family*, ed. Erik H. Filsinger (Newbury Park, CA: Sage, 1988), 119–36; Popenoe, *Life without Father*.

47. Larry Arnhart, "Thomistic Natural Law and Darwinian Natural Right," in *Natural Law and Modern Philosophy*, ed. Ellen Frankel Paul, Fred Miller, and Jeffrey Paul (Cambridge: Cambridge University Press, 2001), 1–33.

48. Bernard Chapais, *Primeval Kinship: How Pair-Bonding Gave Birth to Human Society* (Cambridge, MA: Harvard University Press, 2008).

49. *Public Man, Private Woman*, 70.

CHAPTER FOUR

STRIKING THE BALANCE

Blending Liberty, Tradition, and Reform

Peter Berkowitz

In the preface to her trenchant 1995 book, *Democracy on Trial* (*DT*), Jean Bethke Elshtain proclaims (citing the Polish playwright and novelist Janusz Glowacki) that she has "joined the ranks of the nervous generation" (*DT*, xiv). In the wake of communism's collapse and on the threshold of the dot-com boom, she warns that the main threat to our freedom comes not from some "outside power," but from our failure to appreciate freedom's limits, to respectfully engage with tradition, and to conserve the toleration and independent thought on which democracy depends (xiv–xv).

As she confronted a growing propensity to narrow-mindedness and anti-intellectual partisanship in the university world, Elshtain found herself increasingly discomfited by one-dimensional opinion, including her own. Reaction to the death of Richard Nixon in 1994 gave her an opportunity to reflect on the quality of judgment citizens ought to bring to political life. During the 1970s, she writes in the closing paragraph of her preface, she "was second to none as a Nixon loather" (*DT*, xvii). But over the course of the next two decades she came to view Nixon, and hatred in politics, differently:

In his own way, this complex man, humiliated and disgraced, struggled for the last two decades of his life to regain a measure of respect from his fellow citizens. If we no longer create in America men and women who can be shamed and made to pay a price for dishonoring the public trust, but who, in turn, strive to recover just a few moments of civic grace, we will have lost a culture that is strong enough to censure presidents and kind enough to permit them to recover their dignity through civil accomplishment. I am somewhat abashed now as I look back twenty years or more and recognize how easy it was for me to hate. I do not hate anymore. I have joined the ranks of the nervous. (*DT*, xvii)

Hatred, Elshtain learned, comes to us easily but deforms our grasp of political reality, especially democratic political reality, which requires appreciation of our fellow citizens'—and our own—capacity for virtue and susceptibility to vice.

Because *Democracy on Trial*, indeed Elshtain's work as whole, is committed both to political reform and to conserving what is best in our traditions, it furnishes a lesson of moderation. In this it resembles the work of the great eighteenth-century British statesman and political thinker Edmund Burke, widely regarded as the father of modern conservatism. I do not mean to suggest that Elshtain followed or was directly influenced by Burke. Nor do I wish to imply that Elshtain was in any programmatic or partisan sense a conservative. Even a passing acquaintance with the woman or her writings confirms her irrepressible independence of mind.

My contention, rather, is that central to Burke's moral and political thought is an appreciation of the complexity of human nature, the challenges of self-government, and the determination to reconcile principles and interests that are typically taken to be incompatible. Burke provides invaluable guidance concerning the form of political moderation appropriate to conserving freedom. In these angry and polarized times, he can help us recover an understanding of the qualities of mind and character—virtues if you prefer—on which liberal democracy depends, a recovery that very much advances the preservation and improvement of liberal democracy to which Elshtain was devoted.

CONSERVING LIBERTY

Moderating the tension between liberty (or doing as you wish) and tradition (or doing as has been done in the past) to reform political life in
light of liberty's promise is a hallmark of Burke's speeches and writings.
The conservative spirit is enduring and some have always been
more amply endowed with the conservative inclination to preserve
inherited ways, and others more moved by the progressive impulse to
improve or supersede them, but the distinctively modern form of conservatism emerged with Burke's polemic *Reflections on the Revolution in
France* (1790). Burke concentrated his enormous intellectual and rhetorical gifts on the revolution's brutally destructive political excesses,
which he argued were inspired by prominent elements of Enlightenment philosophy and by leading strands of what subsequently came to
be called the liberal tradition. Yet it would be a grave error to conclude
that he was therefore a foe of the Enlightenment or an opponent of the
liberal tradition. In the *Reflections*, Burke brings into focus a distinctly
modern conservatism, which accepts the Enlightenment and operates
within the liberal tradition while seeking to moderate the tendencies
toward excess of both. His devotion to liberty was even more evident in
the great reform efforts that define his political career—reconciliation
with the American colonies, toleration for Ireland's Catholics, and protection of the natural rights of British subjects in India. But even if all
we had were Burke's *Reflections*, he would still deserve to be counted
among our great teachers concerning the principles and practices that
conserve liberty.

The liberty to whose conservation Burke, as a British patriot and
parliamentarian, was in the first place devoted was British liberty. Yet
Burke did not believe, as some have supposed, that liberty was good for
Englishmen but not for others. Liberty in his judgment was good for all
humans. At the same time, he maintained that the universal principle
had varying application: the *achievement* of liberty, he thought, depends
on the complex interplay of concrete political institutions, moral beliefs
and practices, social and economic arrangements, and religious faith,
all of which do indeed differ from people to people and place to place.
Therefore, honoring the universal principle requires exacting study of

background moral and political conditions, painstaking examination of the intricacies of contemporary opinions and practices, and shrewd statesmanship in crafting laws and adjusting policy to shifting circumstances. Moreover, conserving liberty at home required Britain to give close attention to events abroad. In the revolution in France, Burke found an object lesson for England in how the quest for liberty can go astray. In America, Ireland, and India, he confronted the failure of British policy to respect the legitimate claims of liberty abroad, which in his judgment could only injure Britain's long-term interests in preserving an empire based on liberty.

Burke's *Reflections* and his classic speeches clarify the conditions under which British liberty flourished, the immediate threats it confronted, and the policies that Burke believed would over the long run secure and extend it. They do this not by presenting a theory of freedom but—much as Elshtain's writings delve into the details of the American experience to illuminate the intricacies of faith, justice, and national security—through analysis of the actual British beliefs, practices, and associations that gave British freedom life.

FREEDOM AND THE FRENCH REVOLUTION

Burke's *Reflections* demonstrates that his was not a wholesale critique of the spirit of the Enlightenment and the moral and political principles of John Locke. Indeed, Burke was a Whig who cherished freedom and, in the name of individual liberty, sought throughout his long parliamentary career and in battle after battle with the Tories to limit the political power of altar and throne. But to limit is not to abolish, and can be, as it was in Burke's case, consistent with cherishing. Within their proper boundaries, Burke taught, religious faith disciplined and elevated hearts and minds, and monarchy upheld the continuity of tradition, reflected the benefits of hierarchy and order, and provided energy and focus in government. Both institutions, in his assessment, encouraged virtues crucial to liberty's preservation.

As he sought for the sake of liberty to limit the political power of altar and throne in Britain—and in Britain's affairs in America, Ireland,

and India—he also defended them for liberty's sake in France against what he regarded as the revolutionaries' perverted conception of freedom. Contrary to their doctrine that freedom required the overthrow of inherited beliefs, practices, and institutions, Burke championed "a manly, moral, regulated liberty."[1] It depended more on self-restraint than self-interest. It was secured less through calculation, planning, and ambitious projects than by the steady development of institutions and practice over centuries, the outstanding example of which was the British Constitution. And it included the right to live under the rule of law; to own and acquire property and to pass it on to one's children; and generally to live with one's family as one saw fit provided one did not trespass on the rights of others. The very purpose of political life, Burke argued, was to secure these rights, though just where the exercise of freedom constituted a violation of another's rights, and how best to use one's freedom to live well, could only be determined by prudent reflection on tradition and custom, because they embodied the nation's accumulated wisdom concerning the organization of human affairs.

Prudence, Burke famously proclaimed, is "the God of this lower world."[2] Mediating between principle and practice, it represented moderation in judgment. It guided the reconciliation of liberty with the requirements of order and the need for virtue by taking the measure of all three and fashioning courses of action that, to the extent possible, gave each its due.

In contrast, according to Burke, the French revolutionaries were immoderate in the extreme. Along with monarchy and religion, they sought to overthrow not merely this tradition or that custom but the very authority of tradition and custom. Their aim was to establish an empire built on reason alone. Prudence, which involved the wise and balanced application of principle to circumstance, would be unnecessary. Instead, they would mold circumstances to comply with reason's demands. Marching under the banner of "the rights of man," they set out to deduce the structure of a society of free and equal citizens without regard to the inherited beliefs, contingent passions, enduring attachments, and local practices that form character and color conduct. Rather than counting on education to discipline a recalcitrant human nature, they were prepared to go so far in molding circumstances as to remake human nature to fit reason's supposed revelations about citizens' specific wants, needs, rights, and obligations. The ambition to use the power of the state to create a new humanity, Burke presciently argued, was sure to result in the dehumanization of man.

The quarrel between Burke and the French revolutionaries comes down not to whether liberty is good or even the leading purpose of politics—Burke thought it was both—but to the material and moral conditions and the political institutions most conducive to securing and enjoying it. The French revolutionaries—and progressives to this day—put their faith in government's ability not only to identify and provide for citizens' wants and needs but also to improve their beliefs and educate their sensibilities. In contrast, Burke's conservatism places the emphasis on the moral and political benefits that flow to liberty from the time-tested beliefs, practices, and institutions beyond government's immediate purview that structure social life and shape character. The progressive mind tends to see order and virtue as the antitheses of freedom. In contrast, the conservative mind—on this Elshtain's work comes down decisively on the conservative side—sees them as pillars of freedom. And the conservative mind seeks, as does Elshtain in her writings, to conserve the nongovernmental institutions—the family, religious faith, the voluntary associations of civil society—that sustain order and virtue.

Despite the veneration of the past and excoriation of the French Revolution's moral and political innovations to which he gave expression in *Reflections*, Burke was no reactionary who dogmatically clung to the old and rejected the new. He himself observed in the *Reflections* that, because circumstances alter, "A state without the means of some change is without the means of its conservation."[3] Of course the change in question must be prudent, wisely adapting enduring principles to the ordinary vicissitudes of politics and, in extraordinary times, to substantial shifts in sentiment and practice. Prudent change as Burke understands it, though, is more than a political necessity. It is also inseparable from respect for tradition and custom, because they typically present not a clear-cut path but "a choice of inheritance."[4] Since the right choice must be freely and reasonably made, liberty and tradition are mutually dependent.

This mutual dependence provides an opening for moderating their claims, which frequently pull in opposing directions. Justly moderating, or harmonizing, the competing claims of liberty and tradition avoids unprincipled compromise—though compromises must be made. And it steers clear of thoughtless acquiescence to necessities—though necessities must be recognized. It is built on a recognition of the complexity of the conditions that permit free citizens to flourish. It should not be confused with the absence of strong passion. Moderation rightly understood involves the restraint of desire for immediate gratification in the quest for the satisfaction offered by a greater good or more comprehensive happiness. In other words, the restraint at the heart of moderation also involves the exercise of passion—the passion to strike the best balance among worthy but incomplete ends for the sake of a higher end. This is the government of the self on which self-government in a free society depends.

REPRESENTATION, LIBERTY, AND REFORM

Prudent reform to meet the changing requirements of liberty was the dominant theme of Burke's long political career, which stretched from his election to Parliament in 1765 as a member of the House of Commons for Wendover to his retirement in 1794 as a representative of Malton. The Britain Burke served governed the largest empire the world had ever seen. More than by its reach, it was distinguished from previous world empires by the principle of liberty in which it was rooted. Crucial to conserving the empire, Burke contended, was both England's interest in respecting liberty and its obligation to honor it not only at home but in all its far-flung undertakings. In taking controversial stands as a member of Parliament in support of American self-government, toleration and fair treatment for Ireland's Catholics, ending Warren Hastings's corrupt and cruel administration of India, and in his arguments condemning the French revolutionaries, Burke's target was the abuse of power that subverted fundamental requirements of liberty.

Burke's signature reform efforts rested on the conviction that what a legislator particularly owed his constituents was his sound judgment about the policies that would best advance their interests. The sound judgment of which Burke spoke must not be confused with the view of those many contemporary academic political theorists who, in the tradition of John Rawls, busy themselves deriving from abstract principles public policies that they hold to be truths of reason and invariably turn out to converge with progressive preferences—an arid and delusive enterprise against which Elshtain very much rebelled. For her, as for Burke, sound judgment grows not of theory but practice, not out of the most abstract assumptions about man and morality, but out of the complex tapestry of political life.

In his "Speech on Conciliation with America" (1775), Burke counseled Britain on how to avoid war with the colonists and reestablish on a solid footing the deteriorating relationship with them. The first step was to formulate policy with a view to actual circumstances, at home and in the colonies, and with an appreciation of common interests, "and not according to our own imaginations; not according to abstract ideas of right; by no means according to mere general theories of government, the resort to which appears to me, in our present situation, no better than arrant trifling."[5] The most important circumstance, Burke argues, is the deeply rooted interest Britain shares with America in freedom.

Their common and deeply rooted interest in freedom is crucially connected to their common interest in prosperity. Over the previous seventy years, England's trade with the colonies had increased "no less than twelve-fold," and commerce with America had come to constitute more than a third of England's total worldwide trade. America's rise and the resulting benefits to Britain were owed in considerable part to London's hands-off policy: "Through a wise and salutary neglect, a generous nature has been suffered to take her own way to perfection."[6] This policy, argues Burke, should be maintained. Burke was inclined to view American exuberance, even American obstreperousness, with generosity— "I pardon something to the spirit of liberty."[7]

To preserve the colonies' vital place in the empire in the face of the violence that had broken out across the Atlantic would require "prudent management."[8] The beginning of prudence in the matter was to recognize that because it weakens when it does not ruin the object it subdues, force was to be avoided. Force could nowhere be more counterproductive than in the case of America, where liberty was the colonists' lifeblood and the decisive factor in their critical contribution to the empire.

Indeed, argues Burke, "a love of freedom is the predominating feature which marks and distinguishes" the American character.[9] America's "fierce spirit of liberty,"[10] which only increased with the growth in the colonies' size and prosperity, stemmed from several sources. As descendants of Englishmen, Americans were devoted to the English understanding according to which their liberty depended on their right, exercised through their representatives, to have a say in the taxes imposed upon them. The high degree of participation in the popular governments they established throughout the colonies further heightened Americans' taste for liberty. As a result of their Protestantism, which "had sprung up in direct opposition to all the ordinary powers of the world," Americans were disposed to make strong claims on behalf of "natural liberty."[11] In the south, the institution of slavery paradoxically amplified the attachment to freedom among slave owners by reinforcing their identification of freedom with nobility and high station. Avid reading and study increased Americans' sensitivity to abuses of power and honed their arguments on behalf of liberty. And finally, the three thousand miles of ocean that separated America from Parliament greatly impeded communication, thereby thwarting responsible oversight by London and weakening the authority of central government in the eyes of the colonists.

Given these powerful and diverse supports of their freedom, observed Burke, arguments marshaled in London demonstrating that Americans' demands for greater liberty were unreasonable—including arguments with respectable grounds in traditional British understandings and practice—were bound to fall on deaf ears in the colonies. Consequently, Burke contended, Britain had three choices: to remove the immediate cause of the dispute; to prosecute the Americans as criminals; or to recognize American demands for representation as necessary and devise policies to satisfy them.

The options for removing the causes of the dispute were useless. To restrict trade would enrage the colonists and deprive England of their productivity and bounty. To attempt to change their religion or education or to set the slaves free—to say nothing of draining the ocean the better to reassert authority through improved communication— would be utterly impractical.

Prosecuting the colonists for their acts of resistance was no more advisable. Taking a hard line was inconsistent with maintaining an empire that, Burke asserted, must allow for challenges to government policy. To treat every questioning of authority by the colonists as an act of treason was to "teach them that the government, against which a claim of liberty is tantamount to high treason, is a government to which submission is equivalent to slavery."[12]

The alternative that remained was for Britain to learn to live with Americans' love for liberty. In appreciation of that necessity, Burke favored granting the colonists limited representation in Parliament on questions of taxation, though not as a matter of right. Burke made clear that under British law the colonists had none. At the same time, he stressed that the issue was not a matter of right: "The question with me is, not whether you have a right to render your people miserable; but whether it is not your interest to make them happy."[13] Statesmanship goes beyond the questions of strict legality and, for that matter, crude calculations of utility: "I am not determining a point of law; I am restoring tranquility; and the general character and situation of a people must determine what sort of government is fitted for them."[14] Granting the colonists a measure of representation was consistent with the spirit of liberty that linked America to Britain. And it advanced a surpassing British interest, which was to encourage the colonists to appreciate their interest in remaining a part of the empire.

Such a policy involved a concession, but one, according to Burke, that was rooted in principles and policies favoring the extension of liberty and representative government that had consistently informed British government policy and contributed to the growth of the empire. Indeed, conciliation itself was "the ancient constitutional policy of the kingdom."[15] And consistent with the very nature of politics: "All government, indeed every human benefit and enjoyment, every virtue, and every prudent act, is founded on compromise and barter. We balance inconveniences; we give and take; we remit some rights, that we may enjoy others; and, we choose rather to be happy citizens, than subtle disputants."[16] With America, the deal for Britain was a particularly good one. By allowing English liberties to flourish in the colonies, Britain would encourage the spirit that made America prosperous, reinforce the spirit of liberty at home, and conserve English dominion on the most favorable long-term basis.

Five years later, in his "Speech at Guildhall" (1780), which marked the close of his career representing Bristol, Burke offers a notable defense of toleration for Irish Catholics. This was a delicate matter for Burke. His father, Richard Burke, was a Protestant lawyer, who, a few years before Edmund was born in 1729, almost certainly had converted from Catholicism so that he could practice law. Burke's mother, Mary Nagle, was a Catholic. So too was Burke's wife, Jane. Throughout his career, Burke was highly circumspect about his Catholic connections and was constantly attacked by his political enemies as a Catholic sympathizer. His rousing yet carefully reasoned defense of a bill that provided relief for Catholics from the disabilities imposed by England's Penal Laws is all the more impressive for the personal interests it implicated and the significant political costs it incurred.

His critics, Burke told his constituents at Guildhall, contended that he pushed the demand for justice beyond what prudent attention to the polity and the opinions of his constituents could bear. In reply, he argued that the reforms he sought reflected the imperatives of liberty in the context of the realities of British politics.

The long view, Burke maintained, was relevant to the determination of the proper public policy concerning the freedom of those who belong to the minority faith. The principle of toleration had roots in the Reformation, "one of the greatest periods of human improvement," yet pockets of intolerance in violation of Protestant principles of liberty persisted long after the Reformation, not least in the form of legal disabilities imposed upon Catholics.[17] Passed in 1699, the Penal Laws made the saying of Mass and teaching by Catholics a crime punishable by indefinite imprisonment. They also required Catholics to renounce their Catholicism or forfeit their land, and placed severe restrictions on professional advancement, like those faced by Burke's father.

One did not have to rely only on distinctively Protestant principles, however, to condemn the wrongs inflicted by the Penal Laws, because universal principles also condemned them. The Penal Laws worked out-rages against human nature, crippling in their targets "the rights and feelings of humanity."[18] They had a "tendency to degrade and abase mankind, and to deprive them of that assured and liberal state of mind, which alone can make us what we ought to be."[19] The repeal of the Penal Laws, in short, was necessitated both by the religious principles that a majority of Britons professed and the common humanity all men shared.

Other considerations, grounded in the events of the day, also coun-seled reform. With toleration gaining ground and spreading throughout Europe—in Holland, Germany, Sweden, and France—British toleration of Catholics would lend support to the claims to toleration of Protes-tants in Catholic countries abroad. And as Catholics were England's best manufacturers, toleration advanced Britain's commercial interests.

But if toleration was so important, other critics asked, why did Burke support a bill that provided only partial relief rather than outright repeal of the Penal Laws? Because, answered Burke, prudence so counseled. In the short term, outright repeal was not politically attainable. At the same time, by means of incremental steps, "the people would grow reconciled to toleration, when they should find by the effects, that justice was not so irreconcilable an enemy to convenience as they had imagined."[20]

Still others objected that Parliament was acting with undue haste. Burke replied that "Parliament was too slow," taking eighty years to undertake the repair of laws that should have been repealed at once.[21] And to those who insisted that it was monarchs who posed the true threat to freedom, Burke insisted that freedom can be placed in jeopardy just as much by the "strongest faction," or the tyranny of the majority. Because the true love of liberty is extremely rare, the people are an imperfect guardian of toleration. Their voice must be heard and respected, but their will must be "confined within the limits of justice," which prescribe toleration as a political fundamental in a free society.[22]

In his "Speech on Fox's East India Bill" (1783), Burke once again pressed for reforms based on the conviction that honoring the claims of liberty abroad made liberty at home more secure. The speech, attack-ing what he believed to be Britain's gross malfeasance in India, was a high point of the cause to which he devoted the greater part of the final decade of his parliamentary career. To his many critics, it seemed that he was consumed with the issue. Indeed, Burke went to great lengths to remove Warren Hastings, the first governor-general of India—he was impeached in 1787 and acquitted in 1795—and spoke with uncompromising passion on the question of India. Nevertheless, his speech in support of Fox's East India Bill—Burke was largely responsible for drafting the bill—is a model of reasoned political analysis and advocacy. It is notable, as were his call for conciliation with America and his insistence on tolerance for Ireland's Catholics, for combining an appeal to morality with an appeal to interest.

Britain's interest in robust commerce converged with "the interest and the well-being of the people of India."[23] But, according to Burke, the East India Company, which Britain had chartered to promote those ends, had abused its power. It used its prerogatives to enrich its employees while trampling on native-born Indians, in the process enervating India and corrupting British morals. This was not merely unjust but counter to Britain's national interest. Promoting self-government among the Indians, argued Burke, was necessary to protect British self-government from corruption.

The bill Burke championed would alter the charter that established the East India Company's status as a private company with responsibility for governing India by giving Parliament responsibility for overseeing the company's conduct and the authority to correct its misconduct. In response to those who contended that he championed reforms that represented an "attack on the chartered rights of men," Burke maintained that the chartered rights of men properly so called are those natural rights that are given concrete and effective political expression through their affirmation in fundamental legal documents. The Magna Carta, "a charter to restrain power, and to destroy monopoly,"[24] according to Burke, is an outstanding example. In contrast, "The East-India charter is a charter to establish monopoly and to create power."[25] It works to "suspend the natural rights of mankind at large," allowing the company to administer, as if it were a state power, an enormous territory vital to the commercial interests of Britain and also to "the lives and fortunes of thirty millions of their fellow-creatures."[26] The power to rule over another, or political power, however, is not a natural right. To the contrary, and once again agreeing with the larger liberal tradition, it is "wholly artificial, and for so much a derogation from the natural equality of mankind at large, ought to be some way or other exercised ultimately for their benefit."[27]

The East India Company had enjoyed a trust. By betraying the lawful purposes that brought it into being, the company had nullified that trust. In view of "the plenitude of despotism, tyranny, and corruption" perpetrated by the East India Company, Parliament was obliged to reassert its responsibility for the efficient and equitable administration of India, and thereby to provide "a real chartered security for the *rights of men* cruelly violated" by the East India Company.[28]

Burke recognized revision of the East India Company's charter represented a drastic measure. He justified it on the grounds that the East India Company was engaged in drastic abuse. But the reform he advocated, he stressed, was in no way based on any "a priori" argument against endowing a private company with the political power to administer a vast nation.[29] Not that he failed to appreciate arguments against entrusting a private company with such power. Rather, he distrusted a priori arguments even, or particularly, those concerning universal principles: "With my particular ideas and sentiments, I cannot go that way to work. I feel an insuperable reluctance in giving my hand to destroy any established institution of government, upon a theory, however plausible it may be."[30] And of course no political institution could be indicted for the mere existence of abuses in the exercise of its powers, because "there are, and must be, abuses in all governments."[31]

So Burke lays out criteria, whose application requires observation, evidence, and judgment, for determining whether existing institutions must be fundamentally altered: "1st. The object affected by the abuse should be great and important. 2d. The abuse affecting this great object ought to be a great abuse. 3d. It ought to be habitual, and not accidental. 4th. It ought to be utterly incurable in the body as it now stands constituted."[32] Furthermore, insists Burke, fundamental reform of an existing institution requires that evidence for these propositions must be as clear as "the light of the sun."[33] The bulk of Burke's speech on Fox's East India Bill, which delves deeply into the nitty-gritty of the matter, is devoted to showing that such was very much the case with the conduct of Governor-General Hastings and the East India Company.

Burke's arguments on behalf of reform of British policy toward India are of a piece with those he puts forward on behalf of reform of British policy toward America and Ireland. Combined with his opinions on the revolution in France, they show that preservation and reform are both crucial to the conservation of liberty.

This double imperative imposes formidable demands on the people and on officeholders in free societies. To be sure, under governments of all sorts policy and law must constantly be adjusted, calibrated, and balanced in light of changing circumstances. But liberty guarantees that circumstances will always be changing. That's because liberty is a principle that excites the human love of novelty—for how can I be free if I must submit to the same old routines? And it goads the human love of dominion—for how can I be free if others defy my will? Since freedom encourages a contradictory and destabilizing desire for mastery and aversion to authority, it also tends to provoke an immoderate backlash against freedom. One consequence is that free societies simultaneously generate radicals who make unprecedented demands both to rule over others and to be free from governmental authority and reactionaries who seek to roll back the role of government and reinstate traditional forms of authority. A government devoted to conserving freedom, therefore, will require particular prudence in balancing the demands of preserving and improving.

MODERATION AND LIBERTY

The virtue of moderation is often mistaken, if not for a vice, then for a compromise with virtue, a softening of belief, a diluting of passion, a weakening of will. But these are examples not of moderation but of the failure to achieve it. Moderation is not a retreat from the fullness of life but a balance of the complexities of human nature and the crosscutting realities of political life. It is called into action by the awareness of the variety of human interests; the array of worthy and enduring moral principles; the multiplicity of valuable human undertakings and ends; the indispensableness of the quest to discern a common good in light of which we can make distinctions and establish priorities; and the substantial limits on what we can know and how effectively and justly we can act. It underlies self-government in both senses—the individual's mastery of his own conduct and a free people's rule over themselves. And so it is essential to the conservation of liberty.[34]

In the final paragraph of *Reflections*, Burke portrays moderation in action on behalf of liberty. His opinions about the revolution in France, he declares,

> come from one, almost the whole of whose public exertion has been a struggle for the liberty of others; from one in whose breast no anger durable or vehement has ever been kindled, but by what he considered as tyranny; and who snatches from his share in the endeavours which are used by good men to discredit opulent oppression, the hours he has employed on your affairs, and who in so doing persuades himself he has not departed from his usual office. They come from one who desires honours, distinctions, and emoluments, but little, and who expects them not at all, who has no contempt for fame, and no fear of obloquy; who shuns contention, though he will hazard an opinion; from one who wishes to preserve consistency, but who would preserve consistency by varying his means to secure the unity of his end; and, when the equipoise of the vessel in which he sails may be endangered by overloading it upon one side, is desirous of carrying the small weight of his reason to that which may preserve its equipoise.[35]

To preserve liberty at a time when the French revolutionaries made extravagant claims on its behalf, Burke fervently championed tradition's claims. And when his countrymen failed to grasp its imperatives in their affairs abroad in America, Ireland, and India, he passionately urged reforms that enlarged the sphere of liberty. The fervor of his language can sometimes obscure the moderation of his positions.

The conservative side of the larger liberal tradition rings variations on the moderation contained in Burke's devotion to conserving liberty. Adam Smith examined the mutual dependence of economic life and virtue. He saw that the market economy, which brought prosperity and nourished political liberty, both rewarded moral virtues—rationality,

industry, ingenuity, and self-discipline—and corrupted workers' character by condemning them to monotonous labor. He therefore insisted on
the need for government action—providing education for workers and
limiting the workplace demands imposed on them by manufacturers—
to support the "system of natural liberty."

The authors of the *Federalist Papers* defended a new constitution that
was grounded in the principle of consent and that secured individual
liberty. To do so, it established institutions that refined and elevated the
will of the people, and channeled the personal ambitions of officeholders toward goals that would serve the public interest.

Alexis de Tocqueville understood that democracy was inevitable and
just and that it fostered a certain simplicity and straightforwardness in
manners, but it also encouraged selfishness, envy, immediate gratification, and lazy acceptance of state authority. To secure liberty, without
which in his estimation a life could not be well lived, it was necessary
to preserve within democracy those nongovernmental institutions—
particularly the family and religious faith—that counteracted democracy's deleterious tendencies by teaching moral virtue, by connecting
individuals to higher purposes, and by broadening their appreciation of
their self-interest to include their debts to forbears and obligations to
future generations.

And John Stuart Mill classically made the case that liberty served
"the permanent interests of man as a progressive being."[36] At the same
time, he distinguished between the use and abuse of freedom; defended
a rigorous education continuing through university and combining science and humanities to equip individuals for freedom's opportunities
and demands; and favored political institutions that, though grounded
in the consent of the governed, were designed to improve the likelihood
that elections would bring to public office individuals of outstanding
moral and intellectual virtue.

In sum, if a liberal in the large sense is one who believes that the aim
of politics is to secure liberty, then Burke, Smith, the authors of the *Federalist Papers*, Tocqueville, and Mill are exemplary members of the liberal
tradition. Their exercise of moderation in harmonizing rival principles
and goods is a reflection of their passion for freedom.

So too is the author of *Democracy on Trial* an exemplary member of the larger liberal tradition and so too is her harmonization of rival principles and goods both an exercise of moderation and a mark of her passion for freedom. What she wrote in the concluding chapter of that book, in the aftermath of the collapse of Soviet communism, has lost none of its pertinence:

> "Let freedom ring!"—the cry of democrats throughout centuries —now echoes 'round the world. What do aggrieved peoples want? Freedom. When do they want it? Now. That, at least, is the story of the recent past. From Tiananmen Square to Wenceslas Square, the rhetoric of protesters, dissidents, and new citizens has been cast in the idiom of freedom. But democratic freedom is a particular sort of freedom, tempered by centuries of hard wisdom that stretch from ancient Attica to the modern Western metropolis. It is decocted civic lore that tells us that human beings are not only capable of great deeds of courage and selflessness but are tempted by power, corrupted by greed, seduced by violence, and weakened by coward- ice. (*DT*, 117)

Because of our capacity for virtue and our susceptibility to vice, "the drama of democracy" creates "a permanent contestation between con- servation and change, between tradition and transformation" (*DT*, 136). The contending imperatives must be given their due: "To jettison one side is to live in either a sterile present-mindedness or an equally sterile reaction" (*DT*, 136). Freedom for her is not merely a benefit conferred by the state to be enjoyed but a precious opportunity to engage in poli- tics civilly, imaginatively, reasonably.

Like Burke and those who share his appreciation of freedom's crosscutting requirements, Elshtain keenly appreciates that free soci- eties expose individuals to influences that corrode moral and political order and enervate the virtues on which liberty and self-government depend. She clarifies freedom's dependence on constraint—of law, non- governmental associations, and the internalization of traditional habits and norms. And she illuminates why government must be limited to prevent it from encroaching on liberty but not so limited that it cannot take necessary and proper action in defense of the rights shared equally by all. Consequently, though the balance she strikes might differ from the one Burke would strike, the account of self-government she develops is distinguished, like Burke's, by the premium it places on striking a balance, or moderation.

NOTES

This essay has its origins in my short discussion of Burke in "Constitutional Conservatism," *Policy Review* (February and March 2009), and my chapter in *Constitutional Conservatism* (Hoover Institution Press, 2012).

1. Edmund Burke, *Reflections on the Revolution in France*, in *The Works of the Right Honourable Edmund Burke* (London: John C. Nimmo, 1887), 3:240.
2. Edmund Burke, "Letter to the Sheriffs of the City of Bristol, on the Affairs of America," in *Works of the Right Honourable Edmund Burke*, 2:226.
3. Burke, *Reflections*, 259.
4. Ibid., 275.
5. Edmund Burke, "Speech on Conciliation with the Colonies," in *Works of the Right Honourable Edmund Burke*, 2:109.
6. Ibid., 118.
7. Ibid.
8. Ibid.
9. Ibid., 120.
10. Ibid.
11. Ibid., 123.
12. Ibid., 137.
13. Ibid., 140.
14. Ibid., 141.
15. Ibid., 154.
16. Ibid., 169.
17. Edmund Burke, "Speech at the Guildhall in Bristol, Previous to the Late Election in that City, Upon Certain Points Relative to His Parliamentary Conduct," in *Works of the Right Honourable Edmund Burke*, 2:389.
18. Ibid., 391.
19. Ibid., 396.
20. Ibid., 409.
21. Ibid., 414.
22. Ibid., 421.

23. Ibid., 434.
24. Ibid., 438.
25. Ibid.
26. Ibid., 438–39.
27. Ibid., 439.
28. Ibid., 441.
29. Ibid., 442.
30. Ibid., 442.
31. Ibid., 443.
32. Ibid., 442.
33. Ibid.
34. See Harvey Clor, *On Moderation: Defending an Ancient Virtue in a Modern World* (Waco, TX: Baylor University Press, 2008), chap. 1.
35. Burke, *Reflections*, 563.
36. John Stuart Mill, *On Liberty* (London: Walter Scott Publishing Company, 1901), 19.

CHAPTER FIVE

DEMOCRACY, DEPRESSION, AND DISABILITY

Jean Elshtain on Democracy, Despair, and Hope

Nancy J. Hirschmann

Jean Bethke Elshtain's view of democracy is best summed up by some-thing she says about civil society: "Civil society is a realm that is neither individual in a narrowly relentless individualist sense nor communi-tarian in a strong collectivist sense."[1] I think this describes her view of democracy, too, because she *contrasts* a "plebiscitary system" to a "democratic" one, suggesting that simply tallying the preferences of the majority is insufficient if that majority is not engaged in thinking about the common good, but only about their selfish interests.[2] For Elshtain, democracy is a realm where we talk, listen, respect differences, ham-mer them out, work them through, and come up with solutions, rules, and policies that serve the common good more than the selfish good of particular individuals.

Yet Elshtain opens *Democracy on Trial* by saying that she is nervous. The conditions that caused her nervousness are in many ways remark-ably unchanged today from what they were when she wrote this in 1999—perhaps even worse. Indeed, many of the worries and warnings she made twenty and even thirty years ago are truer today than ever. In rereading these essays and books written over the course of thirty-five years, it is shocking to see how much time has passed and how little has changed about our decaying democratic landscape.

So I am nervous too. But there's nervous, and there's nervous. There is the anxiety of the laboratory animal who will receive an electric shock but is given a way to avoid it by pushing a lever or ringing a bell; it is given a way to deal with stress by exerting some control over what happens. Someone else is still deciding whether and when to shock the animal, and it is living in a laboratory cage, hardly the best life for an animal of any species, but it can make choices that will have predictable effects. That is altogether different from the animal who cannot avoid the shock no matter what it does. It tries pressing the lever, ringing the bell, going through complicated maneuvers, and it still gets shocked. The result is what Martin Seligman called "learned helplessness" and later "learned hopelessness"—the animal gives up trying.[3] If the cage doors are opened, the animal will not even try to leave.

It seems to me that that is an appropriate metaphor for the democratic citizen these days. We are getting shocked into hopelessness, and it does not seem that there is any way to avoid it. Some obvious shocks are economic; as Elshtain wrote in "Families and Trust," workers see themselves as "dispensable" now more than ever, with an unemployment rate hovering around the 10 percent mark in the aftermath of the 2008 recession. And though that rate was cut in half, to below 5 percent by the 2016 presidential election, employment insecurity remained high enough to affect the outcome of that election.[4] Salaries have stagnated for the middle class; many benefits have eroded. Though the Affordable Care Act allowed many previously uninsured Americans to obtain health coverage, each year it costs more and gets us less, and is at the time of this writing under threat of complete dismantling. Though there was some talk in the press when the "Great Recession" first hit of a reemphasis on the values that Elshtain urged in that piece and elsewhere—that the increased downtime from unemployment may have facilitated a refocus on family and the simple pleasures that can be rediscovered when we unplug (because we cannot afford cable anymore)—economic pressures on families are rarely positive, and indeed can drive stress and conflict in interpersonal relations.

But the shocks also come from the political realm. Certainly, economics is political, but I mean political in the narrowest sense of the term. We vote, and the politicians do not do anything about the problems we face, or worse still, they act out of selfish interest with an eye on their donors—and they call it the will of the people. Indeed, they insist it is what the people want, even in the face of polls showing the opposite, as if reiteration of the claim will turn "truthiness" into truth. Our current sitting president would seem to be the logical end result of the "spiral of delegitimation" that Elshtain identified more than twenty-five years ago, electing a television personality who Elshtain would have considered completely unqualified for the job.[5]

In a 1997 essay, Elshtain cites a 1996 study indicating that two-thirds of the American public believe that our elected officials are "incompetent," and that has worsened since; according to a Gallup poll, in August 2017 Congress had an approval rating of only 16 percent.[6] So we keep "throwing the bums out" but new "bums" fill their places. Gridlock, dysfunction, hyperbolic "debate," the intensity of partisan divide: no matter what we do it seems we cannot avoid the shocks.

Who is administering these shocks, however, and preventing us from taking positive action to minimize the shocks? Given the linkage between economics and politics, it is significant that it is no longer the centralized state that is the problem. (That is what Elshtain worries about in the first chapter of *Democracy on Trial*—the Left centralizes economics and entitlements, the Right sexual and moral lives.) Rather, corporations are a significant and problematic part of what Elshtain identified as part of the "democracy matrix." The removal of regulations over the past thirty-five years has turned over incredible amounts of power to the corporations. The Supreme Court shored this power up in its decision in *Citizens United v. Federal Election Commission*, 558 U.S. 310 (2010), to allow multibillion-dollar corporations to have the same free speech rights as individual citizens, thereby vastly increasing corporate influence on the outcomes of political elections. Why should any citizen bother to contribute money to his or her candidate, when the individual donor will be vastly outspent by a corporation?

That is why citizens feel disaffected: it is not just that they are apathetic about elections because they are apathetic about politics; they

are apathetic about politics because the power no longer lies in politics. Whether they vote or not literally does not seem to make any difference.[7] Barack Obama's election in 2008 proved that; the candidate
whose campaign was about "change" was remarkably unable to change
very much, in the view of many Americans. And many of those who
voted for Donald Trump will be the most seriously injured by his efforts
at medical insurance and tax reform.[8] Votes are wasted because they do
not express our participation; they demonstrate our manipulation. So
why bother voting? Apathy is a function of depression borne by a complete lack of control: we are the dog in the cage who receives electric
shocks no matter what he does, who then gives up completely, who does
not bother trying to leave even when the cage door is opened.

I may be overstating, but presumably you can tell that I am very
depressed by the state of American democracy. A measure of this, in my
view, is how I recently reread *Jane Addams and the Dream of American
Democracy* (*JA*): this theme of the failure of democracy leapt out at me
much more prominently than the first time I read it when the book first
came out in 2003. Back then, I was impressed and inspired by Elshtain's
sympathetic portrayal of Addams's dream of "break[ing] down artificial
barriers between people and mak[ing] it possible for human beings to
realize their full sociality" (*JA*, 95), a dream that had long influenced
my own reading of canonical texts and my own feminist reconstruc-
tions of theoretical concepts like obligation and freedom.[9] I found sense
in Addams's assertion that "no decent person throws 'aside all obligation for the sake of her own selfish and individual development'" (*JA*,
104). Addams's "compassion without condescension" invoked my own
fascination with the problem of recognition in political theory and the
contributions that a feminist ethic of care could make to it, echoing
Addams's view "that women's lives revolved around responsibility, care,
and obligation," while simultaneously noting that "these emphases were,
in a sense, thrust upon them." Addams saw care and responsibility as "a
moral necessity that can and often has served as a source of female power
and authority"; that is, as simply part of the human condition and the
moral landscape that dominant discourses such as political theory have
ignored or even denigrated. But Addams holds that "the imperatives of
this realm must be extended more generally," with Elshtain calling such

a view "the rock bottom ground of her [Addams's] civic philosophy and social feminism" (*JA*, 157). Similarly, when Addams notes that behavior that appears to be neglectful parenting may just be illustrating that "the world has closed in on them" so that "in order to put food on the table, they must give succor short shrift," she expresses an understanding of choice and action within constrained parameters that informed my own view of the freedom of welfare mothers and battered women trying to survive in a world that does not want them to, and as a result making "choices" that do not appear, from a middle-class perspective, to be very rational, much less liberating.

The challenge Elshtain hears in Addams's work—"Who is this 'other' after all? Not an abstract artifact of discourse, but rather, one's neighbor" (*JA*, 128)—surely echoes contemporary feminism's rejection of the dichotomy of self and other, its argument for seeing the other and self in a mutually constituting relationship. Her emphasis on "autonomy within relationships" (*JA*, 174) foreshadowed contemporary "relational autonomy" that influenced my own understanding of freedom and obligation.[10] And surely her advocacy for poor mothers to be able to care for their children instead of working in sweatshops anticipates contemporary feminist arguments against workfare and other welfare reforms of the 1990s.[11] The Jane Addams I encountered in Elshtain's writings in 2003 dreamed a recognizable dream of democracy that I shared, and I could appreciate her dedication, strength, leadership, compassion, and commitment to democratic equality that Elshtain portrays so eloquently and effectively. In case it's not clear, I loved this book—inspiring, prescient, smart.

But context, as Elshtain notes, is very important. On rereading this book over a decade later, I could not help but have my focus drawn to those forces that worked against Addams. There was a very strong resonance between the story Elshtain tells and the world around us today. Particularly depressing was Addams's vilification by those on the Right regarding pacifism (*JA*, 226–35). It reminded me so much of our own Gulf Wars and the war on terror, where anyone who raised an objection to the president's actions was seen as unpatriotic, disloyal, a traitor.

This was not an exceptionalism bred by war, however, but the solidification of a trend of hyperbole and incivility that had emerged in the 1990s. Politics has not changed in the past century, much less the past two decades, as "Yes, we can" turns into "Oh, no, you won't," a politics of hope turns into a politics of cynicism, lies, fake news, and manipulation, and democracy seems more a dream than ever. Addams's fight against Johnny Powers, and the way that she was smeared by him (*JA*, chap. 7); her being labeled as an anarchist (*JA*, 199); the extreme uncompromising positions of those on the Left regarding her support of Theodore Roosevelt and her lack of "purity" on socialism (compare the list of accomplishments Elshtain tallies in *JA*, 190, with the socialists' sneering dismissal of her as a "bourgeois" in *JA*, 188): all seemed just too depressingly familiar. This is the kind of absolutist rhetoric, the misrepresentation and twisting of truth—particularly, we might add, against a woman—that undermines and even destroys democracy, and it is the dominant discourse on the political scene today. What hope does Jane Addams's "mitigation" (*JA*, 163) have today? I read Elshtain's observation, "You cannot build a democratic culture if everyone is on the take and cynicism about public life prevails" (*JA*, 184), with a sinking heart, knowing that she, too, was thinking of the world around her when she wrote it. What Elshtain's account of Addams made clear was how much prejudice, hysteria, and hypocrisy are all the enemies of democracy, and yet at the same time its inevitable by-products.

In the midst of this despair, what should one committed to democracy do? Where can we find hope? Certainly we can strive to emulate Jane Addams. As tenured academics, we could give up research and writing and devote our classroom time to teaching our students about the common good and then volunteering in homeless shelters and soup kitchens. But with even tenure on shaky ground now, particularly at state universities in grave financial difficulty, that may become less thinkable. Or we could emulate Elshtain and become public intellectuals, spreading the voice of reason, and moderation, and compassion, and thoughtfulness, but the people who read such pieces are often those who least need to be reached and influenced.

Clearly Elshtain herself thought that strengthening families is vital to fixing this mess; they are the key to repairing a decaying civil society, which in turn is essential to shoring up democracy. And her vision of family embodied Christian values, such as the gift economy. These are

well-made, persuasive arguments, but getting there from here is the perpetual problem. As Elshtain noted, the feminist dream that both men
and women would work for income and share parenting and household
responsibilities has not come to pass; though most married women work
for wages, they also perform the majority of the housework and childcare. What Arlie Hochschild called "the time bind" hits both men and
women, but it impacts women particularly, not to mention children.

But in my view the way to address this problem is not for women to
stay home, because doing so not only creates an imbalance of democratic
power within the family that is likely to impact children in a different,
but equally negative, way, but it also increases the economic vulnerability
of women's children in the event of divorce, death, or a husband's unemployment. It also hurts their daughters: recent studies show that the
daughters of mothers who work will earn more in their own adult working lives.[12] The fact that most married mothers now work is not simply
a function of a desire for more material goods or guilt that feminists
supposedly inspire (a difficult claim to reconcile with the vast amount
of important work feminists have written valuing care work), but of the
demands of an uncertain economy: when employment security is weak,
both parents need to keep their skills up and their resumes burnished to
increase the likelihood that there will always be at least one income. But
to reconcile this economic need with strengthening families, work hours
need to decline for everyone without bringing them below a living wage
and without jeopardizing benefits like health care and retirement. That
sort of structural shift may be difficult to achieve, but it is impossible to
achieve unless we look to government.

FINDING AN ALLY IN JOHN STUART MILL'S "RELIGION OF HUMANITY"

Another place that we could look for democratic hope, one within the
more standard framework of academic life, might be John Stuart Mill.
This might seem a surprising suggestion since we often tend to associate
Mill with such strong individual liberty that he would seem to represent
the very kind of individualism that Elshtain blames for undermining

democracy. And, in fact, she writes very little about Mill. Moreover, Mill did not share Elshtain's belief in the value of organized religion.

But Mill shared a number of ideas with Elshtain, such as the need to understand individual freedom within a context of responsibility to the social; the importance of character to sifting out good and beneficial desires from bad and harmful ones, and the right, perhaps even the duty, of fellow citizens to express their moral disapprobation of the harmful ones within the civic realm (though not the governmental); the importance of inclusion and participation in a democratic culture; and the importance of the best people being put forth to lead, because they would come up with the best ideas for the common good. Though Mill thought that universal suffrage was vital, he no more believed in plebiscitary government than did Elshtain, because of course the majority is often of the self-interested variety. That is why he advocated giving plural votes to the better educated and more intelligent.[13]

There are obviously many criticisms one could make of his views of representative democracy and plural voting—including the link he assumes between education or intelligence and commitment to the public interest, since we know that the hedge fund managers who brought about the Great Recession were very intelligent and highly educated— but it is not simply the more intelligent who should serve as guides in Mill's view. Rather, it was those who had superior character as defined by "the religion of humanity." An idea that Mill got from Auguste Comte, the religion of humanity, according to Joseph Hamburger, "held up duty as an ideal and sought to fundamentally change motives and habits to generate widespread altruism. . . . The goal was to discourage selfishness by making private motives coincide with the public good."[14]

One finds the religion of humanity developed particularly in a series of essays Mill wrote for *The Examiner* entitled "The Spirit of the Age." He opined in those essays that the mid-nineteenth century was "an age of transition."[15] Mill says that in most periods of history, there are elites who can "dedicate themselves to the investigation and study of physical, moral, and social truths, as their peculiar calling," by whom others should, and normally, do, let themselves be guided.[16] However, "In an age of transition, the divisions among the instructed nullify their authority, and the uninstructed lose their faith in them." The age of transition is not a result simply of disagreement among intellectuals. Rather, disagreement among the learned and leaders is a function of the fact that the *world* is changing; economic, social, and political relationships are in transition, and defining the new truths that reflect those changes is fraught with difficulty. As a result, "the multitude are without a guide; and society is exposed to all the errors and dangers which are to be expected when persons who have never studied any branch of knowledge comprehensively and as a whole attempt to judge for themselves upon particular parts of it."[17] This reliance on private judgment is disastrous for social progress: "Men who place implicit faith in their own common sense are . . . the most wrong-headed and impracticable persons." One must not follow the guidance of people who cannot see, but leading yourself when you cannot see is no better. Yet, "in an age of transition . . . the exercise of private judgment" is the only resource people have.[18]

In criticizing the failure of Christian churches to provide this moral leadership, Maurice Cowling argues, Mill's "religion of humanity" was to be led by an elite "clerisy" of intellectual, educational, and moral character.[19] If old truths no longer apply because of radically changing economic and cultural conditions, it is up to the superior members of society to figure out the new truths that apply to this new world as it emerges. This might sound rather antidemocratic and elitist; Cowling in fact argues that Mill "feared that democracy would destroy the higher cultivation" of "good" desires because of "collective mediocrity." But this is less a condemnation of democracy per se, Cowling avers, than a fear of democracy's emergence at a particular time in history when "old opinions are dead" and the new ones are based on, as Mill put it, "the despotism of custom" rather than new and bold ideas that reflected the powerful changes that were occurring in industry and in social formations around the world, such as the struggle against slavery.

In such conditions, to echo Elshtain's terms, we would end up with a plebiscitary system rather than a democratic one. The "religion of humanity" was a positive vision for a world where people think of the common good and see themselves as linked with others. A major goal of Mill's *System of Logic* was to develop an "Ethology, or the Science of Character." But as Hamburger notes, in *On Liberty* and in other writings,

"Mill provided more detailed and concrete accounts of how to promote wholesome and how to prevent depraved qualities of character."[20] The religion of humanity was key to the building of character, for it would lead men and women to "form the desires so that those which were selfish would be diminished and those which were altruistic would become predominant."[21]

Mill's project, then, became "to provide a body of commanding doctrine which, by stimulating the higher intelligence of all citizens, will . . . tell men what their duties are, and induce that sense of common participation, of which the great changes in European society, and the decay of old opinions, have deprived them."[22] But for Mill, again, such "instruction" was tied up not with authoritarianism but with the cultivation of a true democracy and a robust civil society, in which we can "replace customary deference to arbitrarily established authority by rational deference to elevated intellect." The role of education in *On Liberty* takes on a deeper significance in this light, for the purpose of free exchange is not to have an ongoing debate throughout history, but to achieve truth, for "once good principles have been established as a basis for conduct, they will not need to be subjected to critical examination on every occasion." This does not eliminate the need for freedom of thought and discussion, of course, for "a free individual is more likely than an unfree one to contribute to the higher cultivation."[23]

Indeed, following on Cowling's remark about Mill's dismay about the failure of organized Christian religions and churches, Hamburger argues that the purpose of advocating freedom of thought was to loosen the grip of formal religion on morality, so that intellectuals could pursue a "true" morality based on the good of humanity rather than "arbitrary" religious dictates. The key, according to Hamburger, was to create circumstances that would allow the superior to develop new ideas, and that required Mill to advocate a strong philosophy of individual liberty. As Mill notes in *On Liberty*, "Genius can only breathe freely in an atmosphere of freedom. Persons of genius are, *ex vi termini*, more individual than any other people—less capable, consequently, of fitting themselves, without hurtful compression, into any of the small number of moulds which society provides in order to save its members the trouble of forming their own character. I insist thus emphatically on the importance of genius, and the necessity of allowing it to unfold itself freely both in thought and in practice."[24]

For anyone who believes in organized religion, of course, as Elshtain did (often describing herself as "Lutheran leaning toward Catholic") this might seem a rather weak and thin reed on which to hang a claim about the relationship of religion to democracy, and Mill's religion of humanity might seem a rather obnoxious use of the term "religion." But the key link to Elshtain may be civil society. Character is important for Mill precisely because he wanted government to play a relatively minimalist role in people's lives: instead of law, moral approbation and disapprobation were key instruments in getting people to improve themselves and to think about the common good rather than selfish interests, because it was the best way to keep government from doing that job for us. In that sense, the religion of humanity was key to a robust version of civil society, and both were vital to democracy.

So turning more to John Stuart Mill might be one way for democratic theorists, and political theorists more broadly, to fight the desperate state of democracy today. And I hope that it is clear that the account I have given of Mill coheres with the themes I have previously discussed in Elshtain's writings: character, it seems to me, is the central demand of a democratic culture in Elshtain's theory, but it is a demand that has been too infrequently met in recent years. I think, then, that further engagement with Elshtain's and Mill's thought in conversation with each other might be extremely productive.

DEMOCRACY AND DISABILITY

But another direction in which we might turn—if this does not sound too much like a *non sequitur*—is disability studies. Like my Mill suggestion, this too might seem counterintuitive, given Elshtain's harsh criticism of identity politics. I share much of Elshtain's impatience for the frequent facileness of identity politics. And I admit that a great deal of disability activism and even disability studies demonstrates a "for us or against us" mentality; at disability conferences, everyone gets the "in" jokes, they know that "cure" is a dirty word, they uniformly maintain that the difference that disability makes is one to celebrate and even perhaps encourage. It sometimes demonstrates identity politics at its worst, generating "more heat than light," to invoke an Elshtainian phrase.

But identity, rather than objective fact, is often as the heart of disabled persons' exclusion from democracy. Disabled individuals have for decades had to bear the "stigma," to invoke Goffman, of "spoiled identity."[25] Able-bodied individuals routinely express negative reactions, ranging from repulsion to pity. Disabled people have thus been forced into the private sphere of the home or, worse, institutions. Disabled people in ancient Greece were left out to die. In later centuries and cultures they were closed off, out of the public sphere. In the seventeenth century, the "great confinement" locked both mentally and physically disabled individuals in institutions; and in Enlightenment thought of this era, disability was commonly invoked as a metaphor for unfreedom.[26] In the nineteenth century, "ugly laws" legally prohibited disabled people from appearing in public.[27] In the twentieth century, the Nazis began their program of purification by killing disabled people in concentration camps before they moved on to the Jews, but this followed on policies of other twentieth-century democracies where forced sterilization and other sorts of eugenicist policies were already practiced.[28]

In the latter half of the twentieth century things began to shift, with legislative action that outlawed discrimination, though often ineffectively, and eventually the passage of the Americans with Disabilities Act (ADA), which required that public buildings and spaces be accessible to all sorts of bodies, and provided a few more teeth to antidiscrimination legislation in education and employment. It was followed ten years later by the ADA Amendments Act (ADAAA) to close the legal loopholes that the courts regularly found in the laws to make discrimination easier, and which many members of Congress, on both sides of the aisle, found particularly frustrating as the courts routinely misinterpreted the congressional intent of the original act.

Surely, a law like the ADAAA does not make the exclusion of the disabled a thing of the past; lawsuits are expensive and time-consuming, and the people and institutions that they are generally made against have deep pockets. But what I find amazing is that Congress, of all institutions, passed this in the first place, and both the ADA and the ADAAA were signed into law by Republican presidents—despite the widespread (though generally mistaken) belief that having to provide accommodation is antibusiness. Some have explained this as a "welfare reform" effort to get disabled persons off federal support and into the paid labor market.[29] But a number of the legislators were themselves disabled, such as Sen. Daniel Inouye of Hawaii, Sen. Robert Dole of Kansas, Sen. Bob Kerrey of Nebraska, and Sen. John McCain of Arizona—all disabled veterans—and also Rep. Tony Coelho (epilepsy) and Rep. Jim Langevin (paralyzed). Others, such as Sen. Tom Harkin, Rep. Steny Hoyer, Rep. Jim Sensenbrenner, and Sen. Edward Kennedy, had disabled relatives. Others, such as Sen. Orin Hatch of Utah, acted out of love for Ronald Reagan, who was dealing with Alzheimer's disease. So the personal dimension of this legislation should not be dismissed so readily.[30]

But the democratic dimensions of this should not be ignored either: disability is not a phenomenon limited to a small minority, but it is a significant social issue. It was recently estimated that in the United States alone, 51.2 million Americans are disabled, approximately 18 percent of the population; in other words, one out of every five or six citizens —including political theorists—will have a disability, if not yet, then eventually.[31] Disability affects people of all races, ages, religions, ethnicities, nationalities, classes, and genders. Many more also have or will have loved ones and family members with disabilities. So the disabled may be a minority, but it is a rapidly growing one, particularly as baby boomers age, and the democratic polity will need to address this as a collective problem.

So disability can provide a good example of how identity politics can, should, and, in this case, did work to foster democratic debate and dialogue. This bipartisan, bicameral effort was a historic example of the workings of good government that rose above traditional political jockeying and focused instead on substantive policy. It moreover helped bring into the polity many citizens who have historically been excluded. It embodied, in Adam Michnik's words, as Elshtain notes in "In Common Together," "the essence of democracy," which entails the "freedom which belongs to citizens with a conscience."[32] Indeed, rather than disability rights advocates acting as the ones to foreclose debate by requiring political correctness, instead it was those opposed to the legislation who were short-sighted and against democratic debate—for instance, refusing to accept evidence that the cost of providing accommodation was generally more than balanced by increases to employees' productivity, or rejecting studies that routinely show that disabled people have the same levels of happiness as nondisabled people.

It is in this light that I take issue with Elshtain's views of Christopher Reeve's appearance at the Democratic National Convention in 1996. She admits her essay to be "dyspeptic" (her term), but in the process I think she mischaracterizes the disability position and misses its democratic potential in the process—a potential that could be important to her own work, and to democratic theorists' attempt to reclaim hope. It may be that what many people felt was pity, but I think that the dominant theme—and what Reeve was going for—was *advocacy* and the kind of fighting against victimization that Elshtain articulates in "Neither Victims nor Heroes,"[33] which is about her own struggle with polio and postpolio syndrome.

Reeve advocated an issue that, in my view, is at the heart of the democratic project, namely, more funding for medical research of all kinds. I believe that is an important part of the democratic project. If we would spend one-quarter of the money we spend on the military on the National Institutes of Health, just imagine all the citizens who currently are excluded from the public realm who could be brought back into it. If it is assumed that pity was the reason that Reeve was asked to the stage, and that pity is why people cheered him, then we create a circular argument: disabled people by definition become excluded from advocating for themselves. And indeed, that is a complaint lodged against disability activism more broadly: that "those people" are just selfish complainers who don't have the good grace to accept the hand that fate or God has dealt them; they want to waste huge expenditures for special features —like wheelchair lifts on buses—that only a small minority will use, when that money could go toward other (often unspecified) expenses that benefit the vast majority.

Such thinking is reminiscent of pre-Enlightenment thinking about disability, dating back to an era when democracy was hardly a norm. As historian Cathy Kudlick demonstrates in her work on the smallpox epidemic in eighteenth-century France, the "medical model" emerged out of Enlightenment thinking about the power of human agency; rather than simply accept illness as "fate" or "God's will," science and medicine were seen as ways in which humans could construct and change illness by social intervention. In other words, the medical model was "always already" social.[34] But more significant for my purposes here is the idea that the Enlightenment gave rise to democratic ways of thinking about government because it recognized the power of human agency in creating and shaping the world—a creating and shaping that a Jane Addams would admire. In other words, the same way of thinking that motivated such views of science and illness motivated the move toward democratic self-governance.

Advocacy for medical research is only a sign of selfish individualism—or pity—if you assume that disability advocacy is possible without grounding it in a broad notion of group welfare. But it is not. What makes disability advocacy even possible, and what makes it so fundamentally democratic, is precisely the ways in which disability weaves through the lives of people who could and should and want to be active members of the democratic polity—who "just want to be part of the conversation"[35]—but who are shoved aside, excluded, forgotten. And when one includes not just the individuals who have the disabilities but their family members and friends who must provide the resources and care that democracy fails to provide, then we have quite a large number of democratic citizens who are affected.

Elshtain was a great advocate of shedding "light" rather than "heat," and it is clear from her view of the 1996 political party conventions that she thinks Reeve was operating in the land of "heat," and she may be right. As I recall it, an emotional appeal was part of Reeve's approach, and that was a significant part of what Elshtain rejected. But democracy needs both heat and light in order to flourish. Certainly, there is far too much heat (and not enough light) in politics lately, but we do need *some* heat to keep the democratic spirit alive. Democracy is about pushing and pulling, giving and taking, fighting passionately for what you believe in. That you might benefit from it personally, or more than some others, does not necessarily mean that self-interest trumps the common interest. For indeed, if disabled people must depend on the advocacy of able-bodied people to bring about change in disability policy, medical research, and other issues, they are consigned to the same role of helpless dependency to which they have been assigned since ancient times. It is much like arguing that women should be quiet and let men advocate for women's equality—which, of course, Elshtain would never argue.

I would like to think, in fact, that one reason why Elshtain started to turn to this topic later in her career was the democratic potential and democratic energy of the disability movement. Go to a disability conference, for instance, and you will find all sorts of people with all sorts of bodies: some missing limbs, others in wheelchairs, blind, some with dwarfism, others with cerebral palsy who have their translators in tow, and of course a large segment of individuals who look completely "normal"—some of whom are deaf, others who have diabetes, MS, arthritis, PTSD, some of whom have no physical anomalies at all, many of whom are closely related to individuals with disabilities, but others who are just interested in disability. Every panel is crowded, interesting questions are asked, practitioners, activists, and scholars intermingle. At the Society for Disability Studies annual meeting, the biggest disability meeting in the world, the conference culminates on Saturday night with a dance, where nobody feels self-conscious about how they look while engaging in "creative" dance moves. Acceptance, kindness, compassion, inclusion—all of the hallmarks of democracy as Elshtain describes it—are in rich abundance.

Moreover, Jane Addams would be right at home among today's disability scholars and activists. Indeed, as Elshtain perhaps inadvertently shows us, Addams's approach to disability provides an early foreshadowing of today's disability perspective. Certain aspects of her argument anticipate the "social model of disability," which holds that although "impairments" such as blindness or paraplegia may be biologically founded, such impairments constitute "disabilities" only because social arrangements are structured to favor certain kinds of bodies and penalize others. For instance, it is not the fact that I am unable to walk that disables me from entering a building to take a class, but the fact that the building was built with stairs instead of ramps; it is not the fact that I cannot hear that disables me from using a telephone at work, but the fact that my company refuses to install TDD technology. Those social arrangements are a function of power, even, as Mairian Corker says, "a form of social oppression."[36]

When Addams argued against "euthanizing" infants with "mental infirmities" and for social policy that would make it easier for mothers to care for disabled infants, she presaged today's prenatal-testing discourse, where pregnant women are urged to abort infants with potential disabilities because caring for such infants is potentially too difficult. As Addams would argue, and as Elshtain has argued,[37] if resources were provided for disabled infants and their caretakers, taking care of such infants would be much less difficult. Such resources would change parents', and indeed society's, view of such children as not "exceptions" but rather "a type of child that occurs from time to time," thus making "special" children seem "ordinary" (*JA*, 161–62). In Addams's view, disability is simply a "difference," and a good democratic society can and should respond to a variety of differences among its citizens.

Certainly, Elshtain and I agree that one can carry the social model of disability too far. In her account of postpolio syndrome, much of what makes her "disabled" is the lack of response, accommodation, and just plain use of common sense (particularly at airports!). But the body does pose challenges in itself, as Elshtain knew and experienced.[38] People with impairments experience pain, suffering, and limitation that is physiological in nature, that no "accommodation" can redress: an employer can accommodate an employee with diabetes by allowing her to take breaks to check blood sugar, eat a snack, or inject insulin, but low blood sugars occasionally happen to even the most well-regulated diabetic, with their consequent disorientation and confusion. That does not mean the diabetic cannot do her job, but it also does not mean that she is disabled exclusively by her workplace rather than her body.

But what theorizing and thinking about disability does in the context of democracy and democratic theory, regardless of the "model" one follows, is to highlight the relationship of political and private. Certainly Elshtain advocated protection of the private sphere. But she clearly saw, going back to *Public Man, Private Woman*, that there could be "private" things that were nevertheless *political*, even if they were not necessarily *public*. For instance, the sequestering of disabled persons in the private sphere that the ADA was meant to fight was and is intensely *political*: it was a reflection of a judgment that "we" don't want "that sort of person" to have a say in politics, in social customs, in determining practices and norms: what Elshtain calls "the connection in Addams's mind between the quality of human life and the quality of public policy—which could either work to sustain human fellowship or contribute to the break-down of human relationships" (*JA*, 242). The ADA and ADAAA do not only change the workplace, or the architecture of public buildings and spaces, but in the process they also make life livable for a wider diversity of human beings, thereby increasing the range of diversity among the individuals occupying the public realm.

Part of our collective loss brought by Elshtain's death was that she was intending to work more in this area; she would have made valuable contributions to a field that political theorists have been slow to catch onto.[39] Democracy needs "heroes . . . of the quotidian sort,"[40] and this is what we see in disability studies and activism: people with particular physical conditions or bodily differences who are simply fighting to be part of the democratic public, to be participatory members of the demo-cratic polity. If they do that by getting an automatic door installed in an office building, or making their boss aware of how much most vision-impaired people *can* see or how agile people can be in their wheelchairs, or getting a professional academic organization to pay for Internet access so a panelist whose disability "flared up" at the last minute, pre-venting her from attending, can Skype in her talk, or to ask presenters to bring large-print copies of their presentations with them to distribute for hearing- and vision-impaired members of the audience—those small changes add up to a more inclusive polity. Surely, my suggestions are hardly adequate to overcome the cynicism, dysfunction, incompetence, and incivility that we find in U.S. politics today. But if our democracy is still on trial—and I think it clearly is—then perhaps a sliver of hope will help the process of gaining a more favorable verdict.

NOTES

1. Jean Bethke Elshtain, "In Common Together: Unity, Diversity and Civic Virtue," in *The Constitution of the People: Reflections on Citizens and Civil Society*, ed. Robert Calvert (Lawrence: University of Kansas Press, 1991), 67.

2. Jean Bethke Elshtain, "Issues and Themes: Spiral of Delegitimation or New Social Covenant," in *The Elections of 1992*, ed. Michael Nelson (Washington, DC: Congressional Quarterly Press, 1994), 109–24.

3. M. E. P. Seligman and S. F. Maier, "Failure to Escape Traumatic Shock," *Journal of Experimental Psychology* 74 (1967): 1–9; Martin Seligman, *Helplessness: On Depression, Development, and Death* (San Francisco: W. H. Freeman, 1975).

4. Jean Bethke Elshtain, "Families and Trust: Connecting Private Lives to Civic Goods," *Journal of Family Ministry* 12, no. 1 (1998) 31–40.

5. Elshtain, "Issues and Themes."

6. Jean Bethke Elshtain, "Not a Cure-All: Why Civil Society? Why Now?" Brookings Review 15, no. 5 (1997): 13–16; Rebecca Riffkin, "2014 U.S. Approval of Congress Remains Near All-Time Low," Gallup.com, December 15, 2014, http://www.gallup.com/poll/180113/2014-approval-congress-remains-near-time-low.aspx. During the first third of 2017, congressional approval jumped to 28 percent in February but dropped back down to 20 percent by April, continuing down from there. "Republicans' Approval of Congress Drops to New 2017 Low," http://news.gallup.com/poll/215630/republicans-approval-congress-drops-new-2017-low.aspx.

7. I say this despite the claims that voter identification laws and other things suppressed turnout in 2016, resulting in Clinton's loss. Correlation is not causation, and many factors account for low turnout, including voter apathy and disaffection; see Michelle Ye Hee Lee, "Do Voter ID Laws Help or Hurt Voter Turnout?" *Washington Post*, May 30, 2017.

8. Nate Cohen, "Trump Supporters Have the Most to Lose in the G.O.P. Repeal Bill," *New York Times*, March 10, 2017.

9. Nancy J. Hirschmann, *Rethinking Obligation: A Feminist Method for Political Theory* (Ithaca, NY: Cornell University Press, 1992); Hirschmann, *The Subject of Liberty: Toward a Feminist Theory of Freedom* (Princeton, NJ: Princeton University Press, 2003).

10. In Hirschmann, *Rethinking Obligation*, chap. 3, I give central attention to the difference between "relational autonomy" and "reactive autonomy," a theme that was echoed in Hirschmann, *Subject of Liberty* (esp. 35–39), despite my strong assertion that freedom *rather than* autonomy was my focus. See also Nancy Hirschmann, "Autonomy? Or Freedom? A Return to Psychoanalytic Theory," in *Autonomy, Oppression, and Gender*, ed. Andrea Veltman and Mark Piper (Oxford: Oxford University Press, 2014), 61–86.

11. See essays in Nancy J. Hirschmann and Ulrike Liebert, *Women and Welfare: Theory and Practice in the United States and Europe* (New Brunswick, NJ: Rutgers University Press, 2001).

12. Claire Cain Miller, "Mounting Evidence of Advantages for Children of Working Mothers," *New York Times*, May 15, 2015, https://www.nytimes.com

/2015/05/17/upshot/mounting-evidence-of-some-advantages-for-children-of
-working-mothers.html.

13. John Stuart Mill, "On Representative Government," in *On Liberty and Other Essays*, ed. John Gray (Oxford: Oxford University Press, 1992).

14. Joseph Hamburger, *John Stuart Mill on Liberty and Control* (Princeton, NJ: Princeton University Press, 1999), 108.

15. John Stuart Mill, "The Spirit of the Age, I," in *Collected Works*, Vol. 22, *Newspaper Writings, December 1822–July 1831*, ed. Ann P. Robson and John M. Robson (Toronto: University of Toronto Press, 1986), 230.

16. John Stuart Mill, "The Spirit of the Age II," in *Collected Works*, 22:242.

17. Ibid., 238.

18. Ibid., 239.

19. Maurice Cowling, *Mill and Liberalism* (Cambridge: Cambridge University Press, 1963), 15–23.

20. John Stuart Mill, "System of Logic," in *Collected Works*, Vol. 8, *A System of Logic, Ratiocinative and Inductive*, ed. M. Robson (Toronto: University of Toronto Press, 1974), 869; Hamburger, *John Stuart Mill on Liberty and Control*, 118.

21. Hamburger, *John Stuart Mill on Liberty and Control*, 108.

22. Cowling, *Mill and Liberalism*, 10–12.

23. Ibid., 28, 30.

24. Mill, "On Liberty," in *On Liberty and Other Essays*, ed. John Gray (Oxford: Oxford University Press, 1992), 72.

25. Erving Goffman, *Stigma: Notes on the Management of Spoiled Identity* (Englewood Cliffs, NJ: Prentice Hall, 1963).

26. Nancy J. Hirschmann, "Freedom and (Dis)Ability in the Early Modern Era," in *Recovering Disability in Early Modern England*, ed. Allison Hobgood and David Wood (Athens: Ohio State University Press, 2013).

27. Susan Schweik, *The Ugly Laws: Disability in Public* (New York: NYU Press, 2009).

28. Christina Cogdell, *Eugenic Design: Streamlining America in the 1930s* (Philadelphia: University of Pennsylvania Press, 2004); Matthew Thomson, *The Problem of Mental Deficiency: Eugenics, Democracy, and Social Policy in Britain, c. 1870–1959* (Oxford: Clarendon, 1998).

29. Samuel Bagenstos, "The Americans with Disabilities Act as Welfare Reform," *William and Mary Law Review* 44, no. 3 (2003): 954.

30. It should be noted, however, that although Inouye advocated for the bill, he is listed in the Senate roll call as "not voting."

31. Erika Steinmetz, "Americans with Disabilities: 2002," *Current Population Reports*, U.S. Census Bureau (May 2006), https://www.census.gov/prod/2006 pubs/p70-107.pdf.

32. Jean Elshtain, "In Common Together: Unity, Diversity and Civic Virtue," in *The Constitution of the People: Reflections on Citizens and Civil Society*, ed. Robert Calvert (Lawrence: University of Kansas Press, 1991), 81.

33. Jean Bethke Elshtain, "Neither Victims nor Heroes: Reflections from a Polio Person," *Philosophy and Medicine* 104, no. 4, (2010): 241–50.

34. Cathy Kudlick, "Smallpox, Disability and Survival in Nineteenth Century France: Rewriting Paradigms from a New Epidemic Script," in *Disability Histories*, ed. Susan Birch and Michael Rembis (Chicago: University of Illinois Press, 2014).

35. Tobin Siebers, "Disability Trouble," in *Civil Disabilities: Citizenship, Membership, and Belonging*, ed. Nancy J. Hirschmann and Beth Linker (Philadelphia: University of Pennsylvania Press, 2015): 223–36.

36. Mairian Corker, "Differences, Conflations and Foundations: The Limits to 'Accurate' Theoretical Representations of Disabled People's Experience?" *Disability & Society* 14 (1999): 631.

37. Jean Bethke Elshtain, "Genetic Fundamentalism" (lecture delivered at the University of Pennsylvania, March 2009).

38. Elshtain, "Neither Victims nor Heroes."

39. She had agreed to contribute to Barbara Arneil and Nancy J. Hirschmann, eds., *Disability and Political Theory* (Cambridge: Cambridge University Press, 2016), but passed away before she could write the essay she proposed on children's rights and disability.

40. Elshtain, "Neither Victims nor Heroes."

PART II

CITIES OF GOD AND MAN

Introduction

Michael Kessler

A significant thread running through Christian political theology is the multifaceted tension between the two orders of *regnum* and *sacerdotium*. A central problem has been how to envision the legitimacy of the material governing structures when they arise from human will and are thereby shaped through powers that are misdirected and pathological. St. Paul's injunction is clear enough: "Let every person be subject to the governing authorities. For there is no authority except from God, and those that exist have been instituted by God" (Rom. 13:1). Yet theologians and political theorists have had to grapple with the reality of political authority, which is too often seen as the handiwork of the devil.

Jean Elshtain's work, especially in *Sovereignty: God, State, Self* (S), helps sort through crucial aspects of the earthly necessity to organize and chasten human wills and choices and clarifies political configurations that might optimize governance for the types of creatures we humans are. Elshtain envisions politics through the framework of ultimate ends and transcendental goods that exceed material organizational competency, thus limiting the power and rule of the spiritual kingdom in earthly affairs. Unusual for a contemporary political theorist, Elshtain pursued this task in dialogue with a remarkable array of resources—some Christian and many not. She was interested in contemplating good models of human life and flourishing wherever they might arise.

The relation between the two realms of power—human and divine, political and spiritual—ebbed and flowed over the centuries. As Elshtain described, "Although there was no straightforward and simple identification of spiritual and temporal authority, there was overlap between the two that made conflict inevitable between competing jurisdictions. The saga of sorting this out gave the history of the Western half of Christendom a distinctive dynamic that channeled cultural energy, conflict, and contestation" (*S*, 12). Indeed. Much of the history Elshtain goes on to recount traces the rise of sovereignty, from political acts conducted under reason in conformity with transcendental concepts and law given under the form of justice, to modern configurations of authority and legitimacy envisioned nakedly as arbitrary will backed by coercive sanction. This is an old story of how the sovereign self rises to crowd out the divine sovereign, and how humans proceed unmoored from the natural and transcendent anchors that give their lives meaning, purpose, and direction.

Elshtain shares in a host of critical assessments saying that this rise of autonomy has been, at best, ambiguous in achieving fulfillment and flourishing for human beings alone or together with their fellows. As Hans Blumenberg put it in his magisterial *The Legitimacy of the Modern Age*, "The decisions that were once made outside this world in the absolute acts of divinity and are now supposed to be accomplished in and through man, as moral, social, and political actions, did not, as it turned out, permit a successful transition to self-disposition."[1] Self-preservation and autonomy, on this account, have consumed theory and life, and they have become, in Blumenberg's words, "a fundamental category of everything in existence," from "the principle of inertia in physics to the biological structure of drives and the laws of state building."[2] Human contingency, ordered by our own preferences and law-giving, has replaced God's ordered creation of human life. States' political institutions and regulations now reflect the arbitrary will of the lawgivers— reflecting their naked grabs for power and the collective accumulation and securitization of satisfied desires—not the intrinsic justice and ratio-nality of a law made in conformity to eternal order.

The essays here in part II think alongside Elshtain as she dialogues with this ambiguous set of tensions in our history and present. In chap-ter 6, Lisa Cahill captures a basic fact of Elshtain's legacy and why so many hold her in esteem: "At the end of the day, we are left with the confident, outreaching, justice-committed politics of Aquinas, Catho-lic social teaching and Jean Elshtain—and the circumspect, church-preferring, dirty-hands-washing politics of Augustine, Luther, and also Jean Elshtain." This capacious thinking, where (as Gilbert Meilaender points out), "Bonhoeffer sits comfortably beside Camus," is not a sign of eclecticism or confusion; rather, Elshtain engaged a wide variety of serious thinkers in whom she saw the working out of the human drama in a fragmented world. She was neither a nostalgic defender of a distant past that might guide our present age nor an ecclesial separatist hoping to follow that new St. Benedict (for whom Alasdair MacIntyre yearned) onto a theologically pure Masada high above the fallen, dirty political order below.³ She was deeply skeptical of modernity's impulses but also recognized the possibilities that modern modes of *responsible* freedom that sought justice could achieve *and* the deeply troublesome conse-quences that were simultaneously awakened in those human capacities disconnected from deeper sources of thought and life.

Cahill pushes us to consider some of the ways that many people lack control and agency in this era of contemporary global economic and political structures, a situation that necessitates more social and political commitment from Christians and all people of good will, not retreat into ecclesial enclaves.

In chapter 7, Nigel Biggar sees this same tension in Elshtain's work, and he links it to a profound struggle in Augustine, who envisioned the human "stretched between the exhilarating lure of eschatological hope on the one hand, and the drag of sin . . . on the other." For Augustine, the human will is caught between these two poles of the sinful and the hope-ful world beyond. The pilgrim, on Elshtain's account, in a profoundly Augustinian mode, must navigate this tension by discerning how to remain committed to the world and its possibilities for human flourish-ing while recognizing its fragmentary limits and constant ambiguity.

For Gilbert Meilaender, in chapter 8, Elshtain's turn to the Trinitarian model of relationality bears deep significance for her project of
constructing a view of sovereignty that resists a singular, naked will.
Meilaender pushes to the limits of Elshtain's views. Even though she
constructs a view of the self as relational, and one that is deeply rooted
in the Christian idea of what it means to be a person, Meilaender asks
how this model can arise and thrive in a world that finds this model of
personhood foreign, if not hostile. Can a plural, democratic order sustain the space in which the Christian can be a pilgrim, with one's eyes
and heart turned toward deeper matters? And yet, the Christian is called
to love one's neighbor as the "holiest object" of our senses, and, as such,
we remain inextricably called toward them.

In chapter 9, Eric Gregory considers the Augustinian vision of *caritas* residing at the foundation of this hopeful drive that recognizes the
limits of what humans can accomplish by their own lights. Elshtain, following Augustine, holds that humans are "bundles" of drives and loves,
some pathological and needing correction, others graciously driven to
our higher end and purpose. We are, as Gregory puts it, able to "enjoy
the gifts of God even as we are perennially tempted to enjoy them in
the wrong way." There are many temptations in this temporal life, and
a common political variety is to envision what we do as political agents
is morally justified. Gregory thinks alongside Elshtain as she confronts
the problem of "dirty hands" and how we are often confronted with
choices between two competing evils. Elshtain confronts the challenges
of the use of torture in achieving security; sometimes there are supreme
emergencies that merit imperfectly justified tragic choices to protect
creation from disorder. Gregory pushes us to consider how far love goes
to thwart, or recommend, the kinds of power that states wield and that
situations may, at times, demand.

Daniel Philpott points in chapter 10 to Elshtain's work on international relations and just war as one horizon in which she navigated
these tensions, and how she may have erred too far on the side of the
realists. Elshtain called for serious consideration of religion in analyzing
international affairs, she critiqued state ultimacy and pervasiveness, and
she saw that war required some moral criteria in its execution. Philpott
situates the rise of the modern realist, secular state and the international

arena against the background of theological and philosophical thought, which Elshtain was likewise engaging. She pushed against the dominant realist paradigm within which her peers operated, but Philpott problematizes her engagement with the (on Philpott's reading) overly realist Niebuhr as insufficiently critical.

The essays here seek to expand upon Elshtain's vision that the contemporary self "seeks meaning and dignity and finds a measure of both not in total liberation from nature, nor in some utopian attunement and at-oneness with nature but, rather, in growing to become a full person according to our human natures," a nature that is intrinsically social and relational (*S*, 229–30). "We are created to love and to be loved" (*S*, 230), and love leads us out from our own answers to see and respond to the suffering and need around us. Elshtain pushes us to understand that power politics helps address this immense need and is therefore inscribed within the order of love, but politics is only a limited part of the answer to our predicament.

NOTES

1. Hans Blumenberg, *The Legitimacy of the Modern Age* (Cambridge, MA: MIT Press, 1985), 89.
2. Ibid., 183.
3. Alasdair MacIntyre, *After Virtue* (Notre Dame, IN: University of Notre Dame Press, 1984), 263.

CHAPTER SIX

SOVEREIGN NO MORE?

Selves, States, and God in Our Bewildering Global Environment

Lisa Sowle Cahill

Like Jean Bethke Elshtain, I am very committed to a defense of moral realism, a shared human nature, and some sort of revised "natural law." These are essential to the pursuit of justice in our present "global" century, because they express and reinforce the shared human values on which justice across borders depends. Yet Elshtain also brings an Augustinian reminder that the cities of God and of politics are two different realities, whose aims should not be conflated. This creates tensions in her thought that may reflect tensions in our human and Christian realities, a possibility that I will explore in what follows. In addition, I question the premise that selves and states today are best described as "sovereign."

Elshtain has over the years maintained a strong interest in war, peace, and just war, and, more recently, the rebuilding of societies after conflict.[1] This is another area of convergence for us. *Sovereignty: God, State and Self* (S) touches on these themes, inasmuch as a main thread in Elshtain's historical argument is that U.S. constitutionalism, with its tripartite balance of the powers of government (judicial, executive, and legislative), represents the binding of the powers of a sovereign head of state or government by the higher requirements of a natural moral law protecting "prepolitical dignities that belong to human beings as such and that the state can either honor or dishonor" (*S*, 158). Consequently she repudiates, as do I, the "realist" idea that "war knows no law save that of force" (151). It is no simple matter, however, to articulate the content of the moral laws governing use of force in the international arena, and it is even more difficult to understand the nature of the authority or authorities that govern or could govern the moral use of military power.[2] Today the majority of wars are no longer between or among "sovereign states," they are intrastate, and the majority of people killed in them are civilians—up to 75 percent; World War I saw only 5 percent.[3]

Therefore, besides endorsing wholeheartedly Elshtain's call for the recognition of common moral values, including human equality, I share her hope that social conditions of injustice can be changed for the better and her confidence that religious actors, traditions, and organizations can play a positive role in the process. At the same time, however, I might distinguish more strongly than she the views of Aquinas and Augustine on the historical possibilities of politics. I would in fact not only incorporate but actually stress a note of Augustinian pessimism about approximating, what Elshtain calls toward the end of *Sovereignty*, commerce as "trusting and promise-keeping," politics as "commitment to a good that we can know in common," and law as guaranteeing that "each and every one, no matter how lowly, stands as an equal before the law" (*S*, 243–44). Augustine is a good antidote to the overconfidence in human reasonableness and good will often found in developments of the ethics of Thomas Aquinas, especially Catholic social teaching. Related issues I will address briefly are the status of equality as a modern value, a human value, and a religious value; the legitimacy and importance of feminism, not reducible to liberal feminism; the existential conditions under which "the self" today perceives its prospects for sovereignty, autonomy, and choices; the sense in which we are living in a "new world order" in which state sovereignty has eroded but not disappeared; and the potential contributions of Christianity to global work for justice.

First, let's spend some time with the broad argument of *Sovereignty*. Elshtain analyzes the ways both divine and state sovereignty changed in meaning as a consequence of the replacement of medieval theology by nominalism. As she puts it, "the accent shifted from sovereign God as the apogee of reason and love, a God bound to and by his loving creation, to God as force and will, a God less accessible to us and less trustworthy" (S, 58). The shift in conceptions of political or state authority runs parallel: from the idea "that earthly dominion is about *jus* or justice and governed by law," to a more absolutist view of political authority, the notion that there is a "plenitude of power" in earthly authorities, a power that can do all things and cannot be resisted (58, 60). Nominalist power is "monistic," whereas the medieval and Reformation notions of power were pluralistic. The Thomistic idea of the common good includes the interaction of plural sites of authority and social institutions; the Reformation "two swords" view saw the temporal and spiritual swords as operating in distinct if interrelated realms, under independent authorities. This allowed for mutual contestation and opened the possibility of resistance by authority's subjects.

Nominalism did away with the premise that legitimate earthly rule or state sovereignty entails a commitment to "justice and righteousness" and that justice derives from elsewhere than the sheer will of the sovereign (S, 64). In the medieval view, "the king serves as mediator to the transcendent" and is thus accountable to transcendent standards of justice. Yet, according to "modernizing theory . . . the king is an absolute emperor within his own kingdom" (67, cf. 15).

These developments have serious consequences, according to Elshtain, for the individual as moral agent, and for the way individual persons envision themselves in relation to others and to society as a whole. Let me give you three quotes from *Sovereignty*: "As sovereign state is to sovereign God, so sovereign selves are to sovereign states" (159). "As God wills and the state wills, so selves will: we are willful; we make demands; we have wants. But the 'we' is an aggregate of 'I's'" (160). "The self stands alone, sans any mutually constitutive relationship to the world. . . . The language of conquest, control over, complete self-ownership—tests of self-sovereignty—prevails" (204).

In concluding chapters of *Sovereignty* that deal in part with genetics, abortion, and what she calls "radical feminism," Elshtain offers up some extreme outcomes of such a view of the self. For example, the feminist philosopher Alison Jaggar is quoted as saying—in 1983—that if new

134 Lisa Sowle Cahill

birth technologies could enable women to inseminate one another or
men to carry pregnancies and lactate, then there could be "a substantial
reduction in the social domination of women by men," and an increase in
"women's control over their bodies, and thus over their lives" (S, 213).[4]
As I very well also recall, the ethics of abortion was addressed philosophically with analogies to far-fetched cases of people seeds, famous
violinists, and minimally decent Samaritans, all of which made the fact
that a pregnant women had not chosen to get pregnant the key on which
analysis should turn.[5]

Like Elshtain, I thought and still think that the fact that an unborn
child is entirely dependent on its mother, and intimately biologically
related to her, is also a source of moral obligation, whether or not the
pregnancy has been chosen, though this is not necessarily determina-
tive of the morality of an abortion decision.[6] Because human beings are
embodied and inherently social, just as Elshtain says, we often find ourselves in the midst of situations, relationships, and bonds that we did not
choose and that nevertheless exert claims upon us.[7]

Yet feminists do insist that women can be so submerged in perceived
obligations to others that they get lost in a morally problematic ethos
of female self-sacrifice, the best antidote to which is the bolstering of
their self-respect, sense of dignity, and realization that genuine responsibility does not amount to masochism. Valerie Saiving Goldstein famously
argued this point against Reinhold Niebuhr's diagnosis of sin as pride
and self-assertion.[8] Margaret Farley has maintained similarly that true
respect for persons means recognizing both their dignity, integrity, and
relative autonomy, on the one hand, and their relationality, on the other.[9]

SOVEREIGN SELVES

Surely the "I'm all about me and I'm in control" mentality that Elshtain
categorizes under Augustine's view of sin as self-love (S, 161–62) is a
huge contributing factor in the moral outlook of the 20 percent that
controls 80 percent of the world's income, and of the 1 percent that
since 2007 has controlled more than a fifth of Americans' income.[10] Yet
I question whether our twenty-first-century world offers anything near

to a majority of people "a vast arena within which many projects and forms of an absolute self, a law unto himself or herself, beckon" (*S*, 203). For one, the worldwide economic recession took a serious bite out of individual self-determination through drastically diminished economic opportunity. Attaining any meaningful degree of self-sovereignty has become a struggle, and not only for the mentally and physically disabled for whom Elshtain rightly urges our empathy.

If we turn our gaze worldwide, we quickly appreciate the prevalence of the powerless self over the sovereign self. According to UN estimates, extreme poverty rates have been cut by more than half since 1990. This is a remarkable achievement, but more than 700 million people still live in extreme poverty, including one in five people in developing regions, who subsist on less than $1.90 a day. Extreme poverty is most prevalent in sub-Saharan Africa and southern Asia, especially in fragile and conflict-torn societies.[11] To have one's physical safety constantly under threat is a great underminer of the aspiration to be a sovereign self, a condition facing millions in conflict zones, and consider the myriad daily victims of domestic abuse, trafficking, and the sometimes fatal consequences of climate change. More, not less, sovereignty is needed for both individuals and peoples in the global majority living in the developing world.

We also should not think that, although meaningful life-direction choices may be few and far between at the existential level, philosophers are still carrying on in a liberal dreamworld where autonomy is king. I need only mention post-Foucault postmodern and postcolonial theories; hypotheses of the social construction of the self; postliberal communitarian ethics á la Alasdair MacIntyre; sociobiology and its deterministic philosophical fellow-travelers. Charles Taylor has addressed these issues repeatedly and at length over a period of decades, primarily in *Sources of the Self* (1989), *The Ethics of Authenticity* (1992), and *A Secular Age* (2007).[12] Taylor represents a philosophical trend to see the self as a "social construct," and as having a hard rather than an easy time in exercising autonomy or creating a worldview beyond what the social environment provides. This view seeks to overturn the sovereign self, but it also runs counter to ideals of moral realism and natural law that Elshtain defends.

SOVEREIGN STATES: LIMITED IN POWER

Considering the sovereign state, we find likewise that its prospects in the last few decades have changed. Following political theorists like Stanley Hoffman,[13] Catholic social ethicist Bryan Hehir has suggested that since the 1980s and 90s, trends in world politics have impinged on the sovereignty of nations postulated by the Peace of Westphalia. Hehir names humanitarian interventions in Bosnia, Somalia, and Iraq, and the introduction of new standards of international decision and action[14] embodied most recently in the "responsibility to protect."[15]

A similar analysis is advanced by Anne-Marie Slaughter.[16] We are living in a world in which authority in global affairs is not vested exclusively in sovereign states. It is increasingly dispersed as "networked" authority, shared among "disaggregated" states that communicate with one another at multiple levels (judiciaries, legislatures, regulatory bodies, etc.), achieving cooperation piecemeal, in spheres and layers, as states contrive to share power for mutually agreeable ends across borders. Civil society and nongovernmental organizations are also active in transnational networks of influence. Of necessity, expressions of state power are often persuasive exercises of what Joseph Nye calls "soft power,"[17] rather than coercive or overtly self-asserting sovereignty.

Elshtain recognizes these changed global conditions of the exercise of state power, at least partially, in her "Concluding Thoughts on Sovereign States." Though reaffirming the premise of the present world order as essentially "a world of sovereign states," she outlines three ways in which the idea of sovereignty might be adjusted. The first would be simply to hang on to the standard of "classical state sovereignty" and deny any need for or possibility of more diffuse or networked exercises of state political authority (S, 157). By implication, then, relations of states globally would still have the nature of a contest of strength, according to the Thucydidean standard: "The strong do what they will; the weak suffer what they must."

A second option is to recognize that the power of any given state is not in fact supreme, but the relations among states are nevertheless governed by standards of justice, or "generalized benevolence and human rights order of things." The problem here, as she sees it, is that there is no "agreed-upon universal mechanism of enforcement" (*S*, 157). Very true—hence the relative powerlessness of the UN in protecting human rights, protecting civilians from violence, and ensuring the global adoption of environmental controls.

Finally, there is the option of a "chastened version of sovereignty," in which individual sovereign states take responsibility for "indicting leaders of other states for doing politics in ways the indicting state finds unacceptable." The obvious problem here, Elshtain grants, is that "this self-proclaimed authority lacks a generally recognized legitimacy." Nevertheless, "systematic, continuing, and egregious violations" of human rights "demand concerted action in the form of interdiction and punishment." The "most likely" agents of such intervention in the present world order are states that are themselves constituted in terms of limitations of state power by the requirements of respect for human rights (*S*, 157–58).[18]

SOVEREIGNTY, MORAL REALISM, AND LIMITS OF POLITICS AND ETHICS

I find in *Sovereignty* a very strong affirmation of moral realism. Elshtain several times quotes Albert Camus on "the fact" of a human nature, on "the affirmation of a nature common to all men, which eludes the world of power'" that forms the basis for moral realism (*S*, 243).[19] I fully agree with Elshtain that, whatever postmodern deconstructions of "identity" or "the human" may say, there is an evident commonality in the fact of human embodiment. All humans share certain essential needs for food, clean water, shelter, safety from physical violence and disease, and perduring, cooperative relationships with other human beings (224–25, 240). Humans are inherently social and by nature destined for community and "a social compact," respecting all as "equal before the law" (229–30, 252, 244), because "human beings *qua* human beings deserve equal moral regard," corresponding to their "inalienable dignity."[20] On the basis of human nature as involving embodiment, sociality, and basic equality, "we look for commonalities and for sources of renewal" (243). Elshtain has confidence in the capacity of human reason to recognize nature, goods, justice, and equal regard, and the moral ideal of altruistic love of neighbor. It is "heartening that so often human beings rise to the occasion as they answer generously and forthrightly not only the question, Who am I? But also, Who is my neighbor?" (241).

To put forth the "irreducible" dignity of the human person (*S*, 237) as normative for public and political life, and as relevant to international politics, requires it be grounded in human nature, and not only in a particular religious or political tradition or traditions. Elshtain indicates in several places, and I agree, that dignity, equality, and neighbor-love can be religiously backed, transmitted, and reinforced, yet they are nonetheless defining features of common "human" morality.[21] Making the case for this conviction, however, is not so easy.

Elshtain quotes a character in Marilynne Robinson's novel *Gilead*, who says, "Any human face has a claim on you, because you can't help but understand the singularity of it, the courage and the loneliness of it" (*S*, 236). But this is exactly what millennia of human beings and societies (including Christian ones) have failed to understand—willfully failed to understand—as they commit massacres, torture, lynchings, enslavement, child abuse, and rape. Indeed, equal regard is a *modern* value or norm, supportable to be sure by certain biblical narratives, but not really visible even to Christians until an era in which the value and freedom of the individual surfaced culturally and took shape in movements for political and social liberation and for human rights. For instance, although women were regarded by Augustine and other Christian thinkers to be fully human and made in the image of God, nevertheless they (or we) were regarded as inherently destined for a subordinate sphere—which is not true equality and equal regard.[22]

I actually believe that equality or equal regard is a much harder "common human value" to defend than basic goods related to human beings' embodiment, sociality, need for cooperative social institutions, or even the need to, in Aquinas's words, "seek to know the truth about God."[23] Very few societies truly and in practice recognize equality as a social norm or give equality secure legal protection, even today. The unequal position of women in virtually every society, including modern societies, is but one illustration. Many or most defenses of equality amount more to assertions than to explanations.[24] In fact, I am not at all sure there is a knock-down philosophical defense of equality or equal respect; perhaps it is better defended through examples and narratives, like the parable of the Good Samaritan or the young prince Siddhartha's encounter with human suffering.

But if we grant, as probably most of us do, that basic human equality is a moral reality and not just a socially constructed modern Western preference, we still have to explain why this has not been more widely recognized. Can equal regard constitute a "commonality" to guide international affairs, if it is not endorsed in practice, or given only lip service? Beyond the question of equal regard as an objective value, we have a noetic or epistemological question. As moral realists assert, there may be a genuine moral order enshrining the nonnegotiability of dignity, rights, and the common good, but who can and does know that order? Who is motivated to observe it?

AUGUSTINE TO THE RESCUE?

In *Augustine and the Limits of Politics* (*ALP*) and in a more recent article on just war and natural law, Elshtain maintains that Augustine backs a "naturalistic morality"[25] that includes "equal regard." Augustine holds that no man was created to be the slave of another, so Elshtain infers that he is a proponent of essential human equality[26] and "equal regard."[27] Moreover, even "fallen nature" heeds the "call to justice that is embedded in an account of our natures" and discerned "through our God-given reason."[28] Original sin "does not preclude seeking right order—justice—between peoples and between peoples and God,"[29] or rule out the actual achievement of justice, through the use of force, motivated by charity.[30] Thus, morality can be both known and enacted by any human being.

Pondering this fairly sanguine reading of Augustine as a resource for natural law, public ethics, and historical justice, I am reminded of a truly excellent line in *Sovereignty*: "On this earth, if the lion lies down with the lamb, the lamb must be replaced frequently" (*S*, 84). This hints at a more pessimistic Augustine who also appears in *Augustine and the Limits of Politics*, Elshtain's depiction of "political Augustinianism." How much credence did she put in the Augustine she presented to her students back in the 1970s? Did she continue to think it reflects dimensions of the real Augustine? In my opinion, the old class notes were not half bad. They concluded that Augustine "does not believe living in political society transforms or completes our natures. He dissents from strong conceptions of justice. There is a rough and ready justice, to be sure, even in robber bands, but earthly justice is often little more than a principle of retribution as well as an imperfect sign of our sociality—it doesn't touch on the really important stuff" (*ALP*, 22). I still see validity in the question Elshtain then asked of her students: "Even though political Augustinianism is not particularly attractive to us, might it not say something true about the human condition nonetheless?" (*ALP*, 21).

I am acutely aware that Augustine is complicated, even ambivalent. There are multiple schools of thought about his politics and his view of the attainability of justice. To give just one example, the renowned scholar Robert Markus in 1970 wrote a famous book on Augustine, *Saeculum*, in which he maintained that a truly just society is impossible without faith in the God of Christianity and love of that God above all else. More than three decades later, in 2006, Markus wrote another book, *Christianity and the Secular*, defending the autonomy of the secular from a Christian standpoint, and giving a much more hopeful construal of political justice. One reviewer opines that the second book is "in some ways a retraction of his earlier work," since it consists in an appeal to be open to and value the secular. This reviewer, Anthony Meredith, expresses his own reservations in a concluding understatement: "Whether Augustine would have gone quite as far is not absolutely certain."[31]

Is it true, then, that "earthly peace is a real good,"[32] or is such a peace just an instance of distorted loves that at most can clear a space for the building of the church? Does Augustine mostly believe that "even the peace of injustice is worthy of the name of peace as a fragile human achievement," providing "partial order to the universe,"[33] or does he see all politics not oriented by the love of God as essentially vicious? What is striking to me is that for Augustine, the Romans did not merely have "imperfect" virtue—they were vicious, seeking glory, honor, and fame.[34] Not just complete or perfect virtue but any virtue worthy of the name depends on grace for Augustine,[35] and as far as the universal availability of grace is concerned, Augustine is no Karl Rahner.

Furthermore, it is seriously questionable whether Augustine thought the prospects for even Christians to achieve political justice to be particularly good. I am always impressed by the fact that in the same book of the *City of God* (bk. 19) in which Augustine famously holds out the political ideals of "tranquility of order" and "well-ordered concord"[36] he also repeats at least half a dozen times that those engaged in politics will unavoidably be entangled in misery, miseries, and miserable "necessities."[37] Surely the torturing judge he offers as an example is a highly dubious character, having both "tortured an innocent man to discover his innocence" and "put him to death without discovering it."[38]

In a discussion of her book *Just War against Terror* (*JWT*), Elshtain idealizes "tranquility of order" but grants that Augustine saw life as "tragic and violent." Nevertheless, "responsibility" demands that Christians in statecraft not try to evade the reality of "dirty hands."[39] But in a thoroughly Augustinian and nondualistic view of politics, is it possible to maintain that the moral analysis and the intentions are pure, and only the hands get "dirty"? To some critics, morality is on shaky ground once "dirty hands" are simply accepted as the price of doing business, because principled scrutiny of what is really necessary and of what are the nonnegotiable limits (like no torture) go out the window.

If the present international order represents a situation in which states are not only not sovereign, and in which there is no effective "world authority," and also a situation in which states acting alone or even in alliances are as likely to act on *libido dominandi* as on justice, peace, human rights, and love of neighbor, then I think we who are interested in historical justice have some major problems that go beyond the analysis of *Sovereignty*. This book, whose final chapter contemplates "The Human Future," ends not by imagining what more just national and global governments could look like, but with an anecdote about Jean Vanier and the Christian community of L'Arche. Augustine may make "universal claims about human dignity and value" (*S*, 239) but, Vanier warns, "One of the dangers in our world is wanting to do big things, heroic things. We are called to do little things lovingly—to work to create community."[40] Where does this leave politics, political justice, the real place and possibilities of states and of selves as citizens, and the necessary global institutions and actions to preserve peace and avoid war?

What I would be very interested to see is further development of Elshtain's point that it was a good thing that premodern states and societies respected multiple sites of power and authority, and included among these religious institutions and actors. Do we not see at the beginning of the twenty-first century a restoration of pluralism in government and authority, a pluralism badly in need of principles and practices of ethically justified government? Given what Elshtain said in earlier chapters of *Sovereignty* about the dangers of "monism," it seems that the model of a powerful state acting alone should be complemented if not replaced by models of states acting in alliances, preferably at the regional level, and of entities in addition to states working both within nations and transnationally to limit self-interested action by the powerful and to promote justice, peace, and human rights. Joint decision-making, it seems to me, is a better check on *libido dominandi*, bias, and self-deception than the prerogative of a single decider, whether most powerful state or single monarch.[41]

Certainly, religious traditions and organizations would be a part of a pluralistic leadership mix, as they certainly have been in global peace-building efforts.[42] Religious actors are especially effective at networking and building trust in local communities, but they also have or can have a presence at the national, international, and transnational levels. The global infrastructure of the Roman Catholic Church is a great advantage for groups like the CPN, Jesuit Relief Services, Caritas Internationalis, and Sant'Egidio, an international lay Christian group that serves the elderly and AIDS victims and was instrumental in brokering a peace agreement in Mozambique in 1992.

SOVEREIGN GOD REINTERPRETED

As with states, there has been an erosion of divine sovereignty, even if not its displacement. Of course, as with other monotheistic religions, Christians believe God to be sovereign over all creation. But this concept has been expressed in different ways, more often by speaking of divine creation and of divine providence than of "sovereignty." Though the Bible certainly depicts God as ruling over the whole cosmos, the

term "divine sovereignty" is a later historical and theological development, one associated perhaps most strongly with John Calvin and the
Reformed tradition. Elshtain rightly insists that the Christian God is a
God of love and justice, not arbitrary will, but these are difficult concepts to reconcile.

Since the latter half of the twentieth century, God's sovereignty has
been reinterpreted in favor of a God of love and compassion whose
providence includes the determination to heal the suffering of humans
and other creatures, to convert sinners to a better path, and to bring
all human beings into a realm of redemption that begins historically
with reconciled communities (not limited to the Christian churches) of
love, justice, peace, and hope. "Sovereignty" as God's creative power is
interpreted to mean the possibility of a different kind of human politics,
a politics of "the reign of God." Important theologians who advance
this revision include, but are by no means limited to, Jürgen Moltmann,
Gustavo Gutierrez, Jon Sobrino, Elizabeth Johnson, William Schweiker,
and Timothy Gorringe.

The first encyclical of John Paul II, *Redemptor hominis* (1979), states,
"The redemption of the world—this tremendous mystery of love in
which creation is renewed is, at its deepest root, the fullness of justice in
a human Heart—the Heart of the First-born Son—in order that it may
become justice in the hearts of many human beings" (sec. 9). In subsequent encyclicals, such as *Sollicitudo rei socialis* (1987) and *Centesimus
annus* (1991), John Paul II advocated a "preferential option for the poor,"
inspired by the social virtue of active solidarity, that would touch social
structures and international relations, bringing more justice to the international economic system, trade, military intervention, and the development of technology. Like his predecessors John XXIII and Paul VI,
John Paul II was extremely skeptical that war could be an instrument of
justice, but he never ruled it out, particularly in the form of humanitarian intervention. Pope Francis has carried forward this trajectory, calling for a "Church of the Poor" and stressing that climate change, for
example, most affects the poor, in *Laudato si'* (2015).

Such proposals find a basis in biblical narratives depicting Jesus's
ministry of the reign or kingdom of God, consisting in the revolutionary
inclusion in one community of the righteous and the sinner, the elite and

the outcast, the beloved and the "other." As the first-written Gospel has it, "Jesus came to Galilee, proclaiming the good news of God, and saying, 'The time is fulfilled, and the kingdom of God has come near; repent, and believe in the good news'" (Mark 1:14). By the time this Gospel was written, Paul has already recorded an early Christian baptismal formula that showed what the reign of God was to mean concretely: "There is no longer Jew or Greek, there is no longer slave or free, there is no longer male and female; for all of you are one in Christ Jesus" (Gal. 3:28). And lest there be any doubt about whether equal respect and inclusion were to be carried out at a social and not just a spiritual level, Paul berated the Corinthians for having Eucharistic parties where elites ate first, drank too much, and gave the poor the leftovers (1 Cor. 11:20–22).

Though neither Jesus nor Paul was a social reformer, community organizer, or politician in the modern sense, the practices of the communities they formed were certainly radical enough to shake up the status quo, obvious enough from the fact that imperial government put both of them to death. The sovereignty of the God whose kingdom is inaugurated by Jesus is of a very different sort from that of the absolute monarch of early modernity, and from that of the majority of statesmen and politicians, whose virtues more resemble the Romans than the game-changing solidarity with the powerless called for by the last four popes. The international, structural dimension is salient and unavoidable, and a realm in which Christians have the obligation to partner with others. By far the greatest emphasis in the modern papal encyclicals has been on the economic disparities between rich and poor nations, the ways in which the privileged are accountable to people in "developing" countries, and the need for the latter to be empowered as agents of their own development.

Now let me mention some shortcomings of Catholic social teaching, and on that note return to some of the merits of Augustine and their possible relevance to war and peace-building. Catholic social teaching is centered on the correlative concepts of the dignity of the person and the common good, understood increasingly as "the universal common good." All members of society have mutual rights and duties, and the right and duty to participate in and contribute to the benefits a society has to offer. The claims of the encyclicals about justice are inspired and supported by the Gospels, but are also assumed to be evident to "all men of good will," as in the opening salutation of John XXIII's *Pacem in terris* (1963).

Some of the drawbacks of this vision—though ameliorated in *Laudato si'*—are that it too readily assumes that all interlocutors are indeed of good will and reasonable; that rights, justice, and the demands of natural morality will be more or less self-evident, despite variations in cultural perspective or philosophical commitment; that the UN is the ultimate authority to control worldwide inequities; and that the poor can be effectively empowered by popes who write encyclicals with little or no consultation across regions, least of all with the laity, and who address these encyclicals primarily to government officials and other world leaders. This is where a dose of "political Augustinianism" is a good tonic. Yet at the end of the day, I do agree with Elshtain's call for Christian engagement in the public sphere, with the knowledge that our actions are never as clear-sighted, noble, and productive as we wish; nor as myopic, corrupted, or futile as we fear.

CONCLUSION

Perhaps the various exaggerations of sovereignty that have occurred historically, and that still exist to some degree, are not what today most demand our concern. More important and problematic is the acute awareness of many selves and of whole populations of being at the mercy of forces they cannot control. In the United States the recession following the crash of 2008 is a perfect example, as is the disempowerment felt by many in the face of the poisoned polarization of national politics, driven of course by economic interests. In many other places around the globe, powerlessness is caused by the far more horrifying problems of political repression and murderous civil conflict. Globally, individuals, governments, and civil society experience lack of effective agency rather than "sovereignty" in remedying the destruction of the environment, the terrible status of women, slavery, and human trafficking.

In Christian social ethics the glaring danger is not liberal individualism but retreat into small communities of liturgy, prayer, and shared moral values on the small scale, with resulting abandonment of social and political commitments that were so important to both Augustine and Aquinas, and I would argue so necessary in living out the gospel of the kingdom or reign of God. At the end of the day, we are left with the confident, outreaching, justice-committed politics of Aquinas, Catholic social teaching, and Jean Elshtain—and the circumspect, church-preferring, dirty-hands-washing politics of Augustine, Luther, and also Elshtain. I am not at all sure these two can be put together analytically, but I do believe they are both important. The first is essential to Christian advocacy for more just social structures, the latter is a necessary reminder that sin is a great barrier and progress is neither "pure" nor guaranteed.

NOTES

1. See, for example, Elshtain, *World at War*; Elshtain, *Just War against Terror*; Elshtain, "Realism, Just War and the Witness of Peace," in *American Feminist Thought at Century's End: A Reader*, ed. Linda S. Kauffman (Hoboken, NJ: Wiley-Blackwell, 1993), 466–77; Elshtain, "Politics and Forgiveness," in *Religion, Politics, and Peace*, ed. LeRoy S. Rouner (Notre Dame, IN: University of Notre Dame Press, 1999), 32–47; and Elshtain, "The Just War Tradition and Natural Law," *Fordham International Law Journal* 28, no. 3 (2005): 742–55.

2. I have been involved for the past several years with the Catholic Peacebuilding Network, founded by the Kroc Institute for International Peace Studies at Notre Dame and by Catholic Relief Services. This experience has helped me to understand both the human suffering caused by war and the depth and extent of the human hunger for peaceful social life. Theologians were brought together with peace workers in three conferences in Mindanao, Philippines; Bujumbura, Burundi; and Bogota, Colombia. In those meetings I learned that societal violence is usually protracted and intractable; that neither states, nor the so-called international community, nor the UN has much power to end violence; that peace-building must be conducted within conditions of violence, and not only afterwards; and that women are among the most frequent targets of violence, but also the most pervasive and persistent workers for peace.

3. See Monty G. Marshall and Benjamin G. Cole, *Global Report 2009: Conflict, Governance, and State Fragility* (Washington, DC: George Mason University/Center for Systemic Peace and Center for Global Policy, 2009), http://

www.systemicpeace.org/; and Malin Nilsson, "The Trends in Armed Conflicts Today," *Peace Monitor*, October 12, 2011, http://peacemonitor.org/?p=142. See also data from GlobalSecurity.org.

4. Elshtain cites Alison M. Jaggar, *Feminist Politics and Human Nature* (Totowa, NJ: Rowman and Allanheld, 1983), 132.

5. See Judith Jarvis Thomson, "A Defense of Abortion," in *Philosophy & Public Affairs* 1, no. 1 (1971): 47–66.

6. See Lisa Sowle Cahill, "Abortion, Autonomy, and Community," in *Abortion: Understanding Differences*, ed. Sidney Callahan and Daniel Callahan (New York: Plenum, 1984), 261–76.

7. It is not surprising that concrete women in the existential situation of a problem pregnancy do not follow the script of the sovereign self. They do not actually make their decisions on the basis simply of "conquest, control over, complete self-ownership" and "self-sovereignty." Figuring more prominently in women's moral consciousnesses are relationships, obligations to others, and the harm to other beyond the self that a given decision will cause. This throws the thesis that "self-sovereignty" is culturally controlling or controlling for feminists into question. See Meghan Winter, "My Abortion: 26 Women Share Their Abortion Stories," *New York Magazine*, November 10, 2013. Many feminists, especially theological feminists, see relationality as a key feminist value and principle. See Margaret A. Farley, "New Patterns of Relationship: Beginnings of a Moral Revolution," *Theological Studies* 36 (1975): 627–46.

8. Valerie Saiving Goldstein, "The Human Situation: A Feminine View," *Journal of Religion* 40, no. 2 (1960): 100–112.

9. Margaret A. Farley, *Just Love: A Framework for Sexual Ethics* (New York: Continuum, 2006), 211–15.

10. "In 2007, the top 1 percent share of national income peaked at 23.5 percent"; see Marcie Gardner and David Abraham, "Income Inequality," Inequality.org (Washington, DC: Institute for Policy Studies: 2011), http://inequality.org/income-inequality/. In 2008, the top 1 percent had 21 percent of income, and the average income of the top 1 percent of households rose by nearly 12 percent from 2009 to 2010; see Hannah Shaw and Chad Stone, "Incomes at the Top Rebounded in First Full Year of Recovery, New Analysis of Tax Data Shows" (Washington, DC: Center on Budget and Policy Priorities, March 8, 2012), http://www.cbpp.org/research/incomes-at-the-top-rebounded-in-first-full-year-of-recovery-new-analysis-of-tax-data-shows.

11. "No Poverty: Why It Matters," Sustainable Development Goals: 17 Goals to Transform Our World, http://www.un.org/sustainabledevelopment/wp-content/uploads/2016/08/1_Why-it-Matters_Poverty_2p.pdf.

12. Charles Taylor, *Sources of the Self: The Making of the Modern Identity* (Cambridge, MA: Harvard University Press, 1989); Taylor, *The Ethics of*

Authenticity (Cambridge, MA: Harvard University Press, 1992); Taylor, *A Secular Age* (Cambridge, MA: Harvard University Press, 2007).

13. See Stanley Hoffmann, *Duties beyond Borders: On the Limits and Possibilities of Ethical International Politics* (Syracuse, NY: Syracuse University Press, 1981); and Hoffmann, "Clash of Globalizations," *Foreign Affairs* 84, no. 4 (2002): 104–15.

14. J. Bryan Hehir, "World of Faultlines," *Commonweal*, September 25, 1992, 8–9.

15. See Gareth Evans and Mohamed Sahnoun, "The Responsibility to Protect," *Foreign Affairs* 81, no. 6 (2002): 99–110.

16. Anne-Marie Slaughter, *A New World Order* (Princeton, NJ: Princeton University, 2004). See also Jessica T. Mathews, "Power Shift: The Rise of Global Civil Society," *Foreign Affairs* 76, no. 1 (1997): 50–66; and Anne Marie Slaughter, "The Real New World Order," *Foreign Affairs* 76, no. 5 (1997): 183–97.

17. Joseph S. Nye, Jr., *Bound to Lead: The Changing Nature of American Power* (New York: Public Affairs, 2004).

18. In some other writings, Elshtain casts the United States in this role as adjudicator of international human rights infringements. For example, in an article on international justice and the use of force, she states, "Despite all the clamor about U.S. power, and the resentment it engenders in some quarters, the 'we' likely to be called upon to intervene to protect the innocent from harm, the 'we' to whom a country without the means to intervene would likely make its case, is the United States"; Jean Bethke Elshtain, "Military Intervention and Justice as Equal Regard," in *Religion and Security: The New Nexus in International Relations*, ed. Robert A. Seiple and Dennis R. Hoover (Lanham, MD: Rowman & Littlefield, 2004), 127.

19. Elshtain's quotation is from Albert Camus, *The Rebel* (New York: Vintage, 1956), 250.

20. Elshtain, "International Justice as Equal Regard and the Use of Force," *Ethics & International Affairs* 17, no. 2 (2003): 67.

21. Elshtain, "Military Intervention and Justice as Equal Regard," in *Religion and Security: The New Lens in International Relations*, ed. Robert A. Seiper and Dennis R. Hoover (Lanham, MD: Rowman & Littlefield, 2003), 116; Elshtain, "International Justice as Equal Regard," 67; and Elshtain, "The Dignity of the Human Person and the Idea of Human Rights: Four Inquiries," *Journal of Law and Religion* 14, no. 1 (1999–2000): 62.

22. Martin Luther imaginatively challenged this notion in his *Lectures on Genesis*, but that is a topic for another day.

23. Thomas Aquinas, *Summa theologiae* I-II.94.2.

24. Margaret Farley, *Just Love: A Framework for Christian Sexual Ethics* (New York: Continuum, 2006), makes a good stab at a defense, where she foregrounds

human relationality, and the capacities for self-determination, communication, intimacy, love, and self-transcendence.

25. *ALP*, 25; "Just War Tradition," 743.

26. "Just War Tradition," 745; Elshtain is citing from *ALP* (26) and Augustine, *Concerning the City of God against the Pagans*, trans. Henry Bettenson (Hammondsworth: Penguin, 1972), 875.

27. "Just War Tradition," 755.

28. Ibid., 753.

29. Ibid., 750–51.

30. Ibid., 754.

31. Robert A. Markus, *Saeculum: History and Society in the Theology of St. Augustine* (Cambridge: Cambridge University Press, 1992); Markus, *Christianity and the Secular* (Notre Dame, IN: Notre Dame University Press, 2006); Anthony Meredith, S.J., review of *Christianity and the Secular*, by Robert A. Markus, *Journal of Theological Studies* 59, no. 1 (2008): 377–79.

32. Jean Bethke Elshtain, "Why Augustine? Why Now?" *Theology Today* 55, no. 1 (1998): 12.

33. Elshtain, "Realism, Just War and the Witness of Peace," 475.

34. *City of God* 5.4.

35. Ibid., 19.4 and bk. 5.

36. Ibid., 19.13.

37. Ibid., 19.4–6.

38. Ibid., 19.6.

39. Jean Bethke Elshtain, "Response to Reviews of *Just War against Terror*," *Journal of Lutheran Ethics* 4, no. 11 (2004): para. 10.

40. *S*, 248. The afterword to *Sovereignty*, which includes the Vanier quotation, was originally published as a "short reflection" in the *New Oxford Review*, December 1992, 16–17.

41. This of course does not mean that the United States or any other state should not exercise leadership among peers.

42. There is now an abundant literature on the positive capacities of religious entities in global politics. See Douglas Johnston and Cynthia Sampson, eds., *Religion: The Missing Dimension of Statecraft* (New York: Oxford University Press, 1995); Maryann Cusimano Love, *Beyond Sovereignty: Issues for a Global Agenda*, 4th ed. (Boston: Wadsworth, 2011); and Robert J. Schreiter, R. Scott Appleby, and Gerard Powers, eds., *Peacebuilding: Catholic Theology, Ethics, and Praxis* (Maryknoll, NY: Orbis, 2010).

CHAPTER SEVEN

STAGGERING ONWARD, REJOICING

Jean Bethke Elshtain, Augustinian Realist

Nigel Biggar

ANTHROPOLOGY AS *APOLOGIA*?

Abutting the back-garden of the South-West Lodgings in Christ Church, Oxford, is a small building that used to supply my medieval predecessors with beer. Between November 1972 and April 1973, after his departure from New York and before his departure for Vienna, it provided W. H. Auden with a home. Since I moved into the Lodgings ten years ago, therefore, I have been revisiting—and mostly visiting for the first time—Auden's poetry. To date, the poem that has struck me most forcibly is one that he wrote in January 1941, when he was in the United States, "Atlantis." Its forms are ancient Greek, but its substance is Christian: "Atlantis" stands for the heavenly Jerusalem, and the poem concerns the odyssey that is the Christian life. It takes the stance of someone bidding farewell to a voyager. Toward its end, we reach this verse:

> Assuming you beach at last
> near Atlantis, and begin

150

the terrible trek inland
through squalid woods and frozen
tundras where all are soon lost;
if, forsaken then, you stand,
dismissal everywhere,
stone and snow, silence and air,
remember the noble dead
and honour the fate you are,
travelling and tormented,
dialectic and bizarre.

Stagger onward rejoicing . . .[1]

I imagine that I hear echoes of St. Augustine in those words. I imagine it partly because I know that Auden had a high regard for Augustine on account of his ability to show that "the Christian faith can make sense of man's private and social existence."[2] But more exactly, I imagine it because Auden has captured a dialectical vision of human existence that I take to be Augustinian, one where the human being is stretched between the exhilarating lure of eschatological hope, on the one hand, and the drag of sin—some of it volunteered, much of it original or inherited —on the other: "*stagger* onward . . . *rejoicing.*" It is a vision that dignifies without idealizing. It saves at once from cynicism and romanticism. It generates both stringent demands and deep compassion. It is a marvelously, beautifully *humane* vision—humane, not sentimental. And it is one that many of Christianity's most effective apologists have taken up and articulated, each in their own terms—most famously, Pascal, Tillich, and Reinhold Niebuhr. And to this eminent list, I would add Jean Bethke Elshtain, whose work shares the intention of recommending the Christian theological story by displaying its power to explain and make sense of human being and existence—individual, social, and political. And not only its power, but its superior power: its power to *out*-narrate alternative stories, be they Hobbesian, Rousseauian, Kantian, Nietzschean, or Sartrean, as she says in *Sovereignty* (*S*) (6–9). That is why Elshtain takes care, particularly in *Augustine and the Limits of Politics* (*ALP*) but also elsewhere, to show how modern, non-Christian philosophers have often found themselves drawn back to Augustinian Christianity—among them Wittgenstein, Camus, and Arendt (*ALP*, 27, 71, 101, 115).

This is an apologetic strategy with which I have a great deal of sympathy. Indeed, it was the main reason I first came to the University of Chicago Divinity School in the late 1970s: not to study Barth, but, while completing a master's thesis on Pascal, to learn more about Tillich and Niebuhr at the feet of Langdon Gilkey. So I warm to the strategy, and yet I wonder about its efficacy. I wonder how effectively the cogency of Christian anthropology leads to conviction about Christian theology. Wittgenstein, Camus, and Arendt might have admired Augustine, but they still declined to buy into Christianity's theology. Similarly, Hans Morgenthau and other "Atheists for Niebuhr" remained atheists, notwithstanding their admiration for Niebuhr's Christian, and considerably Augustinian, realism. And even now, Jürgen Habermas admits, on the one hand, that religious traditions (by which he means primarily Christianity) "have the distinction of a superior capacity for articulating our [liberal, humanist] moral sensibility."[3] And yet, on the other hand, rather than finding in this phenomenon moral reason for buying *into* religious tradition, he prefers to look for ways of translating the moral kernel *out of* its religious husk, apparently assuming that it will somehow retain its superior intelligibility. So I am wondering if the oblique, anthropological route really works as an apologetic strategy. Does it persuade unbelievers into theology, Christology, and eschatology? Or does it not rather lead to the *down*playing of the peculiarly theological moments of the Christian narrative for the sake of retaining plausibility, as exemplified in Niebuhr's increasing theological reticence after *The Irony of American History*? In short, is Stanley Hauerwas right after all?

MONOTHEISTIC(?) MORAL REALISM AGAINST HOBBESIAN *UN*REALISM AND LEGAL POSITIVISM

To display the explanatory power of Christianity, Augustinian anthropology is one apologetic strategy. To subject social contractarianism to immanent critique could be another. In her Gifford Lectures' critical history of the concept of sovereignty, Elshtain exposes the inadequacies of contractarian political philosophy, whose lineage she traces back to nominalist or voluntarist theology. This story could be used to recommend the explanatory virtues of what I shall call, for want of a better term, "logical" theology—that is, an understanding of God as one freely bound by his own "logos," and whose creation is consequently rational and humanly graspable in terms of law. If that was the intent, however, then it does not seem to have worked for Michael Walzer, who, in his warm back-cover plaudit of *Sovereignty*, writes, "The most remarkable fact about this powerful book is that one can appreciate and endorse its critique of the idolatries of state and self without accepting its view of divine sovereignty."

I had rather hoped the opposite—that one could not appreciate the one without being moved to accept the other. Certainly, there is a one-way logical connection from "logical" theism to culturally transcendent, universal, natural law, and there *might* be a reverse connection too. Part of the meaning of the monotheistic assertion that there is one God, without rival, is that the world of God's creating is basically coherent and rational, not divided and anarchic. Since this created order is not just physical but moral, monotheists are bound to be moral realists—that is, they are bound to believe in a universal moral order or reality. However, it is not so clear that this logic works in reverse. It is not so clear that belief in moral realism logically inclines to belief in one God. On the one hand, some moral philosophers evidently feel able to hold one without the other. On the other hand, many philosophers do associate the concept of God with that of a given moral order, and since they regard the latter as the enemy of human freedom, they repudiate the former.

Whatever its logical connection to theism, Christian moral realism does have the considerable merit of out-narrating the degrading Hobbesian anthropology that many contemporary social and political philosophers are so oddly keen to endorse. If Hobbes is to be believed, human beings are basically motivated by one thing only: the desire for material security—to be safe and fat. Although that might be true in the abstract conditions dreamed up by game theorists in Prisoners' Dilemmas, it is not true as an empirical generalization. Even soldiers in the field usually care more about being loyal to their comrades than saving their own skins—and since their loyalty often involves their own deaths, it cannot be explained in terms of a self-regarding strategy of reciprocity. No, Thomas Aquinas and Joseph Butler were the realists, not Hobbes: we humans are moved both by self-interest and by benevolence, and we care not only for the good of self-preservation but also, and sometimes above all else, for the good of friendship.

Elshtain's Christian assertion of moral realism necessarily and rightly leads her to relativize positive law. Beyond positive law there is a higher law, to which appeal can be made. If that were not so, then Bonhoeffer and his July 1944 complotters were simply criminal traitors and not first and foremost moral heroes. What applies on the domestic stage also applies on the international one, as Elshtain made plain in *Just War on Terror* (*JWT*) (164–65). International positive law cannot have the last word. So Carl Schmitt was not wrong to claim that there must be a sovereign who decides "the exception" to the law, and who therefore stands above it. Any conscience does that. He was wrong, however, to suppose that human sovereigns who stand *over* positive law do not at the same time stand *under* natural law. Those who make exceptions, as sometimes they ought, nevertheless remain responsible and are obliged to give a justificatory account of their decision. So whatever else we think about the legitimacy of the UK and U.S. invasion of Iraq in 2003, it stands to the credit of Tony Blair that he pressed George W. Bush to have the Coalition go before the UN Security Council, to be accountable and to make a case, and it stands to Bush's credit that he agreed.

LOVE'S DIRTY HANDS

About six months after Auden left Oxford, I arrived to begin my undergraduate study of history, at the end of which I took a course on the life and times of St. Augustine. I was immediately hooked. Several things hooked me, but one of them was Augustine's struggle to be responsible *in the midst* of the inherited mess of human life, to be faithful *under* the burdens of history—his struggle, if you like, to honor his fate, personal, social, and human. This struck me as admirably—and movingly—honest and brave. Until I read Elshtain's *Augustine and the Limits of Politics*, I had not noticed that Augustine takes as his model of human being, not the fantasy of the self-sufficient adult, but the fact of the infant, born into a place and time that he did not choose and vulnerable to all sorts of forces beyond his control (*ALP*, 13, 31–32, 53; *S*, 162).

Nor had it occurred to me to say of Augustine, as Elshtain does, that he was "in love with the world," which he once described as "a smiling place" (*ALP*, 89, citing Augustine, *Sermon 169*). In that light, Augustine's resolve to honor his fate was not just honest and brave; it was also and foremost an expression of love for the world, and more exactly for human well-being. It was out of *love* for human welfare that Augustine was willing to remain fully involved in the world, in spite of all its burdens and constraints, its intractable mess and terrible dilemmas. It was out of love that he was willing to risk dirtying his hands.

One passage in Augustine's writings that has haunted me for the past forty years appears in the sixth chapter of book 19 of *The City of God*, where he reflects on the terrible inadequacies and ironies of human justice, but equally on its necessity:

> What of those judgements passed by men on their fellow-men, which cannot be dispensed with in cities, however much peace they enjoy? What is our feeling about them? How pitiable, how lamentable do we find them! For indeed those who pronounce judgement cannot see into the consciences of those on whom they pronounce it. And so they are often compelled to seek the truth by torturing innocent witnesses. . . . And what about torture employed on a man in his own case? The question is whether he is guilty. He is tortured, and even if innocent, he suffers, for a doubtful crime, a punishment about which there is no shadow of doubt and not because he is discovered to have committed it, but because it is not certain that he did not commit it. This means that the ignorance of the judge is often a calamity for the innocent. . . . In view of this darkness that attends the life of human society, will our wise man take his seat on the judge's bench, or will he not have the heart to do so? Obviously, he will sit; for the claims of human society constrain him and draw him to this duty; and it is unthinkable that he should shirk it.[4]

In an earlier letter (95) to Paulinus of Nola, where he discusses the use of coercion against the Donatists, Augustine shows how acutely he feels the anguish of this predicament:

> On the subject of punishing or refraining from punishment, what am I to say? It is our desire that when we decide whether or not to punish people, in either case it should contribute wholly to their security. These are indeed deep and obscure matters. . . . What do we do when, as often happens, punishing someone will lead to his destruction, but leaving him unpunished will lead to someone else being destroyed? . . . "Trembling and fear have come upon me and darkness has covered me, and I said 'Who will give me wings like a dove's?' Then I will fly away and be at rest."[5]

But Augustine did not fly away, nor did he shut his eyes. Such a man—such love, such honesty, such courage—surely deserves to be followed.

And Elshtain follows him. Placing herself in a minority among contemporary Christian intellectuals and feminists, and perhaps even among academics in general, she does not flinch in affirming the necessity of coercion, even while acknowledging its dangers and its moral murkiness. (Here she makes a rare—surprisingly rare—invocation of Niebuhr in her *Just War against Terror* [106–11].) Even more than this—and even worse, in some eyes—she affirms the necessity of *punitive* coercion—for example, against the regime in Afghanistan that was harboring al-Qaeda. The proposal that just war is properly punitive is not popular, even among those who acknowledge that it might be necessary. In the minds of too many, punishment is indistinguishable from retribution, which is indistinguishable from vengeance. Those who have drunk at Augustine's well, however, know that this is untrue. If they have been further enlightened by Richard Swinburne, they will also recognize that a hostile response to one who has caused damage to something valuable—which is punishment—is the only way of paying him the respect of taking his agency seriously. And unless he immediately repudiates what he has done, it is also the only way that he might be prompted to repent.[6] Therefore, not to punish—not to "retribute," in a broad sense—is to fail

in love for the wrongdoer. It is also, of course, to fail in love for the good
that he has damaged.

FORGIVENESS AND JUSTICE, POSSIBLE
IMPOSSIBILITIES

If love sometimes requires punishment—if it must take the form of
"kind harshness," to use Augustine's phrase[7]—then by the same token it
sometimes forbids forgiveness (insofar as forgiveness amounts to abso-
lution). Here is another topic on which Elshtain developed Augustinian
wisdom: the avoidance of cheap forgiveness, its properly "judgmen-
tal" character, and both the possibility and the limits of its political
expression.[8]

Before I focus on the limits, let me dwell for a moment on the possibility. Elshtain's admission of the possibility of forgiveness operating in
political life marks one mild point of divergence from Niebuhr. I speak
of divergence, because Niebuhr contraposed the self-sacrificial, forgiv-
ing love that can operate in interpersonal relations and the coercive justice that must operate in larger-scale economic and political relations.
Against sentimental Social Gospelers, he was at pains to insist that, in
the midst of raging class or interstate conflict, to enjoin mere love upon
the oppressed is to invite them to play doormat. Even though some
of those possessed by greed or fear or hatred might be disarmed by
such love's bold beauty, in most it will inspire violent contempt. History
shows us so. In holding—rightly, in my view—that love-as-forgiveness
can find limited political expression, Elshtain distinguishes herself from
Niebuhr. Still, I say that the divergence is "mild," because we should not
overdraw the contrast. Niebuhr did admit that the "impossible ideal"
of love can and should be efficacious in raising justice's head above the
waters of vindictiveness. So it turns out that the ideal is not so impossible, after all.

Now let me turn from the possibility of political forgiveness to its
limits. In her essay "Politics and Forgiveness," Elshtain tells us that "there
are wrongs suffered that can never be put right"—especially wrongs on

a massive scale[9]—and that forgiveness consists partly in acknowledging this, not simply a forgetting, but a "knowing forgetting."[10] I applaud the forthright acknowledgment of how much justice has not been—and cannot be—done. But I wonder why the acknowledgment is supposed to generate forgiveness, rather than sullen resignation or bitter cynicism or nihilistic despair.

My own view is that atrocious injustice on a massive scale compels us to confront the natural fragmentariness of all human justice. For here the political and financial constraints become plain. For sure, here as elsewhere one may hope to do some justice for some of the survivors, though little for the dead. But here the numbers of dead are too great for us to overlook. Here justice, too, seems a largely impossible ideal. This raises a series of questions. Can we continue to gaze upon the vast sea of unvindicated dead without hope and yet still with care? Or shall we preserve hope by ceasing to care for the hopeless, rationalizing and dismissing them as the inevitable "refuse of an [emancipating] historical process?"[11] But would not such rationalizing of the unrelieved suffering of others diminish our own humanity with callousness?[12] How, then, can we acknowledge the mountainous horizon of unfinished—and, secularly speaking, unfinishable—judicial business, and still prevent our commitment to justice from hardening into utilitarian ruthlessness or sinking into despairing inertia?

One answer to these questions lies in the traditional Christian (and Jewish) notion of eschatological hope—hope that, beyond the world of time and space and by the superhuman power of God, the vast majority of victims who have received no justice in this world and the rest who have received only fragments and tokens of it, will yet be fully vindicated. It was just such a hope to which I instinctively resorted after seeing *Katyń*, Andrzej Wajda's 1999 film about the Soviet massacre in 1940 of 22,000 Polish soldiers, police officers, and intellectuals by the Soviets.[13] Stunned by the film's dreadful climax, I stumbled out of the cinema muttering to myself, "There *has* to be a hell. There *has* to be a hell—for Stalin and all his assembly-line murderers." Well, as Max Horkheimer has pointed out, the "monstrousness" of the thought that there is no final justice, no vindication for the wronged dead, does not amount to a cogent argument for its contrary.[14] That is so, and it constitutes a major

challenge to Christian theology and philosophy. Eschatological fulfil-
ment is essential to a Christian vision of things, and eschatological hope
is essential to Christian moral life. This is something that Christian
theologians and ethicists have not been shy in affirming to each other.
But when they turn to unbelievers, they tend to become tongue-tied
and reticent about it—as did Niebuhr. They fall silent, I assume, because
they lack a robust public defense. My own starting point is to say that, *if*
eschatological hope is necessary to render rational an acceptance of the
severe limits of secular justice that is not acquiescent but expectant, not
resigned but resolute, and *if* the rightness of that resoluteness seems to
us quite as true as anything else we believe in, *then* that is *one* reason for
supposing eschatological hope to be true, too. However, even if that is a
decent start, it is only a start. We need much more if eschatological hope
is to be distinguishable from childish wishful thinking.

PASTORAL EMPATHY FOR EMBODIED
DECISION-MAKERS

Whether treating political forgiveness in South Africa or the United
States' war against Afghanistan, Elshtain displays an admirable sensitivity to the plight of those who carry political responsibility—"the
burden-bearers of the world," as Niebuhr calls them.[15] For example, in
Just War against Terror she rebukes critics of the U.S. attacks on Taliban
Afghanistan for their indifference to the real foreign policy dilemmas
that men and women in government have to face, for ignoring the fog
of war, and for assuming a false clarity (*JWT*, 76, 97). The astute British political commentator, Timothy Garton Ash, has written: "When
you get a few glimpses into the way major foreign policy decisions are
made, you are left with a sense of mild incredulity that this is how the
world is run. It is vital that we all appreciate this simple truth about
our rulers: half the time they really don't know what they're doing."[16]
Now, such a statement tends to give rise to a ripple of smug laugh-
ter, as if to say that if *we* were in their shoes, we would know what *we*
were doing. But, of course, we would not. Anyone who has had charge
of running an organization—even something as modest as a university

department—knows that there are times when you have no choice but to fly by the seat of your pants.

And what is true of a university department is true in spades of a national government in a contemporary democracy. As Blair writes in his autobiography, "The pace of modern politics and the intrusion of media scrutiny . . . mean that decisions have to be made, positions taken, strategies worked out and communicated with a speed that is the speed of light."[17] I believe that I read somewhere, though I cannot now find out where, that the average length of a decision-making meeting in government is thirty minutes.

Before setting out to judge the world—as they must—Christian prophets should stop reading it at a safe distance through the lens of abstract concepts that caricature as much as they describe. And when judging the deeds of rulers, prophets owe the judged due appreciation of the conditions under which they have to act, lest their prophecy become slander. Christian prophets owe this specific form of neighbor-love. Augustine showed it in his pastoral correspondence with military tribunes, such as Marcellinus and Boniface, and Elshtain showed it in her feminist version of Christian realism, with its acute awareness of the embodied nature of human moral agents. Would that such sisterly or brotherly empathy were more common among Christian intellectuals today.

NOTES

1. W. H. Auden, *Collected Poems*, rev. ed., ed. Edward Mendelson (London: Faber & Faber, 2007), 313.

2. Arthur Kirsch, *Auden and Christianity* (New Haven, CT: Yale University Press, 2005), xi–xii.

3. Jürgen Habermas, "Habermas entre démocratie et génétique," *Le Monde*, December 20 2002, "Essais," viii.

4. Augustine, *City of God*, ed. David Knowles, trans. H. Bettenson (London: Penguin, 1972), 19.6, pp. 859–60.

5. Augustine, *Letter 95* (to Paulinus of Nola and Therasia), in Augustine, *Political Writings*, ed. E. M. Atkins and R. J. Dodaro (Cambridge: Cambridge University Press, 2001), sec. 3, pp. 23–24.

6. Richard Swinburne, *Responsibility and Atonement* (Oxford: Clarendon, 1989), 81–86.

7. Augustine, *Letter 138* (to Marcellinus), in *Political Writings*, sec. 14, p. 38.

8. Jean Bethke Elshtain, "Politics and Forgiveness," in *Burying the Past: Making Peace and Doing Justice after Civil Conflict*, rev. ed., ed. Nigel Biggar (Washington, DC: Georgetown University Press, 2003), 45–64.

9. Ibid., 49, 60.

10. Ibid., 50, 51.

11. Helmut Peukert, "Fundamental Theology and Communicative Praxis as the Ethics of Universal Solidarity," in *The Influence of the Frankfurt School on Contemporary Theology*, ed. James A. Reimer (Lampeter: Mellen, 1992), 233.

12. Peukert makes a similar point: "How can one retain the memory of the conclusive, irretrievable loss of the victims of the historical process, and still be happy, still find one's identity? If for the sake of one's happiness and one's own identity this memory is banished from consciousness, is this not tantamount to the betrayal of the very solidarity by which alone one is able to discover oneself?"; H. Peukert, *Science, Action, and Fundamental Theology: Toward a Theology of Communicative Action*, trans. James Bohmann (Cambridge, MA: MIT Press, 1984), 209.

13. I was delighted to discover that Elshtain was also a fan of Wajda, judging by her discussion of his "brilliant" 1983 film, *Danton* (*S*, 139–41).

14. Max Horkheimer: "The thought is monstrous that the prayers of the persecuted in their hour of greatest need, that the innocent who must die without explanation of their situation, that the last hopes of a supernatural court of appeals, fall on deaf ears and that the night unilluminated by any human light is also not penetrated by any divine one. The eternal truth without God has as little ground and footing as infinite love; indeed, it becomes an unthinkable concept. But is the monstrousness of an idea any more a cogent argument against the assertion or denial of a state of affairs than does logic contain a law which says that a judgement is simply false that has despair as its consequence?"; quoted by Peukert in *Science, Action, and Fundamental Theology*, 209–10.

15. Reinhold Niebuhr, *An Interpretation of Christian Ethics* (New York: Seabury, 1979), 15.

16. Timothy Garton Ash, *Free World: Why a Crisis of the West Reveals the Opportunity of Our Time* (London: Allen Lane, 2004), 195.

17. Tony Blair, *A Journey* (London: Hutchinson, 2010), 18.

CHAPTER EIGHT

ENGAGING THE MIND OF ELSHTAIN
ON SOVEREIGNTY

Gilbert Meilaender

Honesty requires that I begin with an admission that may make doubtful much of what follows: I have no idea how the modern period emerged from the medieval. And, since Jean Elshtain explicitly states in her Gifford Lectures,[1] *Sovereignty* (*S*) (58), that she is using the concept of sovereignty to rethink the manner in which modernity emerged from disintegrating medieval structures, and since she develops this thesis with considerable learning and in considerable detail, there is much in her account that I cannot judiciously evaluate.

Were I more confident of my ability to chart the course of several centuries' development, no doubt I would, like almost all right-thinking people today, point an accusing finger or two at William of Ockham (and his Franciscan predecessor, Scotus). Lacking such confidence, however, I will instead have to make my own idiosyncratic way into Elshtain's Gifford Lectures.

In the preface to *Augustine and the Limits of Politics* (*ALP*) (published in 1995, more than a decade prior to *Sovereignty*), Elshtain depicted herself as wandering "the footpath that ambles from Wittenberg to Rome, not knowing whether I will ever see Rome; reverse direction and return to Wittenberg; or simply meander ongoingly in between" (*ALP*, xii). This path has, of course, become rather well-worn in recent years—and, I have to say, often for quite good reasons. Nevertheless, to arrive finally at Rome, fulfilling and satisfying as that may be, can obscure some things we should not forget.

Tracing the history of sacral kingship, Francis Oakley observes that although the modern era has seen increased belief in limited government and the importance of individual consent, even as late as the beginning of World War I most European states remained monarchical. Relatively few of those monarchies survived the two world wars of the twentieth century, however, and those that remained often did so only as weakened and desacralized shadows of their former selves.

There was, however, an exception. If, Oakley writes, "one stands well back and views the royal scene from afar, the one case where a monarchy can be seen to have gained from the nineteenth century to the present in both power and prestige would appear to be that of the papacy."[2] And again: "Though it would doubtless try to shrug off the designation, it remains the case that the papacy, which a thousand years ago launched a frontal assault on the sacral pretensions of the German emperors, stands out in solitary splendor today as itself the last of the truly great sacral monarchies."[3] These observations are not intended, either by Oakley or by me, as what might once have been called an "antipapist" remark. On the contrary, I think it helps us to understand something important about the direction Elshtain's thinking was taking. Oakley may overstate his case, but Elshtain seems to suggest that a genuinely pluralistic society today requires the sacral monarchy of the papacy. That, at least, is the moral of her story as I read it.

I will try to examine that story in three stages. First, I try to think through the point of the basic narrative at work in *Sovereignty*. Second, I raise a few questions about the structure and implications of this narrative. And last, I take up two larger theological issues that are involved in the claims she makes—first, to set the relational talk she favors into the context of Trinitarian belief; second, to explore some of the deeper theological limits to sovereignty, both political and personal.

THE POINT OF THE NARRATIVE

Once upon a time (that is to say, in medieval times) *regnum* and *sacerdotium*, each a form of God's government of human life, were set over against each other as competing jurisdictions. But, Elshtain says in *Sovereignty*, as God moved "from suffusing the whole to taking up residence on the edge or margin of things, at least institutionally speaking," *regnum* did not recede in tandem with *sacerdotium* (*S*, 77). On the contrary, the human longing for transcendence, a longing that never goes away, was simply "relocated in earthly matters" (143), and the sovereign state emerged.

Given this narrative framework, it should not surprise us that in her writings Elshtain paid considerable attention to warfare. For in war the sovereign state asks for our sacrifice, a concept from which the sacred is never far away. This is not entirely bad. We must all locate ourselves within particular communities, which need our service and defense, and Elshtain was willing to support war justly fought, even though, as she says, "no one walks away even from a justifiable war morally unscathed."[4] And when religious concepts such as sacrifice "migrate"—a favorite metaphor of Elshtain's—into the political realm, and the sovereign's will becomes as singular as God's, she believed we should be wary. As she states in *Real Politics*, "Historically, much of the power of the concept of sovereignty lay precisely in its encoding of the absolute, perpetual, indivisible power of a masculinized deity—a deity whose power was absolute as a penultimate political form" (*RP*, 136).

How should one respond to a story that depicts sovereign states beginning to free themselves of countervailing jurisdictions? As Elshtain tells us in a footnote, she was "essentially a counterpuncher" (*S*, 297n36). And counterpunchers are, I suspect, congenital pluralists. For them our concerns must be shaped by our circumstances, and positions needing defense at one point in time may need criticism at another. At least in our time and place—over against that modern sovereign state, which seeks to absorb all the sacredness that once checked it in medieval times—some countervailing authority or competing jurisdiction is greatly needed. That is becoming increasingly clear in the United States, as government regulations on things as different as the funding of health care, the meaning of marriage, or the policies of adoption agencies begin to impinge on the freedom of churches to order their common life in accord with their beliefs. In the absence of "strong formative institutions other than the state, it will be very difficult over time to sustain civic freedom."[5]

A fragmented and increasingly debilitated collection of small Protestant churches will not fill the bill. Hence, we might say, if the Roman Catholic Church did not exist, we would have to invent it. Fortunately for Elshtain it did exist, and, although she did not depict it as a sacral monarchy in the way Oakley does, its presence was essential to her hope for a truly pluralistic society.

One of the accounts given to explain the rise of modern "sovereign absolutism," an account Elshtain characterizes as at least partially accurate, is that the fragmentation of many little principalities in the late medieval period produced a need for sovereign states to maintain order (S, 113–14). Likewise, the fragmentation of Protestant bodies within the United States makes Rome appealing to all counterpunchers, to all who recognize the need for a countervailing sacral power set over against the awesome majesty of the modern state. Only that will make genuine pluralism possible. Rather than posing some kind of theocratic danger, the existence of Rome as that standing alternative authority is the chief bulwark of private conscience. If this reading of the narrative recounted in *Sovereignty* is roughly on target, it helps explain the kind of pluralism whose diminishment concerns Elshtain—namely, a pluralism in which institutionalized religious authority is powerful enough to withstand the tendency toward absolutism in modern political sovereigns.

QUESTIONS RAISED BY THE NARRATIVE

Nevertheless, there are aspects of the argument in *Sovereignty* that I cannot fully work out. "A streamlined version of my thesis," Elshtain writes, "would go like this: As sovereign state is to sovereign God, so sovereign selves are to sovereign states" (S, 159). That is, from that Ockhamite God pictured as singular will grew sovereign political entities, and then "this logic of sovereignty came unbound and migrated, becoming attached more and more to notions of the self" (*S*, 159). Streamlined indeed; perhaps too much so.

The direction of migration is puzzling for several reasons. In part, it doesn't seem to work in some instances. Hobbes, for example, fashions his "mortal God" in response to the sovereign selves who are bumping up against each other in that war of all against all that is the state of nature. Even the family is for him a small, contractual political community of isolated individuals whom it seems accurate to describe in Elshtain's language of hard self-sovereignty: "The self stands alone, sans any mutually constitutive relationship to the world" (*S*, 204). The conceptual migration here seems the opposite of that in her narrative. The sovereign self emerges first, and the sovereign state is created to control it.

More generally, the relation of two kinds of sovereign selves to the state remains unclear, at least to me. What Elshtain calls soft sovereign -selves are "eager to be absorbed in a collective" (*S*, 205). Hence, what she calls a form of sovereignty, I would be inclined to call sloth—a fear of freedom, a falling back into finitude and a loss of individuality. Nor am I certain what makes both this and hard self-sovereignty instances of the same thing—sovereignty. Perhaps they are alike in that each finally ends in isolation.

The notion of hard sovereign selves is more straightforward, but we need to distinguish it from a view that might initially seem similar. To reverse direction and turn back toward Wittenberg for a moment, Luther discerned in human beings—rightly, I think—a free personal center, which a human sovereign can no more govern than he can command the moon to shine.[6] The "blind, wretched folk"—that is to say, political sovereigns!—"do not see how utterly hopeless and impossible a thing they are attempting. . . . The heart they cannot constrain, though they wear themselves out trying."[7] To be sure, in Luther's view that human heart is not fully sovereign in Elshtain's sense; for, though ultimately free of the monarch's power, it remains under the power of God. This does make an important difference, but, nonetheless, it suggests that the process of historical development may be more complex than Elshtain's account indicates.

There is, in addition, a different sort of question raised for me by the development Elshtain traces. Put simply, it is "whither?" Where do we go from here? Or, more particularly, where should the church go from here? Compare Elshtain's Gifford Lectures to those of Alasdair MacIntyre, published as *Three Rival Versions of Moral Enquiry*. His prescription for our ills directs Christians to look to their own resources—chiefly St. Thomas Aquinas—and to focus on the character of their own communities. Elshtain is rather more eclectic; Bonhoeffer sits comfortably beside Camus. And her prescriptions seem to be directed at least as much to the political communities we inhabit as they are to distinctively ecclesiastical communities. Is this good or bad, wise or foolish? Should our focus be more on the internal life of the church or on the *polis*? And must we make such choices? This is a line of inquiry that, at least implicitly, *Sovereignty* poses for others who may want to carry further the lines of thought that Elshtain began to develop.

Her narrative moves from the medieval period to the modern. Although it is no doubt impossible to date such periods definitively, Josef Pieper once suggested that, because of its "special symbolic significance," we might take the year AD 529 as the beginning of the medieval period.[8] In that year—the same year in which the Platonic Academy that had existed in Athens for nine hundred years was closed by the Christian emperor Justinian—St. Benedict founded Monte Cassino. At roughly the same historical moment, Boethius died. He had hoped that his philosophic work could be done in the court of the German ruler Theodoric. His death dashed that hope. But his younger contemporary Cassiodorus did not make the same mistake. Leaving his position in Theodoric's court, he, like Benedict, founded a monastery. And, Pieper writes, "for almost a thousand years to come Boethius remained the last 'layman' in the history of European philosophy."[9]

Pieper also suggests that we consider as a symbol for the end of that medieval period the day when in 1324 Ockham reversed the direction of movement and, fearing the fate of Boethius, fled the cloister, preferring to live at the court of the Holy Roman Emperor. From that time, Pieper notes, philosophy once again took up its residence in the world.[10]

Elshtain's Gifford Lectures invite us, I am suggesting, to ask whether that continues to be a good place to reside. Drawing on Trinitarian imagery, to which I will return shortly, she argues that we live "in and through concrete levels of being" (*S*, 239) that reach out toward a universal community (corresponding to a God who is not limited by boundaries). Acknowledging that the most important institution for early Christians was the Church, and drawing on Augustine's image of Christians as pilgrims (for whom, Augustine thought, the nature of the political sovereign matters relatively little), she herself is concerned that these Augustinian pilgrims not flee "into a realm at least theoretically removed from the vortex of social and political life" (241). She may have been right; I do not know. But the picture of sovereign rulers and sovereign selves that she has painted might at least make us wonder how receptive they will be to her Christian way of understanding human life.

THEOLOGICAL ISSUES

I want to take up two theological matters that are embedded within Elshtain's account of sovereignty. Each is complicated—far more so than I can adequately display—but each points toward themes in her work that merit further attention and study.

At various points along the way in her discussion of sovereignty, Elshtain argues for a renewed attention to God's triune nature. The God who is Father, Son, and Spirit is constituted as a relation in love and is not simply a powerful and singular will. Interestingly, Elshtain was thinking similar thoughts well before her Gifford Lectures. For example, in an article[11] first written in 1991, she mused about the possibility of what she called a "post-sovereign politics" that would shift the accent from sacrifices, which sovereigns eagerly demand, to responsibility—a word which suggests that "one is answerable, accountable to another" (*RP*, 138).

Singular selves—if not by their very nature, at least in a sinful world—are in competition with each other.[12] Their power is not divisible, and one or the other must triumph. The political implications are captured nicely in words of Prince Hal to Hotspur in Shakespeare's *Henry the Fourth, Part I*:

I am the Prince of Wales, and think not, Percy,
To share with me in glory any more.

Two stars keep not their motion in one sphere,
Nor can one England brook a double reign
Of Harry Percy and the Prince of Wales.[13]

No shared glory there—and quite different it is, therefore, from the Athanasian Creed's characterization of Father, Son, and Spirit as "equal in glory, coeternal in majesty."

I do not doubt that this creed's depiction of God's triune life gives us an image of mutual love. Does it, however, accomplish what Elshtain was after—namely, undercutting the notion of sovereign power as isolated will? The three persons in relation constitute *one* God, after all, and we have to say something about the oneness. Although existing only as Father, Son, and Spirit in relation, the one God nonetheless governs and orders the whole creation. Indeed, some critics of Trinitarian doctrine have argued that Christians used a hierarchically structured God as their model for worldly sovereigns. After all, centuries before Ockham, Eusebius of Caesarea argued that because there was one heavenly king there should also be one king on earth, even as Ignatius of Antioch argued that there should be one bishop in any given place, corresponding to the one God.[14]

Nevertheless, Elshtain's instinct that a Christian understanding of the person, drawn from Christian belief in the triune God, offers a way to withstand evils perpetrated by sovereign selves strikes me as sound and worthy of continued development. With respect to many of the issues she takes up in the last few chapters of *Sovereignty*—eugenics, abortion, cloning—she is, in my view, on the side of the angels. I suspect, however, that we need more than an appeal to the fact that human life—like God's life—is best understood as relational. For, as the philosopher Alva Noë has noted, not just human beings but living organisms generally are relational from the start. Even so simple a being as a bacterium "has a world; that is to say, it has a relationship with its surroundings."[15] What Elshtain's case needs, therefore, is not simply relational talk but the Christian understanding of what it means to be a person. On that understanding, to live in relation and relinquish any claim on independence of self does not undermine our identity as individuals; on the contrary, it establishes that identity.

Here again the Athanasian Creed charts the way. The three persons of the Godhead are not distinguished one from another by any characteristic or quality. If we say that the Father is uncreated, we must say the same of Son and Spirit. If we confess that the Father is infinite—well, the same must be said of Son and Spirit. Likewise: "Almighty is the Father; almighty is the Son; almighty is the Spirit." We get the picture. And yet, of course, "there are not three almighty beings, but one who is almighty."

How then are the three to be distinguished? Only in terms of the internal relations of their shared divine life. The Son is begotten of the Father; we may not characterize either the Father or the Spirit as begotten. The Spirit proceeds from the Father and (at least in the West!) the Son; Father and Son do not so proceed.[16] Being a person, then, does not require that one possess—whether actively or even in potency—any particular qualities or capacities. It means rather, to draw on the language of the philosopher John Crosby, that a person is not a mere instance of our shared human nature (with its characteristic capacities) but is an unrepeatable someone knowable only through love.[17] There is no way to evaluate such persons comparatively, and, hence, our very inability to do so establishes a kind of equality among them.

This, I think, is the deep Christian ground for much of Elshtain's concern about the notion of a sovereign self and the deeds of purportedly sovereign selves who suppose that they are self-creators. But I note that, however much it was bequeathed to our civilization and however much it shaped—until quite recently—our understanding of what it means to be a person, it is a distinctively Christian ground. Which raises once again the question I asked earlier: Where do we go from here, and how shall we shape our arguments if we share Elshtain's concern about some of the deeds of would-be sovereign selves in our society?

Whatever answer we give to that question, a second theological issue also deserves consideration—one that focuses our attention very directly on the relation between God, state, and self in our discussion of sovereignty. In relation to our world, the God who exists as three persons mutually indwelling each other is One and is named as Creator. No matter how often we emphasize the relation of the three persons, this remains true, and it complicates Elshtain's account of sovereignty.

She herself recognizes that "the genealogy of the concept [of sovereignty] is nested in the powerful and pervasive construction of God's sovereign dominion, force, and will over what would have remained a formless void had He not exercised His omnipotent volition" (*RP*, 136). Although she commends a God of reason and love rather than unbounded will, the transcendent Creator is not, as she knows, a character appearing only in a post-Ockhamite world. Only with great difficulty did ancient Israel overcome tendencies all around it to identify gods with particular places or with the cycles of nature.[18] As it did, the transcendence of God was sharpened and clarified. That powerful Creator is not just a source from which emerges the concept of sovereignty but is, simultaneously, one who limits sovereigns, who desacralizes both the natural world and political society.

Moreover, however much the lingering influence of Greek philosophy and the Thomistic synthesis may have inclined medieval Christians to conceive of the world—and of themselves—as participating in the divine reason and love, and not just as the product of a commanding will, belief in the Creator had in our history a profoundly desacralizing effect. The archaic sense of the divine as immanent in nature, a belief commonplace among the ancient Near Eastern peoples from whom Israel gradually distinguished itself, was, Francis Oakley suggests, hard to reconcile with "the personal and transcendent God of power and might, upon whose will the very existence of the world was radically contingent."[19] To be sure, Christians did compromise and make a limited peace in various ways "with the nature worship of the pagan past, with the archaic pattern of sacral kingship, with the Roman ideal of imperial universalism, with the Greek philosophy of divine immanence, with the Provençal ideology of courtly love."[20] But the gradual direction of movement was one in which the realms of nature, of society, and even of humanity were no longer part of a "divine continuum."

This complicates the account of sovereignty Elshtain gives, or so it seems to me. For it suggests that the state's struggle for a sovereignty unmatched by any countervailing jurisdiction is not just a story of the movement from medieval to modern, or the movement from Aquinas to Ockham. It is, instead or additionally, rooted in the way Christians picture the world's relation to God. Thus, for example, whereas Elshtain in *Sovereignty* characterizes the idea of divine right monarchy as "an early modern invention" (*S*, 95), as if until then it was unproblematic for Christian thought, Oakley calls it "ultimately pagan in its presuppositions and ancient in its provenance."[21] Hence, our story is not just one of modern political sovereigns setting themselves up in the image of an Ockhamite God, unchecked by any countervailing authority; it is a longer and ongoing story of the biblical God, who created the world out of nothing and whose ends even political sovereigns must serve. To remind these sovereigns of that we may need St. Thomas less than we need the Bible.

Whatever our account of the rise of modern political sovereigns, Christians have good theological reason to deflate their sacral pretensions and to defend whatever countervailing jurisdictions seem helpful in that project—whether originating in Wittenberg, Rome, Geneva, Providence, or even (I am not sure of this) Salt Lake City. For the God that Christians worship—whether they kneel beside Thomas or beside Ockham—is One, who, in order to use political sovereigns as his servants for our good, drains all ultimacy from them.

I am aware that the story I myself have been telling in very abbreviated form is no sure thing and has its own difficulties. For example, on the account I have given the God of Israel whom Christians worship desacralizes not only society but also nature. This is not unproblematic, though it is also one of the sources of modern science, the blessings of which we all enjoy. The God of Israel creates an ordered world, but a contingent one. There is order in nature to be discovered. But it need not have been ordered as it is, and, hence, its order must be discovered. And having discovered it, we may manipulate it in countless ways— some fruitful and creative, others debilitating and destructive.

That is what science as a human project does. The world comes to be thought of as a machine whose workings we seek to discover, to fix when needed, and perhaps even to improve. If, like St. Thomas, we think of the world's order as participating in some mysterious way in the reason of God, we may be drawn to think of the world somewhat less as a machine and somewhat more as a living organism. If, unchastened by the plot of Elshtain's story, we think of the world's order as simply imposed by the divine Commander, the image of a machine may have more appeal for us. But in either case we need not suppose piety demands that we never put nature to the test, never seek to direct and, even, to master it.

If so, however, our difficulties go still deeper. I said that the God whom Christians worship desacralizes not only society but also nature. So far—perhaps—so good. But, at least in the view of some, we must go on to add this: not only nature but also human nature. And if so, then, of course, my account would become part of the problem Elshtain confronts in her concluding chapters on self-sovereignty, and I could not coherently describe the views she puts forth in those chapters as being on the side of the angels.

In *The Abolition of Man*, one of the most incisive accounts of this problem, C. S. Lewis writes, "There are progressions in which the last step is *sui generis* . . . and in which to go the whole way is to undo all the labour of your previous journey."[22] That is, our mastery and manipulation of nature has required that we see it not as a living organism participating in a cosmic, divine order—mother nature—but as something like an object, a machine, to be tinkered with. Now though, and this is a large part of Elshtain's concern, we have begun to make humanity itself a natural object, available for manipulation in answer to our boundless desires.

Elshtain and I are agreed that at least many aspects of this project should be resisted and even, not to put too fine a point upon it, condemned. But on what ground? Consider first her narrative. What resources for resistance does it offer? I am not sure of the answer to that question. As best I can tell, her move is once again an appeal to relationality. "The self I have in mind," she writes in *Sovereignty*, "seeks meaning and dignity and finds a measure of both not in total liberation from nature [the project of sovereign majesty], nor in some utopian attunement and at-oneness with nature [regression to the sacred cosmos from which Israel extricated itself], but, rather, in growing to become a full person according to our human natures." And this nature is "intrinsically social." "We are created to love and to be loved" (*S*, 229–30).

With none of that would I disagree. Indeed, there is an insight here that merits our attention. In *That Hideous Strength*, one of Lewis's space fantasies, William Hingest, himself a scientist, says: "I happen to believe that you can't study men; you can only get to know them, which is quite a different thing."[23] That is to say, if it is *persons* whom we want to know and understand, and if persons are unrepeatabilities distinguished not by their capacities but by their relations, getting to know them is the right way to honor and acknowledge them. So there is something important in Elshtain's appeal to our intrinsically social nature in order to oppose unending manipulation of human beings.

Perhaps, however, we can say one thing more, and more definite— something available for learning both in Wittenberg and in Rome, for it is shared by both. The triune God lives not only *ad intra* but also *ad extra*, as the theologians say. That is, the divine life includes not only the mystery of God's inmost life but also God's "missions" to the world. Chief among these is the incarnation of the Son in Jesus of Nazareth, in and through which our human nature is taken up into his person. This means that every person is made to share in the enjoyment of God; each is a possible future companion in beatitude. To quote Lewis once more: "There are no *ordinary* people. . . . Next to the Blessed Sacrament itself, your neighbour is the holiest object presented to your senses."[24]

The human person is not, therefore, a proper object of our mastery or our manipulation. Quite obviously, that general statement will need to be refined and made more precise in countless instances, but I think it is the theological premise that underlies Elshtain's rejection of so much that we have learned and are learning to do to others in the name of our sovereign selfhood. There is a great chasm fixed between mastery of nature and mastery of human nature. The curtain will one day fall on the natural world, and God—so Christians believe—will create new heavens and a new earth. But that new world will not be one for which new persons must be created. It will be a world inhabited by the persons we live with and know here and now, and—recalling the afterword to *Sovereignty*—we will not then, I think, want to be known as people who consigned to the shadows outside our circle of concern those with "empty pockets" (*S*, 247–48).

NOTES

1. Delivered in 2005 at the University of Edinburgh.

2. Francis Oakley, *Kingship: The Politics of Enchantment* (Oxford: Blackwell, 2006), 160.

3. Ibid., 161.

4. Jean Bethke Elshtain, "Abraham Lincoln and the Last Best Hope," *First Things*, November 1999, 47.

5. "How Should We Talk? Religion and Public Discourse: A Conversation with Jean Bethke Elshtain and William McGurn," *Center Conversations*, Ethics and Public Policy Center, no. 11 (June 2011): 3.

6. Martin Luther, "Secular Authority: To What Extent It Should Be Obeyed," in *Martin Luther: Selections from His Writings*, ed. John Dillenberger (Garden City, NY: Doubleday Anchor, 1961), 384.

7. Ibid., 385.

8. Josef Pieper, *Scholasticism: Personalities and Problems of Medieval Philosophy* (New York: McGraw-Hill, 1964), 14.

9. Ibid., 41.

10. Ibid., 155.

11. Jean Elshtain, "Sovereignty, Identity, and Sacrifice," *Social Research* 58, no. 3 (1991): 545–64.

12. Elshtain seems to believe that they are *in their very nature* competitors. I doubt that. In a sinful world, however, competition no doubt characterizes such singular selves.

13. William Shakespeare, *Henry the Fourth, Part I*, 5.4.68–72.

14. William C. Placher, *Narratives of a Vulnerable God* (Louisville: Westminster John Knox Press, 1994), 73.

15. Alva Noë, *Out of Our Heads: Why You Are Not Your Brain, and Other Lessons from the Biology of Consciousness* (New York: Hill and Wang, 2009), 40.

16. It is worth noting—and perhaps of more than incidental significance when discussing a topic such as sovereignty—that in the Orthodox Church the oneness of God is grounded in the fact that there is one Father. Thus, the Orthodox Church teaches the "monarchy" of the Father, to whom Son and Spirit trace their origin (the Son begotten of the Father, the Spirit proceeding from the Father). For the Eastern Church, to say that the Spirit proceeds not only from the Father but also from the Son would mean that the divine oneness must be grounded in some essence shared by the three persons. That, at any rate, is a standard way of distinguishing East from West on this question.

17. John F. Crosby, *Personalist Papers* (Washington, DC: Catholic University of America Press, 2003), 6–14.

18. Jon D. Levenson, "The God of Abraham and the Enemies of 'Eurocentrism,'" *First Things*, October 1991, 15–21. Unsurprisingly, Levenson observes, when the Nazi regime—whose deeds form part of Elshtain's narrative of the sovereign self—sought to revive attachment to the gods of place, to *Blut und Boden*, Jews had to be targeted. And in good time the Christian Church itself

naturally also had to be radically reconstructed by the German regime, as if—contrary to what St. Paul says in Romans 11—the wild olive shoot of the Gentiles had not been grafted onto the nourishing root of the olive tree that was Israel.

19. Oakley, *Kingship*, 153.

20. Francis Oakley, *The Medieval Experience: Foundations of Western Cultural Singularity* (New York: Charles Scribner's Sons, 1974), 212.

21. Ibid., 113.

22. C. S. Lewis, *The Abolition of Man* (New York: Macmillan, 1947), 91.

23. C. S. Lewis, *That Hideous Strength* (New York: Macmillan, 1965), 71.

24. C. S. Lewis, "The Weight of Glory," in *The Weight of Glory and Other Addresses* (Grand Rapids, MI: Eerdmans, 1965), 15.

CHAPTER NINE

TAKING LOVE SERIOUSLY

Elshtain's Augustinian Voice and Modern Politics

Eric Gregory

My study here has two parts. First, I focus on Jean Bethke Elshtain's reading of the historically distant and enchanted world of Augustine of Hippo. Second, I consider what we might call her applied Augustinianism. I do so by highlighting two important contemporary issues —torture and humanitarian intervention—and their relation to her account of political Augustinianism.

Elshtain dedicates her book *Augustine and the Limits of Politics* (*ALP*) to "those who taught her well." It is an appropriate dedication. Augustine was preoccupied with education. His earliest dialogues presented the liberal arts as the best guide for the difficult journey to happiness. Much of his writing mediates ancient learning refracted through a new theological idiom. Given his combustible mix of Roman and Christian ideals, he was anxious about false teachers. At his most confessional, this suspicion extended to his own influence as a teacher. But his disillusionment with the liberal arts is a case study in his broader assessment of pagan culture. The liberal arts, he came to believe, were too often an occasion for pride. They conceal imperial ambition and violence. They perpetuate the counterfeit virtues of a culture of honor and shame.

For Augustine, false worship fundamentally distorts both ethics and politics. His polemics place him among the Christian culture warriors, to use a sometimes pejorative term. He analyzed the distortions of excessive psychic attachments to finite goods, writing in a time when uncertainty and moral panic abounded. By my lights, he was harsher on the practices of his culture than on its various believers. He also was better at psychologizing injustices rather than historicizing them in ways that might promote alternative practices. Yet he joined theory and practice because he thought imperial culture did not have the conceptual and linguistic resources to adequately name its self-deceptions. Its perversity was repressed, an important theme in Elshtain's own social criticism. Domination comes hidden in the guise of liberty and compassion. Political ills, whether in late antiquity or the contemporary United States, reflect deeply embedded yet contingent habits that escape the surface moral complaints found in any decent Roman philosopher or modern-day pundit. This stance, in part, is why figures like John Rawls considered Augustine one of the darkest minds in Western literature.

Augustine knew the beauty of the world. But it was always a fragile beauty. In a wonderful yet neglected essay, Judith Shklar numbers Augustine among those rare political thinkers who take injustice seriously. Augustine, for Shklar, is rightly impressed by the *scope* of injustice as something more than the mere absence of justice. Like Shklar, Augustine had a keen sense of injustice and "the many ways in which we all learn to live with each other's injustices tend to be ignored, as is the relation of private injustice to public order."[1] She contrasts this seriousness with what she calls a complacent view of justice modeled on a confident trust in institutions of fair rules. Augustine took injustice seriously, even if it eluded any narrative explanation in his telling of sinful conformity to the world (cf. Rom. 12). Augustine's account of the wretchedness of mortal life can and has sponsored otherworldly withdrawal and worldly engagement.

His rhetoric, like Milton's or Lincoln's, brought us into hell. But it hoped to bring us out. The genius of Augustine's politics may be in the very way he frames theology as a kind of sociology anchored by that overarching appeal to the biblical imagery of Babylon and Jerusalem. Two rival entities, shaped by two rival loves, are entangled with one another in hidden ways throughout history. Modern readers find in this Pauline vision the origins of ideology critique: even Noam Chomsky does not resist Augustine's inspired retelling of the pirate's response to Alexander the Great in book 4 of the *City of God*.[2] Others, of course, find only ideology itself, an ideology of exclusion still unconfessed. As Elshtain's former student and political theorist Romand Coles puts it in his treatment of Augustine: "It is difficult to write of generosity today without conjuring up images of terror wrought by a religion that at once placed the movement of *caritas* and *agape*, giving and love, at the foundation of being and swept across the Americas during the conquest with a holocaust of 'generosity.'"[3] Given the history of various crusades of love, often violent, I suspect many people get nervous when a Christian tells them they are going to love them. And "love" is sometimes a word that dare not speak its name among many Augustinian realists and modern political thinkers more generally. They fear accusations of sentimentalism, not unlike those made by Romans troubled by the meek religion of the Sermon on the Mount. What does love have to do with politics?

ELSHTAIN'S AUGUSTINE AND MODERN
POLITICAL THEORY

No one doubts Elshtain's realism. Like many of her contemporaries, she was introduced to Augustine through political realism. She found him through her teacher Kenneth Waltz, international relations realist, and through the writings of Reinhold Niebuhr on the ironies of American history. In *Achieving Our Country*, Richard Rorty casts Niebuhr and Elshtain as writers who "take the notion of sin seriously."[4] Critics of both Niebuhr and Elshtain often claim that sin is the only Christian notion they take seriously. But Elshtain was not embarrassed by Augustine's heart or his other theological confessions.

One of Elshtain's central insights about Augustine and her own Augustinian voice is that she takes *love* seriously. In fact, taking sin seriously and taking injustice seriously are predicated on taking love seriously. Elshtain highlights the way in which even the language of justice demands examination of the character of a people in terms of their objects of love. What you love most is the essence of your character, that to which your will is turned. True virtue is rightly ordered love. Unlike dominant conceptions of persons as sets of interests or utility-maximizers, Elshtain again and again helps us appreciate Augustine's fundamental notion that human beings and the communities they constitute are bundles of loves. They are disordered bundles of loves in need of therapy and constraint, but they are loves nonetheless. We creatures are moved by self-interest, but not only self-interest.

Like Augustine's reading of Cicero, Elshtain's reading of Augustine inspires a new way of thinking about Augustine's subversive relation to modern political thought by this emphasis on the centrality of love. She makes love relevant for Augustine's political thought, not simply for his moral psychology or his ethics.[5] Despite its misleading realist sounding title, *Augustine and the Limits of Politics* is an important example of an emerging consensus that realism and Rawlsian neutrality fail to adequately theorize a needed revival of republican conceptions of civic virtue.

To be sure, I would not want to take Elshtain's reading of Augustine out of a kind of realist camp. But it is a better realism. She knows that "our control over the world is limited" and that "human beings live indeterminate and incomplete lives" (*ALP*, 67). Yet she does not make sin the ground of her defense of a limited politics. Rather, she turns to Augustine's confessional and affective anthropology, criticizing the egoism and the thin selves of liberal political theory by highlighting a "God-given reason and . . . capacity for love, as well as . . . lust for dominance" (27). Taking Augustine away from his Hobbesian readers or world-denying mystics, she charts how his pilgrim theology relies on the claim that "dependence on others is not a diminution but an enrichment of self" (36). Her Augustine is no analytic philosopher, stuffed with propositions. He is an observer of human living, a conversation partner for her alongside Wittgenstein, Havel, Arendt, Sartre, and Camus. Elshtain's Augustine ushers in a valuable moral revolution, a compassion for others that sponsored an intellectual watershed without which we would live in a very different moral and political universe.

Elshtain's casual aside that Augustine's metaphors are "fascinatingly feminine" (*ALP*, 56) and buttress "feminist claims that public and private are not hermetically sealed off from the other" (35) also inspire efforts to read Augustine in a more constructive relationship to contemporary feminist political theory. Elshtain, of course, had her own views on this relationship (see, for example, *Public Man, Private Woman*, and *Women and War*). Augustine is an uncommon ally of feminist ethics in thinking about love's relation to justice. But it is important to note that Elshtain's judgment about Augustine's love affair with the world is a theological claim with significant anthropological and political implications. Her Augustine is the one who writes with wonder about flowers and leaves, oddities and rarities, the quotidian and the final hope. If God is in solidarity with humanity through the Incarnation, then creatures can enjoy the gifts of God even as we are perennially tempted to enjoy them in the wrong way.

These readings offer a different route into thinking about Augustine on love and politics. Most of the twentieth-century interest in virtue and Augustine, in the wake of Anders Nygren's critique of Augustine's notion of *caritas*, was preoccupied with the relation between self-love and love of God. Nygren charged that Augustine corrupted the purity of Christian love (gratuitous *agape*) by lodging it within a Platonic structure of egocentric desire to possess the good (*eros*). Nygren, by contrast, pits the charity of Jerusalem against Athens. One of Elshtain's insights into Augustine was the way he indexed the language of virtue to his account of our sociality, his fascination with ways in which languages and historical communities shape meanings. Our proleptic glimpses of God, like Augustine's vision at Ostia, occur in communion with (rather than without or against) others. Highlighting these incarnational and eschatological perspectives is a way to revive a political Augustinianism that critically affirms civic virtues and a kind of secularity without abandoning suspicion of civic glory and the *libido dominandi* that constrains political communities.

ELSHTAIN'S AUGUSTINIANISM AND MODERN POLITICS: TWO CASE STUDIES

Before political theology became chic, Elshtain refused a rigid separation of religion from politics, and indeed, more importantly to my mind,

of the theological from the political. She did not primarily write intellectual history by way of apologetic or genealogy. There is plenty of that
in her stories about the development of Western politics. Yet she primarily writes as a theorist-citizen, fluidly deploying theological language
as a frame of reference and vocabulary for her contributions to public
life. She relished in the secularity of that public life, to trade upon that
invented Augustinian sense of the "time between the times." Elshtain's
Augustinian voice, always rooted in the particularity of her experience,
is not preoccupied with *her*self as so many of the "self-consumed selves"
of modernity (*ALP*, 6). Against some of Augustine's harshest critics,
Elshtain warns that to find in his *Confessions* only "evidence of a solidification of the triumph of Western logocentrism, is to have a heart of
stone and a head of brick" (15). Her Augustine offers more than ironic
psychological insights into egoism. George Lindbeck once told me, to
my surprise, that he thought Niebuhr was the last public intellectual to
effectively present the Christian faith to a broadly educated American
audience. Here we enter the domain of Nigel Biggar's critical remarks in
chapter 7 of this volume. Lindbeck's claim has always led me to wonder,
despite Barthian sensibilities, if generic theism or even ethical monothe-
ism is as bad as Stanley Hauerwas makes it out to be.

   Augustine's praise of Platonic piety was real, though, of course, in
the end a comic tragedy because it was a prideful piety that endorsed
imperialism. But it had that Churchillian virtue of being better than
other options, perhaps what he elsewhere calls "an imperfect kind of
virtue" on its way to truthfulness.[6] Augustine's pessimism can be exaggerated. In fact, apart from being the great critic of imperial pretension,
we find Augustine writing letters to public officials encouraging them
to use their offices with humility and lamenting necessity for the pro-
motion of Christian morals and unity through social reconciliation. Yet
they should also tolerate earthly peace provided it does "not impede the
religion by which we are taught that the one supreme and true God is to
be worshipped" (*City of God* 19.17; see also 5.17).[7]

   What does Elshtain's "one supreme and true God" language look
like in concrete situations of conflicting goods? Let me briefly raise two
controversial topics that merit further reflection. The first is the use of
torture in wartime, and the second is armed humanitarian intervention.

In her 2004 essay, "Reflections on the Problem of 'Dirty Hands'" (hereafter PDH), Elshtain does not cite Augustine.[8] But she has a recognizably, familiar Augustinian voice, in fact, a deeply Niebuhrian one.[9] The question is whether or not the piece is adequately Augustinian. In her article, I see two main issues raised by the practice of torture. One is whether or not it is ever morally justified, and a second is whether it should be allowed under the law. Everyday life vexes us with situations where doing evil to achieve good, or at least choosing between lesser evils and managing the moral anguish of complicity with an evil, seems the only morally intelligible course of action. The desire for "moral purity" appears unrealistic and, at times, harmful to others and ourselves. Elshtain chastises "legalistic versions of pietistic rigorism in which one's own moral purity is ranked above other goods" (PDH, 87–88). We should be willing to "incur moral guilt, when the lives of others are at stake" (88).

My undergraduates love moral dilemmas; especially the fictional examples conjured by philosophers about trolleys running out of control and fat men in caves. I worry that I indulge their adolescent mentalities with too many of them, but I also assure myself they are pedagogical ways to test our basic intuitions, even if these examples usually bully them into intuitions I think they should not have (namely, "don't worry about moral purity"). Over the past decade, however, we have been having an all too real debate in our churches and in our public life about the use of torture in a war on terror.

In her short article, Elshtain argues that the Christian tradition is neither deontological nor utilitarian. Instead, she argues Christian casuistry seeks to answer the questions about responsibility in particular circumstances. In brief, she concludes that torture is a horror, but there are moments when a rule against torture may be overridden. She writes, "Far greater moral guilt falls on a person in authority who permits the deaths of hundreds of innocents rather than choosing to 'torture' one guilty or complicit person" (PDH, 87). Only pride and disordered love, it seems, would prevent one from choosing to "torture." For Elshtain, importantly, it is not about choosing evil to do good; it is a choice of the lesser evil. This is the task of relative justice, pursued in the spirit of sinning bravely and mournfully. The tone of her piece, however, is more lament than confession. In choosing the lesser evil, we might be sad, but we are not doing bad. We regret that necessity required this tragic choice. We lament our decision, a sign of some violation of a norm, and we should not seek to legalize and thereby normalize what is a horrible decision. Of course, the use of quotes around "torture" and her appeal to "torture lite" and "coercive interrogation" raise the salient questions of phenomenology of torture and the nature of moral guilt.

Legal and moral distinctions in the analysis of human action are the stuff of Christian ethics. But critics argue that there are some scales you just should not be on, especially when certain actions tempt the powerful. Definition hunting can be a sign of moral corruption as much as prudent casuistry is in the face of necessity. A husband should not want to know how much pushing and shoving qualifies as domestic violence. Public officials and democratic citizens should not want to know how much beating and deprivation qualifies as torture. Christians, moreover, are called to see the face of Christ in the most vulnerable. This dignity extends to those enemies who do not seem vulnerable to us. Torture is a defilement of the human creature. Information gained through torture of *suspected* terrorists is both doubted and tainted. Elshtain's recognition of "moral guilt" admits this corruption of legal and moral culture.[10] Is love that strange when confronted by the claims of multiple neighbors?

Augustine and the Limits of Politics is itself a confessional work. The author admits unsure wandering from Wittenberg to Rome with her companion Augustine. There are many Catholic Niebuhrians. But in her writings, Elshtain often compares a Lutheran/Bonhoefferian/Niebuhrian post-Fall Augustine of our justification with a Thomist/John Paul II/natural law/creation-is-good Augustine of our sanctification. In the article on torture, she invokes Michael Walzer's own comparison of the Protestant and Catholic conscience. My question remains: How do these two Augustines relate to her stance on torture, even "torture lite"? Most Thomists (for example, Jean Porter and Robert George) draw a stark line in the sand, adopting strong prohibitions on torture as an expression of our shared humanity even with the accused terrorist about to bomb the schoolhouse. In fact, other Christian intellectuals, such as Jeremy Waldron and George Hunsinger, have argued that the secular debate about torture might benefit from clear Christian language lest we be overwhelmed by soft consequentialism or antinomian appeals to necessity in the face of demands for security. Absolute prohibitions of intrinsically unjust means are necessary precisely for this type of case. Does Elshtain draw a line in the sand? If so, where? She appears to draw one, but that drawing is threatened by her rhetoric of tragedy and necessity. How might her newly Catholic faith now read Augustine's description of the judge's cry, "Deliver me from my necessities" (*City of God* 19.6)? How far apart can we hold our assessment of actions from their agents? Can actions be right even if they are regretted?

These questions bear on a second issue. Elshtain's invocation of just war thinking, like Paul Ramsey before her, trades on its origins in Christian charity. In her writings on humanitarian intervention, Elshtain forcefully invokes an Augustinian conception of neighbor-regard. It is a concern for the most vulnerable that inspired a just war thinking that many find has implications for international justice. I leave to one side judgments about particular interventions, though I admired her candor about the realities of U.S. power and her willingness to get beyond legal frameworks in asking important questions about the kind of society we want to be. Unlike with many so-called prophetic voices, her apt distinctions between the failures of U.S. politics and other societies are compelling. We face dangers of tyranny and empire, but those do not exhaust the pathologies of politics. My interests here are more conceptual than empirical. They are related to the dilemmatic presentation of the torture issue, but from another angle.

Apart from that looming theological question about how what we do in this "time between the times" relates to our eschatological destiny, I think humanitarian intervention presses another question about the character of our loves in terms of our obligations to others. Think of it as the flip side of love's counsel to do no harm. It is Ramsey's Good Samaritan question about inaction: "What do you think Jesus would have made the Samaritan do if he had come upon the scene while the robbers were still at their fell work?"[11] Elshtain appealed to this story in her own writings, and many others have done so in in the face of ethnic conflict, genocide, and the various humanitarian crises in Somalia, Bosnia, Rwanda, Kosovo, East Timor, Iraq, Darfur, Sudan, and, most recently, Libya and Syria. In criticizing the limited NATO bombing of the former Yugoslavia, one professor of international law concretized Ramsey's abstract question:

What would the man going from Jerusalem to Jericho have felt had the Samaritan, instead of putting him on his own beast and taking him to an inn for safety, merely thrown stones at the thieves from his donkey as he passed safely by, which then precipitated murder and sexual abuse because there was no one present to offer the victim effective protection where and when it was needed?[12]

Just war thinking is undergoing a development today in trying to correlate notions of *retribution, self-defense*, and *protection of persons*.[13] Elshtain's welcome appeals to social charity in our public life help us get beyond a stark choice between the spontaneity of love's immediate encounter and practices of charity in complex social wholes. At the same time, exposing the pieties of liberal humanitarian sentiment as pretext for new imperial politics is a major preoccupation of contemporary historians, anthropologists, and philosophers. Charles Taylor's *A Secular Age* is only the most recent example of a Catholic voice that indicts the Protestant Reformation for endowing this frenzied legacy of reform. Humanitarian interventions are notorious for their capacity to cause more harm than good, and many consider them as cheap ways of avoiding long-term tasks of development or structural reform.

A standard view is that humanitarian intervention is supererogatory—a failure to intervene *might* display a lack of virtue but it does not constitute a vice or violation of justice. Most Christian supporters find it "hard to defend an *imperative* to violence as an outgrowth of Christian charity (even in direst situations)."[14] Others have argued that humanitarian intervention is, in fact, a perfect duty (at least, for some international agency) demanded by "respect for humanity" when fundamental human rights are violated.[15] Based on Elshtain's notion of charity, what is the normative status of a humanitarian intervention if all the relevant just war criteria are fulfilled? Is such an intervention an obligation or mere permission for some actor to act? Do we face situations that demand creative moral acts that cannot always be subordinated to existing law?

Whether or not such a prudential judgment can be made *ex ante* is a particularly difficult question for prospective humanitarian interventions. But this difficulty is not unique. The moral life often casts up such difficulties in the face of contingency. The really interesting and difficult moral problem is whether, through no fault of our own, we find ourselves in a genuinely dilemmatic situation regardless of action or inaction. Any Christian response to that problem would implicate a vast array of theological commitments about the nature of God and creation.

CONCLUSION

Elshtain took love seriously. She never abandoned the hope of redemption, even the possibility of redemptive agency in the world. Like Augustine, she wrote for a culture unsure of its deepest commitments. Her generous Christian humanism hoped a shared moral vocabulary might bind us without breaking us, a space for "loyalty and love and care, as well as for a chastened form of civic virtue" (*ALP*, 91). The world is to be worked upon, not just waited out. Here we find the *limits* and the *possibilities* of politics. Elshtain tells us Augustine asks us not "so much how to control an old self, but how to bring a transformed one into being" (11). But that is a hard question, without answers that fit on bumper stickers. How do we change? How do we bring about transformation? Augustinians, by reputation and example, tend not to be utopian about prospects for change. They offer a cautious wisdom, sparing us the thrill of misguided revolutions. Those feed on Pelagian fantasy. We are to use politics, even the violence of the state, but not enjoy it. Augustine's *City of God* never loses its antipagan polemic. From book 10 onward, however, he offers a vision of healing, wholeness, and intimacy that will characterize those shaped by grace. Such love, disciplined by grace, desires the good in the right way at the right time and in right relationships. There is no certain knowledge, but the exercise of political virtues responds to genuine human goods.

Contested genealogies play a significant role in political theology and the academic study of religion more generally.[16] In *Who Are We?*, Elshtain was too careful to jump from origins to application in her own tapping of the "wellsprings of the Christian tradition" (*WAW*, 4). She could describe modern pathologies as Christian heresies. But she aspired to be more than a trustee of historical memory in arguing about both the right and the good in the context of real politics. I do worry that we are entering a time in the academy and in our public life where appeals to intellectual history no longer carry any normative purchase, especially if they have theological origins.[17] Many humanists are now fascinated by theology. But the past has become irrelevant to our best philosophers and ethicists. Most of my colleagues, after we discuss Augustine's views on love or Grotius's view on international law, say that is really interesting, but so what? Elshtain's work always tried to answer the "so what" question. I am grateful for Elshtain's courage as a constructive thinker, willing to risk her loves, giving an example of the so what by interpreting the Church to the culture, and the culture to the Church. Or, as she ends *Who Are We?*, to "love the world enough to want to know it" (168). But, as she and St. Paul remind us, not to be conformed to it. In the tradition in which she was raised, Christians call this "bearing witness."

NOTES

1. Judith N. Shklar, "Giving Injustice Its Due," in *The Faces of Injustice* (New Haven, CT: Yale University Press, 1990), 15. Shklar discusses a number of representatives of the "normal" model in the classical liberal tradition since John Stuart Mill. More recently, we might include the high liberalism of Ronald Dworkin, *Taking Rights Seriously* (Cambridge, MA: Harvard University Press, 1978).

2. See Noam Chomsky, *Pirates and Emperors, Old and New: International Terrorism in the Real World* (Cambridge, MA: South End Press, 2002).

3. Romand Coles, *Rethinking Generosity: Critical Theory and the Politics of Caritas* (Ithaca, NY: Cornell University Press, 1997), 1.

4. Richard Rorty, *Achieving Our Country: Leftist Thought in Twentieth-Century America* (Cambridge, MA: Harvard University Press, 1998), 33.

5. See, for example, Eric Gregory, *Politics and the Order of Love: An Augustinian Ethic of Democratic Citizenship* (Chicago: University of Chicago Press, 2008). In that work, I claim Elshtain as an example of an Augustinian civic liberalism who knows the complex interrelation between Augustine's notions of love and sin.

6. Augustine, *The City of God*, trans. R. W. Dyson (Cambridge: Cambridge University Press, 1998), 5.19. Hereafter cited in text.

7. For Augustine's letters, see E. M. Atkins and R. J. Dodaro, *Augustine: Political Writings* (Cambridge: Cambridge University Press, 2001), and Joseph Clair, *Discerning the Good in the Letters and Sermons of Augustine* (Oxford: Oxford University Press, 2016).

8. Jean Bethke Elshtain, "Reflections on the Problem of 'Dirty Hands,'" in *Torture: A Collection*, ed. Sanford Levinson (Oxford: Oxford University Press, 2004), 77–89.

9. Recall Niebuhr's counsel that "we ought to do whatever has to be done to prevent the triumph of this intolerable tyranny"; see Niebuhr, "To Prevent the Triumph of an Intolerable Tyranny," *Christian Century* 57 (December 18, 1940). Elshtain ends her reflection on torture with an allusion to Niebuhr and the need to rank "concrete responsibility ahead of rigid rule-following" (PDH, 88).

10. See, for example, Jeremy Waldron, "What Can Christian Teaching Add to the Debate about Torture," *Theology Today* 63, no. 3 (2006): 340–43, and Jean Porter, "Torture and the Christian Conscience: A Response to Jeremy Waldron," *Scottish Journal of Theology* 61, no. 3 (2008): 340–58. On the political value of appeals to the "sacred" in debates about torture, see Stephen Bush, "Torture and the Politics of the Sacred," *Soundings* 91, no. 1 (2014): 75–99.

11. Paul Ramsey, *The Just War: Force and Political Responsibility* (New York: Scribner's, 1968), 143. Robert Jenson characterizes this question as a "clichéd cheap shot, but it nevertheless demands an answer"; see Jenson, "Is Patriotism a Virtue?" in *God and Country? Diverse Perspectives on Christianity and Patriotism*, ed. Michael G. Long and Tracy Wenger Sadd (New York: Palgrave Macmillan, 2007), 149. According to Jenson, "a Christian must indeed be a pacifist in his own cause, but can hardly be so in the cause of his neighbors in the world" (ibid.).

12. Christine Chinkin, "The State That Acts Alone: Bully, Good Samaritan or Iconoclast?" *European Journal of International Law* 11, no. 1 (2000): 35.

13. See Eric Gregory, "What Do We Want from the Just War Tradition? New Challenges of Surveillance and the Security State," *Studies in Christian Ethics* 27, no. 1 (2014): 50–62.

14. Timothy P. Jackson, *The Priority of Love: Christian Charity and Social Justice* (Princeton, NJ: Princeton University Press, 2003), 110 (original emphasis). Jackson does not pursue this question per se. But, since he believes that love can sometimes rise above justice, he asserts that "it is better, I think, to see just war as permissible for Christians, rather than as obligatory" (ibid.). It remains unclear to me how this conception of justice remains tethered to charity.

15. Carla Bagnoli, "Humanitarian Intervention as a Perfect Duty: A Kantian Argument," *Nomos* 47 (2004): 117–48.

16. See, for example, Talal Asad, *Genealogies of Religion: Discipline and Reasons of Power in Christianity and Islam* (Baltimore: Johns Hopkins University Press, 1993); John Milbank, *Theology and Social Theory: Beyond Secular Reason* (Oxford: Blackwell, 1990); Eric Nelson, *The Hebrew Republic: Jewish Sources and the Transformation of European Political Thought* (Cambridge, MA: Harvard University Press, 2010); and Giorgio Agamben, *The Kingdom and the Glory: For a Theological Genealogy of Economy and Government*, trans. Lorenzo Chiesa and Matteo Mandarini (Stanford, CA: Stanford University Press, 2011).

17. See, for example, Paul W. Kahn, *Political Theology: Four New Chapters on the Concept of Sovereignty* (New York: Columbia University Press, 2011). Kahn argues that a genealogy of the theological origins of political concepts is "about as interesting and important as learning that English words have their origin in old Norse" (3). Kahn's fascinating turn from genealogy to analogy is decidedly descriptive rather than normative: "to explore the political imagination we have, whether or not we should have it" (18). Phenomenology of the political, of course, need not compete with normativity.

CHAPTER TEN

SUPREMACY AT STAKE

Religion and the Sovereign State in
the Work of Jean Elshtain

Daniel Philpott

My reflections on Jean Elshtain's scholarship revolve around a few major themes in her thought. First is her book *Sovereignty* (S), delivered previously as the Gifford Lectures, where she develops her thinking around a fundamental distinction between absolute sovereignty and ordained, or limited, sovereignty, which emerged in the Middle Ages and continued to shape much subsequent thought and history. Absolute sovereignty emerged from the thought of medieval nominalists on the character of God, which centered on God's will. Law, morality, and ethics, they thought, emanated from God's decrees, by which God is not bound, and have an arbitrary character.

The outcome of absolute sovereignty for politics was rulers who themselves were the source of the law and above the law. These rulers were conceived by early modern theorists like Hobbes and Machiavelli and were actualized in early modern European kingships. Through the thought of Rousseau, sovereignty was transferred to the people, whose general will was now the source of law and which was equally detached from natural law, and even more detached from God. The same concept of sovereignty gives rise to the modern sovereign self—an autonomous, isolated being with isolated interests, legislating his or her own moral law for him- or herself.

What was Elshtain's alternative? Thomism, it turns out. The leading medieval alternative to the nominalists was Thomas Aquinas's God, who is bound by his laws, which reflect and participate in his nature. Political authority, or positive law, was to be grounded in the natural law, accountable to a transcendent God, and it served to further the ends of justice and peace, which were in turn informed by the natural law. This was ordained, or limited sovereignty. Political authority was also subservient to the common good, in which the good of human persons was connected through interrelationship.

The relational character of the human person was another key theme in Elshtain's thought. Human beings are dependent upon and find their good in relationship to other human beings. This dependent relationality shines especially bright in the case of people who are handicapped or do not otherwise exercise their full human capacities. Importantly, the relational character of the human person flows from the relational character of God, not a monistic exerciser of will, but rather a God of three persons, relating to one another through love and gift.

Elshtain's antidote to absolute sovereignty can be understood in light of her conversion to Catholicism late in life. One can see her trajectory toward the Church in her book on sovereignty, where she keeps evoking Thomist principles to stress a contrast with the absolutely sovereign state and the sovereign self. This is not at all to say that her insights were exclusively Catholic; Luther, Bonhoeffer, and Camus were prominent in her pantheon of heroes. Nor did she reject modernity; she was profoundly committed to modern liberal democracy, but thought it required a rooted, relational self, objective morality, an orientation towards God, and a thick notion of the common good.

HISTORY AND THEORY: FROM THE RELIGIOUS TO THE SECULAR

Two other characteristics of Elshtain's thought set the stage for my further reflections. The first is that she brought religion into the analysis of politics. The second is sometimes forgotten: despite her first book, *Women and War* solidifying her reputation as a feminist political theorist, she began as an international relations scholar, having conducted her doctoral studies under Kenneth Waltz, the past generation's premier theorist of international relations, at Brandeis University. These two themes come together in the challenge to the secularized character of international relations that is implicit but strong in Elshtain's work. Waltz stressed that the sovereign state was the fundamental unit in international politics, and he then accepted the sovereign state as an uncritical assumption as he proceeded to analyze international politics in terms of a competition for power and security in an anarchic world. His recommendations for containing war are all rooted in balance-of-power analysis. Religion plays scant role in his work. Elshtain, by contrast, finds the origins of the sovereign state in developments in medieval theology. She agrees that the world of international politics is structured by the sovereign state, but she is highly critical of the absolutist form that this has taken. She thought that the state should be limited, not supreme, in its authority. Her analysis of war is an ethical analysis and is highly informed by religion.

The majority of scholars in the field of international relations have thought about international politics much more like Waltz than like Elshtain. Waltz's 1979 book, *Theory of International Politics*, was a landmark work in American international relations scholarship, known not only for its substantive view of international relations but also for encouraging a methodological revolution in which scientific methods of theory and hypothesis testing came to dominate the field. Elshtain's work, by contrast, always centered upon philosophical and normative concerns. She also took the role of religion seriously at a time when few others in the field did. Thus I will offer some reflections on the secular character of international relations scholarship, the limitations that has imposed on the field, and alternatives to that point of view.[1] Elshtain's understanding of religion allowed her to map more accurately the contemporary political landscape; my intent is to highlight areas where the openings created by Elshtain's work can be further expanded.

Mainstream international relations theory—especially the liberal and realist traditions—is secular because its founding fathers described, celebrated, and incorporated into their thinking a secularizing set of historical events: the development of the international system of sovereign states between roughly 1300 and 1700. These events were secular in three senses. First, they involved a transfer of the authority and power of religious actors into the hands of the sovereign state. Second, they involved the sovereign state's subordination of religious actors within its territory. Third, these first two trends not only took place but were actively celebrated by leading intellectuals of the period. Thus, Thomas Hobbes, Niccolò Machiavelli, Jean-Jacques Rousseau, Immanuel Kant, and others not only described a world in which religious actors had lost their authority but recommended that politics proceed without them.

A consensus of historians and sociologists holds that in Europe between 1400 and 1700, encompassing what is called the early modern period, state institutions strongly increased in their power and authority relative to other kinds of organizations and entities, including religious bodies, especially the Catholic Church, which had held great temporal authority prior to this time. The periodization is not exact and the trend is not linear, but it took place all across the Continent. Whether or not one thinks that the system of sovereign states was consolidated at the Peace of Westphalia in 1648 (as I do), it is very difficult to dispute that in the decades surrounding this date an international system was consolidated in which sovereign states were the dominant entities. And it is very difficult to dispute that, in terms of temporal power, the Catholic Church was the loser. No wonder Pope Innocent X called the Peace of Westphalia "null, void, invalid, iniquitous, unjust, damnable, reprobate, inane, empty of meaning and effect for all time."[2]

Why did the state win? Theorists like Charles Tilly, Hendrik Spruyt, Brian Downing, and others tell a material story.[3] The state best survived a Darwinian struggle through which it became the type of organization best able to fight military battles and in turn to raise the taxes and the troops necessary for this fighting. Others, including me, tell a story in which changes in ideas helped to bring about the change in political organization. My analysis focuses on the effects of the Protestant Reformation. Prior to the Reformation, I argue, the Catholic Church wielded considerable temporal power—the ability to tax, the ownership of large tracts of land, and other prerogatives that we now think of as political—and was assisted by figures like the Holy Roman Emperor, Charles V, who would use his soldiers to enforce orthodoxy, thus reinforcing the symbiosis of temporal and ecclesial authority.[4]

The Reformation did three things to facilitate the transfer of power and authority over to the state. First, it developed a theology—roughly Martin Luther's two kingdoms idea—that delegitimized the temporal prerogatives of the Catholic Church and legitimized the enhancement of kings' and princes' prerogatives. Second, by withdrawing the allegiance of large bodies of people (though still a minority in Europe) from the Catholic Church, the Reformation weakened the Catholic Church's temporal prerogatives. Third, because the reformers had to seek protection from forces allied with the pope, they placed themselves in the hands of princes, whose newfound power and authority they thus bolstered.

Religious ideas were not a sole cause, I argue, and they operated in tandem with material changes to bring about the sovereign state system. Others are more convinced by a "material causes alone" argument. William T. Cavanaugh, in his recent *The Myth of Religious Violence*, seeks to show that the period was not one of religious war. It was rather one of the growth of state power, which took place apart from religion and came to dominate religion.[5] Whatever account to which one subscribes, the fact remains that the sovereign state won and religious authority lost, yielding the arrangement that became the sovereign state system, the subject of contemporary international relations theory.

What does it mean to say that religious authority lost? First, it means that the pope's transnational authority lost much of its temporal relevance and became more purely spiritual. This is the privatization of religion about which Elshtain wrote in *Sovereignty*. No longer would the pope arbitrate wars, excommunicate kings and queens, release the king's or queen's subjects from obedience, or play an active part in the diplomacy and wars of Italian city-states.[6] By and large, the pope ceased to wield authority over rulers, who had come to wield supremacy within their territory, or sovereignty.

Second, religious authorities were largely subordinated to political authorities within states. Historian of the Reformation Euan Cameron has written that churches were little but "departments of state" by the middle of the seventeenth century.[7] Protestant churches often came under the direct control of princes and kings, whether in a friendly fashion in Germany or through the brutal seizure performed by Henry VIII in England. But Catholic churches were increasingly coming under royal control, too. The French king asserted "Gallican liberties" vis-à-vis the pope and did so with the support of the French bishops, who wanted to curtail the pope's authority. The Spanish king asserted sharp control over the Church, as did the Spanish and Portuguese crowns within New World colonies, where they asserted the "patronato real." True, the symbiotic character of medieval church–state relations partially remained. In France, for instance, the king actively supported the Church and acted to uphold its religious monopoly, even expelling Huguenots from the country. But the overwhelming trend of the period—all across the Continent—was the growth of state power and the relative decline of the temporal power of the Christian churches.

This long historical trend can also be captured through an idea that has become popular among scholars in several disciplines: the migration of the holy. The thesis seems to have been launched by the great Catholic theologian Henri de Lubac in his book *Corpus Mysticum*, which he wrote just after World War II.[8] In his research into medieval theology, de Lubac noticed a transformation in the notion of the Body of Christ. First, it had meant the consecrated host—the actual body and blood of Christ in the Mass. Then, during the high Middle Ages, it also came to mean the Church as a body of people or an institution. From there, the concept migrated to the modern state, where it became secularized as the body politic yet retained the sacredness and the attendant claim on the loyalty of the members.

It is a theological story strongly echoed in Elshtain's work—and one that matches what happened in the transformation of the relationship between the Church and political authority from medieval to modern times. Others, who have espoused this thesis or something quite like it, include political philosopher Sheldon Wolin, medievalist Ernst Kantorowicz, theologian William Cavanaugh, theologian Chad Pecknold, and historian John Bossy.[9] In a chapter of his book *Christianity and Politics* entitled "Towards Hobbesian Bodies," Pecknold draws the reader's attention to the famous drawing that appears on the front cover of the

Penguin edition of Hobbes's *Leviathan*. In it, a giant human being, the Leviathan, is composed of scores of tiny human beings—thus he incorporates them into his body. Whereas once it was thought that Christ incorporated human persons into his body as members, now the state claims to do so.[10]

RELIGION'S ABSENCE IN MODERN INTERNATIONAL RELATIONS

Those philosophers who are considered founders of today's international relations traditions, both realist and liberal, wrote roughly during this period of consolidating state sovereignty, especially if we extend it to 1800, and largely incorporated the secularizing historical trends into their theories. Following Michael Doyle's *Ways of War and Peace*, I consider Hobbes, Machiavelli, and Rousseau the founders of realism during this period, and Kant, Locke, and Adam Smith the founders of liberalism.[11] To say that they incorporated secularism means that (1) they described international relations as if ecclesial authorities wielded little control; (2) they generally thought that this was a good thing, either explicitly advocating and celebrating the loss of churches' temporal powers or else just ignoring the churches; and (3) they espoused a morality of international relations that paid little heed to the authoritative teachings of churches and was largely based on autonomous reason. Informing their thinking were the lessons that they learned from their historical context. Whether or not it is true that the wars of early modern Europe were really fought over religion, most of these thinkers thought that religion was a chief cause of war and should therefore be privatized and taken out of politics. This perceived lesson greatly shaped their adherence to secularism. Not all of them were atheists, but all of them adhered to the kind of secularism that I have been describing.

Machiavelli looked around him and saw warring city-states and yearned that Italy might be unified in a glorious republic. He thought that the Church was a problem. It taught a religion that was enfeebling and prevented political leaders from taking needed manly action. The

Church itself, he thought, was little more than another political actor, engaging in the same kind of conniving, manipulative, and sometimes cruel behavior that other leaders of city-states exhibited. Why should it be taken seriously as a religious entity? Better to keep its ecclesiology out of politics. Then, Machiavelli took a momentous turn in the development of modern moral thinking (or so argues Jacques Maritain in his 1942 essay, "The End of Machiavellianism"[12]) when he counseled statesmen sometimes to do what is not good. Machiavelli did not reject morality per se or offer any philosophical arguments as to why it was not valid. Rather he counseled statesmen not to be moral when it was necessary and in so doing rejected the classical tradition of Plato, Aristotle, and Aquinas, all of whom would never have agreed to such a thing. Machiavelli was not a consequentialist, but he did lay the foundations for an enduring theme of realism—namely, that moral absolutes cannot be adhered to consistently in matters of statecraft.

Through the eyes of faith, figures like St. Catherine of Siena saw things differently. During the late fourteenth century she became an advocate of the Church's authority, during a time of nasty wars among Italian city-states in which allies of the pope did their own share of nasty things, like killing all the inhabitants of a city. She told skeptical friends, though, that even if the pope and his friends did not seem very holy at times, the pope was still the pope and had the spiritual authority of the successor of St. Peter, and thus ought to be protected and even situated in Rome. She became a player in the politics of the time and was instrumental in bringing Pope Gregory XI back home to Rome from Avignon. Like Machiavelli, she valued masculinity and encouraged Pope Gregory to be a "manly man" and to go back home to Rome over the opposition of French cardinals. Unlike Machiavelli, though, she saw the pope as more than just another politician.

Hobbes wrote during the time of the English Civil War—largely a religious war, arguably—and also yearned for stability (security and stability have always been big themes for realists). He was also the translator of Thucydides's *Peloponnesian Wars*, the Ur-source of realism. As Elshtain described so well in *Sovereignty*, in *Leviathan* Hobbes advocated that political authority be concentrated in the hands of a single ruler (or body of rulers) and that the churches be utterly subordinated to this single ruler. He did not ignore religion (people argue about whether he was a religious believer), and *Leviathan* is full of scriptural references and arguments. But he envisioned politics without the influence of religious actors, especially bishops. In the beginning of *Leviathan*, he constructs his argument for political authority, beginning with the laws of matter in motion, thus resting the authority of the state on scientific naturalism and not on the ordination of God or the requirements of the common good. He thereby rejected the Aristotelian-Thomist tradition of moral reasoning.

Realists in the twentieth century carry on these commitments. In 1962, Hans Morgenthau wrote: "The moral problem of politics is posed by the inescapable discrepancy between the commands of Christian teaching, of Christian ethics, and the requirements of political success. It is impossible, if I may put it in somewhat extreme and striking terms, to be a successful politician and a good Christian." Morgenthau goes on, "I would . . . maintain that it is particularly difficult to be a Christian in politics, because the aim of man in politics is to dominate another man, to use man as an instrument, as a means to his ends; and this is a direct denial of Judaeo-Christian ethics. The political act is in a specific, particularly acute sense incompatible with Christian ethics, in a sense in which the non-political act is free."[13]

Here we can see the commitments of Hobbes and Machiavelli carried forward. Traditional morality, Christian morality, cannot govern international affairs (or even politics in general). It cannot be expected to be followed, leaving us with a form of consequentialism, "the morality of the national interest." Generally, Morgenthau sought to describe international politics, indeed to develop a scientific theory of it, on the basis of states pursuing power. Religious actors were not influential on this pursuit, nor, largely, were religious ideas.

THE RETURN OF RELIGION?

It might seem that Reinhold Niebuhr, the twentieth-century theologian whom Morgenthau called "the father of us all," might be an exception to realist thinking about religion. He was a theologian, after all. Elshtain invoked his thought in *Just War against Terror: The Burden of American Power in a Violent World* (2003), but in my view she ought to have found more tensions between his analysis and hers. Unlike Elshtain, Niebuhr's thought leaves little more room for religious influence on international affairs than that of other realists. He also thought power was pervasive. He thought that the pursuit of moral goals beyond power would come to ruin, ironically, in a world of sin. Niebuhr did not think that moral norms could or should govern political behavior in any absolute sense; in effect, he counseled states to pursue the least sinful form of action, a morality similar, if not identical, to consequentialism. In both his description and prescriptions for politics, then, he was little different from secular realists.[14] Elshtain, by contrast, accorded morality a far greater role, both descriptively and prescriptively.

As any student of international relations knows, liberal theorists have thought and still think that international norms, liberal domestic regimes, and moral ideas can mitigate the effects of anarchy and the pursuit of power and allow a greater degree of peace and justice to prevail. But they have accorded religion little more role than have realists. The liberals of the Enlightenment did not think religious actors played an important role in politics and said little about them. As for the moral teachings of religion, these were now largely reduced to precepts of reason, norms that any human mind could discern through the exercise of rationality—"religion within the limits of reason alone," as Kant put it. They, too, reflected back on the religious wars and thought that traditional religion was irrational and divisive. As it was then, so it is in the present day.

Liberalism and realism are the dominant traditions of international relations theory today and each have a pedigree of centuries behind them. There are, of course, other traditions. Marxism was prominent for a time, but it needs no pointing out that it did not leave much room for the independent influence of religion. It might seem that constructivism, with its stress on ideas, identities, and culture, might make more room for religion. Theoretically it does. But neither Alexander Wendt, the school's founding father, nor the seminal volume of essays, *The Culture of National Security*, gave play to religion.[15] Peter Katzenstein, the editor of that volume, however, has done much since to advance the study of religion in international relations theory and has done so broadly out of constructivist commitments. Jack Snyder's edited volume, *Religion and International Relations Theory*, contains essays that seek to theorize religion and international relations, though it is not centrally constructivist in its bent.[16]

And yet, a small but vibrant and growing field of scholars in religion and international relations is seeking to overcome the limitations of secularist assumptions and to theorize religion and politics. This effort is important if for no other reason than that religion has come to matter a great deal in contemporary global politics. In our book *God's Century: Resurgent Religion and Global Politics*,[17] Monica Duffy Toft, Timothy Samuel Shah, and I make the case that the last half century has witnessed a resurgence in the influence of religion and politics in every region of the globe and within every religion. Religion's political influence is diverse, including its impact on the last generation's wave of democratization, on peace settlements, on transitional justice, on terrorism, on civil war, on women's rights, and on many other issues.

Religion also matters a great deal to U.S. foreign policy. Examples include the Iranian Revolution of 1979, the crisis that it caused in U.S. foreign relations, and its impact on the alignment of the Middle East was a direct result of the rise of Islam—a phenomenon little understood by the Central Intelligence Agency prior to the revolution. Religion was critical to the Afghan resistance that helped defeat the incursive Soviet army in the 1980s—and to the subsequent rise of the Taliban in the 1990s, which was crucial in sheltering Osama bin Laden. Religion was also critical in toppling the Soviet empire in a different sense—through the democratic revolutions in Eastern Europe, which, in turn, were sparked by Pope John Paul II's pilgrimages in communist Poland. It goes without saying that religion was behind the attacks of September 11, 2001, which spawned a war in Afghanistan that continues through this day and contributed greatly to the United States' decision to invade Iraq in 2003. Religion then fueled a civil war in Iraq that preoccupied the administration of President George W. Bush and lingered into the Obama years. The resurgence of religion has reshaped and intensified the conflict in Israel/Palestine. Religion is also behind the rise of the Islamic State of Iraq and Syria, a steadily growing menace.

All of this influence of religion Elshtain understood. The field of international relations is only beginning to comprehend it. The gap between the headlines, which reveal religion to be persistently influential, and scholarship, remains substantial. The field is ripe for younger scholars to follow in her footsteps and close the gap.

NOTES

1. This portion of the chapter draws from the unpublished report, *Religion and International Relations: A Primer for Research* (The Report of the Working Group on International Relations and Religion of the Mellon Initiative on Religion across the Disciplines, University of Notre Dame, 2013).

2. Quoted from David Maland, *Europe in the Seventeenth Century* (London: Macmillan, 1966), 16.

3. Charles Tilly, *Coercion, Capital, and European States, AD 990–1990* (Oxford: Basil Blackwell, 1992); Hendrik Spruyt, *The Sovereign State and Its Competitors* (Princeton, NJ: Princeton University Press, 1994); Brian Downing, *The Military Revolution and Political Change: Origins of Democracy and Autocracy in Early Modern Europe* (Princeton, NJ: Princeton University Press, 1992).

4. My view of Westphalia can be found in Daniel Philpott, *Revolutions in Sovereignty: How Ideas Shaped Modern International Relations* (Princeton, NJ: Princeton University Press, 2001), chap. 5. For a challenge and a good review of the literature, see Daniel H. Nexon, *The Struggle for Power in Early Modern Europe: Religious Conflict, Dynastic Empires, and International Change* (Princeton, NJ: Princeton University Press, 2009), chap. 8.

5. William T. Cavanaugh, *The Myth of Religious Violence: Secular Ideology and the Roots of Modern Conflict* (Oxford: Oxford University Press, 2009).

6. This last decline is somewhat exaggerated, for the pope would continue to be a diplomatic player in Italy to some extent up through the 1929 Lateran Treaty, which established the Vatican as a sovereign state, but after Westphalia his role greatly diminished.

7. Euan Cameron, *The European Reformation* (Oxford: Oxford University Press, 1991), 153.

8. Henri Cardinal de Lubac, S.J., *Corpus Mysticum: The Eucharist and the Church in the Middle Ages*, trans. Gemma Simmonds, CJ, with Richard Price and Christopher Stephens; ed. Laurence Paul Hemming and Susan Frank Parsons (London: SCM Press, 2006).

9. Sheldon Wolin, *Politics and Vision: Continuity and Vision in Western Political Thought* (Princeton, NJ: Princeton University Press, 2006); Ernst Kantorowicz, *The King's Two Bodies: A Study of Medieval Political Theology* (Princeton,

NJ: Princeton University Press, 1997); William T. Cavanaugh, *Migrations of the Holy: God, State, and the Political Meaning of the Church* (Grand Rapids, MI: Eerdmans, 2011); C. C. Pecknold, *Christianity and Politics: A Brief Guide to the History* (Eugene, OR: Cascade, 2010); John Bossy, "Unrethinking the Sixteenth-Century Wars of Religion," in *Belief in History: Innovative Approaches to European and American Religion*, ed. Thomas Kselman (Notre Dame, IN: University of Notre Dame Press, 1991), 278.

10. Pecknold, *Christianity and Politics*, 69–83.

11. Michael Doyle, *Ways of War and Peace: Realism, Liberalism, and Socialism* (New York: W. W. Norton, 1997).

12. Jacques Maritain, "The End of Machiavellianism," *Review of Politics* 4, no. 1 (1942): 1–33.

13. This and the above quote are cited in Ivan Strenski, *Why Politics Can't Be Freed from Religion* (West Sussex, UK: Wiley-Blackwell, 2010), 126–27.

14. See, for instance, Reinhold Niebuhr, *Moral Man and Immoral Society: A Study in Ethics and Politics* (Louisville, KY: Westminster John Knox Press, 2013); Niebuhr, *Christian Realism and Political Problems* (New York: Scribner, 1953).

15. Alexander Wendt, *Social Theory of International Politics* (Cambridge: Cambridge University Press, 1999); Peter J. Katzenstein, ed., *The Culture of National Security: Norms and Identity in World Politics* (New York: Columbia University Press, 1996).

16. Jack Snyder, ed., *Religion and International Relations Theory* (New York: Columbia University Press, 2011).

17. For the resurgence thesis, see Monica Duffy Toft, Daniel Philpott, and Timothy Samuel Shah, *God's Century: Resurgent Religion and Global Politics* (New York: W. W. Norton, 2011).

PART III

NATIONS AND CITIZENS
AT PEACE AND WAR

Introduction

Marc LiVecche

In the dark days after the planes hit, Jean Elshtain mused to a friend: "Now we are reminded of what governments are for." She forever after insisted that 9/11 made plain that "the primary responsibility of government is to provide for basic security—ordinary civic peace" (*JWT*, 46). This responsibility, a burden really, she understood to be a divine mandate. "This does not mean," she cautioned, "that every government and every public official is godly but, rather, that each is charged with a solemn responsibility for which there is divine warrant . . . a *political* ethic is an ethic of responsibility."[1]

Following the exemplary temper of any of her several heroes—Augustine, Camus, Bonhoeffer, Tom Doniphon, or Václav Havel, among them—Elshtain insisted that human beings, Christians chiefly, cannot, *must* not, remain aloof to the conditions of history.[2] Against the depravity, bloodshed, and injustice of the present age, the security and peace necessary for human beings to enjoy basic human goods requires a basis upon which to reside, and its preservation, if in the last resort human willfulness means nothing else will work, requires force. For Elshtain, the just war tradition shepherds this force toward just expression. But it is no easy row to hoe.

The studies in this part III serve as able guides to help illuminate both the sophistication of Elshtain's use of the just war tradition—as she "freely mingles theological, ethical, philosophical, and political categories and concerns" (*WAW*, ix) to address the problems of history—and the daunting complexity of the very task itself. Each chapter taps into key dimensions of Elshtain's scholarly persona.

In chapter 11, Nicholas Rengger importantly focuses on her commitments to Christian realism, particularly as it draws our attention to questions regarding the possibility of simultaneous commitment to both the sovereignty of God and of the state. As with another of her heroes, Reinhold Niebuhr, Rengger rightly grounds Elshtain's Christian realism in Augustine's exhortation against "moral perfectionism" and the drive to build corresponding political systems. Here we see the stress on Christian *realism*: a political vision at once anti-utopian and pluralistic with regard to political form. This vision emphasizes power and interests; that recognizes the human tendency to war, even if it does not theologically ground this in anthropological dualism; and that commits to a view of the world as it *is* and not as we long for it to be.

At the same time, Elshtain was equally insistent on a *Christian* realism by which the theological qualifier enjoins the recognition that moral claims are indeed *real* claims. Loath to extinguish the charitable and humanitarian impulses of the human heart, Elshtain's moral realism refused to collapse "interests" into a kind of gluttonous self-obsession that clamors for our own security and material prosperity to the exclusion of our assailed neighbors. Any nation, Elshtain opined, that believes it has responsibility *only* for the survival of its own people and none for those outside its borders is quite possibly a nation not much worthy of survival.

For Elshtain, such commitments counseled against withdrawal or retreat by the United States. Believing neither that a hands-off approach to international affairs by the United States would ever be reciprocated by aggressor nations nor that vacuums wouldn't be filled by bad guys, Elshtain posited what she informally called the "Spiderman ethic"—with great power comes great responsibility. What this rendered was a view of American exceptionalism characterized by an exceptional responsibility grounded—as Rengger quotes her with added emphasis—by two truths: "equal regard is the foundation of our own polity and we are the only superpower," and, as such, "America bears the responsibility to help guarantee . . . international stability, *whether much of the world wants it or not.*"

It's a provocative notion and crucial to understanding Elshtain's advocacy of the use of U.S. power, particularly in view of intervention and a responsibility to protect. But Rengger insists it's not without its problems. In light of Elshtain's commitment to limited state sovereignty, Rengger argues her benevolent view of the American use of power is hard to square with her notions of God's sovereignty. To explore this tension, Rengger brings Elshtain into conversation with John Milbank.

In chapter 12, John Carlson allows for continued review of Elshtain's ideas about intervention and similar responsibilities through reflecting on how her casting of "just war as politics" makes room for a more expansive use of force vis-à-vis those who view the just war tradition primarily as a means to constrain the state's belligerence through narrow limits. Detailing a historical development in Elshtain's thought, Carlson argues that her innovative approach to just war politics is "the outgrowth of the seeds she planted" in her early *Women and War* (1987). Guiding us through that work, Carlson explores Elshtain's "abiding interests in how war sharpens our understanding of citizenship, virtue, and politics" and the manner in which she reconsiders the tropes of "the beautiful soul" and the "just warrior" to overturn "the various antinomies that politics artificially establishes and preserves," such as man/woman, public/private, and war/peace.

Against such false, even contrived, antipodes Elshtain proffers to us the "chastened patriot." Even in resisting her endorsement of the aforementioned "Spiderman ethic" as perhaps too glib, Carlson is affirming of such a thoughtful patriot who, in Elshtain's crafting, "seeks to bring together particularist civic identities with more universal sets of moral commitments." Even as he notes Elshtain's own "forceful patriotic voice" was sometimes perceived as overly strident, Carlson insists her ideal of the "chastened patriot" informed and sustained "the deep

scrutiny she cast upon U.S. conduct in several wars" and her own "patriotic commitment to the United States as it exercises global responsibilities to those whose human dignity is trampled underfoot by oppressive
governments."

Focusing on *Just War against Terror*, in chapter 13 Chris Brown
explores the unique battle space created by that war. Situated between
the familiar images of any reasonably well-ordered society policing
criminals and of the conventional battle space created between contending nations, the neither/nor intermediate space of nonstate actors—and
the military and surveillance technologies deployed to fight them
—introduces an array of new challenges to the burden of using U.S.
power in a violent world. Brown makes his own substantial contributions to ethical discussions surrounding complex issues, such as the use
of drones, but his careful dissection of the issue, his nuanced judgments
and attention to detail, and his critique of those without such care calls
to mind Elshtain's own scholarly approach.

Elshtain, ever the careful, plodding, painstaking casuist, Brown
praises, who always insisted that the first task was to get as accurate an
accounting of the facts on the ground as possible, was never one to give
in to "the desire to see a grey world in black and white terms." This
scholarly disposition not infrequently erupted in a certain impatience
against those who failed to respond appropriately to moral evils, such as
Islamist terrorism. Her invective naturally hit hard against the terrorists,
but Elshtain held plenty in reserve for use against her academic peers
and ecclesiastical leadership who rationalized terror as payback for the
failings of the United States, or for those unable, or unwilling, to distinguish between terrorists (who refuse to discriminate and deliberately
target the innocent) and American warfighters (who exercise propor-
tional and discriminate restraint—even at enormous personal risk).

She would also have approved of the assessment that though global
terrorism might not threaten the West's physical existence, it nevertheless poses very real existential threats: the operation of extremists
in our communities, the seduction and recruitment of our young, the
radicalization of mosques—each individually and collectively work to
poison interfaith relationships, sow distrust among neighbors, and hin-
der a nation's zeal to welcome strangers to our shores. This, in turn,

desiccates civil society, that essential space between individuals and the state. Thus, though not a threat to life itself, global terrorism *is* a threat to a *way* of life and hamstrings the peace, order, and justice that make human flourishing possible.

In his reflection in chapter 14 on just war as "commanded war"— that is, commanded by "moral law"—Michael Walzer captures vintage Elshtain in a single sentence: "How could one watch Nazi aggression in Europe . . . and choose to be neutral?" With this sentiment perhaps in mind, Walzer, the morning prior to delivering the study published in this volume, commented to a gathering of doctoral students that growing up in the shadow of the *Shoah* permanently inoculated him against pacifism.[3] He goes on to wonder if a war to stop a massacre is deemed to be just, how can it not also be considered *required?* Indeed, on numerous occasions, as he points out, Elshtain in fact asserted, "There are some things that must not be done," and she carried the assertion to its logical conclusion: "to the extent possible, these things should be stopped."

With many of Elshtain's heroes having been involved in the fight against the twentieth century's fascist and communist regimes, who swallowed dozens of millions in their crematoria fires and lime pits, she affirmed Camus's injunction: "It is essential to condemn what must be condemned, but swiftly and firmly" (*JWT*, vii). To say "firmly" is to insist this condemnation must be backed by more than words. Those kinds of folks who enjoy genocide cannot usually be talked out of it with prayers, gentle coaxing, or harsh language—they most often have to be *forced* out of it. If soft power cannot get those who are murdering the innocent to stand down, then hard power is necessary to knock them down. But, of course, if stopping genocide is a good thing to do, then someone has to actually do it.

Speaking to her own tradition, in which many insist that such belligerence may well be the business of the government, but it is not the business of Christians, Elshtain argued against the suggestion that though God ordained the sword for the maintenance of just order, he simultaneously called Christians away from such business in order to be some alternative, peaceable kingdom. If the peaceable kingdom were a viable alternative to hard coercion, she presumed, then surely God would have ordained such a kingdom *instead* of, rather than *alongside*, the government's sword. Given that God indeed ordained the sword, one must infer, therefore, that the sword is necessary. And if the sword is necessary, then *somebody* has to wield it. For anyone to then say, "Let it be you and not me," makes such a person, and by extension the peaceable kingdom, parasitic—because it cannot remain in a world in which their good hosts do not bear arms. The idea that Christians should allow others to dirty their hands while keeping their Christian souls clean was, in Elshtain's view, morally abhorrent.[4]

Finally, in chapter 15, James Turner Johnson positions his and Elshtain's views of sovereignty side by side to examine whether gaps remain to let light pass through. It's the kind of endeavor that excited Elshtain: the coming together of engaged and engaging minds in a spirit of mutual edification. She liked that sort of thing, she reveled in it—it was the same approach she took to reading books or watching movies— she found in everything a conversation, she was always surrounded by a host of interlocutors.

There is space to be measured, Johnson observes, between his and Elshtain's approach to the study of war. Elshtain, he suggests, was involved in the cultivation of memory—revealing and articulating a particular understanding of historical events that shapes collective purposes and identities—hers was, he posits, a looking back in order to always lean *forward*, her eyes were most often focused ahead. Johnson places himself in history as one seeking understanding drawn from the factual records, examining events in their own context. Johnson takes care not to make these different approaches starkly binary—they are always marbled one with the other, but they do serve different ends and mark Elshtain's style of doing political theory, and also Johnson's vocation as a historian of moral traditions.

There's much to commend this observation. The just war tradition, in Elshtain's view, perceives the human soul as a work to be realized. In the face of evil, just war, trading on our Western cultural patrimony by which we learned what is to be abhorred and what is to be loved, harnesses and deploys our resolve to rise against injustice. Elshtain understood such a disposition to be crucial for our times. Her unease at the prospect of the loss of moral memory helped to keep the terrorist attacks of 9/11 on her working mind. Elshtain feared that with the distance of time many of us would forget what that day was really like. "We shouldn't," she warned. "It was just as bad as we remember it. Our emotions at the time were not extreme: They were appropriate to the horror. Anger remains an appropriate feeling" (*JWT*, 7). But she also knew the human capacity for undomesticated vengeance. She only had to recall the "exterminationalist rhetoric" of certain elements within the United States in the 1940s, endorsing a policy of annihilation of the Japanese, to know that the martial spark, once fanned, can set the whole world alight and consume everything in its lust for retribution (*WW*, 156). The just war tradition, she asserted, is predicated on the notion that love and war can stand together, that evil—whether external to us or that with which we ourselves are complicit—can be restrained: all so that the good can be revealed before us.

Despite their different disciplines and scholarly tasks, Johnson knows he and Elshtain are wedded on this point. For both, sovereignty, rightly understood, must harken back to its Greco-Roman and medieval hinterlands, where it is understood in terms of the moral responsibility of the temporal ruler with no superior to serve the natural law and to do justice, to maintain the peace, and to keep the order for the sake of the common good. Sovereignty is a *moral* concept, and if one does not grasp this one cannot grasp Elshtain. Her concept of just war in the main (and of such things as intervention in the particular) hinges on this. And this brings us back to where we started.

Sovereignty as a moral responsibility results in a conception of political duty that includes the occasion for war. It is a hard row to hoe, indeed. Augustine, especially, understood full well the heavy burden of meting justice in this life, and Elshtain often alluded to his famous lament for the task of human judges, who cannot always know with any real certainty whether they condemn to death the innocent or the guilty but who nevertheless take up the hated necessity because the welfare of human society requires it. Perhaps less well known are his deeply moving letters to Paulinus of Nola, one of which Elshtain introduced to me long ago:

On the subject of punishing or refraining from punishment, what am I to say? It is our desire that when we decide whether or not to punish people, in either case it should contribute to their security.

These are indeed deep and obscure matters: what limit ought to be set to punishment with regard to both the nature and extent of the guilt, and also the strength of spirit the wrongdoers possess? . . . What do we do when, as often happens, punishing someone will lead to his destruction, but leaving him unpunished will lead to someone else being destroyed? In all this I confess my sins and my ignorance every day. . . . How all this makes us tremble . . . surely we are to think that the following words apply: "*Trembling and fear have come upon me and darkness has covered me, and I said, 'Who will give me wings like a dove's?' Then I will fly away and be at rest*" (Ps. 55:5–6).[5]

Cognizant of the terrible weight of it all, clearly yearning, like the philosopher judge, to simply be delivered from his necessary duties, Augustine nevertheless did not fly away—and so he judged and in his judgment he punishes where punishment seems prudentially required. Neither did Elshtain fly from her responsibilities, shirk her duties, or take the safe path. Because of this, her work represents a vocational commitment to resist evil, to do no harm, and to help where one can. And long may it result in beautiful things.

NOTES

1. Jean Bethke Elshtain, "Luther's Lamb: When and How to Fight a Just War," *Common Knowledge* 8, no. 2 (2002): 306.

2. J. Daryl Charles nicely captures the force of Elshtain's conviction on this. He writes, "It is a fundamental assumption of just war thinking, and of Elshtain's work, that human evil must be resisted when and where we have the wherewithal to do so. To fail to act is to serve as an accomplice in the evil itself"; Charles, "War, Women, and Political Wisdom," *Journal of Religious Ethics* 34, no. 2 (2006): 363.

3. Michael Walzer, "Discussion between Michael Walzer and James Turner Johnson," at the University of Chicago, October 17, 2013.

4. Some of this wording is drawn from Nigel Biggar's *In Defence of War* (Oxford: Oxford University Press, 2013), 43. Elshtain and I discussed the passage on the peaceable kingdom from a prepublication draft of the chapter in which it appears.

5. Augustine, *Political Writings*, ed. E. M. Atkins and R. J. Dodaro (Cambridge: Cambridge University Press, 2001), 23–24.

CHAPTER ELEVEN

Two Sovereigns?

Violence and the Ambiguities of Jean Bethke Elshtain's Christian Realism

Nicholas Rengger

My aim in this chapter is to reflect on one particular aspect of Jean Elshtain's work over the years—her commitment to a certain form of Christian realism, in particular in the context of her Gifford Lectures on the topic of sovereignty. It raises, I think, profound questions as to the possibility of combining a commitment to, as she might herself have put it, "the sovereignty of God" with the "sovereignty of states," and it thus invites us to reflect on the character of each and what each implies. And such reflection inevitably has serious implications for how we might think about international politics in particular, and perhaps all politics in general. To do this I want to break down what I have to say into three parts. The first offers a reading of her account of the relationship between a sovereign God and the sovereign state. The second offers a reading of Christian realism and her relation to it. And the third explores what I take to be an ambiguity the previous two readings expose and assess how damaging that ambiguity is for her account. To tip my hand in advance, I suggest that Elshtain wants to hold to both God's sovereignty and to the state's sovereignty, but that the way she argues this makes it very difficult for her to do so, since her presentation of the state's sovereignty retains too much of what we might term a "strong" notion of state sovereignty. As Hobbes, perhaps most presciently, saw, the Leviathan is a "Mortall God" and it is hard to see how holding this is truly compatible with the sovereignty of an immortal God. The significance of this I will return to at the end of the chapter.

THREE SOVEREIGNS?

For Elshtain, the notion of "sovereignty" has to be read in a number of different registers.[1] And the first thing to emphasize about her account of it is that it has to be seen against the backdrop of a crucial medieval debate, the so-called realist versus nominalist debate, and to understand its significance, a small philosophico-theological detour is necessary. The debate arose out of the medieval discussion of the character of creation and in particular of the character of so-called universals, itself parasitic on the medieval understanding of ancient Platonism,[2] which held that "universals" alone are truly real, existing *ante res*—prior to particular things. Thus, for defenders of this view—the so-called realists[3] —particular things are fixed by their participation in the essence of the universally real, which is God's creation. Individual men and women, for example, participate in the general idea of "humanity," which is the relevant universal and which allowed talk of human beings at all: God in essence was, for the realists, the supreme universal. The antirealist position, however, argued that what were called universals are in fact simply names that appear *post res*—after the existence of particular things— hence the term "nominalism." Man or women, in this instance, would simply be a convenient name for things that we have deemed a relevant collective.

It is important to emphasize that this debate was, in the medieval period, a debate between Christian theologians. It was not that the nominalists were not Christians, quite the contrary, but they did want to assert—as against the traditional assumptions of the time—that if God was all powerful, He could (if He so chose) change the nature of the universe as a consequence of a decree emanating from an unfettered divine will. In which case, there could be no eternal or universal essences that particular things participated in. To suppose there was threatened to make God subordinate to aspects of his creation (or so they claimed)—the omnipotence of God could only be vindicated if there were not extramental universals.

However, the effect of nominalism according to Elshtain (and there are not dissimilar arguments in recent work by Michael Allen Gillespie—expressly thanked in the acknowledgements of *Sovereignty* [*S*]—Charles Taylor, and John Milbank[4]) was to begin the process of separating out created order from constructed order and in the process to open a space for an increasingly voluntaristic, instrumental conception of human agency, which paves the way for modern natural science and which also introduced distinctions between the "natural" and the "supernatural" that had not been present in previous thought. This also produces a notion of order (including political order) as the creation of human reason—rather than the discovery by human reason of a pre-given pattern of order—which notion becomes central to the emerging political ideas of the Renaissance and early modern periods, which ideas reach a culmination of sorts in Hobbes. It is the origin of the tradition of thought in the West that depended, in Michael Oakeshott's phrase, on "will and artifice."[5]

Elshtain foregrounds the rise of nominalism in her account and suggests that the characteristic of the modern state "sovereign"—its "absolute" character and complete autonomy—echo the classical treatment of God's sovereignty asserted by nominalist theologians in the Middle Ages. Thus theological understandings migrated into early modern politics, and, she then argues, the move continues from the autonomy and absolute character of the state to the autonomous and absolute character of individual political agency in the modern world. Elshtain offers a reversal of Gillespie, but very much works with the same tools. For Gillespie, nominalism emphasizes individual autonomy and voluntarism, and from that we get the early modern state and the states system that goes with it. Elshtain's picture is rather that the theological underpinnings migrate first to the community and then to the individual. As she puts it, "A streamlined version of my thesis would go like this: as sovereign state is to sovereign God, so sovereign selves are to sovereign states. Given that sovereignty in the political sense 'named' self-determination for a territorial collective entity, it is altogether unsurprising this logic of sovereignty came unbound and migrated, becoming attached more and more to notions of the self" (*S*, 159).

In the main part of *Sovereignty*, she fleshes this thesis out to admirable effect, drawing on both classical texts in political thought and—a characteristic Elshtainean device—aspects of contemporary and popular culture. Yet, like Gillespie and to a lesser extent Taylor, however, Elshtain is not wholly critical of the "sovereignty" that nominalism made. She tells us at the end of chapter 7:

> Political sovereignty is a great historic achievement. It helped to bind millions of people to a particular "place" creating a civic home for which they had direct responsibility. In its constitutional form, it provided and provides for a type of civic identity not reducible to the terms of race, gender, ethnicity or religion. . . . In its pluralist, constitutional forms of limited government and recognition that there are prepolitical dignities that belong to human beings as such and that the state can either honor or dishonor, sovereignty offers about as 'good a deal' as human beings can reasonably expect in a world riven by conflict and confronted daily with the specter of wars of all sorts. (*S*, 158)

Whether this is a wholly consistent position, given her general argument, is something I shall return to later, but it is certainly a well-made one. But Elshtain is most certainly critical of the second migration, the shift to the "sovereign self." The later parts of *Sovereignty* are often witheringly critical of this move. Without denying that self-sovereignty in some hands (Emerson, she particularly mentions) can be ennobling, she thinks that in general it is not. Especially in its radical forms, she thinks it wholly misguided. She illustrates what, in her view, is wrong with the radical sovereign self with a quotation from Cormac McCarthy's novel *No Country for Old Men*. At a conference, the main protagonist of the novel falls into conversation with a clearly "liberal" woman who is being very critical of the "right." Finally, (Elshtain quotes):

She told me: I don't like the way this country is headed. I want my granddaughter to be able to have an abortion. And I said well mam I don't think you got any worries about the way the country is headed. The way I see it going I don't have much doubt she'll be able to have an abortion. I'm going to say not only will she be able to have an abortion; she'll be able to have you put to sleep. Which pretty much ended the conversation. (S, 203–4)

Elshtain's point is to emphasize that the woman's language of "self-sovereignty" is one of control over self, complete self-ownership, a view she regards as characteristic perhaps of all claims to self-sovereignty, and she relates it to notions like eugenics (and now positive genetic enhancement), the debate over abortion (obviously), and forms of radical identity politics (such as radical feminism). In some respect this echoes her earlier critiques of some forms of state sovereignty, though it is expressed with more polemical edge. The point she emphasizes in her final chapter is that sovereignty has to come with limits if it is to be legitimate at all. For, as she puts it:

Personal autonomy (rightly understood) and national sovereignty are achievements rather than presuppositions. We presuppose—we believe—God is sovereign (and this for hundreds of reasons), but we cannot assume a nation-state is sovereign until it demonstrates its ability to be independent from the protection of another state, to treat its citizens decently, and to foster a vibrant civil society: sovereignty as responsibility. This marks a state as a mature member of the international community. Something analogous is also true for the person—persons are not born as mature members of society, but they can grow to become such. (S, 228)

In particular, Elshtain thinks, persons—and in some respects also collectivities—are relational. In an earlier chapter she had discussed Dietrich Bonhoeffer's critique of Kant's theory of autonomy precisely for denying this and for emphasizing the independent and absolute character of individual moral agency. And in some respects she can be read as seeing Kant and Nietzsche as perhaps the two most powerful

"philosophers of self-sovereignty" (her argument here parallels Gillespie's), who forget the relational aspect of sovereignty. Though she
doesn't quote it, she might agree with the wonderfully polemical critique of Kant from Iris Murdoch's *The Sovereignty of Good*, to the effect
that "Kant's man had already received a glorious incarnation nearly a
century earlier in the work of Milton: his proper name is Lucifer."[6]
    But for international relations (and for the academic field of interna-
tional relations) this has profound implications. International relations
in the modern world—and indeed a good deal of politics in general—is
effectively a hybrid between a system built on will and artifice yoked
together with at least a rhetoric that effectively assumes older "realist"
transcendent conceptions. One can see this in many respects throughout
the seventeenth and eighteenth centuries, where the likes of Grotius
and Vattel (Kant's "sorry comforters") consistently try to fuse a voluntaristic sense of human agency with a sense of transcendent truth. And
the whole history of the idea of natural law from the thirteenth century
to the present is clearly marked by this dilemma. Hobbes is in this, as
in many other things, the most far-sighted and the most consistent of
his contemporaries in refusing the hybrid and saying point-blank that
(for example) the "Mortall God," the Leviathan, *creates* what is good and
what is just, rather than, as the (now intellectually hollowed out) tradition of natural law would suggest, *discovers* what is good and what is just.
    By the nineteenth and twentieth centuries, the hybrid would be
ever flimsier, yet increasingly central to debates about international
relations.[7] What Michael Barnett has recently called the "humanitarian
big bang,"[8] essentially the rise of "compassion" in the late eighteenth
century and after, is absolutely saturated with the ambiguities the hybrid
creates, and that remains true, I think, of—for example—human rights
activism today. Can one coherently have a fully and only constructed
and artificial sense of agency and society and a belief that anything is
universal? This surely raises, at the very least, a powerful problematic for
those in the contemporary international order—most of all for those in
the West, at least, who wish to hold onto both. Inasmuch as the world
of international relations *is* a hybrid, therefore, Elshtain's portrayal of
sovereignty would seem to suggest that the "real" world of international
relations is the "Hobbesian" one (or at least the nominalist one) of the

radical sovereign—though sovereign states, to be sure, rather than selves, and the rhetoric of obligation and responsibility that dominates so much of contemporary international relations is empty: a realist ghost in the nominalist machine. But if so, wherein does the role of the "Sovereign God" lie?

CHRISTIAN REALISM

Before I come back to this, however, I want to turn to Elshtain's presentation of Christian realism—and her identification of her own position with it. To do this I need to offer a general presentation of what this view is thought to entail, and the obvious place to look for that, of course, is at the work of Reinhold Niebuhr. It is certainly not the case that Niebuhr is the only Christian realist, but he was the person who in a sense defined the term, and so it seems reasonable to start with him.

To put it very briefly, I think Niebuhr's "realism" emerges principally out of his encounter with two of his formative influences: his role as pastor and preacher in Detroit in the 1920s and his ongoing debates with his brother, Helmut (H. Richard) Niebuhr. The former experience, as is well known, radicalized Niebuhr and led him to take on board the various aspects of socialist and even Marxist ideas that marked his first major book, *Moral Man and Immoral Society*. To this should be added the sense Niebuhr had—gleaned very much from his Detroit days—that it is not cynicism or even the propensity for evil itself that is the biggest problem for human societies, but rather the persistent self-image people have that they are doing good when manifestly they are not. As he once remarked to his future biographer, June Bingham, "Most of the evil in this world . . . does not come from evil people, it comes from people who consider themselves good."[9]

Niebuhr thus embarks on a persistent critique of what he would term the "Utopian" images people have of themselves and their societies. In *Moral Man and Immoral Society*, this takes on a very critical "socialist" form, but it persists even after Niebuhr has turned his back on the progressivism that was his intellectual and spiritual origin and embraced a much more explicitly "theological" orientation to his work, from the late 1930s onwards (after he received an invitation to deliver a set of Gifford Lectures). However, this socialist form turns outward as Niebuhr becomes increasingly convinced that the source of the "crisis" facing human kind is not merely American idolatry and hypocrisy but rather will to power in its most damaging form and on a global scale. As he puts it in his introductory essay to the inaugural edition of the journal he founded, *Christianity and Crisis*:

> We are well aware of the sins of all nations, including our own, which have contributed to the chaos of our era. We know to what degree totalitarianism represents a false answer to our own unsolved problems—political, economic, spiritual. Yet we believe the task of defending the rich inheritance of our civilization to be an imperative one, however much we might desire that our social system was more worthy of defence.[10]

This view bespoke a belief in active involvement in the world and its struggles, rather than a refusal of that world. And this belief was founded, I think, on two imperatives: the first, a desire to avoid both the simple progressivism of his early opponents in the Social Gospel movement and the pessimism and "tragic" view of action he had imbibed to a large extent in the 1920s, and to which, in his darker moments, he was still prone; the second, an engagement with, but dissent from, the position his brother, H. Richard Niebuhr, had developed in dialogue with him for much of their adult life.

This part of the story is by far the most complex and is discussed well by Cox in his biography of Niebuhr. I only mean to gesture towards its significance here. Simply, Niebuhr had always inclined towards the activism of the progressives and H. Richard had not. As the 1930s went on, Niebuhr's progressivism waned as did his activism, but in the fight against totalitarianism he found another cause to engage him. But at the same time, he had been provoked by his brother's (sympathetic) critique—that his ethics lacked theological bite and that his "activism" was almost a denial of the promises of God—to ground his position much more theologically than he had done before. This coincided with the invitation to deliver the Gifford Lectures in Edinburgh for 1939 (the first set were delivered April/May, the second October 1939). He and H. Richard had argued their respective cases in print a couple of years before—over the Manchurian crisis—and the Gifford Lectures provided Niebuhr with the best platform possible to further ground his evolving ideas in a new theological context.

Thus, in the two volumes of *The Nature and Destiny of Man*[11] Niebuhr develops the central ideas that underpin what becomes "Christian realism," a theology of history as the meeting place of sin and the grace of God, where human agency is possible but flawed, where structures shape our actions but do not determine them, and where hope is possible but utopia is not: a world where, as Niebuhr was later to put it (in *The Children of Light and the Children of Darkness*): "The Children of Light must be armed with the wisdom of the children of darkness, but remain free from their malice."[12] As Yale's R. L. Calhoun remarked in his powerful (and largely laudatory) review in the *Journal of Religion*, "In temper and method and results this is the work of a mind in which liberal Protestantism and radical but sophisticated Paulinism, both deep rooted and long in fierce conflict, are moving towards reconciliation."[13]

As Robin Lovin has remarked in a recent book,[14] Niebuhr's Christian realism united three different realisms: (1) a political realism that is profoundly anti-utopian and pluralist with regard to political form, emphasizing power and interest; (2) a moral realism that argues that moral claims are genuine claims (and thus not reducible to interest or power) and that among human interests are the pursuance of such moral claims—though not, of course, in a utopian direction; and (3) a theological realism that asserts, over and above the first two, the reality of God, of sin, and of grace.

In his mature thought, Niebuhr tries to steer a course between a simple *machtpolitik*—though he is often accused of succumbing to that —and various different forms of progressivism and utopianism that are echoes of that self-deluding idolatry that he so powerfully lacerated in moral man and immoral society. In this respect he resembles more obviously political realists like Morgenthau. But at the same time he seeks to champion the role of Christian engagement in politics in mediating human society and societies, and he rejects both the quietism of his brother and the much more fully fledged neo-orthodoxy of his great theological and ecclesiological opponent, Karl Barth. It is in the attempt to move beyond utopianism, progressivism, and quietism, or so it seems to me, that we should locate the real source of the power of Christian realism in its classical Niebuhrian form.

And it is very much this that frames Elshtain's own understanding of Christian realism. Like Niebuhr, she frames it through Augustine[15] and, like Niebuhr, thinks it facile—and dangerous—to assume a "moral perfectionism that seeks to build political systems" (*JWT*, 111),[16] and finally, like Niebuhr, she sees the Christian realist position as one that accepts the inevitability of action in a plural and divided world without denying that this brings moral costs that we must bear, and she emphasizes that "the primary reason Christians enter politics is to . . . restrain evil" (*JWT*, 108). Just as Niebuhr's Christian realism is predicated on the attempt to steer a course between progressivism and utopianism, on the one hand, and *machtpolitik*, on the other, *coupled with* an attempt to recognize the power of Christian agency while turning away from "otherworldly" resignation (of his brother, of Barth) and the "tragic pessimism" (of, say, Morgenthau), it is very much a contemporary version of this, I think, that we find in Elshtain's work, for the most part. The studied quotidian element in her work is a permanent feature and one that steers us away from the "tragic" elements of a Morgenthau, but there is no question that one so robustly engaged in the struggles for a civic democracy is committed to engagement and has eschewed withdrawal.

But at the same time, in *Just War against Terror* (and even more in *Woman and War*) she is insistent that politics is about power: her introduction to the book is titled "Politics Is Not the Nursery," a retort of Hannah Arendt's, she tells us, to those humanists and liberals who failed to understand the reality of social and political evil and the role of power in political life. And when she calls Niebuhr in aid (as she does in chapter 7 of *JWT*, for example), it is the Niebuhr who insists that Christians must use the power of power politics, even at the risk of "dirtying their hands."

In his recent book,[17] Lovin suggests we see contemporary Christian realists as being divided into four groups. The first group, which he terms the "antirealist" politics of Christian witness—he has Stanley

Hauerwas in mind—is really not a version of Christian realism at all, except that it is so dependent on a repudiation of it (I confess I am not sure why this counts). The second group he terms "anti-utopian realists," the more direct descendants of Niebuhr, and they are the largest group and do not merely include theologians but also many commentators and even some politicians—they might include, for example Anatol Lieven (in his recent book on "ethical realism" for example), and he also suggests Elshtain belongs in this group. The third group, called "counterapocalyptic realists," suggest that the tension between power and virtue will always favor power and that Christian realists should be wary of any attempt to tie together realism, power, and virtue. Finally, the fourth group, "pluralist realists," tries to split the difference between anti-utopian and counterapocalyptic realists and to suggest a more optimistic reading of the possibilities of our time than the traditional Niebuhrian Christian realist does. Max Stackhouse and William Schweiker are cited as pluralist realists, and it is fairly clear that this is also where Lovin sees himself. Niebuhr, for Lovin, advocated both anti-utopian realism *and* counterapocalyptic realism versions as two sides of the same coin, and one might, I think, see Elshtain as arguing something similar in a contemporary context. Lovin's point, however, is that in the contemporary context these two cannot be run together, which is why pluralistic Christian realism becomes the default position. The question is first whether one should agree with this and, second, whether, if one does, Christian realism still allows one to hold, as it were, to a thesis asserting "two relevant sovereigns" rather than essentially to be forced to choose one.

VIOLENCE AND AMBIGUITY

In this final part of the chapter, I want to consider one answer to this question as to whether anti-utopian and a counterapocalyptic realists are incompatible in the contemporary context, leading to Christian pluralism as the default position. I will suggest that, on the assumptions Elshtain herself makes in *Sovereignty*, the answer is strictly speaking no, and that, therefore, Elshtain should give up on her loyalty to the "two sovereigns" (and, indeed, to Christian realism). As we shall see, I don't agree with the answer she offers to the question, but I do agree that it discloses an ambiguity in Elshtain's work on these issues that threatens to undermine it at precisely its most central point.

This answer is the one offered by John Milbank in many of his books and papers, most significantly *The Future of Love* and his recently published *Beyond Secular Order*.[18] I choose Milbank in part because he has a good deal in common with aspects of the argument that Elshtain makes, and that I have already outlined, with one crucial difference. Rather than holding that one can sustain both God's sovereignty and state sovereignty, Milbank thinks God's sovereignty must trump the state's. For Milbank, theology should eschew the nominalizing process that gave birth to modernity and hold fast to the truths of metaphysical realism, the *philosophia perennis*, which in his terms bears the name "radical orthodoxy."[19] But this should not be seen as a "going back," for his view is that we still inhabit the "nominalizing" Middle Ages. As he puts it in his first Stanton Lecture, delivered in Cambridge in 2011: "We still live within a Franciscan Middle Ages, and this can be shown to be as true of our politics as it is of our philosophy. The question is whether an alternative, Dominican Middle Ages can yet be revived in order to shape, in the 21st Century, an alternative modernity."[20]

For Milbank, Christian realism represents an unholy alliance of Kantian (idealist and absolutist) and utilitarian (pragmatic and calculating) viewpoints, which actually tends to dissolve ethics altogether. It depends upon what he calls a "Stoic" attitude to ethics that Niebuhr (he argues) effectively adopts. Milbank, of course, offers in its place "attendance to the realities spoken of by the (genuinely) Christian narrative" and a superbly clever critique that suggests that there is no "reality" to which Christian—or other—realists "bring" their insights. Rather, for Milbank, for the Christian, there is no reality to which Christianity must be accommodated; rather there is only the Christian reality because we are all "scions of language bound to structures in which reality is already worked over." For Milbank, as for some others, the Christian story is the *alternative* political narrative and so to step outside that narrative is to step into another (though he does not use the term) language game. Much of his recent work consists in an attempt to critique the aspects of the "Franciscan" Middle Ages that dominate our current modernity or to flesh out what shape a "Dominican" modernity might take.[21]

Thus, "Christian realism"—and Elshtain's commitment, in however qualified a form, to notions of state sovereignty—represent for Milbank a "Franciscan" modernity, and he is insistently, and persistently, critical of this. For Niebuhr, and for Elshtain, we have to work with the grain of the world order—we have to understand that states are what we have to work with and that the world they make, though, of course, imperfect, is the only one we have. And we can expect—or at least hope—that we can help them make a better world. But Milbank does not see the world order like this at all. A good deal of his work, from some of his earliest essays to his present work, emphasizes, albeit briefly or *en passant*, a conception of world order that is highly diffuse, filled with local, regional, corporate (in the original and not capitalist sense) bodies, and where the structure of authority is filtered through the notion of gift. As he puts it in one recent collection:

> The Christian principles of polity stand totally opposed to any idea of the nation-state as the ultimate unit and rather at once favour at once the natural pre-given region on the one hand and the universal human cosmopolis on the other. Likewise they oppose the manipulative politics of human rights and propose instead the distribution of specific liberties, offices and duties to certain individuals and groups in certain circumstances according to the discernment of what is specifically desirable and has a tendency to cement human solidarity.[22]

Of course, we are no more required to accept Milbank's account than we are to accept Elshtain's, but the point of raising it is to emphasize that the significance of talking about "sovereignty" at all is to focus on *exclusive* authority. The problem with attempts to combine God's sovereignty with the state's is that it begs the question of who (or what) is "really" sovereign. Elshtain herself, as we saw in the first section of this chapter, essentially agrees with this, but if she does, it is very hard to see how she can gainsay the basic thrust of Milbank's charge, which is simply to suggest that the "absolute" character of the nominalist sovereign is, essentially (as Hobbes saw), one of power and thus (in his terms—and hers) one of evil. In *Just War against Terror*, Elshtain, astonishingly, almost seems to accede to this.

For Elshtain, true international justice is defined as the "equal claim of all persons to (have) coercive force deployed on their behalf if they are victims of one of the many horrors attendant upon radical political instability" (*JWT*, 168). And in this less than ideal world, absent an international body that could act as guarantor (and we *are* absent it), then

> the one candidate to guarantee this principle is the United States, for two reasons: equal regard is the foundation of our own polity and we are the only superpower. . . . As the world's superpower, America bears the responsibility to help guarantee . . . international stability, *whether much of the world wants it or not.* This does not mean that we can or should rush around imposing solutions everywhere. It does mean that we are obliged to evaluate all cries for justice and relief from people who are being preyed upon whether by non-state enforcers (like terrorists) or by state-sponsored enforcers. We, the powerful, must respond to attacks against persons who cannot defend themselves because they, like us, are human beings, hence equal in regard to us, and because they, like us, are members of states, or would be states, whose primary obligation is to protect the lives of those who inhabit their polities. (*JWT*, 169–70; emphasis added)

Here, she is ceding to one state—one sovereign—the power to act in the world in an unlimited way—"whether much of the world wants it or not"—in ways that surely cannot be squared with the notion of limited sovereignty she outlines in *Sovereignty*. There, remember, she tell us that "we cannot assume a nation state is sovereign until it demonstrates its ability to be independent from the protection of another state, to treat its citizens decently and to foster a vibrant civil society: sovereignty as responsibility" (*S*, 228). But the short answer is why? On her own argument, to be sovereign is certainly to be autonomous, but why should treating citizens decently or fostering a vibrant civil society be any part of sovereignty. No answer is given. In her own way, Elshtain seems to be caught up in what I earlier called the "hybrid"—asserting at one and the same time the validity of a system built on will and artifice yoked together with at least a rhetoric that effectively assumes older "realist" transcendent conceptions. Milbank's argument, for all its obvious problems, at least has the virtue of clarity. Elshtain's seems balanced on a perpetual knife edge constantly threatening to tip one way or the other. The ultimate ambiguity of her position, or so it seems to me, is that she wants both to assert the value of "God's sovereignty" without giving up on the sovereignty of the state. Although I would not agree with the specifics of Milbank's alternative to this, it does seem to me that he raises in a particularly powerful form the fact that we perhaps need an alternative. That perhaps Elshtain needed one. And in truth, much of her work—that part which focused on differing modes of civic engagement—does not seem to really *need* the "sovereign state" in the strong sense that she deploys it in her writings on international relations. Perhaps the way forward for an Elshtainean notion of political community, wedded to notions of God's sovereignty, lies in the direction of a more civil and less statist form of politics—what I would like to call a "nomocratic" form of politics as opposed to the "teleocratic" forms that are increasingly dominant, including, at least in some moods, in Elshtain's own work. The integral humanism of a thinker like Jacques Maritain might possibly be a model here, one that certainly has had an influence on another similar writer, Charles Taylor, and there might be other possibilities. What does seem clear is that Elshtain's commitment to her "two sovereigns" is not sustainable, at least in the form in which she sought to establish it.

NOTES

1. Aspects of the following section draw on Nicholas Rengger, "On Theology and International Relations: World Politics beyond the Empty Sky," *International Relations* 27, no. 2 (2013): 141–57.

2. Largely, in fact, dominated by Neoplatonic readings of Plato. A good general essay that surveys this is the excellent one by John Rist, "Plotinus and Christian Philosophy," in *The Cambridge Companion to Plotinus*, ed. Lloyd Gerson (Cambridge: Cambridge University Press, 1996), 386–413.

3. Not, of course, realists in the sense of the field of international relations, but philosophical realists.

4. Elshtain discusses nominalism and its fruits in *Sovereignty*, 1–2, 25–27, 36–40, 50, 79–80, and 105–7. Michael Gillespie, *The Theological Origins of Modernity* (Chicago: University of Chicago Press, 2008), is largely concerned with this debate and its ramifications. Charles Taylor, *A Secular Age* (Cambridge, MA: Harvard University Press, 2007), has a short chapter at the end where he relates his version of the secularity story—which he terms the "Reform Master Narrative" (RMN)—to this version, specifically in the version put forward by Milbank and radical orthodoxy, which he terms the "Intellectual deviation" story. He is sympathetic to it, but thinks it needs the RMN in addition to really explain secularity. For Milbank's version of this thesis see, especially, Milbank, *Theology and Social Theory* (Oxford: Blackwell, 1990; 2nd ed., 2005), Milbank, *The Suspended Middle: Henri de Lubac and the Debate over the Supernatural* (London: Eerdmans, 2005), and his as yet unpublished Stanton Lectures delivered in Cambridge in the early part of 2011. The texts can be found on the website of the Centre for the Study of Theology and Philosophy, which Milbank directs: John Milbank, "John Milbank's Stanton Lectures 2011," March 12, 2011, http://theology philosophycentre.co.uk/2011/03/12/john-milbanks-stanton-lectures-2011/. I will come back to its significance for Milbank in a moment. It is also probably worth adding that the story has something in common with the argument propounded by Alastair Macintyre, *After Virtue* (London: Duckworth 1981).

5. See Michael Oakeshott, introduction to *Leviathan*, by Thomas Hobbes (Oxford: Blackwell, 1960). See also Francis Oakley, *Politics and Eternity* (Leiden: Brill, 1999), chap. 10, which makes explicit the significance of the tradition Oakeshott is pointing to for medieval thought.

6. Iris Murdoch, *The Sovereignty of Good* (London: Routledge and Kegan Paul, 1970), 23.

7. Of course, there was no formal field of international relations in the nineteenth century, but there was a good deal of writing about international relations, from a wide variety of standpoints. The point is that in almost all of these the hybrid is distinctly visible.

8. See Michael Barnett, *Empire of Humanity: A History of Humanitarianism* (Ithaca, NY: Cornell University Press, 2011).

9. June Bingham, *Courage to Change: An Introduction to the Life and Thought of Reinhold Niebuhr* (New York: Scribner, 1961), 8

10. Reinhold Niebuhr, "The Christian Faith and the World Crisis," *Christianity and Crisis* 1, no. 1 (1941): 6.

11. Reinhold Niebuhr, *The Nature and Destiny of Man* (London: Nisbet, 1941).

12. Reinhold Niebuhr, *The Children of Light and the Children of Darkness* (New York: Scribner's, 1944), 41.

13. R. L. Calhoun, review of *The Nature and Destiny of Man*, Vol. 2, *Human Destiny*, by Reinhold Niebuhr, *Journal of Religion* 24, no. 1 (1944): 59.

14. Robin Lovin, *Christian Realism and the New Realities* (Cambridge: Cambridge University Press, 2008).

15. In particular, see her excellent *Augustine and the Limits of Politics*.

16. Elshtain is here quoting Niebuhr, "To Prevent the Triumph of an Intolerable Tyranny," in *Christian Century*; reprinted in Reinhold Niebuhr, *Love and Justice: Selections from the Shorter Writings of Reinhold Niebuhr*, ed. D. B. Robertson (Philadelphia: Westminster, 1957), 272–78.

17. Lovin, *Christian Realism and Contemporary Realities*.

18. The published version of his 2011 Stanton Lectures at Cambridge.

19. The name he gave to the movement in contemporary theology he inspired and in part created and developed along with other theologians, such as Graham Ward and Catherine Pickstock.

20. John Milbank, "Stanton Lecture 1: The Return of Metaphysics in the 21st Century" (University of Cambridge, January 19, 2011), http://theology philosophycentre.co.uk/papers/Milbank_StantonLecture1.pdf.

21. See "John Milbank's Stanton Lectures 2011." See also John Milbank, *Beyond Secular Order: The Representation of Being and the Representation of the People* (Chichester, West Sussex: Wiley-Blackwell, 2013), 44.

22. John Milbank, *The Future of Love: Essays in Political Theology* (Eugene, OR: Cascade, 2009), 246–47.

CHAPTER TWELVE

THE EDUCATION OF A JUST WAR THINKER

Politics and Patriotism through the Lens of Gender

John D. Carlson

On a drizzly September morning, just days after the terrorist attacks that would set the course of history in the early twenty-first century, two dozen American religious leaders gathered at the White House to offer counsel to the president as he sought to guide the country and prepare for its response. Among those assembled, though not a "religious leader" per se, was Jean Bethke Elshtain, whose appointment in a divinity school and whose ethical writings on war and peace had garnered the attention of the meeting's organizers. Elshtain later recounted the events of the morning, including an intriguing, unscripted premeeting among the various invitees while waiting for the president. For about forty minutes, religious leaders representing every major faith tradition crafted, edited, and signed a statement condemning the terrorist attacks. Elshtain recalls, quoting liberally from the statement:

> We offered up our prayers for the bereaved. We lifted up those who "selflessly gave their lives in an attempt to rescue others." We expressed our gratitude that "the President has spoken out early and clearly to denounce acts of bigotry and racism directed against

Arabs, Muslims, and others in our midst. To yield to hate is to give victory to the terrorists." We called the attacks of September 11 acts against all of humanity—over sixty other countries lost citizens in the attacks—and we argued that there was a "grave obligation to do all we can to protect innocent human life" because "the common good has been threatened by these attacks . . ." We called for a response that was just and peaceful—understanding, as many of us do, that the claims of justice and of peace must guide any reaction.[1]

It is not surprising that Elshtain, as someone who had drafted and organized the signing of several prominent public statements reaffirming American civic values, contributed to this collective effort among the White House meeting participants.[2]

The group then moved to the meeting room, whereupon President George W. Bush arrived (without press) and joined them in a circle for a searching and, at times, emotional conversation. He spoke first—extemporaneously, for twenty-five minutes or so—reflecting not about the war to come but about the need to address the fears of Americans: "He indicated that he would oppose anyone who singled out those of the Muslim faith or Arab background for acts of vigilantism and bigotry." He articulated, as he had on other occasions, that Islam "is a 'religion that preaches peace' and those who had hijacked Islam to murder nearly seven thousand people did not represent Islam." When he was finished speaking, he asked to hear from his guests. As her turn came around, Elshtain picked up on the instructive tone of the president's remarks, urging him to see that "a President's role as 'civic educator' has never been more important. That he must explain things to the American people; teach patience to an impatient people; the need to sacrifice to a people unused to sacrifice." The president nodded in assent.[3]

Such civic-minded themes, as they emerged in this important meeting, were a staple of Elshtain's political thought going back to her early work: the virtues on which citizens' engagement in public life depends; the moral presuppositions on which democratic society is based, such as justice, human dignity, and human equality; the need to restrain patriotic fervor so as to protect vulnerable minorities; and the willingness of individuals to prioritize the community and the common good over the self. These concerns were also at the core of Elshtain's convictions about the use of force, a far-reaching position she called "just war politics" that would later take its most detailed form in her *Just War against Terror*.

After mingling and shaking hands with the president, his guests shuffled out into the rain, sobered by the occasion but hopeful that the unity experienced in this poignant meeting would proliferate throughout broader circles of society. The president returned to his schedule of events. Hours later, he addressed Congress—and by extension the nation and the world—in a special State of the Union address that laid the groundwork for what would become the "war on terror." The speech called the armed forces to alert: "The hour is coming when America will act, and you will make us proud." And it included Bush's memorable lines, "Every nation in every region now has a decision to make: Either you are with us or you are with the terrorists."[4] For her part, Elshtain would go on to write a strident defense of this war, morally explicating the attacks of September 11 and setting the justificatory stage for the ensuing invasion of Afghanistan. Indeed, she commented that the September 11 attacks "reminded me of what it means to be an American citizen."[5] She would go further. Her views gradually hardened, as she took controversial stances in support of the invasion of Iraq in 2003.[6] After her death in 2013, Elshtain was remembered as "an intellectual beacon for neoconservative policy makers in the post-9/11 era," as *The New York Times* reported in her obituary, for, perhaps more than any other scholar, she had inscribed "just war" principles and reflection into the "war on terror."[7]

Where did these ideas come from? What were the markers along the way—the biographical, intellectual, and political developments leading up to the moral positions she took as a public intellectual and the persona she adopted as just war advocate for the war on terror? Critics and even friends of Elshtain found themselves asking, Where or how did she go wrong when it came to supporting the highly controversial Iraq War? That is, if indeed she did go wrong. In this chapter I address these questions by exploring Elshtain's early writings and the thematic trajectories that shaped her unique view of "just war as politics." In particular, *Women and War* (*WW*) was the launching pad for a journey that culminated in her public recognition as a leading just war thinker of her day.[8] I begin by tracing the heritage of two key wartime tropes in this work, that of the "Beautiful Soul" and the "Just Warrior" and then show how Elshtain pushed beyond the binaries these tropes presume and reinforce. Within this gendered analysis of war, Elshtain's vision of civic virtue, politics, and patriotism emerge; they undergird her approach to just war, which begins as a form of civic virtue and develops over time into a vision of politics more broadly. This fuller picture of her progression as a just war thinker enhances our understanding of this complex and controversial figure, such that we might hazard more satisfactory responses to the pointed questions about what Elshtain got right and where she went wrong. In particular, we can appreciate what such evaluations would mean in terms that Elshtain herself would apply.

THE AMBIVALENT BEAUTIFUL SOUL

In her *Women and War*, the Beautiful Soul is one of two central tropes that serve as lenses through which Elshtain examines the gendered history, politics, and experience of war. Her effort to explore and ultimately shake off the trappings of the Beautiful Soul was a crucial move in the development of her just war position. Borrowed from Hegel, Elshtain appropriated the Beautiful Soul for her own uses to assess, critique, and ultimately reconfigure recurring political and wartime representations of women and female identity.[9] The Beautiful Soul embodies, she claims, "values and virtues at odds with war's destructiveness, representing home and hearth and the humble verities of everyday life" (*WW*, xiii). As an individual, the beautifully ensouled self inhabits the private domains. But in her collective being, the Beautiful Soul reinforces, in Hegel's words, "the appearance of purity by cultivating innocence about the historical course of the world" (quoted in *WW*, 4). This collective representation establishes clear social expectations and fulfills vital political functions. For many women, such innocence was preserved by remaining outside the realm of the *polis*—in the *oikos* or domestic sphere. Within Elshtain's conception of the Beautiful Soul, as we will see, a commitment to home life need not be mutually exclusive with civic participation.

Much of *Women and War* is devoted to historical, literary, political, and autobiographical recoveries of individuals who, in some way, embodied this highly moralized form of beauty. Certainly the Madonna is the archetype. But Elshtain turns up many other manifestations, as in the "Ten Commandments of Womanhood," a 1918 document prepared by the Connecticut Congress of Mothers, which urges women to be thrifty and frugal, neither wasteful of time nor of bread or other materials of the home. Revealingly, the sixth and seventh of these commandments warn against overlooking the woman who stands behind the man, whether as sustainer in good times or as prop or salve in the bad: "*Hearten Thy Men and Weep Not*, for a strong woman begetteth a strong man, and the blasts of adversity blow hard and swift across the world." The next reads: "*Bind Up the Wounds of Thy Men and Soften Their Pain*, for thy presence by the light of their campfires is sweet and grateful, and the touch of thy hand deft in the hour of need" (quoted in *WW*, 147). Even pioneering feminists such as Elizabeth Cady Stanton played the part of Beautiful Soul, embracing the pacifying tendencies of womanhood and motherhood through their civic devotion to the suffrage movement. In contrast to the "male element"—known by its "destructive force, stern, selfish, aggrandizing, loving war, violence, conquest, acquisition, breeding in the material and moral world alike discord, disorder, disease and death. See what a record of blood and cruelty the pages of history reveal!"—Stanton augured "a new evangel of womanhood, to exalt purity, virtue, morality, true religion, to lift man up into higher realms of thought and action" (quoted in *WW*, 6). Beautiful Souls striving for greater equality were motivated by more than justice. Improving their own political lot would improve the condition of men and political life more broadly. One of Elshtain's great civic heroes, Jane Addams, spoke forcefully of women's "maternal affection," "remembering heart," and "imperative to preserve human life" as ways of transforming men's militaristic political pursuits and conforming their ill-tempered social existence to the natural and civic order of peace.[10]

   Elshtain's Beautiful Soul trope emerges amidst the feminist discourse of the 1970s and 80s, even as it also puts pressure upon it. She enables us to see from whence the assumptions about men's violence and women's pacific zeal originate and the tremendous work they have done in popular culture and scholarly discourse. To set the scene, one might simply recall some of the gendered bumper stickers of those days: "What would missiles look like if women designed them?" or "It will be a great day when our schools have all the money they need and the Air Force has to hold a bake sale to buy a bomber." If this sounds glib, consider one reviewer's appraisal that Elshtain "forces us to do some hard thinking. In a world that spent $900 billion for military programs in 1986 when one adult in three could not read and write and one person in four was hungry, understanding women's participation in and resistance to war is crucial."[11] Oversimply, if women ruled the world, war would become a topic of history, not of contemporary affairs and international relations.

Elshtain, of course, was eager to counter such simplistic thinking, pointing to bellicose proclivities in the steely Elizabeth I and in the Iron Lady, Margaret Thatcher. Since then, secretaries of state Condoleezza Rice and Hillary Clinton and UN ambassadors Susan Rice, Samantha Power, and Nikki Haley have helped to bury the assumption that women who occupy the halls of power will extend the Beautiful Soul's reign of domestic peace over the political realms they help govern—at least by resisting all use of force. Elshtain does not cobble together the stuffing of a straw man—or straw woman—only that she might set it alight, though her prose at times suggests she has matches at the ready. Rather, she insists upon understanding the hopes and aspirations of the Beautiful Souls she recovers, for there is much to be retained, reconsidered, and even redeemed in the civic dispositions they exhibit and the political visions, often irenic, they propose. Such a project, though, begins with critique and the respect that critique commands. Critique should be distinguished from contempt, which comes from ignoring an idea altogether (a tendency exhibited by men, including male scholars, who refused to engage these ideas at all). Critique militates against idealization. Elshtain, for example, worried that Addams's idealizations "weakened the cogency of her case" by assuming that women's suffrage "would automatically humanize governments." Addams's location of feminism and militarism in "eternal opposition" provided—in Elshtain's words—"a license to evade many tough questions about power and responses to the use of force" (*WW*, 235–36), urgent problems to which Elshtain herself would dedicate much of her later scholarly career.

Elshtain shows how the simplistic equation of women with peace cannot bear the weight of a more complicated history. For in wartime, the Beautiful Soul puts her balms and maternal comforts toward the love, support, and care of her husband—and, by extension, her country, too, as one Mrs. F. S. Halowes makes clear, writing near the end of the Great War in her *Mothers of Men and Militarism*:

> Women equally with men have a passionate love of mother-country. . . . Though we loathe slaughter we find that after men have done their best to kill and wound, women are ever ready to mend the broken bodies, soothe the dying, and weep over nameless graves! . . . God made two, a man and a woman, to rule the home—the state is but a larger home. . . . A mother's love is at its best the most selfless love of humanity. (quoted in *WW*, 146)

As well, there are those whose actions run counter to socially prescribed norms of the Beautiful Soul—for example, an eight-year-old Jean Bethke, who, wielding a croquet mallet she imagines to be a sword, challenges her sister to a duel and who, after watching *Joan of Arc*, rushes out for an Ingrid Bergman–style chop cut that instills in her "a new sense of freedom" (*WW*, 17). Such behavior implicitly acknowledges the norm of the Beautiful Soul in its explicit challenge to it. Other counterevidence to the putatively peace-loving women (and worryingly war-mongering men) that Elshtain unearths include the sisterhood of the "ferocious few" along with a small coterie of pacific brethren.

Generalizations aside, overlooking the impulses that war arouses in women as well as men risks ignoring the ground they hold in common, albeit through historically different roles. More important than preserving or retrieving the past, Elshtain makes clear, becomes the task of forging new roles and identities and nurturing common aspirations, ideally of a less militant vein. War has a way of opening up new ways of being that must be appraised carefully in any effort to affirm or transcend the experience of war. Elshtain affirms,

> War retains the power to incite parts of the self that peace cannot seem to reach. Wartime's Beautiful Soul is no ordinary wife

or mother or secretary or nurse: she becomes a civic being; she is needed by others; she can respond simultaneously to what Jane Addams called the "family claim" and the "social claim," for, she is told, without her unselfish devotion to country and family each would be lost.

Elshtain then goes on to ask,

Might it be possible to crank up this vision again, to make it stick as a compelling ethos for most women? Many women yearn for public identities as civic beings serving ends that take them beyond the borders of private lives. One deeply rooted conviction, sustained by veterans of battle fronts and home fronts and transmitted to others, is that wars—good wars that unite us—offer a communal endeavor, the sharing of sacrifice and danger. Modern society appears to have found no other way to initiate and sustain action in common with others on this scale. (*WW*, 9–10)

This intellectual undertaking aspires to a bold civic purposefulness that goes well beyond the feminist discourse of the era and the scholarly studies of war that then defined her field. Yet the civic purpose Elshtain sought seems not to have been fully realized in *Women and War*—at least not in ways that compare to the energy and tone captured in her White House meeting or the many public engagements in which she lectured and debated the "war on terror" and the invasion of Iraq. Nevertheless, *Women and War* powerfully gestures to these civic purposes in ways that escaped the attention of many critics, including those who overlooked or underappreciated what she was up to.

Elshtain's gender analysis produced some consternation among reviewers when the book first appeared. Despite the many favorable reviews, some feminist scholars wanted Elshtain to unpack the relationship between patriarchy and war.[12] Some criticized the book for failing to show how the study of gender enhanced our understanding of the causes of war—as if that was Elshtain's primary task or one she thought her book was obliged to pursue. Not to say that Elshtain was uninterested in the causes of war. She had studied with Kenneth Waltz, whose work on the different images of war exploring different causal theories, was a part of her research and teaching throughout her career. In fact, she later returned to Waltz's *Man, the State, and War* to offer her own reflections and corrections in an aptly titled essay, "Woman, the State, and War."[13]

Yet though she made clear that the cause of war was never her animating question in *Women and War*, it was hard for Elshtain to escape the presumption that it should have been. As one political scientist wrote at the time, "This is not a book about war; at least, it is not a serious sorting of the causes of the violent conflicts in our international system."[14] Yet, to critique Elshtain for not fitting her project into this (male) reviewer's expectations betrays more about the provincial thinking she was up against in her field and its constrained expectations of scholarship than any failings in her own scholarship. Elshtain doesn't even try to prove her case, he claims. Worse: "She simply scoffs at the power-politics theories of international politics," such as prisoner's dilemmas.[15] The reviewer closes by repeating the original charge: "This is not a book that treats the dilemmas and problems of domestic political conflict or international relations so very seriously in their own right; rather, it dwells on the epistemological problems of approaching this subject as males or females in our culture."[16] Interestingly, the reviewer does credit Elshtain's effort to be self-critical—to attempt to distance herself from the "standard feminist positions" and prejudices about women and war. In the end, though, he judges that Elshtain cannot fully disown the gendered analysis that requires female stateswomen to accept the violent international system imposed upon them by men.[17]

Nowhere does the reviewer consider *his own* epistemological prejudices about the book's subject matter or the standards of "serious" scholarship at the time, including the standard for what qualifies as "a book about war." Nevertheless, this reviewer and others may have stumbled onto a subtler point: namely, that *Women and War*—with its comprehensive-sounding title—was not essentially a book about women and war at all but, rather, one about the ways in which men and women conceive and experience war differently. Clearly, these differences extend even to the academic study of war. To this point, Elshtain later admitted that *Gender and War* would have been a more fitting if less alliteratively compelling title.

Over the course of the book, the Beautiful Soul weathers the decon-structive tendencies of Elshtain's gender-based analysis, though not without experiencing significant attenuation and qualification. This was certainly apt in many ways. For, a too rosy view of woman as a collec-tive repository for all peace or antiwar sentiments, Elshtain urged, was something we must be prepared to shake off. *Women and War* helped facilitate this loss through its broad historical sweep and significant empirical evidence (not to mention its normative commitments). But the book also refuses to close the door entirely to the civic-minded and civic-hearted features that the Beautiful Soul lifts up. Civic virtue—and the longings, meanings, and obligations attached to it—emerge as overarching concerns that recur throughout Elshtain's lifelong corpus. Attention to these themes in *Women and War* yields crucial insights about the relationship among citizenship, virtue, and war in her later just war writings. And the tool with which she pries open this abundant storehouse of civic concepts is the study of gender. Enter here a second trope: the male counterpart to the Beautiful Soul.

THE JUST OR VIRTUOUS WARRIOR?

Elshtain's gender analysis relies similarly on male tropes, notably the "Just Warrior," who offers a restrained form of civic virtue. This figure "takes up arms reluctantly and *only* if he must to prevent a greater wrong or to protect the innocent from certain harm" (*WW*, 127). Interestingly, Elshtain offers few historical paragons of Just Warriors or modern coun-terparts to the Beautiful Souls she details at length. Augustine and other figures in the "just war" tradition provide some conceptual outlines, but even these sources are discussed rather briefly. The men and male motifs subsumed under her Just Warrior heading are presumed to be honorably fighting in support of a just cause, but they are not foremost concerned with the morality of war in the rigorously reflective way that just war thought invites. The Just Warrior of *Women and War*, rather, is a political being with deep claims of allegiance to the nation, fellow citizens, and one's brothers in arms. He is concerned with the moral enterprise of war as it raises questions about service to country, the brutal hardships of battle, and the formation of one's identity.[18] Morality is sifted through the screen of patriotism, sacrifice, and solidarity—not ethical theory or political philosophy. For these reasons, it is important to distinguish the work the Just Warrior performs in *Women and War* from just war thought proper as Elshtain and others later developed it.

The male cognate *virtú*—especially armed civic virtue—is the reigning concept in most of Elshtain's analysis of male warriors: from Homeric warriors to Tommys, doughboys, and World War II GIs; from Nathan Hale to Ernie Pyle, John Wayne, and Rambo. *Virtú* often entails manly aspirations for personal honor and glory that are realized in battle on behalf of one's country (e.g., in Crane's *Red Badge of Courage*). Alternately, such hopes may be unveiled as false promises as when men in battle lose their manhood (e.g., in Ron Kovic's *Born on the Fourth of July*). The warriors who most intrigue Elshtain are tragic figures (as in Remarque's *All Quiet on the Western Front*) or those few—"we happy few" (to recall Shakespeare's *Henry V*)— who experience war and sacrifice as a form of brotherhood, intimacy, or even "communal ecstasy," to borrow a term from J. Glenn Gray's classic *The Warriors*.[19] War and Human Identity—one of Elshtain's favorite classes to teach (and for students to take)—relied upon deep moral readings of many of these texts (alongside *Women and War*) and the viewing of films, ranging from *Glory* and *Saving Private Ryan* to John Ford's wartime documentaries. It was an ethics class, to be sure, but "just war" was not a prominent theme.

For these many reasons, "Virtuous Warrior" is perhaps a more comprehensive term for the many multisided characters whose diverse experiences she weaves into her narratives. It is also an apt analogue to the Beautiful Soul since the Virtuous Warrior encompasses male just warriors, compassionate warriors, and even fiercely committed pacifists who imagine ways within or beyond war to limit human violence. With Beautiful Souls and Virtuous Warriors alike, Elshtain's project is to find more chastened, less militant ways of embodying virtue and more robust means for integrating ethical concerns into the political discourse, judgments, and actions of citizens (in war and peace alike). Finally, for my purposes here, distinguishing the more expansive and variegated category of the Virtuous Warrior from Elshtain's limited treatment of just war scholarship in *Women and War* enables us to appreciate the seminal stage this book represents in her intellectual development as a just war thinker.

Traditionally, the Virtuous Warrior taps into the oldest conception of what it means to be a citizen: the willingness to kill and die in defense of one's polity and fellow citizens. The massive mobilization of male citizen soldiers fighting in World War II—the "good war"—is a frequently cited example (often overshadowing, Elshtain points out, the women who worked in munitions factories and other industries supporting the war effort). Military service also has established enduring conceptions of what masculinity entails, or at least the courage, strength, and mettle that war tests in men. To be a citizen is to be a warrior is to be a man.

Virtuous warriors hail from polities across the ages: Spartans and Athenians, Franks and Turks, the North and South, Axis and Allies. At an individual level, the warrior's honor does not depend upon the particular side on which one fights or the justice of its cause. Yet such visions of civic virtue are by no means synonymous with moral virtue. In one particularly vivid articulation, Machiavelli intrinsically links *virtù* to masculinity and virility, which, he enjoins, must seize and overpower the feminine *fortuna*, whose "violent rivers" and ungovernable nature lurk in waiting, threatening to upend the security, self-rule, and glory of the *civitas* to which the prince and his men above all must be committed. In Machiavelli's own offending words, "it is better to be impetuous than cautious, because fortune is a woman; and it is necessary if one wants to hold her down, to beat her and strike her down." It follows, the Renaissance child of darkness goes on, that young risk-takers are apt to be better rulers, "because they are less cautious, more ferocious, and command her [*fortuna*] with more audacity."[20]

This form of civic virtue must be distinguished from that of the Beautiful Soul or Just Warrior, whose appeals to moral virtue would leaven the life of the commonwealth. Elshtain cites a famous passage from Machiavelli's *Discourses*: "When it is a question of saving the Fatherland, one should not stop for a moment to consider whether something is lawful or unlawful, gentle or cruel, laudable or shameful; but putting aside every other consideration, one ought to follow out to the end whatever resolve will save the life of the state and preserve its freedom" (quoted in *WW*, 57). However devout their commitment to the *polis* might be, Machiavelli's virtuous prince, citizen, and warrior all stand outside the frame of anything approaching just war standards.

Elshtain begins her story of armed male virtue with the Greeks: "In the beginning, politics gave birth to war. Better: in the beginning, politics was war" (*WW*, 47). She distinguishes this period from the ensuing era of Christendom that gives birth to the tropes of the Just Warrior and Beautiful Soul. But as is clear from Machiavelli—who dwelled in Christendom even as he criticized the effeminizing propensities of Christianity—there is no historical line that distinguishes the era of classical virtuous warriors from that of Christian just warriors. For Elshtain, many are those who possess "armed civic virtue" yet remain in need of moral restraint. Even many who waged battle under the putative flag of the Just Warrior have been less than fully worthy of the title. Whether one speaks of Christian knights, "who seem not to have tormented themselves overmuch concerning the justice of their cause" (by virtue of their "oaths of liege loyalty"), or of the Tommys and doughboys in the Great War whose nation "sanctified their war effort, turning it toward the crusading extreme" or "a war for purity" (137), many who have claimed the mantle of Just Warrior would find no place in Elshtain's later just war project.[21]

Thus, male citizens who answered the call to arms under Machiavelli's realism, or who responded to Bernard of Clairvaux's appeal to holy war (women, too, accompanied men in the Crusades), or who participated in wide-scale conscription on which industrial nations rely to wage their wars—all invoked the mantle of honorable or virtuous warrior. But none should be confused with just war exemplars simply because they presumed their causes were just. This inchoate positioning of just war vis-à-vis realism and holy war (and pacifism) would become an important foundation to Elshtain's later just war project.

Perhaps the moral icon in *Women and War* who bears the closest connection to just war ideas is the "Compassionate Warrior," a morally reflective example of the "pacific few" whom Elshtain extols for his reluctance to take up arms or fire his weapon, his willingness to sacrifice for others, and his special maternal kind of "preservative love" that, following J. Glenn Gray, Elshtain describes as "an impersonal passion to preserve and to succor, to hold back the annihilation" (*WW*, 209). This exemplary sort of Virtuous Warrior feels the pull of conscience, morality, religion, perhaps the universal brotherhood of arms—even as he locates the enemy (his fellow man and brother in arms) in his gun-sights.[22] In a particularly bracing analysis, Elshtain lays bare the commonalities between mothers and warriors: both are reduced to their bodily concreteness and suffer intense pain, whether from the wounds of battle or of giving birth; both are prone to experience intense feelings of duty and guilt; and, finally, existing on the cusp of life or death, both undergo liminal experiences that irrevocably alter their identities. She professes:

> The ideal of the Good Officer like that of the Good Mother emphasizes *caritas*, Christian caring, giving such action an "almost religious" aura. The abstract words—like honor, glory, mother love—give way, when the soldier or mother is *in the throes*, to the concrete activity of staying alive, or keeping others alive, of tending to *this* moment, *this* comrade, *this* child—no abstraction but a living being to whom I am responsible. (*WW*, 223–24)

Through their concrete experiences, stirring moral sensibilities, and intense relational bonds, just and compassionate warriors become attractive modern alternatives to Homeric, Spartan, and Machiavellian forms of "armed civic virtue."

BEYOND BINARIES: RETHINKING CITIZENSHIP AND PATRIOTISM

Having laid out the Beautiful Soul and Virtuous Warrior tropes, I want to pursue in more depth the purposes they served for Elshtain. The first use is a tropological frame for empirical analysis—for validating, debunking, or qualifying the reigning narratives of gender and war. Where do generalizations hold up? Where do they falter or invite critique? For there have always been countertypes and counternarratives that defy generalizations—war-hating men and war-loving women; "Mama's boys," or male conscientious objectors unwilling to fight, and martial mothers eager, or at least willing, to send their boys to war. Women certainly have aspired to and embodied civic virtue, even in times of war, with some presumptively Beautiful Souls not living up to their irenic expectations. Even if they were themselves noncombatants, they certainly were not pacific, given their support of, or association with, war. Elshtain's discussion of the Spartan mother, earlier excavated and extolled by republican thinkers such as Machiavelli and Rousseau, makes clear that many women conceived it as their civic duty to give birth to citizen-soldiers, whose highest calling was to serve the *polis* or nation.

Elshtain frequently recalled in print and in the classroom the passage from Rousseau's *Émile* in which the Spartan woman rebukes a messenger who quivers in fear as he informs her that all of her five sons have been killed in battle. In Rousseau's telling, the Spartan mother responds, "Base slave, did I ask you that? We won the victory," as she decamps to the temple to give thanks to the gods. Rousseau's admiring response— "This is the female citizen"—shatters modern essentializations of women's pacific identity (quoted in *WW*, 70). And it was vintage Elshtain to observe how such female accounts of "armed civic virtue" reappear in modern-day Spartan mothers. She recalls the words of Confederate wife and mother Mary Boykin Chesnut as she channels Hecuba: "To fill a patriot's grave the noblest fate a man could crave." Elsewhere *Women and War* observes the celebrity status of a twentieth-century American Gold Star mother who, having lost five sons in World War II, is thronged by supporters eager to shake her hand. Some women among the "ferocious few" even served as combatants in war. Elshtain recollects the American Revolutionary Deborah Samson, who fought under a male guise and suffered sword and gunshot wounds only to be discovered and later honorably discharged by General Washington. And again to recall when, as a young girl, Jean Bethke imitated Joan of Arc—was this really such an outlier? We do well to consider the civic impulses and aspirations of women who have sought and found in war *some* conception of armed civic virtue, whether directly or indirectly, in history or on screen, on the front lines or on the playground.

As Elshtain shows, when digging into the complex histories of men, women, and war, overdependence on the Beautiful Soul and the Just/

Virtuous Warrior concomitant dulls the critical edge of these tropological tools. We need still other tools for mining the myriad experiences and competing accounts of war. The ideal tropes serve certain purposes, as made clear when Elshtain (then a Lutheran) critiques Luther's attack against the veneration of Mary. Nevertheless, over the span of history, such ideal tropes become strained and must be qualified, nuanced, and attenuated. Thus one key use of them was to chronicle and explain their historical and empirical limitations—to deconstruct them, if you will.[23] But not to do away with them altogether, either.

We can appreciate the ongoing utility of the Beautiful Soul by considering the epilogue of the second edition of *Women and War* (1995). In taking up the Gulf War, Elshtain attests to social transformations in the U.S. military surrounding questions of women combatants. This issue surged to the fore in 1991, while 32,000 women were serving in the Persian Gulf. Interestingly, at a time when many female members of the armed forces were eager to jettison whatever residue of the Beautiful Soul lingered in the minds of military and congressional leaders— in order to further the cause of equal opportunity within the military profession—Elshtain now found herself clinging to some of those Beautiful Soul vestiges. She welcomed the "final defeat of various myths— that women are weaker, need protecting, and are physically incapable of handling combat" (*WW*, 259). At the same time, she warned citizens of the costs to society and human relationships when new mothers are shipped off to war. The Gulf War became a signature moment of this recognition, as some women were sent overseas just weeks after the birth of their children.

Equal rights for women in uniform remained a worthy pursuit, but when the country mobilizes for war, she worried that concerns about career advancement, legally reinforced by "rights talk," could overwhelm other goods and concerns, negatively affecting mothers, children, and even other citizens: "'Rights talk' has become a juggernaut that flattens principled opposition and even forestalls an open and robust discussion. . . . [A] society that puts the needs of its children last is a society 'progressing' rapidly toward moral ruin. . . . If anything, then, the question of women *and* war is by no means archaic in light of woman *in* war" (*WW*, 263). In response, Elshtain proposes "to make possible a more generous citizenship," for example, one in which mothers in uniform might be granted certain dispensations:

> By all means, those women who want to serve and to make the military their lives should do so. But our vast social experiment in absorbing women into the military who have no such aim and no such ambition and who are pregnant or the mothers of preschool infants (who are most vulnerable in cases of prolonged absence) is surely misguided and needs to be rethought. (*WW*, 264)

Since the Gulf War and the book's second edition, moves have intensified to open up to women military professions previously restricted to men. The ban on female combatants has been lifted throughout the services, including on combat aircraft, ships, and submarines, and there have been efforts to admit women to army and Marine Corps infantry positions. These changes recognize the reality of recent wars in Iraq, Afghanistan, and on other fronts in the war on terror where murky battle lines have eroded traditional distinctions between combatants and noncombatants. This point was first brought home when Private First Class Jessica Lynch—a supply clerk who traditionally would not engage in combat—was ambushed and taken prisoner during the 2003 invasion of Iraq. Lynch was later rescued, but her friend and fellow soldier, Lori Piestewa, died from injuries sustained in the ambush. Since this incident, over one hundred women have died in combat against terrorist adversaries such as al-Qaeda, the Taliban, and other insurgent groups that, in their own way, further blur traditional distinctions between combatants and noncombatants.

What Elshtain resisted through her exploration of the Beautiful Soul was the prevailing range of alternatives available to women— the idea of an either/or proposition: *either* the Madonna *or* the Spartan mother; *either* Jane Addams *or* Joan of Arc; *either* the new mother suckling her newborn *or* the soldier forced to leave her young children behind to serve and possibly die for her country. For every PFC Lynch, there are war's opponents, such as a Cindy Sheehan, an antiwar activist whose son was killed in the Iraq War. Yet traditional dichotomies between the public man and private woman fail to capture the stories of virtuous warriors like Andrew Bacevich, a retired army colonel and international relations scholar, who also lost a son in the very Iraq War he criticized in his scholarship. These rigid gendered categories could never be preserved as they had been handed down, for they presumed a gender gulf that does not reflect reality. Not fully anyway. There may still be more male hawks than female hawks and more female doves than male doves, at least as reflected in polls of Americans' support for the 2001 invasion of Afghanistan. But these are the extremes. What is more remarkable is the virtually equal gendering found among those in the middle—the 65 percent of the population who described themselves as either "Reluctant Warriors" or "Willing Supporters."[24] A year later, the gender gap among those supporting the Iraq War in November 2002 hovered around 5 percent—not significant enough to suggest women form some collective Beautiful Soul that opposes war.[25] Elshtain's creative categories and her critical analysis provide a context for appreciating these findings and reflecting thoughtfully upon what they mean. Elshtain sought to show how "traditional" conceptions of gender and war enjoyed a certain historical standing even as she sought to challenge, complexify, and deconstruct categories when they did not pertain. *Women and War* preserved potent elements of the Beautiful Soul mythology even while recognizing its significant limitations.

Elshtain is best remembered as a political philosopher whose deep knowledge of religion and ethics illumined the moral dimensions of political life. But she actually began her graduate training in history, which continually formed the basis of her trenchant sociopolitical analysis and cultural commentary. She enabled her readers and listeners to understand the society we inhabit, including our vital linkages to the past and the points of departure they set for the future. The historian in Elshtain was often front and center, if occasionally hiding in plain sight. She also sought to bring such empirical approaches to bear on the present. "There is no substitute for the facts," she once claimed. "If we get our descriptions of events wrong, our analyses and our ethics will be wrong too."[26] The ethicist cannot escape—indeed must aggressively engage—the question of *what is going on?* History first; ethics after. Lying beyond efforts to understand historical and contemporary contexts are the normative questions: What shall we do now? Where do we go from here? Hence, the ethical burden of the tropes she lays out.

This brings us to the constructive work that Elshtain's tropes of the Beautiful Soul and the Virtuous Warrior perform, not only in *Women and War*, but as iterative stages in her larger just war project. Might there be a more capacious *via media* between these two tropes, she seems to ask? What does Elshtain have in mind when she wonders whether the Beautiful Soul trope might be "cranked up" again "as a compelling ethos" for women? And what of the Just or Virtuous Warrior? In her efforts to nuance, scramble, and reform these two tropes, Elshtain retains vital elements of each and a critical respect for both. What she argued needed retaining from both tropes and for both sexes was the mutual quest for civic virtue, particularly in the face of war. She lobbied for innovative ways of "disarming civic virtue" as she simultaneously stipulated that such pursuits must engage more ethically robust forms of civic reflection when force is necessary. It is not surprising, then, that, after beginning with Hegel's Beautiful Soul, and moving through an examination of the male Virtuous Warrior, she ends *Women and War* with a neo-Hegelian synthesis: what she calls the "chastened patriot" a third trope that lays the groundwork for Elshtain's further scholarly forays and deep dive into the just war tradition.

To adumbrate the chastened patriot, Elshtain lifts up wartime president Abraham Lincoln and nonviolent civil rights leader Martin Luther King, Jr., noting how patriotism "taps love of country that yields civic concern *for* country." She distinguishes chastened patriotism from zealous forms of patriotism that border on nationalism or too easily reinforce the excesses of Machiavellian *virtù* or holy war fervor.[27] "The chastened patriot is committed *and* detached: enough apart so that she and he can be reflective about patriotic ties and loyalties, cherishing many loyalties rather than valorizing one alone." This frame is available to both "men and women who have learned from the past," who reject "counsels of cynicism" and who "modulate the rhetoric of high patriotic purpose by keeping alive the distancing voice of ironic remembrance" (*WW*, 252–53). At best, Elshtain only gestures to the norms this trope entails. But, with clarity of hindsight, what a gesture this turns out to be.

For what Elshtain presumes is that chastened patriots will slough off the binary framing of Virtuous Warrior and Beautiful Soul that have served as reigning repositories for all manner of other pernicious, oversimple binaries that cramp our moral understanding of war. Elshtain performs a masterful takedown of the ways in which, in time of war, man and woman (or male and female) have been carriers of various problematic dualisms. Overlaid onto man and woman are public/private; active/passive; civic paragon/second-class citizen; life-taker/life-giver; armed virtue/pacific love. War throws such binaries into stark relief, which is why *Women and War* (and the gendered analysis of war) affords an apt frame for examining them. If war is but a way of understanding politics, then these bothersome binaries are illustrative of and active within politics more broadly.

In this light, *Women and War* is not a narrower investigation of themes Elshtain undertook first in *Public Man, Private Woman*. Rather, it is a continuation, if not an intensification, of the ways that gender-based tropes constrain our assumptions about the possibilities of politics writ large. If, as *Women and War* sets out, "in the beginning politics *was* war," then war throws open perhaps the widest, most revealing window onto politics. Yet, if that is true, then alongside her effort to overcome the gendering of civic engagement and political life, an even more resilient binary also must be overcome: the perennially problematic bifurcation of war and peace. "A civic life animated by chastened patriotism," she says at book's end, "bears implications for how we think of peace and war . . . and the pitfalls in how each has been construed" (*WW*, 253). This line precedes the book's penultimate section on Kant, titled "The Problem with Peace"—a subject to which she would return many times, including in a chapter by the same name in *Just War against Terror* that explores the injustices that can traffic under the banner of peace.

These various ideas—war's window onto politics; our understudied assumptions about peace; and the obligations of chastened patriots to think critically *and* affirmatively about their countries through a civic language appropriate to the task—all of these seeds, first planted in *Women and War*, would grow deeper roots in her later ethical writings. The most publicly visible blossoming of these ideas grew into her contribution to contemporary moral reflection, known as "just war politics."

JUST WAR AS CIVIC VIRTUE AND POLITICS

Despite Elshtain's reliance upon the so-called Just Warrior as counterpart to the Beautiful Soul—fabled by his call of duty, willingness to
sacrifice, love of country, devotion to the moral and civic values of the
nation, his reluctant if not tragic disposition—the just war tradition
receives limited treatment in *Women and War*. Again, we distinguish the
broad category of the Just (or Virtuous) Warrior from her brief assessment of the state of the just war tradition in the mid-1980s. To be fair,
just war thought then was not the highly developed field it is today.
Women and War was first published five years before the Gulf War—the
first major U.S. war since the Vietnam War (to which the Gulf War was
compared throughout its run-up). Indeed, one crucial legacy of that war
was the confirmation that the United States could still wage and win a
just war.[28]

The field of just war thought at the time was largely shaped by
Michael Walzer's landmark *Just and Unjust Wars* and by the U.S. Catholic Bishops' 1983 pastoral letter, *A Challenge to Peace*. Elshtain does not
seem to have reckoned yet with James Turner Johnson's deep retriev-
als of just war history nor his mentor Paul Ramsey's ethical reflections,
including his defense of the Vietnam War. This was a male-dominated
field (as it remains today). So, it should be no surprise that Elshtain's
entry into the fray—initially dubbed "just war as civic virtue"—was
shaped by her gendered discussion of war undertaken in *Women and
War*. Beyond her brief engagements with just war thought there, the
deeper issues she explored in *Women and War* would dramatically influence her own unique approach to just war as a form of civic virtue. This
position refers to a form of "*deep reflection* by Everyman and Every-
woman on what his or her government is up to. This, in turn, *presupposes*
a 'self' of a certain kind, one attuned to moral reasoning and capable of
it; one strong enough to resist the lure of seductive, violent enthusiasms;
one bounded by and laced through with a sense of responsibility and
accountability. In other words, a *morally formed civic character* is a pre-
condition for just-war thinking as a civic virtue" (*WW*, 152; emphases
in original). Many of the attendant moral dispositions and civic orientations of this approach are found within the Beautiful Soul's reservoir, the

narratives Elshtain explores under this trope, and the conclusions about morality and human identity that she draws.

To be sure, she follows certain leads, such as Walzer's view of just war as political philosophy or "practical morality." However, she remained critical about the "many horrors that slip through" under Walzer's "supreme emergency" caveat, which under certain conditions and "given the *nature of the Nazi* threat" could legitimate saturation bombing of German cities (*WW*, 155). In spite of her immeasurable respect for Walzer, she was troubled by his "impoverished" reliance upon rights, which she views as an uncertain bulwark for holding back arguments justifying use of atomic weapons—which both Walzer and Elshtain opposed. She was more taken, at least initially, by the civic character of the U.S. Catholic Bishops' letter that, addressed to many and all citizens, took an absolute line against methods of total war that transgress the distinction between combatants and noncombatants.

Yet, over time, the bishops' approach to just war also would prove wanting for Elshtain. Her starting place for thinking about force was *not* the "presumption against war," as it was for the bishops. She was, like Augustine, too troubled by the ambivalence of peace, and by the evils that an unjust peace permits, to give peace, rather than justice, the higher ground in just war reflection. What she found most compelling and would develop in her own approach was not a view of just war that simply set limits and restraints on the resort to and conduct of force when war was in the offing. Elshtain understood and embraced all the traditional *jus ad bellum* criteria, but she didn't view them as fixed fence posts that form a cordon around our ethical thinking, as some just war proponents suggest. Nor was just war only a tool for statesmen and stateswomen, nor simply a professional ethic for soldiers (though her concern with *jus in bello* remained an abiding concern throughout her writings—something that often escaped her critics' notice). Just war as civic virtue, rather, was an ethic for all citizens, men and women, combatants and civilians, Just Warriors and Beautiful Souls, statesmen and -women, *and* everyday people, such as mothers, farmers, and tradesmen. Just war as civic virtue afforded "chastened patriots" an alternate moral vocabulary to the political discourse dominated by classical political realism, nuclear deterrence strategies, and game theory. This approach also served as an ethically grounded and religiously authentic alternative to pacifism and holy war. Rather than viewing just war as an ethical casuistry for justifying a given moral or political judgment or as political window dressing to reinforce whatever actions the state was already undertaking for its own interests,[29] Elshtain viewed just war as a civic framework for anchoring and extending moral debate. Just war drew from a body of ethical ideas that, going back to Augustine, had the potential to inculcate civic dispositions and provide a moral framework citizens could use to think deeply about their government's wars.

As Elshtain's thinking developed, the seeds planted in her just war as civic virtue approach would grow; grafted onto it was a larger project and more expansive position that came to called "just war as politics." That move looks something like this. Elshtain's analysis of gender in *Women and War* informed her understanding not only of civic virtue but how deeply human identity was wrapped up with civic and political identity, including with patriotism. This convergence of moral and civic virtue, identity, and patriotism opened up new possibilities, notwithstanding certain perils. Though wary of *armed* civic virtue and the lure of nationalistic excess, Elshtain's study of men and women in times of war had uncovered patriotism's noble side, which again balances love of country with concern for country.

Just war reflection was, for Elshtain, a promising way of disarming civic virtue and chastening patriotism because it provided a moral compass that was independent of the national interest and thus could guide and check political decision-making. Even in her brief just war discussion in *Women and War*, she finds inspiration in the ways the tradition opened up a larger moral vista onto the horizon of politics. Over time she worked to expand that moral horizon considerably through her "just war as politics" position, an approach that was on full display by the time of the Gulf War and is evidenced in the epilogue to the reprinted edition of *Women and War* (1995). Just war thought need not be limited to those discrete moments when nations were confronting or waging war, Elshtain maintained; rather, it could serve as a frame for thinking ethically about political life writ large: in times of war *and* peace; in international *and* in domestic settings; in universal contexts *and* in more particular formations. In words she uttered many times and in many places throughout her career, "Just war is not just about war. It is a way of thinking that refuses to separate politics from ethics." Perhaps the first time these words appear was in a 1992 essay revealingly entitled "Just War as Politics: What the Gulf War Told Us about Contemporary American Life."[30]

Elshtain's idea of just war politics was distinctive. Yet, she often wrote about just war as if her position and interpretation of the tradition was more settled than perhaps it was. Just war *is* this—or *is not* that, she would say. "Just war politics suggests that we back off rights absolutism," Elshtain maintained as she worried about the career aspirations of women warriors during the Gulf War and the toll taken on children (*WW*, 263). Or, in another formulation, just war as politics embraces "the standpoint of the child and the child's needs."[31] I know of no other just war thinkers who say this. Where are such ideas located within the just war canon? It would be more precise to say that *Elshtain's* just war politics claimed *this* or *that*. She simply wanted her reader or audience to sign on to this more encompassing approach. But this is perhaps a minor complaint compared to the insights that this more expansive school of just war thinking proffers. For example, in leveling sharp distinctions, say, between war and peace, Elshtain's approach to just war expands the aperture of moral reflection available in peacetime. Consider these compelling lines:

> As of this writing, Iraqi citizens are suffering greatly under a continuing set of economic sanctions that appear to have had little effect on Saddam Hussein's ability to hold on to power. Just-war thinking would suggest that this form of (apparent) benign intervention, by contrast to actual war-fighting, is not in fact ethically pristine, even apart from whether or not it is politically effective. The rush to use embargoes and sanctions that target whole populations, harming the least powerful first, requires more justification than it has received from past and current policy makers. (*WW*, 265)

One might assume these lines were part of Elshtain's controversial case for invading Iraq in 2003, a position for which she was castigated in many quarters of the academy and in many religious institutions.

254 John D. Carlson

Or that they were offered as part of a dialogue when other just war thinkers were giving serious attention to *jus post bellum*, that is, the problem of seeking justice after war ends. But Elshtain was already pondering *jus post bellum* when she penned these lines soon after the Gulf War ended. Indeed as early as 1992, she argued that "just war thinking must not be hauled out on various rhetorical or ceremonial occasions and then shelved once the rhetorical or political moment has passed, or the case made. If just war is evoked, as the President [George H. W. Bush] and many of our opinion leaders evoked it, then they should stay within the framework they have endorsed." Just war politics required, in her view, attending to malnourished Iraqis whose condition was aggravated by economic sanctions; the infrastructure devastated by U.S. and Coalition air strikes; and the plight of Kurds in the north and Shias in the south (after rising up as the United States had urged, the Shias were later crushed by Saddam Hussein).[32]

This expansive view of just war politics makes clear how Elshtain could challenge those who view just war as a checklist that gets pulled off a dusty shelf to legitimate a war or, from the other direction, those who conceive just war as a confining moral theory to be wrapped like an iron corset around the decision-making process to prevent the state from using force. For Elshtain, however, just war politics had been in play as part of the moral evaluation of U.S. policy in Iraq long before the "war on terror" ever began, just as coercion and force had been in use for the dozen or so intervening years between the Gulf War and the U.S. invasion that overthrew Saddam Hussein.

Much as Elshtain used just war to extend the moral horizon of politics—a project, we saw, already forming in *Women and War*—her "just war as politics" also made possible more permissive uses of force. This move would extend to supporting the George W. Bush administration's controversial case for preemptively invading Iraq, which Elshtain defended not only for national security reasons but also on humanitarian grounds. Elshtain knew well that the case for invading Iraq was not an easy one. She bore no umbrage against those who disagreed with her—or at least respectfully disagreed. If she was wrong to support the Iraq War, she was not alone. Many from across the political spectrum supported the war, including a long list of liberal hawks who pressed the humanitarian issues they hoped war would ameliorate.[33] But unlike many who later publicly recanted their initial support of the war—calling it a mistake—Elshtain never did. Perhaps this is because she believed just war calls for making the best decisions one can with the information available at a given time. Perhaps she thought the fate of the war stemmed from its flawed execution or failed policies and strategies rather than the moral case for intervention itself. Or, maybe she was just too willing to place her trust in the president and commander in chief, with whom she met, prayed, and deliberated at the White House. To assess if and where she went wrong with the Iraq War, we might judge Elshtain on her own terms by returning to the trope of the chastened patriot.

ELSHTAIN AS CHASTENED PATRIOT?

Just as the Beautiful Soul and the Virtuous Warrior served as carriers of certain gendered norms and presumptions, Elshtain's trope of the chastened patriot culled the strengths of both tropes to became a carrier of the values, norms, and claims underwriting her just war politics position. This third trope also became a vehicle for Elshtain's deepening Augustinianism. Already in *Women and War*, Elshtain was attentive to how Augustine's moral anthropology informs complex relational views of domestic life and the polity, which also extend beyond these spheres to include linkages to the human family. She extolled how "women figure centrally in Augustine's world," particularly his understanding of the peace of the home that contributes to the peace of the political sphere —a contrast to Greek or republican theories that starkly separate *oikos* from *polis* (*WW*, 131). Elshtain returned later in her *Augustine and the Limits of Politics* to dwell at length upon the ways in which Augustine used women in his discussion of human nature to advance an "ontology of equality." Men and women rise and fall together: from the false perch of human pridefulness to the sublime mark of the *imago dei*, with its imparted nature and relation to God that instills a sacredness and worth to all people.[34] Men and women occupy this ambivalent human condition together: their collective pursuits to affirm human dignity are challenged at every turn by sin, evil, and human error.

What has any of this to do with patriotism? Elshtain's chastened patriot is committed to concrete social and political relations that define her immediate contexts even as she extends her reach and concern to broader moral claims and loyalties, including universal ones. Indeed, localized experiences of solidarity and fellowship serve as stepping stones for more all-encompassing claims about human dignity. Politics serves an indispensable role in the preservation of such dignity. In her epilogue to the second edition of *Women and War*, Elshtain recommits to this patriotic aspiration:

> The ideal I here recommend embraces universalistic aspirations and possibilities, affirming the idea that we can and must reach out in gestures of solidarity, friendship, and citizenship to those different from ourselves. . . . What is at stake could scarcely be more impor-tant, namely, to put critical pressure on all forms of nationalistic absolutism even as one recognizes the legitimacy of particular and concrete loyalties and attachments. (*WW*, 269)

Universalism *and* particularism: "Neither trumps the other."

One way this vision would be instituted would become Elshtain's "international justice as equal regard" position, which argued for extend-ing just war thought from a more restrictive account of self-defense to a staunchly interventionist ethic of international justice in which force is used against humanitarian dangers, such as genocide and oppression, that violate the "equal regard and inviolable human dignity" owed to all. Here, she distinguished international justice from the prevailing model of humanitarian intervention that relied upon pity, sympathy, or compassion—of the kind that might move the Beautiful Soul. Nor does she invoke the Virtuous Warrior who fights for his own country and fel-low citizens. Rather, Elshtain privileges the patriot who is both stirred and chastened by universal sentiments, obligations, and claims of justice that are fulfilled through one's own particular national military force when it renders succor to distant neighbors in need. Rather than begin-ning with a "presumption against war," as found in the U.S. Catholic Bishops' statements, Elshtain's chastened patriot argues for a "presump-tive case in favor of the use of armed force by a powerful state or alliance of states who have the means to intervene, to interdict, and to punish in behalf of all those under assault."[35]

One can see here how, over time, the chastened patriot that Elshtain initially promotes in order to tame, temper, and disarm civic virtue ultimately might give way to a more confrontational, even combative ethic in service of a now globalized vision of just war politics. As she does in *Women and War*, Elshtain again proposes a "citizenship model," albeit one intended to address human rights challenges of the twenty-first century. It could even be called a model of global citizenship. Extending the political cosmology first sketched out in *Women and War* (which conceives politics as war and war as politics), she proposes how notions of citizenship are embedded centrally within an interventionist ethic that informed her support for the NATO-led intervention in the Balkans, the Iraq War, and potentially for other military interventions to stem gross human rights abuses.

Recalling her words that the September 11 attacks "reminded me of what it means to be an American citizen," it is clear that, for Elshtain, the American experience of war provided a foundation of her understanding of citizenship. *Women and War* chronicles early signs of this view through her diary entries and personal recollections. At times, her patriotism was anything but chastened. Elshtain recalls that, at age fifteen, she became preoccupied with the American Revolutionary soldier Nathan Hale, who, after being apprehended by the British for spying, was immortalized for his last words at the gallows: "I regret that I have but one life to give for my country." Hale's brave proclamation and martyrdom, she relates, "incited me to fever pitch for nearly a year" (*WW*, 27). But she also reflects ambivalently on World War II, "the good war" that nonetheless ended with the use of atomic weapons: "I'm not sure about Truman. . . . I am offended by the sloughing off of Hiroshima" (*WW*, 38). Finally, her condemnation of the Vietnam War was unstinting. These personal reflections all provided a footing for her just war politics project. At times, her support for U.S. power and American exceptionalism could seem flippant, as when she embraced *the Spiderman ethic* to explicate her view of international justice as equal regard: "with great power comes great responsibility." But subtler accounts of the American moral experience of war are also on display in *Women and*

War, as when she culls the experiences of wives and mothers of Confederate soldiers, such as Mary Chesnut, who exhibit a deeply loyal, loving, and local devotion to the *patria*. She combines these highly particular narratives with a civic identity that channels a "more universalist, democratic prospect," including more inclusive visions of citizenship found among abolitionist women in the North. "Northern women were patriotic, too," she comments. The chastened patriot is one who seeks to bring together particularist civic identities with more universal sets of moral commitments. This synthesis would become an abiding concern in her just war politics position, evident in the deep scrutiny she cast upon U.S. employment of force in numerous wars, including World War II, Vietnam, the Gulf War, Kosovo, and Iraq—all of which failed at times to honor moral commitments upholding a universal regard for human dignity. Her negotiation of particular and universal loves was part of her critical yet patriotic commitment to the United States as it exercised global responsibilities to those whose human dignity is trampled underfoot by oppressive governments (as she contended was the case in the Balkans, Kosovo, Afghanistan, and Iraq).

To be sure, Elshtain's at times forceful patriotic voice struck harsh chords with some critics who claimed that she, of all people, was in need of chastening for her support of the Iraq War and other policies of the George W. Bush administration. Such critiques came in spite of her professed efforts to "to put critical pressure on all forms of nationalistic absolutism." In her defense, her love of country was never grounded in nationalistic chauvinism or exclusivist visions of citizenship, as her recollections from her White House visit make clear. Over the course of her career, Elshtain's intellectual positions, civic activities, and public engagements reflected a tone heard in the famous interwar hymn "This Is My Song" by Lloyd Stone: "This is my home, the country where my heart is / Here are my hopes, my dreams, my sacred shrine." But Elshtain also recognized that, as the verse continues, "other hearts in other lands are beating / With hopes and dreams as true and high as mine." Elshtain's model of a chastened patriot can hold simultaneously the idea that "My country's skies may be bluer than the ocean" while also appreciating that other countries' "skies are everywhere as blue as mine." Such lyrics reflect the tenor of the chastened patriot as she or he negotiates commitment *and* detachment; holds in tension universal ideals *and* particular affections; and considers both national *and* international obligations.

Such themes, so central to the chastened patriot, are what connect *Women and War* to the much later and more developed *Just War against Terror*. This connection is evident in an epilogue to the latter, which Elshtain devotes to "Four Brave Women" from Algeria, Uzbekistan, Somalia, and Iran. Hailing from diverse parts of the world, all of these women shared universal aspirations for basic freedoms, rights, security, education, and the promise of citizenship—what most women desire for their children and themselves. These women also all asked for U.S. support and engagement in their nations' affairs, including, when necessary, perhaps "American presence and power."[36] Elshtain's moral vision of politics, which combines universal aspirations with highly particularized civic loves and loyalties, does not flow from conceiving just war narrowly as a moral casuistry or a corset for limiting political engagement and coercive force in the world. Rather, just war politics proposes a more expansive view of political ethics. Given her sustained meditation upon the gendered experiences of politics and war, her just war position also supports a more expansive role for women in politics. For example, Elshtain's critique of the Taliban's treatment of Afghan women and girls illustrates her effort to use just war thinking as a frame for morally evaluating and critiquing political life—in this case a theocratic political order.[37] And, of course, when humanitarian concerns are at stake, such a broad vision of just war politics may entail a more permissive use of force in more controversial situations—as occurred in the case of the Iraq War.

In one area, however, Elshtain urges the chastened patriot to ask difficult questions of one's own country that Elshtain herself did not seem to ask, at least not publicly: "A nation must learn how to endure defeats—better that than how to crow in victory and war-bought unity." Invoking Lincoln, Elshtain proposed how a nation's defeats (and victories) might be occasions for introspection—"but only if we chasten the nihilistic disillusionment or blind triumphalism each invites; only if we put away the grand narrative of armed civic virtue" (*WW*, 251). The conditions in Iraq were in significant decline throughout Elshtain's final years and until she died in 2013, one year before ISIS rose to power. It

seems fair to ask what it would mean to acknowledge U.S. failures in the
Iraq War on Elshtain's terms. For the chastened patriot must be committed to an honest facing up to such uncomfortable realities. The Iraq
War, and later the war in Afghanistan, became occasions for both disillusionment *and* triumphalism at the same time. For even as these wars
dragged on with anemic signs of progress at best, the United States'
celebration of the cult of the service member and veteran has buoyed
a citizenry that is otherwise largely detached from and indifferent to
the nation's wars. As a young woman, Elshtain engaged these kinds of
critical concerns directly and courageously with respect to Vietnam, a
war she deeply opposed on moral and patriotic grounds. I'm not sure,
though, she ever devoted comparable time or thought discussing what
went wrong in Iraq or what it would mean for the United States to
redeem itself from the mistakes it made there in a war she supported,
again, on moral and patriotic grounds. By standards of judgment that
she set for herself and for all of us, that would seem to be an occasion
for regret.

At the time it was published in 1987, *Women and War* solidified Elshtain's
reputation as a prominent political philosopher whose keen insights
and commentary could significantly enrich public discourse. To read
this work today yields a different set of insights. In retrospect, *Women
and War* colorfully narrates the education of a distinguished just war
thinker—a luminary of her time. Through so many facets of Elshtain's
intellectual development and moral formation—seminal childhood
experiences; vast engagements with literature and film; first-person
accounts of personal and public affections; her deep grappling with historical and contemporary events; her fluid movement across academic
disciplines (from history, international relations, and political philosophy to women's studies, religion, and ethics); and a persistent attention to
how gender offers a lens onto politics and human identity—*Women and
War* planted the seeds of what would grow into the position she called
just war politics. Through two recurring themes—Elshtain's abiding
interest in how war sharpens our understanding of citizenship, virtue,
and politics; and her challenge to the various antinomies that politics

artificially establishes and preserves (man/woman, public/private, life-taker/life-giver; and war/peace)—*Women and War* serves as an early forerunner to the project consummated in *Just War against Terror*.

Elshtain's novel approach to just war politics emerged as both a form of civic virtue and a discourse for chastening patriotism. As a chastened patriot herself, she was fluent in this language, even if perhaps she spoke too stridently at times. This was why we stand in need of other chastened patriots to debate, refine, and even correct her positions; she would surely agree. This chastened patriot is not constructed ex nihilo but rather is born of its maternal and paternal forebears: Beautiful Souls and Virtuous Warriors. However much these two tropes have evolved in certain ways or dissolved in others, they remain part of the chastened patriot's DNA. Elshtain understood this genetic makeup and even located it within herself. For despite her early childhood experiences playing war and her success in male-dominated academic fields, she also drew deeply from her own maternal experiences and instincts. The Beautiful Soul, we recall, "is no ordinary wife or mother or secretary or nurse [or professor]: she becomes a civic being; she is needed by others; she can respond simultaneously to what Jane Addams called the 'family claim' and the 'social claim,' for, she is told, without her unselfish devotion to country and family each would be lost." For those who knew her, Elshtain was just such a civic being. She traveled in circles with women from many other nations who also "yearn for public identities as civic beings serving ends that take them beyond the borders of private lives" (*WW*, 9–10). So, it was not simply her just war contributions that made Jean Bethke Elshtain a model citizen. Devoted to family and country, she was, in turn, deeply appreciated and needed by both. Through her public and private roles—as scholar and patriot but also as devoted wife, mother, and grandmother—she remained until the end a Beautiful Soul.

NOTES

1. Jean Bethke Elshtain, "An Extraordinary Discussion," *Sightings*, October 3, 2001, https://divinity.uchicago.edu/sightings/extraordinary-discussion-jean-bethke-elshtain (accessed July 31, 2017).

2. Elshtain was a lead writer of two key documents published under the auspices of the Institute for American Values, including a much discussed non-partisan statement, signed by sixty prominent academics and other public figures after the 9/11 attacks, entitled "What We're Fighting For: A Letter From America." The statement appears as an appendix in Elshtain, *Just War against Terror* (2003), 182–207. Earlier she had spearheaded the crafting and signing of a document by the Council on Civil Society, *A Call to Civil Society: Why America Needs Moral Truths* (New York: Institute for American Values, 1998).

3. Elshtain, "An Extraordinary Discussion." These original casualty estimates in the immediate aftermath of the attacks were later downsized to just under 3,000 people.

4. George W. Bush, "Address to a Joint Session of Congress and the American People," September 20, 2001, http://georgewbush-whitehouse.archives.gov/news/releases/2001/09/20010920-8.html.

5. Quoted in Paul Vitello, "Jean Bethke Elshtain, a Guiding Light for Policy Makers after 9/11, Dies at 72," *New York Times*, August 16, 2013, A15.

6. Jean Bethke Elshtain, "A Just War?" *Boston Globe*, October 6, 2002; Elshtain, "Thinking about War and Justice," Religion and Culture Web Forum, May 2003, https://divinity.uchicago.edu/sites/default/files/imce/pdfs/webforum/052003/commentary.pdf; Elshtain, "But Was It Just? Reflections on the Iraq War," *Nexus* 9 (2004): 69–77.

7. Vitello, "Jean Bethke Elshtain."

8. Jean Bethke Elshtain, *Women and War* (New York: Basic, 1987).

9. *Women and War*, Elshtain's second monograph, builds upon and focuses more narrowly on many of the themes taken up in her first book, *Public Man, Private Woman*.

10. See her landmark intellectual biography: Jean Bethke Elshtain, *Jane Addams and the Dream of American Democracy: A Life* (New York: Basic Books, 2002).

11. Kristin Herzog, review of *Most Dangerous Women: Feminist Peace Campaigners of the Great War*, by Anne Wiltsher; *Women in War: First-Hand Accounts from World War II to El Salvador*, by Shelley Saywell; *Women in the Resistance*, by Margaret L. Rossiter; and *Women and War*, by Jean Bethke Elshtain, *Signs: Journal of Women in Culture and Society* 13, no. 4 (1988): 877, http://www.journals.uchicago.edu/doi/abs/10.1086/494480.

12. Mona Harrington and Mary Lyndon Shanley, review of *Women and War*, by Jean Bethke Elshtain, *American Political Science Review* 82, no. 1 (1988): 271.

13. Jean Bethke Elshtain, "Woman, the State, and War," *International Relations* 23, no. 2 (2009): 298–303.

14. George H. Quester, review of *Women and War*, by Jean Bethke Elshtain, *Ethics* 98, no. 3 (1988): 609.

15. Ibid. Elshtain once recounted to me a conversation with a faculty colleague whose game theory model had failed to predict Saddam Hussein's behavior during the Persian Gulf War. The incredulous international relations theorist sought exoneration by claiming, "It isn't the fault of the model. How could anyone know Saddam wouldn't act rationally?"

16. Quester, review of *Women and War*, 610

17. It's not that Elshtain overlooked this objection. I just doubt she thought it worth taking seriously. What the critical reviewer calls her "prejudices," Elshtain would have called history. That is, there is no alternate history within which one can stand to test whether a reversal of men's and women's roles would have yielded different outcomes. We are where we are. We must begin at the point to which history has brought us.

18. "Viewing themselves through the lens of this construction, men see edifying tales of courage, duty, honor, glory as they engage in acts of protection and defense and daring: heroic deed doing" (*WW*, 165).

19. J. Glenn Gray, *The Warriors: Reflections on Men in Battle* (New York: Harcourt, Brace, 1959).

20. Machiavelli, *The Prince*, 2nd ed., trans. Harvey C. Mansfield (Chicago: University of Chicago Press, 1985, 1998), 101.

21. For a deep exploration of civil-religious sanctification and redemption, see Jonathan H. Ebel, *Faith in the Fight: Religion and the American Soldier in the Great War* (Princeton, NJ: Princeton University Press, 2010). Ebel makes use of Elshtain's Beautiful Soul trope. Decades later, the citizen-soldier GI of World War II was part of a great "crusade in Europe," as Gen. Eisenhower called it, to defeat Nazism and fascism.

22. Elshtain always enjoyed teaching Michael Walzer's discussion of naked soldiers, in which one soldier finds himself incapable of shooting the enemy whom he has caught unawares in a bath on the front lines; see Michael Walzer, *Just and Unjust Wars: A Moral Argument with Historical Illustrations* (New York: Basic, 1977), 138–43.

23. In returning to *Women and War* when writing this chapter, I was struck by Elshtain's recourse to the language of constructed identities and to her own self-appointed charge of deconstructing such representations. In her early career, she spoke at times of unraveling grand narratives. By the time she moved to the University of Chicago, she spoke far more about moral anthropology and the formation of the human person than of constructed identities. Occasional references to Foucault in *Women and War* gave way to more frequent invocations of Augustine and John Paul II in later work. Not a complete transformation, to be sure, but a notable shift in emphasis.

24. From the Gallup News Service, see David W. Moore, "Eight of 10 Americans Support Ground War in Afghanistan," Gallup, November 1, 2001, http://

www.gallup.com/poll/5029/eight-americans-support-ground-war-afghanistan
.aspx.

25. In November 2002, 61 percent of men supported invading Iraq compared to 56 percent of women; David W. Moore, "Gender Gap Varies on Support for War," November 19, 2002, http://www.gallup.com/poll/7243/gender
-gap-varies-support-war.aspx.

26. *JWT*, 9.

27. "Attached more to the sense of a political and moral community than to
a state, patriotism can be, and has been, evoked to bring out the best in us—even
as, when it shades into nationalism, it brings out the worst" (*WW*, 252).

28. In her autobiographical chapter in *Women and War*, Elshtain recalls her
journal entries on the Vietnam War and how they both alienated and engaged
her, politically speaking. In protest, she wrote letters to editors, walked in silent
vigils, and expressed horror at images of massacred Vietnamese villagers on the
cover of *Life*—"I was ashamed of my country. It is terrible to feel such shame,
she recalls" (*WW*, 37). Elshtain had belonged to a community of protesters. At
her funeral, several of her friends from what she called her "hippy days" turned
out to pay their respects. Their hippy bona fides were confirmed when they told
me about the large house they had all once shared, endearingly dubbed "Brook
Farm II." As well, during the funeral Mass, when the priest invited the congregation to show each other a sign of peace, a few of Jean's friends in the pews could
be seen quietly flashing a peace sign with their fingers.

29. Writing about George H. W. Bush in the Gulf War, Elshtain worries:
"For President Bush, just war was a powerful instrument of legitimation for U.S.
policy . . . it is troubling to see just war criteria brought forward and proffered as
vindication of one side in so cavalier a manner"; Elshtain, "Just War as Politics:
What the Gulf War Told Us about Contemporary American Life," in *But Was
It Just? Reflections on the Morality of the Persian Gulf War*, ed. David E. DeCosse
(New York: Doubleday, 1992), 48.

30. Elshtain, "Just War as Politics," 43.

31. Ibid., 55.

32. Ibid., 52–53.

33. See John D. Carlson, "The Morality, Politics, and Irony of War: Recovering Reinhold Niebuhr's Ethical Realism," *Journal of Religious Ethics* 36, no. 4
(2008): 619–51.

34. *ALP*, 42–45.

35. Jean Bethke Elshtain, "Military Intervention and Justice as Equal
Regard," in *Religion and Security: The New Nexus in International Relations*, ed.
Robert A. Seiple and Dennis R. Hoover (Lanham, MD: Rowman & Littlefield,
2004), 121.

36. *JWT*, 174–79.

37. Ibid., 38–44.

CHAPTER THIRTEEN

A NEW, BUT STILL A JUST WAR AGAINST TERROR

Chris Brown

Jean Bethke Elshtain's *Just War against Terror* (*JWT*) is a work that is difficult to classify. It was published in 2003, but written in 2002 as a companion piece to "What We're Fighting For: A Letter from America," organized by Elshtain and signed by sixty leading figures in American intellectual life, and as such can be seen as a *pièce d'occasion*, an expression of anger at the failure of so many American and non-American intellectuals to respond adequately to the task of confronting Islamist terrorism. But it is much more than a polemic; in a relatively small compass it encapsulates virtually all of the themes that over a forty-year writing career Elshtain made her own. Here you will find women and war, just war theory, democracy on trial, real politics, Augustine and the limits of politics—one could continue but the point is made; *Just War against Terror* is a kind of compendium of Elshtain's thought and a very suitable starting point for a reflection on the story she tells in that book and has told in many other ways. Here, this task of reflection is approached not by looking back, but by examining the world of 2015, an approach wholly in the spirit of the original. Do we still need to fight a just war against terror? And if so, how? These are the themes of this chapter, and the answer to the first question is yes, we do; the second question is more difficult, and some of the ways in which the war is currently being fought need to be closely examined.

SETTING THE SCENE, 2002–2015: IRAQ, OBAMA, AND THE WAR ON TERROR

Just War against Terror condemns al-Qaeda for the terrorist organization it was and is, but the main target of Elshtain's ire was not the terrorists but those who make excuses for terror, the intellectuals who rationalize terror as payback for America's failings in its dealings with the rest of the world. She provides American examples of this tendency; for a set of British opinions on similar lines, a symposium in the *London Review of Books* will suffice.[1] The most controversial comment in this symposium came from Mary Beard, a Cambridge classics lecturer; it is worth quoting at length:

> The horror of the tragedy was enormously intensified by the ring-side seats we were offered through telephone answering machines and text-messages. But when the shock had faded, more hard-headed reaction set in. This wasn't just the feeling that, however tactfully you dress it up, the United States had it coming. That is, of course, what many people openly or privately think. World bullies, even if their heart is in the right place, will in the end pay the price. But there is also the feeling that all the "civilised world" (a phrase which Western leaders seem able to use without a trace of irony) is paying the price for its glib definitions of "terrorism" and its refusal to listen to what the "terrorists" have to say.

This is a compendium of the rationalizations that Elshtain objected to in *Just War against Terror*. In the key quote, it is the United States that "had it coming," rather glossing over the fact that although the attack on the Pentagon could possibly be seen as an attack on "the United States," the victims in New York City and in Pennsylvania were civilians (and not all U.S. citizens for that matter). But what is most interesting is the assumption that the "terrorists" were motivated by resistance to the "world bully," as opposed to the desire to establish a theocracy in the Middle East against the wishes of most of the local inhabitants, and that they had something to say that a liberal intellectual such as Beard ought to listen to and presumably act upon. This is characteristic of the mentality Elshtain attacked in *Just War against Terror*, namely, a refusal to take seriously, or even to read, the pronouncements of al-Qaeda and similar groups, and instead to project on them views that a Western liberal can sympathize with; Beard opposes what she calls American imperialism, terrorist groups oppose what they call American imperialism, and Beard simply assumes that therefore common ground can be found if only we listen for it—but we don't actually have to listen very hard to hear what they are saying, we only have to listen hard if we want to turn what they are actually saying into what we (or she) would like them to say.

In the years since *Just War against Terror* was written, the tendency Beard exemplified has become more pronounced. The Iraq War of 2003, combined with some specific George W. Bush administration policies, such as support for "enhanced interrogation," provided a great deal of ammunition for those who wished to deny the legitimacy of the war on terror. The U.S.-led coalition that intervened in Iraq and overthrew the Baathist regime of Saddam Hussein failed to find the expected weapons of mass destruction (WMD), came with insufficient force to occupy and establish direct control over the country, unwisely disbanded the Baath Party and the Iraqi army, and unwittingly set the scene for a protracted conflict between Shia and Sunni. All this gives us good reason to doubt the judgment of the key players, from Donald Rumsfeld whose plans for the occupation willfully disregarded the advice on the numbers of troops required from those who had hands-on experience of peacekeeping in the Balkans in the 1990s, to Tony Blair, who, amazingly, admitted to the Chilcot Inquiry that he had not anticipated that either Iran or al-Qaeda would take advantage of the intervention to pursue their own goals. In short, there are many good reasons why any concerned citizen should be critical of what was done in this period; still, the mythology that has grown up around Iraq 2003, nurtured by the same figures who apologized for 9/11, goes well beyond anything justified by the facts. In most intellectual circles in Europe and North America it is now regarded as a simple fact that Bush and Blair lied about WMD, that the "humanitarian" justification for the war was an afterthought when this lie was exposed, and that all the deaths in Iraq post-2003 can be attributed to the Coalition.

In fact, on the first two issues the evidence clearly points in a different direction—there is plenty of evidence that Bush and Blair, like most other observers, genuinely believed in the existence of WMD,[2] and there is even more evidence that they, and other coalition leaders repeatedly made the humanitarian case for regime change well before the actual intervention.[3] As for the deaths that have accompanied Sunni–Shia violence post-2003, the primary responsibility for the many atrocities that took place surely rests with those who committed them—although one can agree that a high degree of responsibility attaches to those whose policies created the power vacuum that so many ill-intentioned people attempted to fill. Still, these nuances are lost on those for whom Iraq was not just a failure of judgment but a crime, and this is a legacy of the war that has shaped a great deal of the debate on the war on terror since 2003. Before that date, the writers, intellectuals, and theologians criticized in *Just War against Terror* were somewhat on the defensive in arguing the "blowback" thesis—they needed to be careful not to seem to be actually justifying the murder of so many people on 9/11 (hence the substitution of the term "the United States" in Beard's quote for the 3,000 actual dead, noted above, even Beard would not have said that the actual casualties, mostly civilians and 12 percent non-American, "had it coming").

Thus, intervention in Iraq was a game-changer—critics of U.S. policy had something much more substantial to lay into, and the intellectual burden of proof moved against those who would defend the war on terror. For the latter, the war on terror was (and is) a "war of necessity" not a "war of choice"; there was (and is) a genuine threat from people who are not simply opponents of specific U.S./Western policies, but whose worldview is fundamentally opposed to Enlightenment values—as the cliché has it, they are opposed not just to what we do but to who we are, and the threat this poses must be met, by whatever means are consistent with the values we wish to defend. This judgment was always contested by those critics who convinced themselves that "terrorism" (in scare quotes) was a function of Western policy, and the war in Iraq, seen by all but a few officials in Washington and London as a war of choice, seemed to strengthen their case insofar is it gave our enemies more reasons to hate us. And the Bush administration's unconscionable endorsement of torture rightly caused deep concern for those who wished to see a necessary war fought in a manner that was morally defensible. There are a number of issues concerning breaches of international humanitarian law and the use of detention without trial at Guantanamo Bay that deserve censure, but these can just about be defended as a necessary and temporary evil, as can some forms of interrogation that a human rights activist would disapprove of, such as sleep deprivation.[4] But no defense of "waterboarding" as an enhanced interrogation method is possible. Waterboarding was torture when the Gestapo employed it and it remains so; the Bush administration's denial of this obvious fact inflicted great harm on the cause the president and his advisers believed this repulsive tactic would serve.

This impact of this tidal shift away from support for the war on terror can be felt through to the present day. During the second George W. Bush administration, support for the war waned (and with it support for liberal interventionism more generally). In the United States, Barack Obama beat the more experienced Hillary Clinton to the Democratic Party nomination, largely on the back of his opposition to the Iraq War. In the UK, working-class voters remained loyal to Blair and he was reelected, albeit with a smaller majority, in 2005, but the steady poison directed against him and dripped into the political atmosphere by the media (assisted by his successor, Gordon Brown, it has to be said) finally succeeded in driving Blair out of office a couple of years later, thereby removing one of the most articulate defenders of the war on terror from the scene.

The very term "war on terror" had never been popular in some circles (although the same circles seem not to have been particularly upset by the "war on drugs" or the "war on poverty"), but by 2009 it had been officially discouraged by both the UK and U.S. governments. Still, although the term may have been discouraged, it continued to be echoed in official pronouncements; in his inaugural address in 2009,

President Obama opined that "our nation is at war against a far-reaching network of violence and hatred," and many similar statements can be found uttered by officials on both sides of the Atlantic.

The current state of play on the existence or nonexistence of the war on terror can be found in a speech given by President Obama on May 23, 2013, at the National Defense Academy—given before the rise of so-called Islamic State in Syria, but still relevant. Characteristically thoughtful, and, at times equally characteristically ambiguous, he covered a great deal of ground, first noting very clearly that "under domestic law, and international law, the United States is at war with al-Qaeda, the Taliban, and their associated forces. We are at war with an organization that right now would kill as many Americans as they could if we did not stop them first. So this is a just war—a war waged proportionally, in last resort, and in self-defense."[5]

Still, he also opines that although "our nation is still threatened by terrorists," Osama bin Laden and most of his lieutenants are dead and the nature of the threat from terrorists has changed. The idea that we need to summarize the various campaigns we are fighting under one big heading is to be set aside, partly because it no longer measures up to the strategic reality, but also—and here Obama was, I think, on strong ground—because "we have to be mindful of James Madison's warning that 'no nation could preserve its freedom in the midst of continual warfare.'" Again very sensibly, and implicitly rejecting some of the unwise rhetoric of George W. Bush, he adds, "Neither I, nor any President, can promise the total defeat of terror," or the eradication of evil.

The rest of the speech discusses the nature of the specific threats in particular places that the United States and the rest of the world still face—and here the occasion of the speech is highlighted. The reason the president felt the necessity to give a major speech on this subject was because of heavy criticism of the use of unmanned aerial vehicles (UAVs), or "drones"—and the policy of "targeted assassination." In the preceding weeks, a number of American and European commentators had begun to assess the scale of the use of these weapons and had come to the conclusion that Obama was, as they sometimes put it, "every bit as bad as, or actually worse than Bush."[6] The honeymoon Obama had enjoyed with liberal commentators had finally ended, and he was now having to defend himself on two fronts— from those on the political Right who rejected the "worse than Bush" rhetoric and accused him of weakness, and from those whom he might have considered as coming from his end of the political Left but who refused to accept his interpretation of the nature of the threat that the United States still faced.

By facing up to his critics on the Left, Obama identified and challenged one element of the opposition to the continuing just war against terror—those intellectuals who, after fourteen years of conflict, still find any exercise of U.S. power in the world to be illegitimate, who are still firmly mired in the mind-set identified and excoriated by Elshtain in *Just War against Terror* back in 2002. In this speech, as in his earlier address on the occasion of his accepting the Nobel Peace Prize in 2009, Obama demonstrates that he understands "the burden of American power in a violent world" (to quote the subtitle of *JWT*) in a way that many of his critics on the Left do not.[7] But within a few months of the controversy over drones reaching the boiling point, another occasion for a demonstration of the same oppositional mind-set arose. The revelations of the surveillance activities of U.S. National Security Agency (NSA) and the UK Government Communications Headquarters (GCHQ) by the former analyst Edward Snowden opened up a second front in the war against the just war on terror. Some of Snowden's revelations attracted criticism from libertarians of the political Right, but many of his supporters—and the supporters of the WikiLeaks founder, Julian Assange, who was holed up in the Ecuadorean embassy in London in order to avoid facing prosecution for sexual offenses in Sweden—are the same radical journalists and intellectuals who have been in opposition to the war on terror since it was first mooted.

Drones and the NSA—these became the new battlegrounds, within the West and also in Syria, Pakistan, and Yemen, where the war on terror was being fought and opposed. In both cases there are genuine dilemmas to be explored. Although I will, for the most part, defend the Obama administration's record on use of force and on surveillance and information gathering, the story is by no means as clear-cut as partisans on both sides would like it to be. Drone warfare may be the least-worst option in dealing with many threats, but it still illustrates some of the worst aspects of the postindustrial way of making war. Extensive surveillance may save lives, but it also potentially threatens the liberties that the war on terror is designed to protect. There are difficult issues here, and no easy answers.

DILEMMAS OF FIGHTING A JUST WAR ON TERROR: UAVS AND TARGETED ASSASSINATION

Drones can be used for surveillance, and targeted assassinations can be carried out by manned warplanes or special forces, but still the association of this technology with that tactic does accurately summarize a distinctive feature of the Obama administration's conduct of the war on terror. By 2013, when his speech to the National Defense Academy was delivered, Obama had authorized more 400 drone strikes since taking office, targeting high profile al-Qaeda and Taliban leaders or technical specialists (bomb-makers, etc.) in Pakistan, Yemen, and Somalia, with an estimated 3,000 operatives killed, including 50 high-level leaders.[8] So-called signature strikes had also been conducted, in which groups of individuals who were suspected of being Taliban or al-Qaeda operatives were targeted; these strikes were not technically targeted assassinations because they were not aimed at specific named targets; on the other hand, since the individuals concerned were identified as enemy combatants on the basis of their behavior patterns rather than by such indicators as wearing a uniform, they were also difficult to classify as regular military operations. Drone strikes put a great deal of psychological stress on their operators but did not put the lives of U.S. servicemen at risk.[9] Removing capable leaders and specialists undoubtedly damaged the capability of the groups that were targeted, but it may also have acted as a recruiter for these groups—and, in any event, sometimes removing experienced leaders is not a good idea if an eventual negotiated settlement is sought. The legality of drone strikes in countries with which the United States is not at war has been challenged, as has been the extrajudicial killing of at least one U.S. citizen. Some have argued that the policy of targeted assassination is a logical consequence of the ending of "enhanced interrogation" techniques by the Obama administration and the decision to at least try to close the camp at Guantanamo, decisions which made the taking of prisoners both pointless and potentially legally embarrassing.[10]

All of these issues are important in the context of the politico-strategic efficacy of the drone campaign, but they do not address the question of justice—can a policy of targeted assassination be seen as consistent with a *just* war on terror? And, does the pursuit of this policy via drone strikes affect our judgment in this case? Picking up the latter point first, the reliance on drones represents the latest version of the U.S./Western desire to fight a risk-free war, a desire critiqued briefly by Elshtain in *Just War against Terror*. Her point there was that the Kosovo intervention fell short of what was needed precisely because casualty-avoidance was taken to extremes. She quotes approvingly Paul W. Kahn, "If the decision to intervene is morally compelling, it cannot be conditioned on political considerations that assume an asymmetric valuing of human life" (*JWT*, 157). In Kosovo, there should have been boots on the ground as well as planes in the air—on the other hand, over the last decade-plus there have been plenty of boots on the ground in Iraq, in Afghanistan, and occasionally in Pakistan (for example, in the raid on Abbottabad that killed bin Laden), and drones were for the most part used in places where there are local political (or geographical) reasons for not committing actual soldiers. And on the positive side, the capacity that drone pilots have for maintaining extended periods of surveillance before actually striking should mean that civilian casualties are easier to avoid. In fact, it seems that this potential for increasing human security is not actually realized, largely because of the training of at least the CIA drone pilots, which does not put as much stress on the laws of war as that of regular air force personnel—but still, in principle, drones are weapons that make the discrimination that is central to just war thinking easier to achieve.[11]

In spite of these positives, it is still not too difficult to see why so many people worry about excessive reliance on drones. There is already something intuitively distasteful about the idea of killing without at least some risk of being killed, and this is somehow magnified when the "killer" is sitting in a darkened room two continents away. It is important not to get too romantic about this—notions of chivalry and a warrior's honor have very little purchase where al-Qaeda, the Taliban, or ISIL are concerned—but the impersonality of drone warfare and also of long-distance cruise missile strikes is an issue, and not just because the sense that such killings are "unfair" acts as a driver for recruitment to terrorist groups. This will become an even more pressing issue in the not too distant future when drones are replaced or supplemented by "robots"—that is to say, when the machines themselves are programmed to make the decision to kill. However subtle and sophisticated the programming, the use of robots will increase exponentially the sense of revulsion that the use of drones already clearly generates. Still, it is the use to which drones have been put—the policy of targeted assassinations—that is the more difficult issue for those who would wage the war on terror justly.

International humanitarian law (the law of war) operates on the principle that combatants are essentially anonymous, defined by the uniforms they wear or by other symbols that distinguish them from civilians. The principle of anonymity is also tied up with the idea of the moral equality of combatants.[12] Anonymity also plays a part in the informal code with which combatants of (at least Western) armies have equipped themselves, hence the well-documented distaste in World War I and II for the infantry sniper, who identifies and kills in a way that is disturbingly personal. By the same token, the assassination of heads of state and individual army leaders in times of war is also regarded as morally ambiguous, perhaps justified in the case of a tyrant but generally undesirable. The key question is, how do these legal prohibitions and moral restraints play out in the war on terror?

In fact, they illustrate better than almost anything else the problems we have in coming to an intuitive moral understanding of how we should characterize the war on terror. Obviously, neither terrorists in general nor their leaders in particular wear distinctive uniforms or symbols that could convey anonymity; nor do they usually operate in the kind of context where direct contact between opposing forces is routine and where informal patterns of behavior can thus emerge. On the other hand, they equally obviously carry out or order acts contrary to the laws of war, ignoring the requirement to discriminate among targets. In all three respects, they resemble members of a criminal gang rather than an army, which is one of the reasons why critics of the war on terror dislike the term and think it should be replaced by one that points towards the model of law enforcement rather than war fighting.[13] But the law enforcement model only makes sense in those contexts where a judicial and police system exists that can identify and arrest members of a terrorist group, and this is a context that obviously doesn't exist in many parts of the world today, and, more specifically, that certainly doesn't exist in parts of Yemen, Somalia, Syria, and the frontier districts of Pakistan. These are regions where the writ of the central governments in question simply does not run, and, of course, there is the added complication that those governments, in any event, may not wish to exercise their legal powers when these groups are involved—had the United States gone to the Pakistani authorities with the evidence they had on the probable presence of bin Laden in Abbottabad, it is difficult to believe that this would have led to his capture.

In short, the war on terror is neither a "war" in the conventional sense—if it were, it would tell against a systematic policy of targeted assassination—nor a police operation—where the targeting of criminals is a perfectly legitimate tactic, but where the aim is the arrest and conviction of the wrongdoers and where their assassination would be a form of judicial murder. It is mostly fought not in a conventional war zone, nor in a zone of peace of the sort that might be found in relatively well-ordered societies adhering roughly to the rule of law, but rather in a kind of intermediate zone, neither of peace nor of war.

Perhaps what that suggests is that there is no big story to be told about targeted assassination; rather than trying to work out whether this is a morally acceptable policy in general terms we should instead focus on the specific. The moral demand should be that when killing takes place it should be on the basis of very good evidence as to the standing of the proposed victim, that civilian casualties should be avoided (difficult though that is when the status of noncombatant is so difficult to define), and that the wider political context should be taken into account, in other words, the benefit from the operation should exceed potential political costs in terms of local support. Such a position would not satisfy those critics for whom any use of the tactic of targeted killing is illegitimate, but it would represent the best fit with the principle that the war on terror should be fought justly. It would also rule out so-called signature strikes, where there is no direct evidence that the individuals concerned are members of a terrorist group.[14] Modern campaigns against terrorist groups take place in a grey area where it is unacceptable to regard the local inhabitants as enemies unless they explicitly act as such—being in the wrong place at the wrong time may be suggestive, but it shouldn't be enough on its own to warrant a death sentence.

SURVEILLANCE, SECURITY, AND CIVIL LIBERTY

Does terrorism pose an existential threat to Western societies? At the most obvious, material level the answer to this question is no. Whereas, for example, during the Cold War the possibility of nuclear war certainly did pose an existential threat in the most literal sense of the term, terrorist attacks are on an entirely different scale, less deadly than any number of threats to life produced by the terms of modern living—dying in an automobile accidents being the case that is often cited by those who argue we take the risk posed by terrorism too seriously. Of course, there is an important moral difference between an accident and a deliberate killing, but in terms simply of scale the former is indeed more of a threat to life than the latter, and neither constitutes an existential threat to our societies. On the other hand, existential threats are not necessarily to be defined quite so literally, as threats to one's physical existence; threats to a way of life as opposed to life itself can be equally existential. Does terrorism pose this kind of threat? The operation of extremists within communities, the radicalization of individuals, especially the young and impressionable, the "capture" of mosques, the poisoning of interfaith relations, these are all factors that impinge on everyone's lives in ways that actually constitute a more significant threat than the risk of dying in a terrorist attack.[15] There is, however, a further point, well expressed by Philip Bobbitt, who argues that the real existential threat posed by terrorism is that Western societies will find themselves obliged to change their nature in order to combat terrorism, that the very freedoms that define the West will be sacrificed as a result of the demands of an effective antiterrorism policy, undermining the legitimacy of Western governments.[16]

Responding to this danger in his first inaugural address, President Obama rejected as "false the choice between our safety and our ideals,"

but for some critics the revelations about the level of surveillance conducted by the NSA and its associates in the Five Eyes program suggested
that under his administration our ideals had indeed been compromised
putatively in the interests of our security, and Bobbitt's fears have come
to pass.[17] For these critics, Snowden, and his predecessor, the serviceman
Bradley (Chelsea) Manning, who provided the vast quantities of diplomatic and military information disseminated by WikiLeaks, were heroic
"whistle-blowers" acting in the public interest, rather than the criminals
that the Obama administration believed them to be. Interestingly, the
critics on this occasion may have been led by the usual suspects,[18] but
they included important figures on the libertarian Right in the United
States, most obviously Rand Paul, the Tea Party–supported senator from
Kentucky.[19] Realist international relations scholars also piled in to support Snowden—Stephen Walt argued in the *Foreign Policy* that Snowden
should have received a presidential pardon.[20]

Those libertarians such as Sen. Paul who held elective office backed
away somewhat in their support for Snowden once it became clear that the
latter was seeking sanctuary in countries overtly or covertly hostile to the
United States (and which, incidentally, had seriously bad records themselves from a libertarian point of view), but even so it is clear that the
critique of U.S. surveillance and data-collection policy struck a chord with
public opinion in a way that earlier critiques of the conduct of the war on
terror had not.[21] The Pew Research Center has since 2004 polled U.S.
opinion on the conduct of antiterror programs, asking in a rather simple-
minded way whether these policies "have not gone far enough to protect
the country" or "have gone too far in restricting civil liberties": following the Snowden revelations, for the first time the latter position received
more support than the former, by 47 to 35 percent.[22] Interpreting this data
is not easy—the fact that Republicans were less supportive of the NSA
than Democrats may simply have reflected hostility towards President
Obama—but it does seem that these programs aroused serious concerns,
concerns that reached some people who normally supported government
action in the war on terror.

How should this issue be assessed from the perspective of a concern
with the normative foundations of the war on terror? The first point is
that very little evidence of actual illegal activity had been uncovered.

The various programs of data collection existed within a legal frame-work established by the Obama administration and under the oversight of the Senate Intelligence Committee. Collecting intelligence on foreign nationals based abroad does not constitute a breach of U.S. law. Some Europeans were apparently outraged by U.S. activities in Europe but, as Secretary of State Kerry remarked, all governments conduct espionage against their friends and their enemies, a fact highlighted by the revela-tion in *Le Monde* that the French government had its own data-collection program, and without the cover of legality.[23] However, the legality of U.S. (and UK) programs may actually be formal rather than real—it seems that permission for specific operations is almost always given, and the suspicion was that the Senate Intelligence Committee had, in effect, been "captured' by the NSA. Moreover, the suspicion remains that the close relationship between the NSA and the GCHQ allowed the former to operate in the UK outside of British legal control, and vice versa; in effect, the two organizations can work together to frustrate restrictions placed on each. This is denied by all concerned, but unfortunately there is no independent way of checking those denials.

Even if all the programs run by the NSA are wholly within the law —and, to stress again, there is no evidence to the contrary—they still raise serious issues about the conduct of the war on terror, and it is clear that the blanket assertion that such programs are necessary to preserve our security will no longer pass unchallenged, and nor should it. Bob-bitt's argument that it is in such programs that the existential threat posed by terrorism lies deserves to be taken very seriously. As with the use of drones and the policy of extrajudicial killing, there are complex choices to be made here, which in this case come down to quite basic issues about personal freedom and security. The Internet security that allows us to manage our bank account online relies on encryption algo-rithms that can also be used by other people to organize pedophile rings and terrorist plots. We do not like the idea that the security services are tracking our e-mails and could, apparently quite easily, get permission to actually read them or to look into our finances; on the other hand, we also don't like the idea that we might one day be murdered on a Pic-cadilly Line tube train at Russell Square Station, as happened to twenty-six Londoners on July 7, 2005. Unfortunately, the capacity to prevent such atrocities (or at least make them less likely) may actually involve the security services possessing powers that impinge on the privacy of ordinary citizens—there is no obvious way out of this dilemma, except to hope that the constitutional guarantees that countries such as the United States and the UK have built up over the centuries will actually hold, and that the authorities will not betray the trust we are obliged to place in them.

Of course, the Snowdens of this world simply do not recognize that this is a dilemma. In their worldview there is no threat that needs to be met and the only danger we face comes from an overmighty state apparatus. They regard the constitutional restraints on the exercise of power by the executive in both the United States and the UK as flimsy to nonexistent. This may be wrong, but the mind-set behind it is well entrenched. As with the issue of drones and targeted killing, the desire to see a grey world in black-and-white terms is very strong. As a result of Snowden's revelations and shifts in public and congressional opinion, some elements of the surveillance and data-collection programs run by NSA have been scaled back—but they will not be eliminated altogether. A relatively small adjustment to the programs would probably be enough to regain wide public support, but, of course, it will not satisfy the critics; figures such as Snowden, Greenwald, and Assange clearly hold that no forms of government secrecy are ever justified—in their monochrome world, the U.S. and UK security establishments are essentially instruments of evil, and the threats that they combat are nonexistent. Fortunately, their capacity to persuade others of this point of view is compromised by their extremism, and by their association with regimes that have absolutely no respect for the values they claim to promote.

THE NEW JUST WAR AGAINST TERROR

The subtitle of *Just War against Terror* is *The Burden of American Power in a Violent World*; Elshtain's aim in writing the book was to defend the taking up of that burden, to criticize those who believed that the past failings of U.S. policy disqualified the United States from responding vigorously to attacks upon its citizens, those who mistook the pursuit of justice for the pursuit of revenge. There is no reason to believe that this defense and these strictures are no longer valid or needed; the United States and its allies are still fighting a war—but is a different war from the one that they were fighting in 2002. Then it was a matter of fighting a well-funded, structured—albeit loosely structured—enemy, al-Qaeda, along with its allies in the Afghan and Pakistan Taliban. But, as President Obama outlined in his speech on May 23, 2013, bin Laden was dead and so were most of the leaders of al-Qaeda; the central organization of al-Qaeda had been severely degraded, if not actually eliminated, and the leadership of the Taliban had been decimated. There was still an enemy, but it consisted of "lethal yet less capable al-Qaeda affiliates; threats to diplomatic facilities and businesses abroad; homegrown extremists."

Al-Qaeda in the Arabian Peninsula (AQAP) was the best organized such affiliate, but the Maghreb franchise had become more important, and the Syrian civil war had revitalized al-Qaeda in Iraq and given it a base in Syria itself—to what extent these organizations were actually accurately characterized as franchises is questionable, but they were all capable of attacking Western interests locally, and AQAP carried out a number of attacks on the United States, unsuccessfully to that point. A more disturbing development since Obama's speech is the rise of so-called Islamic State, or ISIL—actually more extreme than al-Qaeda and in conflict with the latter in Syria. ISIL is unusual in so far as it occupies a territory, which it is capable of defending. From this territory, the self-proclaimed caliphate is able to propagandize effectively in the rest of the Muslim world, and among Muslim communities in Europe and North America, and has already attracted many volunteer fighters from the latter.

Although ISIL and other groups may wish to promote terrorism in the West, it is unclear whether "homegrown extremists," such as the Boston marathon bombers and the murderers of Trooper Lee Rigby in London, actually have had much contact with groups outside the United States and the UK, respectively, but what is clear is that whatever relationship they had, it was very different from that of the 9/11 terrorists with al-Qaeda. Mohammed Atta and his fellow suicide-murderers were sent into the United States explicitly in order to carry out the attacks

on the World Trade Center and on Washington, DC, targets—the Boston and Woolwich attackers were local residents, albeit foreign-born;
they were radicalized in the United States and the UK, respectively,
although, again, the individuals concerned claimed it was events outside
of those two countries that were influential in that radicalization. So a
different war is being fought, and it is being fought with air power in
Syria, drones in Yemen and Pakistan, and with surveillance techniques,
data-collecting, and mining at home. In the UK it is also being fought
with programs that are designed to turn Muslims away from extremism,
most obviously the not-very-successful Prevent Program set up after the
7/7 bombings.[24]

How does this shift affect the justice of the war? Less than one
might think—the essential story is still the same. Terrorists should
still be defined as people who refuse to discriminate, who deliberately
target the innocent, and in democratic societies the innocent includes
police and soldiers outside a war zone—and we should still have no
truck with those who repeat clichés about one man's terrorist being
another man's freedom fighter. Societies under attack from terrorists
are entitled to defend themselves with all means consistent with the
moral codes they live by, and, specifically, as far as possible given the
nature of the enemy, consistent with international humanitarian law.
Free societies under attack from terrorists should, again as far as possible, preserve their basic institutions, the rule of law, and constitutional
guarantees. These principles remain as valid as they were in 2002, and,
for that matter, as they were decades earlier during the Provisional IRA's
campaign in Northern Ireland and Great Britain, or the campaigns of
the Red Army Faction against the Federal Republic of Germany in the
1970s. The techniques employed by terrorists and counterterrorist
authorities change over time, but the essentials do not change. Those
essentials were set out in *Just War against Terror* and remain valid—only
the detailed application needs revision; the moral heart of the matter
remains untouched. The clarity with which Elshtain delineated that
heart at a time when many others faltered deserves our admiration, and,
although there are many reasons to regret that she will not contribute
to the discourse in the future, this is an area where she has already said
what needs to be said.

NOTES

I am very grateful to Stephanie Carvin, Norman Paterson School of International Affairs, Carleton University, for comments on an earlier draft of this paper; I, of course, remain responsible for any errors that remain.

1. "11 September," *London Review of Books*, October 4, 2001, http://www .lrb.co.uk/v23/n19/nine-eleven-writers/11-september. In *Just War against Terror*, Elshtain quotes Beard's line about the Unites States having it coming, but the wider quote is more revealing.

2. Accounts of the campaign make it clear that both leaders genuinely feared that WMD would be used against coalition forces, which gives the lie to the idea that they knew that there were no such weapons; see, e.g., Michael Gordon and Bernard Trainor, *Cobra II: The Inside Story of the Invasion and Occupation of Iraq* (New York: Atlantic, 2006). Perhaps Bush and Blair fooled themselves in this respect, but see ibid. (65) for evidence that the nonexistence of WMD also came as a shock to Iraqi generals when revealed to them by Saddam in December 2002.

3. U.S. statements on the need for regime change are legion. For Tony Blair, see Christoph Bluth, "The British Road to War: Blair, Bush and the Decision to Invade Iraq," *International Affairs (Royal Institute of International Affairs 1944–)* (2004): 871–92.

4. Elshtain, "Reflections on the Problem of 'Dirty Hands,'" in *Torture: A Collection*, ed. Stanford Levinson (Oxford: Oxford University Press, 2004), has an illuminating discussion on this topic.

5. "Obama's Speech on Drone Policy," *New York Times*, May 24, 2013, http://www.nytimes.com/2013/05/24/us/politics/transcript-of-obamas-speech -on-drone-policy.html?pagewanted=all.

6. UK example: Mehdi Hasan, "On Wiretaps and Drones Strikes It's Time for Liberals to Accept That Obama Is Worse Than Bush," *New Statesman*, June 13, 2013.

7. "Barack H. Obama—Nobel Lecture: A Just and Lasting Peace," Nobel prize.org, Nobel Media AB, 2014, http://www.nobelprize.org/nobel_prizes /peace/laureates/2009/obama-lecture.html.

8. These figures are taken from Daniel Byman, "Why Drones Work," *Foreign Affairs* 92, no. 4 (2013): 32–43. Numbers and types of casualties in the drone debates are difficult to verify because of the problems of distinguishing combatants from noncombatants in this kind of warfare.

9. James Dao, "Drone Pilots Found to Get Stress Disorders Much as Those in Combat Do," *New York Times*, February 22, 2013, http://www.nytimes .com/2013/02/23/us/drone-pilots-found-to-get-stress-disorders-much-as -those-in-combat-do.html.

10. The charge that the Obama administration killed rather than captured was made by the Left, but also by disgruntled Bush administration officials; see "Watching 'Zero Dark Thirty' with the CIA: Separating Fact from Fiction," American Enterprise Institute, video, http://www.aei.org/events/watching-zero -dark-thirty-with-the-cia-separating-fact-from-fiction/.

11. The claim that drones kill more civilians than manned strikes is made in an interview in *The Guardian* based on an unpublished Department of Defense analysis; see Spencer Ackerman, "US Drone Strikes More Deadly to Afghan Civilians than Manned Aircraft–Adviser," *The Guardian*, July 2, 2013, http:// www.theguardian.com/world/2013/jul/02/us-drone-strikes-afghan-civilians. It is assessed by the most reliable commentator on the human security aspect of drone strikes on the *Duck of Minerva* blog; see Charlie Carpenter, "What We Know, Don't Know, Can't Know and Need to Know About the DOD's Classified Study on Drone Deaths," *Duck of Minerva*, July 15, 2013, http://duckof minerva.com/2013/07/what-we-know-dont-know-cant-know-and-need-to -know-about-the-dods-classified-study-on-drone-deaths.html.

12. The presumptive moral equality of ordinary combatants is argued for in Michael Walzer, *Just and Unjust Wars* (New York: Perseus, 2000), and contested in Jeff McMahan, *Killing in War* (Oxford: Oxford University Press, 2009).

13. But criminal gangs often wear identifying marks (e.g., gang colors) and can operate within quite elaborate command structures.

14. Walzer comes to much the same conclusion in an online *Dissent* article; see Michael Walzer, "Targeted Killing and Drone Warfare," *Dissent*, January 11, 2013, http://www.dissentmagazine.org/online_articles/targeted-killing -and-drone-warfare.

15. The Quillam Foundation, several of whose members are former Islamists, documents this effect in the UK; see http://www.quilliamfoundation .org.

16. Philip Bobbitt, *Terror and Consent: The Wars for the Twenty-first Century* (London: Allen Lane, 2008).

17. The "Five Eyes" program refers to intelligence cooperation between the United States and four "Anglosphere" partners, the UK, Canada, Australia, and New Zealand, which was very highly structured, reflected high levels of mutual trust, and accordingly was somewhat resented by the intelligence services of other U.S. allies.

18. E.g., see Glenn Greenwald at *The Guardian*, http://www.theguardian .com/profile/glenn-greenwald.

19. For Paul's initial position, see Eliana Johnson, "Rand Paul: Our DNI Lied, Snowden Told the Truth," National Review Online, June 23, 2013, http:// www.nationalreview.com/corner/351778/rand-paul-our-dni-lied-snowden-told -truth-eliana-johnson.

20. Stephen Walt, "One More Reason Why Obama Should Pardon Snow-den," *Foreign Policy* July 9, 2013, http://foreignpolicy.com/2013/07/09/one-more -reason-obama-should-pardon-snowden/.

21. For Paul's backing away, see his warning in Sam Stein, "Rand Paul Warns Snowden: Don't Cozy Up to the Russians (Video)," *Huffington Post*, June 23, 2013, http://www.huffingtonpost.com/2013/06/23/rand-paul-snowden_n_348 6455.html.

22. "Few See Adequate Limits on NSA Surveillance Program," Pew Re-search Center, July 26, 2013, http://www.people-press.org/2013/07/26/few-see -adequate-limits-on-nsa-surveillance-program/.

23. As reported in "France 'Has Vast Data Surveillance'—Le Monde Report," BBC News, July 4, 2013, http://www.bbc.com/news/world-europe-23178284.

24. *Prevent Strategy* (London: Stationery Office Limited, June 2011), https://www.gov.uk/government/uploads/system/uploads/attachment_data/file /97976/prevent-strategy-review.pdf.

CHAPTER FOURTEEN

JUST WAR AND RELIGION
Reflections on the Work of Jean Elshtain

Michael Walzer

MOTIFS

In this chapter, I want to wrestle with just war theory and religion, and I will write in a more personal way than I usually do, pulled away from academic impersonality by Jean's death in 2013 and by my reading of her book on St. Augustine, *Augustine and the Limits of Politics*, which is her most personal book. Let me begin with the village described in that book's preface—Jean's instance of Augustine's *saeculum*: the here and now, the world as it is between the Fall and the end time. In this village, which Jean discovers as she "meanders" from Wittenberg to Rome, there is a Lutheran, a Catholic, and a black Baptist church, also a synagogue, and a pub, the Town Tavern, where people gather to argue about politics and religion—I assume, though she doesn't say so, that most of these are the people who don't go regularly to the churches or the synagogue. I imagine that Jean spends time in both the Lutheran and Catholic churches and sometimes visits the pub. I shall move back and forth between the pub and the synagogue—thinking about just and unjust wars. I will try to invoke or, better perhaps, exemplify in my arguments certain key features of Jean's thought.

Rereading the books and articles that she wrote over the years dealing with or touching upon just war theory, I tried to construct a list of central or characteristic themes or motifs—I got to nine before I stopped, but more could be added.

(1) The engagement with and appeal to exemplary figures—Jane Addams, Eleanor Roosevelt, Dietrich Bonhoeffer, Václav Havel, Martin Luther King, Jr., John Paul II. Here are models of compassion, courage, truth-telling, and justice-seeking, men and women whom we ought to admire and emulate.

(2) A deep commitment to human equality and at the same time a deep belief in human frailty, both of which shape her view of politics as the normal form of social interaction, which will never be transcended. Here we are all participants entitled to equal regard—though our interests will always clash and the institutions we create will never be free of the lust for domination. There will never be a time beyond politics, a "magical moment," when the "beautiful souls" will "take charge and retain their nurturing goodness throughout."[1] "Politics," Jean writes, "confronts us with intransigent otherness, with people who have their own cultures and opinions."[2] These "others" must be treated with respect, but they also, often, have to be criticized and opposed.

(3) A conviction that goodness can be present, can be displayed, though it most often isn't, in the political world: the exemplary figures demonstrate the falseness of moral cynicism.

(4) A passionate patriotism "chastened" by the uncertainties of politics and the crimes committed by people who call themselves patriots—and a similar, related, endorsement of other particularist connections to friends and family.

(5) A rejection of the absolutism of "rights"—and of any doctrine that claims to override all other human commitments, most importantly those commitments produced by the love of particular other people: children, friends, members of a religious community, fellow citizens.

(6) A recognition that there really is evil in the world, and that it must be resisted—even if the men and women who resist it are themselves radically flawed human beings.

(7) A belief that some wars are just, but their justice is no reason for fighting them with crusading zeal or for claiming exemption from the constraints on how all wars should be fought.

(8) A robust impatience with anyone whose politics is not marked by the seven themes and arguments I have just listed—and a fierce dislike of anyone who becomes an apologist for terror, injustice, or tyranny.

(9) And pervasive through all this, shaping all of it, a religious sensibility and a set of religious beliefs that are visible in everything she wrote —though it is a feature of this sensibility that she was not impatient with or critical of those of us who come to moral and political issues from a nonreligious perspective (so long as we get them right).

RELIGIOUS PERSECUTION

I learned just war theory from Catholic writers; the doctrine derives from Catholic moral theology, but it has a special place in that theology —which is very much like the place that the moral commandments of the Torah occupy in Jewish legal and philosophical thought. According to the Talmud (Tractate Yoma 67b), the moral laws did not depend on revelation: "If they had not been laid down, [they] ought to have been laid down."[3] This means that we can grasp the moral laws without recourse to what God said to Moses at Sinai. Similarly, Catholic just war doctrine is a part of natural law; it is accessible to and therefore obligatory for all rational beings, whether or not they are Christian, whether or not they believe in God.

Jean argues that the Augustinian account of just war is in some tension with this (can I say?) secular understanding of it. "The obligations of *caritas* in Christian theology," she writes, "are defining features of the just war thinking of . . . St. Augustine"[4]—and, she adds, of Thomas Aquinas. But Augustine is her favorite; she says of him that he gave a "powerful theological jolt" to notions of just war derived from theories of human nature. His is a deeper version of the doctrine than the one that follows simply from natural law, the one that is equally available to secularists and rationalists; it is a more specifically Christian version, which holds, for example, that we should be reluctant to fight even just wars, and when we fight them we should do so with great sadness, avoiding every other emotion, whether it is anger, or righteousness, or triumphalism—for war is a great evil.

In her early book *Women and War* (*WW*), Jean is critical of the version of just war theory that I defended in *Just and Unjust Wars*. The language of rights and rules is impoverished, she argues, "too abstract, too finely tuned" (*WW*, 156) to capture the moral reality of war. She prefers a more religious tuning, more attentive to the experience of evil, to the lust for domination, to the barbarities of war. Perhaps she is right; perhaps a theory of just war infused, as it were, with religious emotion would be a better theory. But there is a problem here: religious emotions connected to war don't always or often make for justice. One might say quite the opposite: the most common, perhaps the most authentic, religious war is the holy war, the jihad, the crusade, all of which give expression to the strongly felt need of many pious men and women (mostly men) to coerce or kill heretics and infidels for the sake of God's dominion. Continuing in the same vein, one might say that just war theory is the secular and rationalist response to and rejection of holy war. Jean worried about these issues in the Augustine book, but I am not sure that she worried enough about Augustine's own vacillations on the subject of religious coercion.

Now let me do my own worrying, wrestle with my own demons, for there is a Jewish version of holy war, which is, some say, the original version, though I doubt that—"originalism" is usually bad history. I first encountered this Jewish version when I was studying to become a bar mitzvah, a son of the commandments and the covenant. The portion of the Torah that I was to read included Exodus 32, the story of the golden calf. Some of you will know the story—how Moses lingered on the mountain; the people grew impatient and frightened and demanded that Aaron make them "gods which will go with us"; Aaron weakly agreed, collected gold jewelry from the Israelite women, and made the golden calf—and the people worshiped the idol and danced around it. Moses heard about all this from God himself, and rushed down the mountain, and when he saw the people dancing (it was a sexual orgy, some commentators say), he was very angry, and he smashed the tablets, and rallied the Levites (his own tribe) with the cry, "Who is on the Lord's side, let him come unto me," and he told them: "Put every man his sword by his side, and go in and out from gate to gate throughout the camp and slay every man his brother, and every man his companion, and every man his neighbor" (KJV, Exod. 32:27).

When I first read those lines I told the rabbi who was my teacher that I could not possibly read them at my bar mitzvah: a bloody, religiously inspired purge was not an edifying spectacle, I thought at age thirteen. The rabbi was a wise man; he didn't tell me that I had to read them; he argued with me over many weeks, and eventually I did read them (proving that I would be a Menshevik and not a Bolshevik when I grew up). But that brief protest may well have been the beginning of my defense of just war over holy war.

We can think of religious persecution as the domestic version of holy war, which is, in the Hebrew Bible as in Christian doctrine and in Islam, a war against idolaters, infidels, and heretics; it isn't an ethnic or national war. Forty years before the holy war of the Israelites against the Canaanites, there was a holy war of Israelites against Israelites. This Exodus text has played an important part in the long history of the persecution of heretics and infidels—and, as I discovered years after my bar mitzvah, one of the first people to appeal to it was St. Augustine. Not Jean's St. Augustine, not the Augustine of the *City of God*, as she describes him and that otherworldly city: the community of true Christians has nothing to gain from the sword. War could bring only worldly victories. It might be just, if it was fought against the wicked for the sake of peace. But it was not an activity sponsored or endorsed by the Church, it was in no sense holy.

On this issue, however, Augustine was not of one mind, and at times he extended the war against secular wickedness to a war against religious wickedness in defense of God's city—specifically against the Donatist heresy. He justified this argument in one of his letters (93) by citing Exodus 32:

When good and bad do the same actions and suffer the same afflictions, they are to be distinguished not by what they do or suffer, but by the causes of each: for example, Pharaoh oppressed the people of God by hard bondage; Moses afflicted the same people by severe correction when they were guilty of impiety [Augustine refers here to Exod. 32:27]: their actions were alike, but they were not alike in the motive of regard for the people's welfare—the one inflated by the lust of power, the other inflamed by love.[5]

"Inflamed by love" is an extraordinary phrase. Jewish commentators had a similar, though quieter, view of Moses, as a leader who pleaded with a furious God for the sake of his people even as he himself was capable of great anger at their waywardness. But it is difficult to make the case that Moses's inflamed love actually extended to the three thousand men who were killed at his command—and to all their friends and relatives. Surely the friends and relatives lived in fear thereafter, though they had stiff necks, the Bible tells us, and so "murmured" against Moses again and again. And they were killed, or many of them were killed, again and again. Is this true love? The idea of *caritas* seems to fit much better with Augustine's argument (Jean's Augustine) that Christians should struggle against heresy armed only with the word of God.

This same Exodus text, my bar mitzvah text, was used, a little more cautiously, by Thomas Aquinas to defend religious persecution, and years later, very incautiously, by John Calvin, who preached a sermon on Exodus 32: "You shall show yourselves rightly zealous of God's service," Calvin told his Genevan congregation, "in that you kill your own brethren without sparing, so as in this case the order of nature is put underfoot, to show that God is above all."[6] Of course, the "order of nature," according to Catholic moral theology, is God's creation, and it is the source of natural law, which is the source of our common conceptions of justice and right. What religious zeal puts underfoot here is justice itself.

In the course of chasing down references to Exodus 32, I came upon a text that is the very opposite of Calvin's—a commentary on the story from a writer whom I have always admired, whom I think of as exemplary, even when I disagree with him (and here I don't disagree). So John Aubrey, in his *Brief Lives*, reports the opinion of Thomas Hobbes: "I have heard him inveigh much against the Crueltie of Moyses for putting so many thousands to the Sword for Bowing to the Golden Calf."[7] I don't know if Hobbes was an atheist, as some of his contemporaries and some of our contemporaries believe, but this was surely a secular response to a religious story.

COMMANDED WAR

The doctrine of holy war is reiterated in the book of Deuteronomy, chapter 20, where it is entangled with an account of a more limited form of warfare. Michael Fishbane has disentangled the two types of wars in his very fine book *Biblical Interpretation in Ancient Israel*.[8] The rabbis of the Talmudic period produced their own version of the two wars, which they called "commanded" wars and "optional" or "permitted" wars. Commanded are the wars of Joshua for the conquest of the Land; permitted are the wars of David for conquests farther afield. According to Deuteronomy, commanded wars should be, and, according to the book of Joshua, commanded wars actually were, wars of extermination directed against the idolatrous Canaanite nations. Fortunately, extermination seems a rhetorical exaggeration, since the Bible tells us that Canaanites were living in the land for many years after the conquest. The Israelites are commanded to "destroy" the Canaanite nations, leaving alive "nothing that breathes," but they are also commanded not to marry the Canaanite daughters. Neither commandment was actually obeyed, but we need to focus on the first, clearly intended by its Author, according to its authors, to produce a holy war, the biblical version of the jihad and the crusade.

The idea of a war commanded by God is common to the monotheistic religions. It follows from the idea that God not only has adherents, faithful men and women, but he also has enemies. Jean writes that "Augustinian realists are not crusaders," and yet Augustine did defend the domestic version of holy war, and Aquinas seems to have defended the Crusades, though probably without enthusiasm. Realism saves Augustine's truest followers (like Jean) in that it teaches them to distrust the motives of the people who claim to deliver God's commands: they are more likely to be men lusting for dominion than humble servants. As just war theory developed in the course of the Middle Ages and the early modern period, it became more and more clearly a doctrine directed against holy wars. The Spanish Dominican Francisco de Vitoria flatly declared that wars could not rightly be fought for religious purposes—such as for the conversion of the native peoples of Central and South America. God's warriors used only spiritual weapons. I am not sure, though, that his was the majority view among Catholic theologians in the sixteenth and seventeenth centuries. One might well argue that the people most immune to holy warfare are those who don't believe in God at all.

But I have to admit that secular theorists, intellectuals, and publicists have their own versions of what the rabbis called "commanded" war. One of these is the ideological crusade against the enemies not of God but of mankind—tyrants, imperialists, capitalists, the local bourgeoisie. Think of the Red Army marching on Warsaw to bring communism to Poland or the U.S. Army marching on Bagdad (here Jean and I had one of our few disagreements) to bring democracy to Iraq. These were unjust wars whether the warriors were driven by the lust for power or by love's inflammations. They are unjust because of their presumptuousness and their cruelty; they aim at more than the force of arms can achieve; they fail the just war test of a reasonable prospect of success. In cases like these, the end cannot justify the means, but it can determine the means that might be justifiable. The best political regime, like the kingdom of God, can only be sought by persuasive arguments and political (or spiritual) struggle. Armed force can only produce caricatures of justice and truth, of communism and democracy—as Jean's Augustinian realists could tell us. In response to people who argue that religious or ideological crusades are commanded, we have to reply: maybe so, but they are nonetheless unjust. If that isn't written, it should be written.

There is, however, another kind of commanded war that I want to consider in more detail: it is precisely the just war or, better, one version of the just war. The more standard version, which is reflected in international law, holds that war is generally bad for all concerned, but that some wars, for self-defense or the defense of others, are permitted. The doctrine of neutrality is built on this idea, that just wars are optional. Countries can decide to stay out of the fighting, choosing to remain neutral, as Sweden, for example, did during World War II, or choosing to surrender, as many Finns wanted to do when threatened by the

Soviet Union in 1939, though their country's leaders decided otherwise. On this view, either of the decisions available to the Swedes and the Finns, to fight or not to fight, would have been permitted. Neutrality or surrender may be inglorious or dishonorable, but standard just war theory holds that countries have a right to choose a life without glory and honor.

Still, the idea of a just war presses us toward the idea of a commanded war—commanded, that is, by the moral law. How could one watch Nazi aggression in Europe, how could one learn about the evils of Nazi rule, and choose to be neutral? If a war is just in the sense that it is a war against aggression or a war to stop a massacre, isn't it also, shouldn't it be, required? Remember the biblical maxim: "Do not stand by the blood of your neighbor" (Lev. 19:16). Neutrality means standing by: How can that be a moral option? Jean doesn't discuss neutrality in her book *Just War against Terror*, but much of what she says in that book suggests that she thought the war against terror was a commanded war.

Over the years, I've defended the right to be neutral as a general rule, for reasons I won't go into here, but in the case of a humanitarian crisis, in the case of mass murder, I've argued that anyone who can intervene to stop the killing, should intervene: this is a moral must. And Jean agrees, with what I take to be a Christian qualification, which is also available to secular theorists. "There are things that must not be done," she says, and so, "to the extent possible, these things should be stopped."⁹ "To the extent possible" is Jean's bow to political prudence, which she takes to be a feature of Augustinian realism. This is for her a deeply felt qualification. Human beings are fallible, and even in their righteousness, they are given to self-righteousness, and then we get the zeal of those who are far too confident that they know what must be done and exactly how to do it.

There is a tradition of the Left, and also a philosophical tradition, according to which the classic Leninist question, What ought to be done?, always has a single, right answer. All things considered, all historical circumstances taken into account, there is only one thing to do. I know a lot of people who argue like that; I sometimes argue like that myself, and I suspect that Jean did too, sometimes. But the main thrust of her political arguments, over many decades, is against certainty and singularity. No doubt, Christian humility plays a part here, but so does an exquisite sense of the realities, complexities, uncertainties, and ambiguities of political life. But still, for all that, the killing of the innocent is an evil, and it "should be stopped"—even if the stopping can only be done by political leaders who have, in their own time, killed the innocent.

Some of Jean's most powerful writing is directed against the idea that moral motives must always be pure. This is an idea that is generally invoked for a political purpose—to make forceful action in this or that case impossible, since no one's motives are pure. But of course, it also has another, opposite purpose—to defend the actions of those who claim to act purely, exactly as morality commands, with no ulterior motives. Jean's commitment to a realistic politics is a rejection of the moralism that justifies a refusal to act at all, because no action is morally safe, and it is also a rejection of the moralism that justifies reckless and imprudent actions by leaders who claim to know with absolute certainty what needs to be done. I doubt that it makes much difference whether this knowledge has divine or secular sources, just as I doubt that it makes much difference whether the better self-knowledge that leads us to think again, before acting, comes from God or from practical reason.

The classification of wars into commanded and permitted makes more sense than I first thought when I read the rabbinic texts—though it isn't in fact a neat or a complete classification. Some wars are indeed morally necessary and therefore commanded, and all wars are subject to prudential calculations that are always judgment calls and therefore in some sense optional—though the prudential calculations and the judgment calls are themselves commanded, that is, morally required. But the rabbis neglected to provide a third class: prohibited wars. Perhaps they had what Jean might call an Augustinian understanding that war is a great evil, and so all wars are prohibited, except for those that are specifically declared to be commanded or optional. Still, we need to mark clearly the full range of prohibited wars, for it is radically inclusive: most wars are or should be prohibited.

It is the commanded wars that worry me, even though I do believe, as Jewish tradition teaches, that we live "under the commandments," and that sometimes we are commanded to fight—and I believe this whether or not there is a Commander (I suspect that there isn't). Jean and I defended together the idea that some things must be stopped. And yet the zeal of the righteous is always frightening, even when we think that we are among the righteous. What are we frightened of? We are frightened by what Calvin zealously demanded of his congregation—and so the best way of expressing the necessary restraint upon righteousness is this: you are not allowed, no one is allowed, to put nature underfoot.

When we are commanded to fight, we are also commanded to fight with restraint. The two commands are in tension, and that tension is central to the arguments that go on not only among just war theorists but also among citizens and soldiers. If we are fighting a just war, isn't it especially important, morally important, to win—and even to win quickly? And mightn't it then be necessary to put nature underfoot and "kill every man his neighbor"? I don't think that Augustine's insistence that soldiers must be melancholy fighters addresses these questions. One can, with great melancholy, commit great crimes. So it is critically important to insist that the restraints on warfare, the rules of *jus in bello*, apply to the just warriors in exactly the same way as they apply to the unjust warriors. For otherwise self-righteousness and moral certainty will overwhelm and break through all the moral restraints.

But there is another restraint on those just and commanded wars, which has to do with *jus ad bellum*, with what we might think of as the project of the warriors. What are they fighting for? The end of war, says St. Augustine, is peace. But any decisive victory will bring peace or, at least, peace of some kind. We need a more specific description of the ends we can rightly seek when we are fighting under the commandments. It is only a description of this sort that will enable us to distinguish commanded wars that are just from holy wars, jihads, and crusades, which are always unjust.

The project of war is different in different cases. When we are fighting to stop a massacre, to bring down a murderous regime, we must aim at a nonmurderous regime, at a government committed to protecting, and capable of protecting, the lives of all its citizens. It doesn't have to be (what I would wish it to be) social democratic, liberal and tolerant, committed to social and gender equality. It just has to free its people, as Hobbes thought all governments had to do—it is their central purpose—from the fear of violent death. More than that is a matter for political struggle, not for military struggle.

If fighting against aggression is sometimes a commanded war, with neutrality ruled out, then the goal can't be anything more than the defeat of the aggressor and, so the classical texts say, the reestablishment of the status quo ante. But the source of the aggression, or its causes, must lie in the status quo ante, and so it is surely right to aim for a little more: an improved version of what existed before, improved by constraints on the aggressor state's capacity to make war—demilitarized zones along its borders, say, or limits on its production or deployment of weapons— and also by treaties that guarantee mutual security. The goal is a status quo less likely to give rise to war—not so much a world made safe for democracy but rather a world made safer for humankind. This is a goal achievable through the effective use of force. What lies beyond is, again, a matter for political struggle.

When I came, many years after my bar mitzvah, to write a book about the Exodus from Egypt and the long march across the wilderness to the Promised Land, I argued that the goal of the march, the promise of the land, was nothing like paradise; no biblical version of utopia was on offer, no perfectly just state. The goal was simply a better place than Egypt. The biblical writers, at least these writers, Jean might say, were Augustinian realists. We can think of the goal of just wars in a similar way, even when these are commanded wars, wars that must be fought. The goal is a better peace than the peace that preceded the war. It isn't eternal peace, or a communist society, or the messianic kingdom.

A better peace, which requires the defeat of conquerors, tyrants, zealots, and terrorists, isn't in fact such a modest goal. I would even argue that it can be pursued without melancholy, with anger against its enemies, and with strong hopes for the betterment that victory can bring. It is hard to imagine men and women deprived of anger and hope preparing themselves emotionally for the necessary fighting. That makes the rules of *jus in bello* all the more important. Living under the commandments is a complex business, but I think that we can live there with both passion and restraint. And, if I read *Just War against Terror* rightly, Jean would not disagree.

NOTES

This essay was offered as a keynote lecture for a conference entitled Just War against Terror: International Relations, Gender, and the Challenge of Ethics, on October 18, 2013. Elshtain hand-selected the speakers for this fourth and final conference of the Engaged Mind series that addressed her work, but she passed away several months before the conference took place. Given the circumstances, many of the papers, including this one, took a more personal note.

1. Jean Bethke Elshtain, "On Never Reaching the Coast of Utopia," *International Relations* 22 (2008): 152.

2. Jean Bethke Elshtain, "Just War, Realism, and Humanitarian Intervention," in *The Sacred and the Sovereign: Religion and International Politics*, ed. John Carlson and Erik Owens (Washington, DC: Georgetown University Press, 2003), 108.

3. *The Jewish Political Tradition*, Vol. 1, *Authority*, ed. Michael Walzer, Menachem Lorberbaum, and Noam Zohar (New Haven, CT: Yale University Press, 2000), 53.

4. Jean Bethke Elshtain, "Military Intervention and Justice as Equal Regard," in *Religion and Security: The New Nexus in International Relations*, ed. Robert A. Seiple et al. (New York: Sheed & Ward, 2004), 122.

5. Philip Schaff, *A Select Library of the Nicene and Post-Nicene Fathers of the Christian Church* (Grand Rapids, MI: Eerdmans, 1969), 384.

6. John Calvin, *Sermon 194*, in *Fifth Book of Moses* (London, 1583), 1203–4.

7. John Aubrey, *Brief Lives*, ed. Oliver Lawson Dick (Ann Arbor: University of Michigan Press, 1957), 157.

8. Michael Fishbane, *Biblical Interpretation in Ancient Israel* (Oxford: Clarendon, 1985).

9. Elshtain, "Just War, Realism, and Humanitarian Intervention," 108.

CHAPTER FIFTEEN

The Effect of Perspectives on Thinking about Sovereignty

A Dialogue with Jean Bethke Elshtain

James Turner Johnson

I first met Jean Elshtain when we were both invited to give presentations at a conference in November 1988 at Chaminade University in Hono-lulu. Over the years after, we crossed paths in similar circumstances a number of times—circumstances in which we were invited to speak on a common theme but from the different perspectives from which we approached that theme. I mention this background not only to honor the relationship that grew up between us over a quarter century but also as a prelude to the reflections I will offer here on the subject of sovereignty—another topic we have both addressed, but addressed from different perspectives, with somewhat different results. More specifi-cally, my focus will be several benchmark subjects we have both treated in getting to our understanding of sovereignty: Elshtain in her *Sover-eignty: God, State, and Self* (*S*), and I in a book on the idea of sovereignty in moral and historical perspective published in 2014, and in several articles published since 2003.[1]

To provide differing perspectives on a common topic is, of course, how academic collaborations work—including this one: the participants are drawn together not only because they are judged to know something

about the topic being examined but because they offer different perspectives on that topic. The aim is to create an intellectual interaction
and ideally a substantive conversation on the basis of both what is common and what is different, and the hope is from this interaction and
conversation to produce new thinking and perhaps new knowledge
about what falls between the fields of vision of the competing perspectives. But academic interactions typically do not address this matter of
the interstices directly; rather, they stop with the expression of the differing perspectives. What I want to do in this chapter is precisely to
consider what remains in the space between Elshtain's approach to the
subject of sovereignty and mine. I will highlight several matters we both
treat, but treat differently, noting what the matter in question looks like
from each of our perspectives and then raising the question of what
remains to be examined and why this may be important to consider. I
deeply regret that it is no longer possible for Elshtain to engage in this
discussion, for she undoubtedly would have had her own perspective to
add there.

The specific matters I will discuss are, in their chronological order,
our respective treatments of Augustine, the Gelasian principle, the work
of the twelfth- and thirteenth-century canonists, the contributions of
Aquinas and Grotius to the development of Western thinking about
sovereignty, and the conception of sovereignty itself. My concerns cross
over all three of the kinds of sovereignty addressed in Elshtain's *Sovereignty*, though, as we shall see, I think of each of these and of their relationship somewhat differently from how they are presented in her book.
The difference between us is not in the moral judgments we reach, for
there we have agreed remarkably well, but we have arrived at those judgments in different ways. And so my study here.

How to think in general terms of the difference in perspective
between Elshtain and me? I think a suggestive way of putting this is
to consider the distinction the Civil War historian Gary W. Gallagher
makes between memory and history in describing the Battle of Gettysburg and its effects.[2] He notes that in our national memory, supported
by many popular and scholarly depictions, Gettysburg is understood as
the turning point of the war: Lee's army was defeated, the Gettysburg
Address was delivered, slavery was abolished, and so on. But a closer

look at the actual events—what Gallagher calls the "history"—presents a different story: Lee's army suffered a tactical defeat and was badly bloodied, but it left the field of battle in good order and remained a formidable fighting force for months to come; the Union army that won the battle was also left with many losses that required a major regrouping before it could again meet Lee's forces in a major battle; and how the war would end was by no means obvious to either side at the time.

What Gallagher calls "memory" is a conceptual construction of the historical events, put together after the fact, for the purpose of defining an understanding that shapes the collective purpose for the future. It has more to do with this looking forward than with understanding the past on its own terms. By contrast, what Gallagher calls "history" is this latter kind of understanding, shaped by examining the records of past events in their own context, with their own interrelations and implications there. From this perspective the way to understand developments in the future is to examine successive historical events on their own terms, describing the line of historical movement by connecting these histori-cal dots. So far as it is possible to determine a purpose in a specific set of events, this is known by looking back after one is able to see where the earlier events have come out.

In Gallagher's terms, Elshtain is engaged in the construction and refinement of memory, but I am engaged in uncovering history. I am not entirely happy with the way Gallagher uses these terms, because I think that, in practice, history and memory are always mixed together, but the distinction he makes highlights the different purposes, and thus the dif-ferent perspectives, interpretive methodologies, and outcomes of these different ways of treating and understanding the past. To use another set of more academic terms, Elshtain uses history as a political theorist; I work as a historian of moral traditions—specifically, where the concept of sovereignty is concerned, as a historian of Western moral tradition, particularly that of just war. The upshot is the same: we have different purposes, and this colors what we consider meaningful from the past, how we understand what is important in it, and the resultant picture we draw. Again, though, my concern is with what we both may be missing and what might be said about that.

In the list of topics I provided earlier, Augustine comes first chrono-
logically, and how each of us uses his work provides a sharp example
of our differences. But before looking at what Elshtain and I make of
Augustine, I believe it may be suggestive to recall how Paul Ramsey
interpreted Augustine in his first work on the subject of just war, *War
and the Christian Conscience*.[3] Ramsey's subject there was "the just war
according to St. Augustine," and he developed this topic through an
extensive discussion of book 19 of *The City of God*, often relying heavily
on Arthur Barker's analysis of it. Ramsey was not interested in the actual
history of the just war idea but rather in describing the Christian idea
of just war in terms of the implications of Christian love of neighbor. In
the context of the widespread pacifist leanings found among Protestant
elites of an earlier time (discussed in chapter 1, "The Problem of Protestant Ethics Today"), but also in the context of a focus on love of neighbor as a distillation of the ethics of Jesus prevalent in the Christian ethics
of that time, Ramsey used Augustine's understanding of the influence of
charity (*caritas*) on politics and history and the movement from the City
of Earth to the City of God to produce a Christian conception of just
war that itself rested on charity. Ramsey's example is useful to recall in
our present inquiry, because Elshtain similarly, in both *Just War against
Terror* and *Sovereignty*, privileges Augustine's idea of charity/*caritas*.[4]

Both Ramsey and Elshtain make good use of Augustine's thought
as the basis of their theoretical constructions of just war, but Augustine himself did not in his writings anywhere provide a comprehensive,
systematic just war theory. Unlike the subject of sexuality, to which he
devoted no fewer than five distinct treatises and which he addressed
more briefly in other contexts, what Augustine said about just war is
limited to fairly short passages found in works of various sorts on diverse
subjects. The first step in drawing these together, along with similarly
brief passages from other Christian sources, into a coherent, systematic
whole was not taken until the twelfth-century canonist Gratian's *Decretum*, pt. 2, causa 23.[5] The passages cited by Gratian from Augustine come
from his *Seven Questions concerning the Heptateuch*, *Questions on Numbers*,
his commentary on the Sermon on the Mount, *Questions on Exodus, Contra Faustum, On Free Will, Sermon on the Child of the Centurion, City of
God* book 1 (not 19), and certain of his letters. All these citations are

relatively brief; they come from collections of canons, or rules of guidance for Christian living, collected in various sources from the fifth century to Gratian's own time to encapsulate the gist of the growing body of Christian moral teaching.

If we scroll forward to Aquinas's treatment of just war in *Summa theologiae* II-II, q. 40,[6] we should note three things: first, what he says here in the context of his own theology summarizes the conclusions reached in the canonical work of the previous century and a quarter; second, textual analysis shows that the citations he provides from Augustine all come from the versions found in the *Decretum*; and third, these citations, albeit used in a way that emphasizes their authority, are brief and but a few: Aquinas's citations from Augustine are only from letters to Marcellinus and to Boniface, from the *Questions on the Heptateuch*, from the commentary on the Sermon on the Mount, and, most importantly, from *Contra Faustum* 22.70, 74, 75. Aquinas does not cite the *City of God* in this connection at all.

Now, which of these interpretations of Augustine on just war is right, the medieval one or that found in Ramsey and Elshtain? Both in fact reflect Augustine, but they do so in different ways; they offer different perspectives. Which is better depends on one's purpose. I ground the origin and development of a coherent, systematic conception of just war in the work of Gratian and the two generations of canonists who built on that work, the Decretists and the Decretalists, with Aquinas's question "On War" succinctly summarizing the conclusions reached by the canonists in the form of a classic statement that remained normative up into the era of the Reformation. This is an interpretation that does not seek to explore the meanings that may be found in Augustine's thought as such, but it is one that tells us a great deal about medieval thinking on sovereign rule, which is a major focus of the canonical debate over just war and whose importance is reflected in the fact that Aquinas lists the "authority of a prince"—that is, a temporal ruler with no temporal superior, already called in the French of his time a *souverain*, a sovereign—first in his three requisites for a just war. I will return to this point later, when we look more closely at the Middle Ages, and again at the end of this chapter. But again, this approach tells us much more about the medieval context than it does about Augustine in himself, and a considerable gulf lies between the use of Augustine found here and in the work of Ramsey and Elshtain.

In other connections discussed later herein, I will suggest that the existence of such a gulf—or what I earlier called the "interstices" between different scholarly perspectives—suggests the need for scholarship directed to what is not covered between our two approaches. In this case, though, at least so far as an interpretation of Augustine on war is concerned, there is no lack of scholars tilling in the field, and on the specific topic of Augustine's thinking on war the work of the British Augustine scholar R. A. Markus will be hard to surpass.[7] Farther out in the gulf and toward the side of Gratian and the canonists, there is also already a growing body of literature replacing the outmoded conception of this period as the "Dark Ages" in which nothing of intellectual importance happened, and so far as the twelfth century is concerned, this period is now widely understood as a kind of early renaissance marked by the rediscovery of Roman law, new developments in the conception of rights, new institutionalization in both the political and church sphere, and so on. Ethicists and political scientists typically don't have the knowledge of the languages needed to contribute to this kind of work, but they might at least pay more attention to it as it evolves, because our conception of this period and its implications for later developments has been growing increasingly more sophisticated.

These remarks get a bit ahead of our chronology, but the way Elshtain sets up her treatment of just war and of sovereignty necessarily draws us into a kind of dialogue between Augustine and medieval developments. We see this also in the next figure on the list I gave above, Gelasius, to whom the Gelasian principle traces. Gelasius was pope for four years toward the end of the fifth century (492–96)—that is, a bit more than sixty years after the death of Augustine. In the sphere of doctrine, Gelasius is remembered as a proponent of the "two natures" of Christ against the position that was widely held in the Eastern Church, that the divine and human natures in Christ were fused into one (a position known as Monophysitism). But in the sphere of politics he is remembered as the author of the "Gelasian principle," following a distinction he made in a letter he wrote in 494, midway through his papacy, to the Emperor Anastasius. The relevant passage follows:

There are two powers, august Emperor, by which this world is chiefly ruled, namely, the sacred authority of the priests and the royal power. Of these that of the priests is the more weighty, since they have to render an account for even the kings of men in the divine judgment. You are also aware, dear son, that while you are permitted honorably to rule over human kind, yet in things divine you bow your head humbly before the leaders of the clergy and await from their hands the means of your salvation. . . . If the ministers of religion, recognizing the supremacy granted you from heaven in matters affecting the public order, obey your laws, lest otherwise they might obstruct the course of secular affairs by irrelevant considerations, with what readiness should you not yield them obedience to whom is assigned the dispensing of the sacred mysteries of religion?[8]

Elshtain quotes the first two sentences of this passage early in her *Sovereignty*, using a slightly different English translation (*S*, 13). In her comments on it she makes much of the distinction made there between the emperor's "power" (*potestas*) and the religious "authority" (*auctoritas*), assigning the latter to "the papacy" (Gelasius mentions only "the priests" and "the leaders of the clergy") and going on to describe the distinction made by Gelasius in terms of the "two swords" doctrine.

The "two swords" doctrine is, though, a much later medieval idea, and Gelasius did not use this term. The distinction Elshtain finds between priestly "authority" and imperial "power" also does not appear in the medieval discussions. In the pages that follow her introduction of Gelasius, Elshtain moves quickly to the medieval debates, examining Aquinas and others on temporal and spiritual power, then turning to the idea of papal "fullness of power" (*plenitudo potestatis*) and citing the "extraordinary claims" made on the basis of this idea in Boniface VIII's 1302 bull, *Unam sanctam*, to assert papal supremacy over the Holy Roman Emperor. She links this idea to Gelasius with the following words: "The doctrine of a papal plenitude of power pushed Church doctrines in a monistic direction: Is there to be but one and all others subordinate rather than the two of Gelasian doctrine? The Monistic answer is yes" (*S*, 24). Indeed. Then why does she earlier draw a link

between Gelasius and the "two swords" doctrine, for this medieval doctrine in fact dates to *Unam sanctam*, where it is explained as follows: "We
are taught by the words of the Gospel that in this Church and under her
control there are two swords, the spiritual and the temporal. . . . Both
[of these] are under the control of the Church."[9] That is, here the "two
swords" doctrine appears in the service of papal supremacy, its "plenitude of power."

I never encountered Gelasius before discovering the use of his letter
to Anastasius by the late twelfth- and early thirteenth-century canonists
in connection with their effort to define the necessary authority for a
just war to lie only with temporal rulers having no temporal superior. In
this effort the canonists' concern had nothing to do with the later dispute over papal *plenitudo potestatis* in the form defined in *Unam sanctam*.
Rather, what they wanted to do was to limit the right of subordinate
temporal authorities to initiate use of the sword in the settlement of
disputes in a culture where every man of the knightly class might, in
principle, claim the right of the sword, and, in fact, regional nobles down
to the rank of baron frequently operated as local warlords.

Because my interest has been to clarify the concerns and the thinking that shaped the coalescence of the just war idea in its first comprehensive and systematic form, I have read the canonistic use of the
Gelasian principle as establishing a strong basis for an idea of temporal
sovereignty understood as the ruler's responsibility, defined by the terms
of the natural law, for the common good of the political community
ruled. On this conception, sovereign authority for the use of armed
force resides in the role of the ruler with no temporal superior to act as
ultimate judge regarding matters of injustice and to choose and employ
the means needed to set matters right: in other words, the ruler acts to
interpret for the political community what natural law requires in the
case at issue. The canonists of this period indeed used the term *plenitudo
potestatis* for papal power, but they understood it as meaning fullness of
power within the Church. As they used this term it functioned in much
the same way as their position on the right to use armed force functioned for the temporal sphere: to give the pope dominion over other
claimants to authority and power within the frame of the Church itself.
In short, the perspective of my work has led me to a somewhat different

view of the debates over sovereignty, *plenitudo potestatis*, and the Gelasian separation between governance in the temporal and spiritual realms than Elshtain's, forged from a somewhat different perspective.

Meanwhile, as to what neither of us has really treated, what of Gelasius's letter in his own time? We should remember—and the work of Peter Brown is an invaluable guide here—that the papacy in the late fifth century by no means possessed the authority and power it later developed in the West, certainly not that claimed by *Unam sanctam*.[10] The territory then nominally under the see of Rome had been significantly reduced by the triumph of the Vandals in North Africa, for the Vandals were Arians. Other Arian Germanic tribes were effectively self-ruling in parts of Italy and the Balkans, though still technically within the empire. Roman troops had left Britain, leaving only remnants of Roman-style government there; western France and Spain too, although still maintaining some of the structures of the empire, had become effectively local principalities. Even where the rulers and populace remained Catholic, the fracturing of what had been a common society meant the breakdown of lines of communication, and increasingly local centers of Christian authority developed, with the papacy in Rome a distant presence at best. Already by Augustine's time the imperial seat of government in the West had moved north, away from Rome itself, and papal interaction with the imperial government had to rely on ambassadors who were days or weeks of travel away from Rome. In Gelasius's time the seat of imperial government was Constantinople.

Nor was the position of the papacy nearly so prominent in the structure of the Church as a whole in Gelasius's time, for the East/West schism had not yet occurred, and the patriarch of Rome had to contend with the various patriarchs of the Eastern Christian world. In the imperial capital, Gelasius in particular had to deal with the influence of the patriarch of Constantinople, the supreme leader of the Church in that city. This posed particular problems within the Church, since this prelate espoused Monophysite doctrine, while Gelasius was a strong champion of the "two natures" doctrine. Emperor Anastasius was also a Monophysite. So we have to ask ourselves just what Gelasius's claim, in his letter to Anastasius, was about. Was it an effort to maintain his right to hold and teach a different doctrine from that of the emperor (and that of the patriarch of Constantinople)? Was it an effort to assert the primacy of the Roman patriarch over the Eastern Church? Both these seem more likely, in historical context, than the later use of his letter for essentially political purposes.

In any case, as to the subsequent development of the "Gelasian principle," we have to acknowledge that, just as it seems not to have been recognized as definitive in the West till late in the twelfth century, it *never* had any effect in the East, where the Byzantine emperors operated as the effective heads of both state and church, exercising authority over the various patriarchs in various ways and providing a template which the early Abbasid jurists adopted for their understanding of the role of the caliph in the Dar al-Islam. The gap between Elshtain's and my perspectives leaves room for all the questions implied here, and more, and for answers the scholarly literature has not yet produced.

I have already commented briefly on the difference between how we understand the work of the canonists, and I will not examine this further here. There are also real differences between how we understand the rediscovery of the concepts of natural law and *jus gentium* as seen in the canonists, in Aquinas, and later, and I also can only note this here. There is, I think, an important difference to be found in Elshtain's emphasis on will and my own focus on the development of the idea of rights in medieval thought, and this too I will simply mention for the present context. I also pass over what Elshtain says about the major Reformation figures, though I do not think there is much daylight between our perspectives on them. I conclude the present discussion by drawing attention to the difference between her treatment of Hugo Grotius and mine.

In *Sovereignty*, Elshtain discusses Grotius briefly in chapter 7, her last chapter on the state. This is a wide-ranging chapter that draws together a variety of people not normally spoken of in the same breath, but among whom Elshtain discovers linked ideas and a pattern of development: they are Voltaire, Camus, Hegel, Bonhoeffer, Clausewitz, Blackstone, and, of course, Grotius, who is introduced here both as a representative of the natural law tradition and as a just war thinker. For Grotius, writes Elshtain, the natural law opens an area of "autonomy for human action that is not entirely managed by the will of God," for "not even God can change the binding nature of natural law" (*S*, 149). She goes on to identify what she sees as, for Grotius, the critical component of the natural law as it bears on war: "States have a right to defend themselves. A society of human beings may punish a member who has committed a crime against another internally. In the same way, a nation or a group of nations has the right to punish a state or ruler that has injured it, or them, unjustly" (ibid.). A bit later she continues, "The judgment between states in any controversy must turn on natural reason as the arbiter between good and evil" (150). At the end of the section on Grotius she returns to the theme of punishment, arguing that it is necessary for a workable form of international law (ibid.).

I agree with Elshtain that punishment or the threat of punishment must be part of a moral understanding of the right of a state or a grouping of states to resort to military force. Unlike her, I trace this back to the classic statement of the just war idea, where by the time of Aquinas the recognized just causes for a just war are only two: recovery of that which has been wrongly taken and punishment of evildoing. Defense had been included in Gratian's listing of just causes, via a passage from Isidore of Seville that included it.[11] But by Aquinas's time Innocent IV had changed the landscape, ruling that self-defense while an injury is under way is a natural right for everybody, but that only sovereign rulers may go further, punishing an injustice already completed. The former is *defensio*, the latter *bellum iustum*.[12]

What is especially interesting about Grotius for me is that he turns the tables decisively back the other way. For him the first just cause for war is "defence of self and property."[13] Only after an extensive discussion of this and its implications does he turn, eighteen chapters later, to the matter of war waged to inflict punishment,[14] and to my reading what is striking here is how much effort Grotius expends on limiting war for this reason: "wars should not be undertaken for [just] any sort of delinquency" (sec. 38); "it is more honourable to avenge wrongs done to others than done to oneself" (sec. 50); he cites "Vitoria, Azor, Molina, and others" as holding that "no enemy will have the right to punish another" (ibid.); that care must be taken not to confuse the law of nature from "widely current national customs" (sec. 41); that the law of nature must be distinguished from "the voluntary divine law that is not recognized by all" (sec. 42); and, finally, that "in the law of nature we must distinguish between what is evident and what is not evident" (sec. 43). The upshot is that the "first just cause for war," namely, defense against attack, turns out to be the one that matters most, and this is certainly the judgment of the later writers on the theory of the law of nations who built on Grotius, and it is the position eventually reached in what we have come to call "the Westphalian system." The effect of Grotius's reasoning is thus to sharply limit the breadth of what natural law tells us regarding the use of force, effectively truncating it to the right of self-defense against an attack that is immediately offered or already in progress. The possibility of war for punishment, the focus of the earlier tradition, remains but is sharply limited.

There is also an important implication of this for the understanding of sovereignty: whereas the earlier just war tradition, following the canonists and Aquinas, had defined sovereignty in terms of the personal moral responsibility of the temporal ruler in every political community to serve the common good by making and enforcing judgments about violations of justice known through the natural law, Grotius relocates the role of the ruler to actions serving the collective self-defense of the political community, with the concept of sovereignty redefined as violations of the political community's territory and the "ancient rights and privileges" of its people. Again, later theory of the law of nations follows this lead, and what we call "the Westphalian system" of sovereign territorial states is the result. In fact, "the Westphalian system" owes far more to this line of thinking in Grotius and the subsequent theorists of the law of nations than it does to the three treaties that make up the Peace of Westphalia itself. All this is why I think Grotius is a pivotal figure, one who defines a significant turning point in the development of just war tradition toward international law and the state system, and who fashions a redefinition of sovereignty in terms of each political community's right to defend its territory and the people, together with their "ancient rights and privileges," contained there.

Now, as to the space between what I have just said and Elshtain's treatment of Grotius in *Sovereignty*, I have suggested that there is already a significant body of scholarship occupying that space. Unfortunately for contemporary readers, not only those from the field of religion but also for political scientists, this body of scholarship is out of fashion today and largely unread. The last major effort to recall it comes mostly from the period between the two world wars, when the series Classics of International Law,[15] begun under the editorial leadership of James Brown Scott, published the relevant sources, together with scholarly commentaries probing their meaning, interrelationships, and significance. But not even many international lawyers today recognize this intellectual tradition and the link made in it between just war thinking and international law, since present-day international law has succumbed to a form of legal positivism.

Let me say a concluding word on the concept of sovereignty. Elshtain notes in the preface to her book that early in her research on sovereignty she searched the Library of Congress catalogue for titles on the subject. She writes, "This message came back: 'Your search retrieved more records than can be displayed. Only the first 10,000 will be shown'" (*S*, xv–xvi). She goes on to confide in readers that she decided not to read all the available volumes but to pursue a different research strategy. In researching my own book on sovereignty, I too did not seek to read everything that has been published on the topic, but what I have found especially striking in looking over the literature on it is how "sovereignty" is nearly universally understood by those who have recently written on the topic to be a concept that belongs to the Westphalian era alone, to pertain to states, and to be defined in terms of the right of states to territorial integrity and to defense of it. There is in fact, though, an older conception of sovereignty, one that has its roots in classical Greek and Roman thought and appears in Augustine, one that is defined in the high Middle Ages in terms of the moral responsibility of temporal rulers with no temporal superiors to serve the natural law and thus to do justice, maintain peace, and thereby satisfy the common good. In the Middle Ages this was defined as the responsibility of a *princeps*, a prince, and to have the authority of such a ruler was the first requirement for a *bellum iustum*, a just war. Aquinas, laying down the idea of just war in this way, used the term *auctoritas principis*, the authority of a prince, a term the canonists had defined as referring to a temporal ruler with no temporal superior. By the time Aquinas wrote, though, the word *souverain*, sovereign, was in use in French to carry this same meaning, and it is from this usage that we get the word "sovereignty."[16] An important value in Elshtain's examination of the idea of sovereignty is that she recognizes these historical roots of the idea of sovereignty and works out her thinking in its context. I share with her this wish to give more attention and emphasis to this medieval and early modern conception of sovereignty, one so different from the conception that dominates the modern era and scholarship on it. For in the end sovereignty is a moral concept, not simply a political or legal one, and Elshtain's very title, linking sovereignty to God, state, and self, serves as a reminder of this. In going forward, whether from perspectives in the study of religion, politics, or law, it would be good not to forget it.

NOTES

1. Elshtain, *Sovereignty*; James Turner Johnson, *Sovereignty: Moral and Historical Perspectives* (Washington, DC: Georgetown University Press, 2014).

2. Gary W. Gallagher, *Causes Won, Lost, and Forgotten* (Chapel Hill: University of North Carolina Press, 2008); cf. Gary Gallagher, morning lecture, Chautauqua Institution, July 10, 2013, https://www.thegreatlecturelibrary.com /index.php?select=speaker&data=1533.

3. Paul Ramsey, *War and the Christian Conscience: How Shall Modern War Be Conducted Justly?* (Durham, NC: Duke University Press 1961).

4. See, e.g., Elshtain, *Sovereignty*, 9–11, 58; *Just War against Terror*, 51, 101.

5. Gregory Reichberg, Henrik Syse, and Endre Begby, eds., *The Ethics of War: Classic and Contemporary Readings* (Malden, MA: Blackwell, 2006), 109–24.

6. Ibid., 176–82.

7. For example, see R. A. Marcus, "Saint Augustine's Views on the 'Just War,'" in *The Church and War*, ed. W. J. Sheils (Oxford: Basil Blackwell for the Ecclesiastical History Society, 1983), 1–13.

8. "Gelasius I on Spiritual and Temporal Power, 494," trans. J. H. Robinson, in *Readings in European History* (Boston: Ginn, 1905), 72–73, https://legacy .fordham.edu/halsall/source/gelasius1.asp.

9. Boniface VIII, *Unam sanctam* (1302), http://www.newadvent.org/library /docs_bo08us.htm.

10. See Peter Brown, *Through the Eye of a Needle* (Princeton, NJ: Princeton University Press, 2012), chap. 7.

11. *Decretum*, pt. II, causa 23, q. II, canon 1; Reichberg, Syse, and Begby, *The Ethics of War*, 113.

12. Reichberg, Syse, and Begby, *The Ethics of War*, 150; see further James Turner Johnson, "The Idea of Defense in Historical and Contemporary Thinking about Just War," *Journal of Religious Ethics* 36, no. 4 (2008): 543–56.

13. *De jure belli ac pacis*, bk. 2, chap. 1; Reichberg, Syse, and Begby, *The Ethics of War*, 401–5.

14. *De jure belli ac pacis*, bk. 2, chap. 20, sec. 38; Reichberg, Syse, and Begby, *The Ethics of War*, 405–9. Further citations are given by section number.

15. See Classics of International Law, 22 vols., ed. James Brown Scott et al. (Oxford: Clarendon and other publishers, 1917–50).

16. The English translation of the *Summa theologiae* found on a widely used Web site renders Aquinas's *auctoritas principis* as "the authority of the sovereign"; see http://www.newadvent.org/summa/3040.htm. Originally published as Fathers of the English Dominican Province, trans., *The "Summa Theologica" of St. Thomas Aquinas* (London: Burns, Oates & Washburne, 1920).

PART IV

THE END(S) OF POLITICAL LIFE

Introduction

Erik Owens

Jean Bethke Elshtain's inquiry into the proper ends of political life shines as one of the brightest and most persistent threads in the rich tapestry of her career. In her many books and articles, and in her teaching, she explored the contours of this fundamental question along with its diverse answers as propounded in theory and enacted in history. It shaped her studies and framed her accounts of democracy, secularism, civil society, and Christian theology, even as it rooted her critiques of liberalism, totalitarianism, nihilism, and utopianism.

Elshtain recognized that political theories are rooted in theories of human nature, and in each of the former we can see evidence of the latter. Her Gifford Lectures (published in 2008 as *Sovereignty: God, State and Self*) offered an extended critique of the moral anthropology and political theory attached to certain forms of liberalism. As others in this volume have mentioned, she published widely on many theories and theorists, finding insights into the human condition—and thus the politics suitable for it—in the work and life of Dietrich Bonhoeffer, Hannah Arendt, John Paul II, Albert Camus, Václav Havel, Alexis de Tocqueville, Abraham Lincoln, Jane Addams, Reinhold Niebuhr, Martin Luther King, Jr., and many others. But Augustine was Elshtain's lodestar; his views on the postlapsarian human condition and the limits of earthly politics profoundly shaped her own, as her book *Augustine and the Limits of Politics* (1997) makes clear.

Augustine's eschatological and teleological frameworks for political analysis anchor his vision of humanity as on pilgrimage in this world while awaiting the next. During this in-between time, fallen humans make imperfect politics that may nevertheless still hold out the possibility of procuring the good of (earthly) peace, however transient. In chapter 19, Robin Lovin concludes this part IV by lauding Elshtain's Augustinian embrace of the limited ends of earthly politics, which are written into our nature as fallen creatures. Peace under these conditions, Lovin writes, is about seeking "limited goods of limited duration, achieved by compromises that only partly solve the problems, put in place by decisions that will have to be made over again." It is precisely this embrace of compromise that stands opposed to the "tendency today to see theology as an *antipolitics*, withdrawing legitimacy from political power or withdrawing from society into a sectarian community that lives out its own moral resources."

Elshtain believed that democracy is the imperfect political form most amenable to earthly peace, because its limited political ambitions allow for (but do not automatically produce) a culture of equal respect, freedom, and dignity. Democracy, however, is constantly threatened by disintegrating internal and external forces. In *Democracy on Trial* (1993) she argues that the recent collapse of communism—and the end of the Cold War—was no cause for triumphalism about the state of our own society. On the contrary, she pointed to troubling trend lines regarding civic engagement, marriage, crime, and other social indicators, and she worried that civil society might be too moribund to correct these trends without deeper engagement with moral traditions that seemed to be slipping away. Citizens, in her view, needed to recommit to democracy as a shared space for peaceful contestation, one that respects diversity but does not celebrate or promote it.

Francis Fukuyama writes in chapter 16 that Elshtain was right to worry then, and her analysis was correct, but in retrospect we can see that most of the worrisome trends she identified had reached their nadir just when her book was published. In the ensuing two decades, Fukuyama argues, civil society actually seemed to heal itself in many ways, but with two crucial exceptions. First, some elements of civil society —namely, special interest groups—have actually grown so strong that they are overwhelming the institutional constraints envisioned by the Founders. Political parties now seek power by assembling coalitions of narrow interest groups rather than forging broad compromises that conduce to the common good but require sacrifice. Second, repairs to the social fabric that can be seen in decreasing crime, divorce, and abortion rates, for example, are unevenly distributed. As Fukuyama states, "It is clear now that social class (whose proxy is education) has now displaced gender, race, and ethnicity as the most powerful predictor of life chances. In some ways, civic life has never been better for those with higher educations, a fact that masks from them the continued existence of civic breakdown for the rest."

Carl Gershman is even less sanguine than Fukuyama about the state of democracy today. In chapter 17, he argues that Elshtain believed Christianity was the most important source of civic activism and revival in American political life, and that "secularism" continues to erode the moral and cultural foundations of democracy. Pointing to the violent looting and riots that took place across London in August 2011 (following the police killing of a young black man during a traffic stop), Gershman notes, "Here we have 'democracy on trial,' but at a later stage of decay and in a different, much starker context." Taking a cue from British rabbi Jonathan Sacks, Gershman contends that a "reinvigoration of religious faith" is required if democracy is to be saved from within; nothing less than a "remoralization of society" will do.

Alas, writes Patrick Deneen in chapter 18, that quest is pointless without the wholesale rejection of liberalism, a corrosive force of individualism that is slowly destroying our democracy. Deneen takes Elshtain to task for identifying (in *Democracy on Trial* and other work in the mid- to late-1990s) some of liberalism's most egregious faults but nevertheless embracing them, as when she calls out the specter of multicultural disintegration but later appears to accept multicultural-ism as a robust conception of culture. He takes her affirmations of civic engagement as an antidote to civic decay to be an endorsement of the "American Creed" that values nationalism as paramount, and an asser-tion of the need for a renewal of the "liberal consensus" at the heart of mid-century political economy. For there is no compromise, and so he writes: "Liberalism of all varieties contains at its core some version of the autonomous choosing individual that stands in contradiction to the long Aristotelian and Catholic tradition that preceded it and that it explicitly rejected and sought to overturn."

These comments capture, of course, only a fraction of the complex arguments made in the four chapters that follow. Each chapter offers sustained reflection on the ends of political life as Elshtain understood them, and on the upshot of this understanding for our daily lives today. They are at times critical and admiring, but always incisive. Together, the chapters make connections among themes she took up across many books and articles, and point to new avenues for argument about civil society, democracy, liberalism, and, above all, the limits of politics. Elshtain would have it no other way.

CHAPTER SIXTEEN

CIVIL SOCIETY AND POLITICAL SOCIETY

Francis Fukuyama

For at least the past three decades, Jean Elshtain was one of America's premier public intellectuals, someone who combined genuine scholarship with a willingness to engage on contemporary issues of broad concern. There are few people who can flow as seamlessly as she between deep consideration of theoretical issues and matters of everyday concern, using the one to enrich understanding of the other.

Being asked to comment on the question of civil society has been an excellent occasion to reread (and in some cases read for the first time) her voluminous writings on the subject. I want to begin my own discussion with her 1995 book, *Democracy on Trial*, since it lays out with great clarity and insight most of the important arguments she made concerning the role and crisis of American civil society.

Doing so has been something of a nostalgia trip for me. Around that time, I published two books whose major theme was civil society, *Trust* (1996) and *The Great Disruption* (1999). The latter in particular took up many of the issues discussed in *Democracy on Trial*; since then, however, I have focused on different matters and have not gone back to that well. Doing so now has been an extremely interesting exercise, and I want to share some of my reflections on how the whole civil society debate looks at a remove of more than a decade and a half.

DEMOCRACY ON TRIAL

The primary concerns articulated in *Democracy on Trial* were not, in the first instance, political. They centered, rather, on the nature of American society at a subpolitical level. In the early 1990s, many of the big political and economic issues that had earlier divided the Left and the Right in American society seemed to have been resolved. The Reagan Revolution in a certain sense had been consolidated in the "New Democrat" Clinton administration, one that accepted Reagan's reliance on markets and continued his skepticism about the welfare state. After the failure of Clinton's health-care initiative, the administration moved quickly to the center and was soon on the road to supporting the Republicans in repealing one of the New Deal's signature programs, Aid to Families with Dependent Children. It would go on to collaborate with them in deregulating financial services with the passage of the 1999 Gramm–Leach–Bliley Act, which dismantled another signature New Deal achievement, the Glass–Steagall Act.

But if economic issues did not seem pressing in this period of a rising stock market and the dot-com boom, there was a broad sense that many fundamental American social institutions were simply disintegrating or breaking down. This began with the family: half of all marriages were likely to end in divorce; the rate of single-parent families had gone from single digits in the 1950s to nearly 30 percent of all households. The great crime wave that began in the mid-1960s seemed to be rising inexorably; urban areas were emptying out and with them the sort of associational life that Jane Addams, or indeed Jane Jacobs, would have recognized. Social trust was fraying and many of the civil society institutions that had supported American democracy, from the Boy Scouts to the Elks and Kiwanis International, appeared to be in terminal decline.

What Elshtain's book did was to put all of these developments in a broader context, and link them to the political system and to a body of theory about the nature of healthy democracy. She reminded us of

Tocqueville's observation that American individualism was a two-edged sword: it freed people from their pasts, but it also threatened to isolate them and depoliticize them as they retreated into a small world of friends and family. Indeed, given the fact that neighborhoods and nuclear families were disintegrating, the kind of social atomization that seemed to be developing was in many ways unprecedented in human history.

Elshtain's analysis pointed to many of the sources of these interrelated phenomena. Feminists, of whom she always counted herself, had in some cases turned into extreme partisans who were so intent on asserting victimization that they were willing to undercut traditional social institutions, beginning with the two-parent family. Multiculturalism and identity politics failed to take account of the need of democracies to have a common language and culture within which people could deliberate and interact; rather, it emphasized difference and its own form of victimology. And finally, the post–Great Society welfare state that was supposed to protect the weak ended up exacerbating the problem by creating both dependency and moral hazard, substituting the horizontal bonds tying citizens together with vertical ones subordinating them to the state.

By and large, the solution that Elshtain saw to these problems was not primarily a political one. It was true that the government should stop doing foolish or counterproductive things, like subsidizing illegitimacy or promoting the divisive ethnicization of public school curricula. But ultimately the state was not going to mend fractured families or create a sense of national purpose—indeed, many of Elshtain's writings warn precisely of the dangers of this particular form of communitarianism.[1] The solution as she saw it had to come at the level of society itself, and in a recommitment on the part of Americans to a concept of democracy as a shared space for peaceful contestation, in which we would respect difference without celebrating or promoting it.

Democracy on Trial and other of Elshtain's writings on civil society were part of a larger literature produced during the 1990s that revolved around a common set of concerns. I would include in this group Robert Putnam's *Bowling Alone* (and the extensive debate that book generated), Mary Ann Glendon's *Rights Talk* and *Seedbeds of Virtue*, Gertrude Himmelfarb's *The De-Moralization of Society*, Alan Wolfe's *One Nation After All*, Alan Ehrenhalt's *The Lost City*, among others.[2] Each of these authors had a different take on the scope and gravity of the problem, each attributed the situation of American society to somewhat different causes, and each proposed different solutions—Elshtain's of course being one of the most coherent and best grounded theoretically. But all perceived excessive individualism as a key problem, leading to civic disunity and increasing social isolation as the central challenges facing American democracy.

THE FATE OF CIVIL SOCIETY

So what do we make of these arguments from this period from our perspective now, in the second decade of the twenty-first century? If asked to say what the biggest problems facing the United States today are, I would not today focus on a crisis of civil society. Indeed, one could argue that American civil society is today too powerful: private interests are so well organized that they have captured large parts of the state and make impossible sensible reforms on a range of issues, from the budget to health care, that would clearly be in the public interest, all the while promoting a dangerous polarization of the political elite. The damaging fractures today are not within families and neighborhoods; they are much more overtly political, between Democrats and Republicans, red states and blue states, diverse urban society and rural America. One thread does unite the two periods: *Democracy on Trial* and other of Elshtain's writings bemoan the absence of democratic deliberation and civility that are necessary for the functioning of a democratic community. This problem has indeed gotten much worse since that book was published, but instead of being confined to primarily cultural issues like abortion and religion, it has escalated to include debates over economic policy and the proper role of government.

A funny thing happened on the way to the present with regard to civil society: it started to heal itself. *Democracy on Trial* was written not more than a couple of years after the nadir of many of the social trends that it chronicled. This is evident in many domains.[3] The most dramatic turnaround was with respect to crime. The great American crime wave that began in 1966 peaked, depending on the type of crime and the city, sometime in the late 1980s, and then basically continued to decline almost every year for the next fifteen. Even the onset of the 2007–08 recession did not alter this pattern on a national basis. Many cities, such as New York, Washington, and Chicago, reclaimed important parts of their inner cities and saw a reverse wave of middle-class immigrants from the suburbs. The American "art of association" has not gone into terminal decline, with individuals sitting in gated communities in front of television sets, as once suggested. There has instead been a mushrooming of electronically mediated sociability. Much has been written about the quality and character of online communities, e-mail, and social media, such as Facebook and Twitter. There are many reasons to believe that the quality of this type of association is often low, and some of it is clearly harmful.[4] But Americans have used these new technologies for political mobilization, social support, and a host of other perfectly legitimate functions served by more traditional types of civic association. The idea that Americans are somehow less interested in combining with one another in civil associations seems to me quite fanciful.

Perhaps the rise of the Tea Party in 2009–10 is the best proof of the enduring strength and health of American civil society. Contrary to certain liberal conspiracy theorists, this movement was not one manipulated from above; rather, it started as a classic populist grassroots uprising that depended on the public-spiritedness and organizational abilities of ordinary Americans across the country. And whether or not one likes the Tea Party's politics, growth of the movement had a Tocquevillian outcome, propelling thousands if not millions of people out of narrow concern with their private lives into engagement in the public sphere.

But even though many trends over the past twenty years have been positive with regard to civil society, a new and very ominous development has occurred. The social breakdown and dysfunctionality that Elshtain chronicled has reversed itself, but only for that part of the country that has some form of higher education. For working- and middle-class Americans with a high school education or less, these problems have spread at an alarming rate. It is clear now that social class (whose proxy is education) has now displaced gender, race, and ethnicity as the most powerful predictor of life chances. In some ways, civic life has never been better for those with higher educations, a fact that masks from them the continued existence of civic breakdown for the rest.

These trends have been chronicled in two books by observers at opposite ends of the political spectrum: Charles Murray in *Coming Apart: The State of White America, 1960–2010*,[5] and Robert Putnam in *Our Kids: The American Dream in Crisis*.[6] What these books do is to document two things. The first is the fact that, among the college-educated, there has been an enormous healing of both family life and civic association. Divorce had already peaked in the late 1980s on a national basis, but for the educated it has been trending steadily downwards ever since, as have the number of households headed by a single parent. Drug use has fallen overall. For this group, latchkey children are less a problem than helicopter parents, who worry excessively about their offspring's ability to get into the Ivy League. It is this group that is more likely to participate in voluntary organizations, make use of social media, and participate politically.

The trends are just the opposite for those with a high school education or less. Concerns raised back in the 1980s about social breakdown centered first and foremost around African Americans—the overall rate of households headed by a single parent reached 30 percent, but the rate among American blacks had shot up to as much as 70 percent. One of the most shocking statistics in Putnam's book is that this is now the rate for working-class Americans as a whole. Drug use has skyrocketed among working-class whites (the only difference being that they tend to use methamphetamines rather than crack cocaine), as has crime and truancy. The disadvantages of growing up in disordered families and neighborhoods then transmits itself across generations.

The African American community, for its part, has bifurcated into a middle and upper class, which shares in the same positive trends as their educated white counterparts. The old "underclass," which was the focus of so much attention in the 1980s, has not disappeared, but a significant black upper-middle class has come into being. A similar story can be told about women, Hispanics, and virtually every other social group in the United States: there has been a sharp divergence in behavior and outcomes that is determined above all by income and education rather than other markers of identity.

What is insidious about the growing class divide in the United States is that the intelligentsia—the media, academics, and pundits who comment on social trends—all live on one side of it. There has been a huge increase in awareness of police abuse of African Americans as a result of incidents in Ferguson, Missouri, New York City, and Baltimore, leading to a "Black Lives matter" mobilization, but relatively little attention had been paid to the meth epidemic that has been taking place in rural white America. One of the ironies of American exceptionalism is the fact that many working-class whites vote Republican and live on the other side of a cultural divide, defined by guns, abortion, and patriotism, from the chattering classes, despite the fact that Republican policies like free trade and anti-unionism have arguably contributed to their economic plight.

During the debate in the 1980s and 90s over the decline of civil society, the Left and the Right were polarized between those that blamed the problem on structural factors, such as deindustrialization and middle-class job loss, and those that pointed either to cultural factors or to counterproductive government policies that encouraged dependence. Elshtain tended to put herself on the cultural side of this argument and did not focus on the economic dimensions of the problems she was describing.

In retrospect, it seems to me that both sides of this argument had a point. Those who argue that the problem was simply structural have to explain why an even higher level of joblessness during the Great Depression did not result in high levels of family breakdown, drug use, and crime. There were, back then, strong norms of responsibility and institutions, such as the shotgun wedding that kept even the unhappiest of families together; this began to change only in the 1960s with the sexual and feminist revolutions.

On the other hand, those who think that the problem is simply a cultural one (i.e., that we are witnessing a general decline of religion, Western civilization, or some other traditional source of values) have to explain why the upper classes in the United States have been renorming themselves, strengthening family life, participating in groups, and generally reversing the trends that so worried conservatives a generation ago. This suggests that the kinds of employment opportunities made possible by higher education make a big difference, and that a great deal of today's social dysfunction has economic roots.

THEN AND NOW

If declining civic life does not seem to be a *general* threat at the moment to American democracy, what is? I would argue that our problems are today much more classically economic and political than social. What is problematic is not civil society but a political society that is deeply paralyzed and unable to achieve consensus on policy issues of central concern to the republic. And unless this problem is solved, the country is in big trouble.

THE RETURN OF ECONOMICS

Following on the great economic crisis of 2007–08, and the ensuing period of stagnation and high unemployment that, many classic economic policy issues we thought were settled during the 1990s are in fact still open, and have returned as a dividing line in American politics.

This is not the appropriate place to enter into a long discussion of economic policy, but I believe that the most serious problems confronting American democracy are caused by the changes in the labor market that have occurred as a result of a combination of technological advance and globalization.[7] The stagnation in median wages since the 1970s, particularly for white males, has long been recognized, but we have also seen the extraordinary growth in incomes for the top 1 percent of earners, indeed for the top tenth of the top 1 percent. As Rajan Raghuram has persuasively argued, American policymakers were reluctant to deal with this problem in a European fashion through straightforward redistribution, so they did it through subsidized lending, which gave many low-income households the illusion that their real standards of living were steadily rising.[8] All of this was facilitated by the seemingly limitless willingness of foreigners to hold U.S. government debt. The long boom from the end of the 1982 recession up through 2007 was in many ways an illusion, fueled less by real productivity increases than by the availability of cheap credit.[9] This system of debt-fueled growth went on for an extraordinarily long time, but it was unsustainable and all came crashing down during the crisis of 2007–08.

There is a stream of conservative analysis that points the finger of blame at institutions like Fannie Mae and Freddie Mac and their supporters in Congress, which used implicit government guarantees to expand low-income lending.[10] But these agencies were only trying to deal with a much deeper structural problem, which was the disappearance of low-skill, high-wage jobs that had been the economic basis of the postwar American middle class. Unconstrained free markets were not on their own providing broadly shared growth; rather, they were producing a society in which the share of national wealth going to the top 1 percent of earners increased from 9 percent of GDP in 1974 to almost 24 percent in 2008.[11] Moreover, failure by the state to adequately regulate financial markets produced huge negative externalities and hurt the interests of people far from Wall Street.

What is troubling about these economic trends is that even when the United States recovers from the current crisis, there will be structural changes to labor markets that may mean that these middle-class jobs will *never* come back. We are facing a bimodal labor market, with high-paying jobs for talented and well-educated people, and lots of low-skill employment in occupations that can't be exported or automated, but a decreasing number of jobs in between. The baby boom generation —my generation—lived beyond its means not just during the 2000s but for much of its lifetime; it is their children and grandchildren who will bear the burden of the deleveraging we are experiencing today. These facts do not make for happy politics, and there is rightly a lot of populist anger at the elites who allowed this to happen—though whether that anger is finding the right targets is another matter. The notion that a strong democracy depends on the existence of a strong middle class remains true today.

THE POLITICAL PROBLEM

Since the showdown over raising the debt ceiling in 2013, there has been a lot of talk about the U.S. political system being "dysfunctional." I believe that the system is dysfunctional, but only in a very specific sense. Many of our problems are in fact rooted in the way that the design of our political institutions interacts with the country's current political culture.

It is common to say that our political dysfunction lies in the society's underlying polarization. It is certainly true that the tenor of political discourse has become steadily nastier and more conspiratorial over time. But there is also a fair amount of evidence that on many issues, including central ones like solving the current debt crisis, there is actually a fair amount of centrist consensus. A healthy democratic political system is supposed to mitigate conflict between social actors and allow the community as a whole to come to consensus decisions, but there is a lot of evidence that our system is doing the opposite, that is, amplifying disagreement and making it harder to reach agreement on difficult decisions. A Congress in which the most conservative Democrat is now more liberal than the most liberal Republican—a situation that has not existed for much of the twentieth century—would not seem to reflect the wishes of a public for which 60 to 70 percent majorities can be found on many issues.[12]

Part of the reason this is true has to do with the basic design of the U.S. political system. If one compares the United States to other liberal democracies, it is way over at the far end of the scale with respect to the number of checks and balances we establish to limit executive authority, or what political scientists call "veto players." This is particularly true when the U.S. system is compared to a classic British Westminster system, which greatly concentrates power in the hands of the parliamentary majority. In the latter system, there is no separately elected president (and therefore no possibility of gridlock), no delegation to state and local levels of government, no judicial review, and no upper house capable of vetoing legislation. In Britain, the government, typically commanding a large majority in Parliament, will formulate a national budget, which will then be passed by the House of Commons within a week or two of its promulgation. (The coalition governments since 2013, due to the failure of any party to win a large plurality in the 2009 election, have been anomalies in British practice.) In the United States, by contrast, the president announces a largely aspirational budget, which is then picked over by 535 individual legislators, each of whom has multiple opportunities over a several-months period to insert favored tax breaks or spending measures into it.[13]

By empowering so many veto players, what the U.S. system does is to provide organized interest groups with an extraordinary number of entry points into the political system, from which they can extract rents. The economist Mancur Olson many years ago wrote about the tendency of stable democracies to accumulate rent-seeking interest groups,[14] and the impact of money and interest groups on Capitol Hill has of course been a long-standing complaint about Washington. Yet this trend has continued unabated for decades, abetted by courts that regard money politics a constitutionally protected right.

THE FUTURE OF AMERICAN DEMOCRACY

Hence, it seems to me that most of the serious problems faced by American democracy today are actually the result of a civil society that is too strong rather than too weak. The political system works as planned: it encourages citizens to come together to promote common interests, and gives them opportunities to influence decision-making, which they do with abandon. This does not lead to deliberation on a national level over serious common problems; rather, groups are empowered sufficiently to extract a protection or benefit for themselves, but are unable to pool interests to reach broader decisions. This is why we have a serious fiscal crisis today, and a broken health-care system: we can't eliminate the mortgage interest deduction because of the real estate and banking industries; we can't eliminate fee-for-service treatments because of the medical lobby; we can't improve teacher accountability because of the teachers' unions. One of the most egregious cases is the single wealthiest and most powerful lobby in the United States today, that of the financial sector. Despite having contributed heavily to a crisis with grave consequences for ordinary Americans, the major financial interests have succeeded in staving off forms of regulation that would prevent such a crisis from happening again.[15]

This then points to one of the big unresolved issues of the civil society debate from the 1990s. Almost everyone who saw a crisis in U.S. civil society back then either implicitly or explicitly made a distinction between a "good" civil society that supported American democracy and a "bad" world of interest groups that undermined it. The first type of association supported friends and neighbors, provided social services, encouraged civic participation, and was ultimately a Tocquevillian "school for democracy." The latter, on the other hand, was made up of large organizations representing corporate or other private interests whose purpose was economic rather than social, or else were what Putnam called "membership organizations," like the AARP, that did not involve face-to-face contact among its members.

In the end, I am not sure that it is possible to make a clear distinction between good civil society and bad interest groups. The distinction cannot rest on whether the organization represents private profit-making interests, as if all nonprofit NGOs were somehow virtuous, and interest groups representing the private sector were bad, selfish actors. Nor can one distinguish on the basis of size: small groups can engage in small-scale rent-seeking as well as large ones do, while groups with noble purposes necessarily need to scale up if they are going to have political impact. Nor can we say that good civil society should operate only at a social rather than a political level. Bowling leagues serve certain purposes, but Tocqueville saw private association not as an end in itself but as a gateway to political participation.

One of the big changes that has occurred in the nature of American civil society over the past forty years has been the shift from broad-based, apolitical associations like the Elks or the Kiwanis to narrower, targeted advocacy groups with very specific political agendas, from promoting organic gardening to funding kidney research to protecting handgun ownership. They tend to fall into the category of Putnam's "membership organizations," organized nationally rather than regionally by a professional staff that does not promote face-to-face contact among members. These groups are not profit-making; they are, however, overtly political and use their power to lobby for their objectives on multiple levels of government.

Morris Fiorina has argued that although there is little evidence that the American public has grown polarized on most issues over the past two generations, the political class, which includes the two political parties, the media, and those who make their livings from politics, is polarized as never before in the twentieth century. He notes that most advocacy groups are far more passionate about their particular issues than the vast majority of Americans, and that the two political parties now seek power by assembling coalitions of such groups. So even though larger numbers of Americans are participating in politics today than previously, not for individual patronage benefits but on behalf of public policy causes, the total effect is to create an uncivil and polarized political system deeply out of touch with the broad public.[16]

The cumulative impact of these groups has very negative implications for American democracy in a number of ways beyond increased political class polarization. James Madison famously argued in *Federalist* 10 that what he called "factions" in a broad and diverse country like the United States would largely offset each other and prevent the emergence of strong, concentrated power. In this he was right: the power of these interest groups lies more in their power to veto and to protect narrow interests than in their ability to dominate the political system. But due to the extraordinary concentration of wealth that exists in an advanced capitalist society, they exercise political influence way out of proportion to the size of the social groups they represent.

Moreover, democracies cannot survive on the basis of widely dispersed veto power. They occasionally need to make difficult decisions and achieve collective action in ways that harm the interests of particular factions (like passing prudent and sustainable budgets). Historically, the United States has been able to do this less through any formal powers conferred on the government by the Constitution, than through the ability of individual presidents to appeal over the heads of existing institutional players and achieve a degree of consensus. But if that leadership is not forthcoming, the system on its own tends to promote weak government dominated by special interests.

To return to Elshtain's work on civil society, the analysis I have just presented is not meant to suggest that she was off target or wrong in any of her analysis. It seems to me that her work and that of other thinkers and observers was critical to the (partial) recovery that subsequently happened. Some of the trends she noted were products of large and unmovable social forces, but others were due to policies and choices made by individuals who were influenced by ideas concerning rights, the family, autonomy, community, and the like. A very important debate occurred in the United States that played a role in restraining some of the hyperindividualistic tendencies that were affecting the society at the time.

Democracy remains on trial today much as it was in the early 1990s. But in my view the terrain has shifted substantially. We still have grave problems at a social level, but this has morphed into a class issue. Among elites, the vigor of American civil society has reasserted itself. The threats to American democracy that are today front and center are economic and political, issues of a sort that we thought had been settled back in the halcyon 1990s.[17]

NOTES

1. See Jean Bethke Elshtain, "Citizenship and Armed Civic Virtue," *Soundings* 119, nos. 1–2 (1986): 99–110.

2. Robert D. Putnam, *Bowling Alone: The Collapse and Revival of American Community* (New York: Simon & Schuster, 2000); Mary Ann Glendon, *Rights Talk: The Impoverishment of Political Discourse* (New York: Free Press, 1991); Mary Ann Glendon and David Blankenhorn, *Seedbeds of Virtue: Sources of Competence, Character, and Citizenship in American Society* (Lanham, MD: Madison, 1995); Gertrude Himmelfarb, *The De-Moralization of Society: From Victorian Virtues to Modern Values* (New York: Knopf, 1995); Alan Ehrenhalt, *The Lost City: Discovering the Forgotten Virtues of Community in the Chicago of the 1950s* (New York: Basic Books, 1995).

3. My own book *The Great Disruption* was written just as many of these trends had started to become evident in the statistical data; some of the numbers referred to here can be found in that book; see Francis Fukuyama, *The Great Disruption: Human Nature and the Reconstitution of Social Order* (New York: Free Press, 1999).

4. See, for example, Evgeny Morozov, *The Net Delusion: The Dark Side of Internet Freedom* (New York: Public Affairs, 2011).

5. Charles Murray, *Coming Apart: The State of White America, 1960–2010* (New York: Crown Forum, 2010).

6. Robert D. Putnam, *Our Kids: The American Dream in Crisis* (New York: Simon & Schuster, 2015).

7. For a longer discussion of the financial crisis and its causes, see my chapters in Nancy Birdsall and Francis Fukuyama, eds., *New Ideas in Development after the Financial Crisis* (Baltimore: Johns Hopkins University Press, 2011).

8. Raghuram Rajan, *Fault Lines: How Hidden Fractures Still Threaten the World Economy* (Princeton, NJ: Princeton University Press, 2010).

9. This argument is made most forcefully by Tyler Cowan; see Cowan, *The Great Stagnation: How America Ate All the Low-Hanging Fruit of Modern History, Got Sick, and Will (Eventually) Feel Better* (New York: Dutton Adult, 2011).

10. See Peter J. Wallison, *Bad History, Worse Policy: How a False Narrative about the Financial Crisis Led to the Dodd–Frank Act* (Washington, DC: AEI Press, 2013).

11. Thomas Piketty and Emmanuel Saez, "Income Inequality in the United States, 1913–1998," *Quarterly Journal of Economics* 118, no. 1 (2003): 1–39; see also Jacob S. Hacker and Paul Pierson, "Winner-Take-All Politics: Public Policy, Political Organization, and the Precipitous Rise of Top Incomes," *Politics and Society* 38, no. 2 (2010): 152–204.

12. On the general subject of polarization, see Morris P. Fiorina, with Samuel J. Abrams and Jeremy C. Pope, *Culture War? The Myth of a Polarized America*, 3rd ed. (Boston: Longman, 2010); see contributions by Thomas E. Mann and Gary Jacobson in *Red and Blue Nation?*, Vol. 1, ed. Pietro S. Nivola and David W. Brady (Washington, DC: Brookings Institution Press, 2006); and William A. Galston, *Can a Polarized American Party System Be "Healthy"?* (Washington, DC: Brookings Institution Issues in Governance Studies, no. 34, April 2010).

13. Perhaps the most extreme example of Congress's veto authority is the fact that any of 100 senators can put anonymous holds on second- and third-tier appointments to the executive branch.

14. Mancur Olson, *The Rise and Decline of Nations* (New Haven, CT: Yale University Press, 1982).

15. This argument is made most forcefully by Simon Johnson, *13 Bankers: The Wall Street Takeover and the Next Financial Meltdown* (New York: Vintage, 2011).

16. See Fiorina, *Culture War?*; and Fiorina, *Disconnect: The Breakdown of Representation in American Politics* (Norman: University of Oklahoma Press, 2009).

17. This essay was written before the 2016 election that brought Donald J. Trump to the White House. Needless to say, his election represents the culmination of many of the trends described, such as deepening class divide and political polarization. In my view, this election has only deepened the country's ongoing political crisis.

CHAPTER SEVENTEEN

RELIGION AND DEMOCRACY

Beyond the Clash of Civilizations

Carl Gershman

When Jean Bethke Elshtain's *Democracy on Trial* (*DT*) appeared in 1995, it attracted great attention because it challenged the democratic triumphalism that still prevailed in the United States in the aftermath of the collapse of the Soviet Union and the dramatic expansion of democracy around the world. The book's central message was that, although the threat to democracy from without had diminished, the threat from within had grown more acute. Democracy was vulnerable to a variety of internal crises—a weakening of democratic civil society; the disintegration of the family and other social webs that had once helped to ground individuals morally and prepare them for democratic citizenship; the rise of political cynicism and even despair; and a societal vacuum that was being filled by an increasingly ubiquitous state.

If *Democracy on Trial* was a fire bell in a night of pervasive complacency, today we no longer feel so confident and invulnerable. The 2008 financial crisis in the United States, the worst since the Great Depression, has been followed by a protracted period of sluggish economic growth. Even more worrisome has been a deepening crisis of governance marked by paralyzing political polarization and a loss of confidence in the United States' capacity to solve its internal problems and provide leadership in an increasingly unstable world. Matters are even worse in Europe, where populist parties of the Left and the Right are gaining strength and the Greek bailout crisis has highlighted the danger of growing debt in relation to output, a problem that is compounded by demographic trends that are shifting unfavorably the ratio of workers to pensioners. Elsewhere in the world, the rising power of China, Russia's aggression in Ukraine and its threat to countries on its periphery, and the rise of ISIS in the Middle East and Iran's growing influence all point to a shift in power globally away from the United States and Europe, democracy's traditional heartland, and they raise questions about the future of democratic civilization.

Such trends are not unrelated to the decline of citizenship and moral responsibility that Elshtain first identified in *Democracy on Trial*. Her worry two decades ago that "America's position in the world will falter" as a result of its trials of democracy at home now seems prophetic (*DT*, 37). Elshtain was an integrative thinker, a public intellectual who tried to explain the relationship of political and economic crises to underlying intellectual and moral trends that affect the capacity of democratic societies to act responsibly and to defend democratic values. As such, she was drawn to moral leaders like Václav Havel and Pope John Paul II, who were able to connect the defense of human dignity to the survival of democratic society in the face of threats from totalitarian political forces and nihilistic social movements. She was also a great admirer of thinkers like Alexis de Tocqueville, who understood the importance for democracy of a vibrant civil society and the extent to which democratic culture needs to be rooted in religious traditions and values. Like these thinkers, she worried that the growth of secularism could erode the moral and cultural foundations of democracy.

One such thinker is Jonathan Sacks, England's former chief rabbi, who has drawn special attention to the decline of religion. Following the London riots in the summer of 2011, Sacks wrote that the violence was "the bursting of a dam of potential trouble that has been building for years," especially "the collapse of families and communities [that] leaves in its wake unsocialized young people." He called these young people "the victims of a tsunami of wishful thinking that washed across the West saying that you can have sex without the responsibility of marriage, children without the responsibility of parenthood, social order without the responsibility of citizenship, liberty without the responsibility of morality and self-esteem without the responsibility of work and earned achievement." The financial troubles, he added, simply grew from that failure of responsibility: "Good and otherwise sensible people were persuaded that you could spend more than you earn, incur debt at unprecedented levels and consume the world's resources without thinking about who will pay the bill and when. . . . We have been spending our moral capital with the same reckless abandon that we have been spending our financial capital."[1]

For Rabbi Sacks, the charred ruins of London neighborhoods are a symptom of a process of civilizational decay that is affecting, to one degree or another, all of the established democracies of the West. Here we have "democracy on trial," but at a later stage of decay and in a different, much starker context. In Sacks's view, the solution will require nothing less than "the remoralization of society," a process that will have to be driven by a religious revival, since it is religion, he believes, that fosters "moral character, self-discipline, willpower and personal responsibility."[2] The loss of faith is responsible for the weakening of such attributes, according to Sacks, and only its revival will enable modern democracy to recover its strength and viability. The very existence of democracy, in other words, is tied to the reinvigoration of religious faith.

The issue of religion and its relation to democracy is a central issue in the thought of Elshtain, but she believes that the most important antidote to the decline of democratic values is a revival of civil society activism. In *Democracy on Trial*, she suggests that the restoration of democratic citizenship and a sense of community can be achieved "when men and women, acting in common as citizens, get together and find a way to express their collective hopes and possibilities" (*DT*, 123–24). As examples of such common actions, she celebrates the nonviolent freedom struggles of the American civil rights movement, the Mothers of the Disappeared in Argentina, and the dissident movement led by Havel in Czechoslovakia. Such struggles, she writes, provide evidence of democracy's resilience, for democracy is "the dream dreamed by democrats everywhere" and "the great source of political hope in our troubled world" (*DT*, 117–18).

Elsewhere, though, she writes that such struggles are not self-generating but are inspired by religious faith. "If we look at the saga of U.S. history," she asks in her Seymour Martin Lipset Lecture delivered in 2008, "what do we see? We see that every major social movement in American history (until recent decades, perhaps) has been inter-laced with religious language, inspiration, and enthusiasm."[3] She cites the American Revolution with its rallying cry of "No King but King Jesus," abolitionism, women's suffrage, the Social Gospel movement of the early twentieth century, and the civil rights movement of the 1960s (which was headed by the Southern Christian Leadership Conference). Social movements may generate the moral purpose and common action that a healthy democracy requires, but they themselves are the product of religious faith.

Moreover, her parenthetical qualification—"until recent decades, perhaps"—implies that something has changed in America, and that the faith-based social movements that have had such a positive influence on American society may be a thing of the past. In *Democracy on Trial*, Elshtain writes a great deal about how feminism, identity politics, and other movements of recent vintage have not helped avert democracy's crisis but rather have contributed to the very ills she decries: the divisive multiculturalism, the shift from an ethic of personal responsibility to a system of state entitlements, and the politics of "displacement" (*DT*, 40) and "victimization" (46). Her problem with such movements is that they treat rights as nothing more than wants, demands, and grievances. The rights they talk about stand alone, she observes, because "the dimen-sions of sociality and responsibility are missing" (15). They are missing because there is no connection to a religious tradition that sanctifies all life and, by so doing, carries with it a moral code that obliges citi-zens to take responsibility for the well-being of others. That tradition is expressed in Christianity, which, according to Elshtain, "created a new vision of community that sanctioned *each* life as well as *everyday* life," and also in other faiths that share the universalist belief that all human life is holy and must be respected and protected.[4] That same belief is contained in the American Declaration of Independence, which links the idea of equality to the belief that all human beings are endowed with rights "by their Creator." This belief has been called America's civil religion, meaning that rights are not entitlements, that people are subject to a higher being, and that citizenship carries with it certain obligations and responsibilities.

If Elshtain was concerned in *Democracy on Trial* with the domestic challenge of reviving democratic citizenship, her focus quickly shifted in the aftermath of the 9/11 terrorist attacks on the United States to the defense of democracy against a foreign threat, a danger that was the subject of her later book, *Just War against Terror: The Burden of American Power in a Violent World*. Suddenly the central problem was no longer the erosion of a moral code rooted in traditional Christian values but the assault on democracy by terrorists in the grip of an extremist interpretation of Islam. These were two very different problems, but in each case the threat to democracy came from a breakdown in the proper relationship between democracy and religion—the decline of religion in the first case and its extreme politicization in the second. Understanding the proper relationship between democracy and religion is therefore the starting point for thinking about how democracy can be renewed and defended in the present era.

No one has spoken more eloquently on how indispensable religion and religious values are to democracy than Havel, the playwright and former president of the Czech Republic. He writes, "The relativization of all moral norms, the crisis of authority, the reduction of life to the pursuit of immediate material gain without regard for its general consequences—the very things that Western democracy is most criticized for—originate not in democracy but in that which modern man has lost: his transcendental anchor, and along with it the only genuine source of his responsibility and self-respect."[5] The institutions of democracy, he adds, "are merely technical instruments that enable man to live in dignity, freedom, and responsibility. But in and of themselves, they cannot guarantee his dignity, freedom and responsibility. The source of this basic human potential lies elsewhere: in man's relationship to that which transcends him. I think the fathers of American democracy knew this very well."[6]

The view that democratic society depends very powerfully on the influence that religious faith exercises on the individual and on society as a whole was set forth in the most compelling way by Alexis de Tocqueville in *Democracy in America*. Tocqueville famously declared that when he arrived in the United States, "the religious aspect of the country was the first thing that struck my attention; and the longer I stayed there, the more I perceived the great political consequences resulting from this new state of things." What he found in America surprised him because the philosophers of the eighteenth century had predicted that the spread of liberty and knowledge would inexorably be accompanied by "the gradual decay of religious faith."[7] But in America this clearly had not happened. He was also surprised because in France he "had almost always seen the spirit of religion and the spirit of freedom marching in opposite directions," but in America he found them "intimately united" and reigning "in common over the same country."[8] How could this be?

His answer was that in the new era of democracy that was beginning to unfold, religion had an indispensable role to play in instructing people "in the art of being free" and in the requirements of self-government.[9] "Despotism may govern without faith," he wrote, "but liberty cannot." Advocates of democracy in France could not understand this, and so they continued to attack religion, which they saw as a bulwark of the status quo, even if in so doing "they obey the dictates of their passions and not of their interests." What his countrymen failed to understand, in Tocqueville's view, was that "religion is much more necessary in the republic which they set forth in glowing colors than in the monarchy which they attack; it is more needed in democratic republics than in any others" because it is the way "to prepare men to be free."

He then posed two questions that showed both his belief in the desirability of democracy and his awareness of its profound vulnerabilities: "How is it possible that society should escape destruction if the moral tie is not strengthened in proportion as the political tie is relaxed? And what can be done with a people who are their own masters if they are not submissive to the Deity?"[10] Democracy requires that people have the character and wisdom to govern themselves, and in Tocqueville's view such qualities could not be nurtured, strengthened, and preserved without religion, which he saw as the foundation of moral character and democratic stability.

Tocqueville identifies three ways that religion prepares people for democratic citizenship. The first is that it cultivates the "habits of restraint" that are "favorable both to the tranquility of the people and to the durability of the institutions they have established."[11] Tocqueville was impressed by the bold and enterprising spirit of the Americans, and he saw in them the capacity to become the world's "most daring innovators" and its "most persistent disputants." Given the boundless energy and ambition that liberty released in people, he thought it a good thing that Americans were restrained by an obligation "to profess an ostensible respect for Christian morality and equity, which does not permit them to violate wantonly the laws that oppose their designs." No one in the United States, he said, has dared to advance the maxim that "everything is permissible," which he prophetically called "an impious adage which seems to have been invented in an age of freedom to shelter all future tyrants." Religion checks any tendency Americans might have to abuse their freedom. It "prevents them from conceiving, and forbids them to commit, what is rash or unjust."[12]

The second way religion serves democracy, according to Tocqueville, is that it shapes the behavior of citizens by directing what he called "the customs of the community." In this way it has a powerful "indirect influence" on the politics of Americans, so much so that Tocqueville called religion "the first of their political institutions," even though it "takes no direct part in the government of society." Although religion keeps aloof from parties and refrains from the advocacy of policies to promote freedom, it nonetheless "facilitates" the use of freedom by fostering "great austerity of manners," and "by regulating domestic life, it regulates the state." In this connection Tocqueville emphasized the great influence religion has on women, who are "the protectors of morals," and the importance for democracy of marriage and stable families, an area where he saw Europe as being woefully deficient. Unlike Americans, he wrote, Europeans "despise the natural bonds and legitimate pleasures of home," with the result that they have a greater "taste for excesses" and a tendency to forget their "domestic troubles by agitating society." In

America, by contrast, the "love of order" that exists in the home carries over into public affairs.[13]

The third and "greatest advantage of religion," according to Tocqueville, was that it inspires "diametrically contrary principles" to certain "dangerous propensities" that are encouraged by conditions of equality, and that if left unchecked could lead to human degradation and even servitude. One propensity that Tocqueville warned against was an excessive taste for "physical gratification" that "soon disposes men to believe that all is matter only," trapping them in an obsessive materialism that Tocqueville called a "pernicious" and "dangerous disease of the mind." A second is that the condition of equality "tends to isolate [men] from one another, to concentrate every man's attention upon himself," thereby feeding his "love of material gratification" and causing him to neglect "the duties which are due from man to man." And the third is that in the absence of religion people are beset by doubt that "cannot but enervate the soul," leading to fear and confusion, a loss of will, and a readiness to accept servitude. When "everything is at sea in the sphere of the mind, they determine at least that the mechanism of society shall be firm and fixed; and as they cannot resume their ancient belief, they assume a master."[14]

Since Tocqueville believed that the disappearance of religion in democratic societies would have catastrophic consequences, he stressed the vital importance for new democracies of guarding and preserving traditional faith "as the most precious bequest of aristocratic ages." He also said that it should be "the unceasing object of the legislators of democracies and of all the virtuous and enlightened men who live there to raise the souls of their fellow citizens and keep them lifted up toward heaven." In a passionate appeal that can be read today as both an anticipation of democracy's present trials and a recommendation for how to respond to them, he urged "that all who feel an interest in the future destinies of democratic society should unite, and that all should make joint and continual efforts to diffuse the love of the infinite, lofty aspirations, and a love of pleasures not of earth."[15]

Tocqueville wanted political and intellectual leaders to appreciate the importance of religion in a democracy, but he did not put the burden of preserving faith entirely on their shoulders. He also appealed to religious leaders to understand that their best interests, and also the goal of preserving influential and respected religious institutions, would be served if they would refrain from getting "mixed up with the bitter passions of the world." He urged that they "confine themselves within their own precincts" and steer clear of the bitter controversies and transient loyalties of politics.[16] Religion's influence should be based "only upon the desire of immortality that lives in every human heart." If it "clings to the interests of the world, it becomes almost as fragile a thing as the powers of earth." This is especially true if a nation becomes democratic and political authority is consequently subject to constant change and competition. "Agitation and mutability are inherent" in democratic republics, he observed, and religion would lose respect "amid the struggles of faction."[17]

Tocqueville's warning about the harm that religion would do to itself by seeking to exercise sovereign power was not addressed to Americans, since they did not need to hear it. Every American he had met, without exception, agreed that "the peaceful dominion of religion" in their country was the result of the separation of church and state. Rather, his entreaties were addressed to the clergy in Europe, where the Catholic Church had formed a union with the temporal powers, for which it was paying the price. Since those powers were dying and democracy was inexorably being born, Tocqueville thought it would be a fatal error if "the living body of religion" tied itself 'to the dead corpse of superannuated polity." He would not dare to predict if the Church in Europe could regain the energy it once had by breaking its bond to the *ancien régime*. But the wisest policy for the Church, he wrote, would be "to leave to faith the full exercise of the strength which it still retains."[18]

We know today, nearly two centuries later, that the Church in Europe has not been able to recover that energy, and that the Continent's deep and growing troubles may well be intimately related to the virtual disappearance in Europe of a living Christian faith. The consequences of this disappearance were described with disturbing clarity by Pope John Paul II in *Ecclesia in Europa* (*The Church in Europe*), an apostolic exhortation issued in 2003 and summarized by George Weigel in his book *The Cube and the Cathedral*. The pope spoke of a civilization facing "grave uncertainties at the level of culture, anthropology, ethics, and spirituality," all rooted in a loss of hope that he called "the most urgent matter Europe faces." Among the signs of this hopelessness were "fear of the future," an "inner emptiness that grips many young people," a "weakening of the very concept of the family," "existential fragmentation" and "loneliness," "selfishness that closes individuals and groups in upon themselves," and a "diminished number of births" as the result of "an obsessive concern for personal interests and privileges."[19] Weigel added to this list the influx of Muslim immigrants who are filling the demographic vacuum and altering the cultural identity of Europe, with many becoming radicalized in the process. He wonders if the vaunted human rights ideals contained in the preamble to the EU constitution can survive in a culture of moral relativism that has lost any connection to its roots in Christianity.[20]

Nothing in the existential crisis of Europe described in Pope John Paul II's exhortation is inconsistent with Tocqueville's dark premonitions about the consequences of the abandonment of religion. As noted earlier, democracy in the United States is also "on trial," though not to the same extent as in Europe, and a revival of interest in Tocqueville's thought could have the salutary effect of focusing closer attention in this country on the importance of religion to the health of American democracy.

Such attention would challenge the commonly held view that the decline of religion is an inevitable and desirable by-product of democracy's advance in the world. Elshtain has described a person who holds this view, often called a secularist, as "someone who wants to go beyond the separation of church and state and to effect a thoroughgoing separation of religion and politics at the level of civil society."[21] Not only does such a position fail to appreciate the essential role that religion plays in building and preserving freedom, it is also inconsistent with the way Tocqueville properly understood the relationship between religion and democracy as a finely balanced system of institutional separation and mutual interdependence, with religion helping democracy by preparing the people to assume the obligations of citizenship, and democracy helping religion by giving it the freedom to minister to the people and to uplift their spirits.

Not only is this "secularist" view not good for democracy, but it also narrows the support for democracy internationally. Havel has said that democracy is often presented to the world "as something given, finished, and complete as is, something that can be exported like cars or televisions, something that the more enlightened purchase and the less enlightened do not." This approach, he adds, "betrays an attitude of superiority and contempt for all those who hesitate to accept the offered goods automatically," and it lacks something that would give democracy "universal resonance" and convey the message that all the people who are involved in supporting democracy are bound together by human solidarity. What's needed, Havel says, is "the spiritual dimension that connects all cultures and in fact all humanity." Democracy, therefore, "must rediscover and renew its own transcendental origins."[22]

Such a renewal, according to Havel, will give the West the ability to address humanity in a more universal way and to connect the Judeo-Christian belief that man was created in the image of God with similar beliefs in other faiths. These include the Muslim belief (stated in Qur'an 49.13) that God created all mankind "from an individual male and an individual female"; and the Buddhist belief, expressed by the Dalai Lama, that democracy and Buddhism are "rooted in a common understanding of the equality and potential of every individual."[23]

Nowhere today is there a greater need to understand and appreciate the necessary link between religion and democracy than in the Middle East and the larger Muslim world, where a debate is raging over the proper relationship between politics and faith. Tocqueville himself was skeptical that the Muslim faith could adapt to democracy, since the Qur'an, in his view, contained "political maxims" and various laws that went beyond spiritual matters. But it is not as if other religions that have successfully adapted to democracy are without such maxims. And as Phil Costopoulos has reminded us, the system of "twin tolerations" (a term first used by political scientist Alfred Stepan) that today exists in all established democracies—he calls it a system of "differentiation that gives due regard to both religious and political authority while rejecting any attempt by one to dominate or interfere unduly with the other"— was only embraced in the Christian West after "a terrible effusion of blood."[24] This process is now working itself out in the Muslim world, and the results so far offer cause for modest hope.

Despite the failure of the Arab Spring to fulfill its democratic promise, there has been over the last two decades an accumulation of evidence refuting the view that democracy and Islam are incompatible. No single development has been more significant in demonstrating their compatibility than the surprising success of democracy in Indonesia, the world's largest Muslim country. The resurgence of Islamist political forces following Suharto's fall in 1998 was just one of many reasons that few people expected democracy in Indonesia to succeed. The transition followed a devastating economic collapse. The country inherited from the Suharto era a strong military that many assumed would consolidate control in the new period. Not least, the unity and very existence of the country were threatened by severe ethnic, religious, and separatist violence. Despite all these challenges, though, Indonesia has succeeded in building a stable democracy. The former Indonesian president, S. B. Yudhoyono, extolled this achievement in a speech delivered in Jakarta in 2010 to a gathering of the World Movement for Democracy: "We in Indonesia have shown that Islam, democracy, and modernity can grow together. We are a living example that there is no conflict between a Muslim's spiritual obligation to Allah, his civic responsibility as a citizen in a pluralist society, and his capacity to succeed in the modern world. It is also telling that in our country Islamic political parties are among the strongest supporters of democracy—and they have every reason to be."[25]

Indonesia is one of many Muslim-majority countries where Islamist parties have been integrated as minority parties into a democratic process. A survey published in 2010 of the electoral performance of Islamic parties in eighty-nine parliamentary elections in twenty-one countries over the past forty years found that they averaged about 15 percent of the vote in each, and that they tended to do worse the freer and more routinized elections were. Interestingly, Islamist parties have tended to do best in first elections after a period of authoritarian rule, in which they used their access to the mosque and the street to become the best organized opposition force. In addition, their popularity is greater, as a general rule, when democracy is suppressed, suggesting that the more extreme Islamists benefit when they can proclaim Islam as "the solution" without having to explain how they will provide jobs or protect the basic political rights that people are fighting for. Nonetheless, the Islamist parties in all these twenty-one countries have embraced participation in democratic elections.[26]

The tumultuous events in the Middle East since the Arab Spring are not inconsistent with these findings. Democratic transitions failed in Egypt, Libya, Yemen, and other countries, but the region's first democracy has now been established in Tunisia, where the major political forces were able to overcome deep political and social divisions to build a consensus for a democratic constitution and to choose a new leadership in peaceful parliamentary and presidential elections. Interestingly, the Islamists of the Ennahda Party in Tunisia, according to a report in the *New York Times*, have rejected "the name 'Islamist' to stake out what they see as a more democratic and tolerant vision." The party's leader, Rached Ghanouchi, asked why Ennahda should be linked to a radical Islamism "that is far from our thought, like the Taliban or the Saudi model, while there are other successful models that are close to us, like the Turkish, the Malaysian and the Indonesian models, models that combine Islam and modernity."[27] Secularists in Tunisia have accused Ennahda of engaging in a deceptive "double discourse" that hides its real agenda, which they say is to impose Sharia law on the society. But in Indonesia and other Muslim-majority countries, Islamist parties have lost support when they have pursued such an agenda, and Ennahda's very cautious strategy shows that its leaders appreciate this danger.

The story of Tawakkul Karman, the young Yemeni journalist and activist who was awarded the Nobel Peace Prize in 2011, is illustrative of the profound changes that are sweeping the Middle East. She started out in Islah, an Islamist party that includes the Muslim Brotherhood, but she soon became an advocate for women's rights, and in 2005 started an activist NGO called Women Journalists without Chains. Eventually she decided to replace her long black head-covering with colorful scarves that framed her face, and her thinking continued to evolve after she joined with secularists in a broad-based movement against an authoritarian regime. Writing in *Foreign Policy*, Marc Lynch notes that her decision to remove her face-covering

> will likely be widely cited . . . as an example of her evolution, and will likely be misunderstood—she was certainly not abandoning or

repudiating Islam, but rather moving within an ongoing and ever changing Yemeni and Arab Muslim society. Her Nobel Peace Prize could become a landmark in the vital effort to prevent a "clash of civilizations"—proving to politically engaged young Islamists that they can be accepted as full equals in Western international society and showing many in the West that such Islamists can be passionate advocates of shared values such as democracy and human rights.[28]

If the Arab Spring offers some modest hope that democracy and Islam may be able to reach a new accommodation with each other in the Muslim region that has been most resistant to democratic change, the very different situation in Iran may ironically offer still further hope that such an accommodation is possible. There is a growing body of evidence, some of it based on opinion surveys, showing that the effort forcibly to impose Islam on the Iranian people has led to an anti-Islamic reaction. One study, based on data from the World Values Survey, concluded that "the heavy regulation of religious belief leads to a decrease in religious participation."[29] A second study, based on a national survey of more than 2,500 Iranians conducted in 2000–2001, concluded that "the experience of having lived for more than two decades under an Islamic fundamentalist regime has had a counter-productive effect, making the Iranians *less* religious and less concerned about Western cultural invasion instead of more so."[30] The Iranian political scientist Saeid Golkar has reached an even harsher conclusion, writing that "imposing Islam in every sector of Iranian society has . . . encouraged the flourishing of non-Islamic and even anti-Islamic behaviors," an example being that Iran has one of the highest crime rates of all Muslim countries. "This 'immoral' behavior," according to Golkar, "is often used to express discontent with the regime and symbolizes individuals' resistance to state power."[31] The experience of Iran confirms Tocqueville's view that efforts by clerics to intervene in politics will harm genuine religious faith, and it also suggests that Islam would fare better in a more tolerant democratic system.

The compatibility of Islam and democracy is demonstrated by a final example from Pakistan, where democratic activists are countering Pashtun extremists in Khyber-Pakhtunkwa, the frontier province where Osama bin Laden was killed in 2011, by offering an alternative, nonviolent vision of Islam. Their group, the Baacha Khan Trust Educational Foundation, is named after Abdul Gaffer Khan, a devout Muslim and nationalist leader during the period of British colonial rule who preached social and political change through nonviolence and education. Called the "Frontier Gandhi," he organized a grassroots movement called the "Servants of God" that was inspired by Qur'anic verses extolling compassion and that sought not just to oust the British from the Indian subcontinent but to transcend the Pashtun tribal culture of blood feuds and violent retribution. The reformers acting in his name today are working with schools and communities in the epicenter of militant activity, organizing volleyball and cricket tournaments, poetry readings, musical events, and public discussions on such topics as the "Compatibility of Islam and Democracy," "Terrorism and Militancy," and "Democratic Institutions and Social Change." The goal is to recapture political, social, and cultural spaces that were ceded to militants and their intolerant ideologies during the past decades of war and violence, with the result that young people have been cut off from education and economic opportunity. Though the various events organized by the Baacha Khan Trust have been repeatedly attacked by these militants, the work is continuing and demonstrates both the courage of the activists and the extremists' vulnerability to an ideological challenge that links Islam to democracy.[32]

These examples, drawn from across the Muslim world, show how people from very different Muslim societies are trying to fashion new ways of adapting Islam to the desire for greater democratic participation and economic progress. Of course, it is not yet clear if these societies, especially those in the Middle East, will be able to adapt their traditional faith and culture to the requirements of democratic processes and respect for minority rights, and there will certainly be setbacks and difficult conflicts along the way. The plight of Christians and other minorities in the Middle East, the rise of ISIS in Iraq and Syria, and the growing influence in the region of Iran's theocratic dictatorship are certainly cause for grave concern. But the reliance of jihadist movements and regimes on violence and extreme intolerance is actually a sign of ideological weakness, and the threat that they represent makes it all the more urgent for modernist Muslims to explore new ways of embedding democratic rights, participation, and accountability in societies where Islam remains the dominant religion.

Tocqueville's view that democracy is strengthened by religion and that religion benefits by abstaining from politics is not well known in the Muslim world, but there might well be a receptive audience for his insights, which could provide a framework for a new vision of Muslim democracy where politics is secular but infused with religious values, and Islam respects democracy while only "indirectly" influencing the state. Rached Ghanouchi actually referenced Tocqueville in an important address on secularism and the relationship between religion and the state that he delivered to a meeting of the Center for the Study of Islam and Democracy in Tunis on March 2, 2012. He distinguished between secularism in France, where religion is "totally excluded from the public sphere," and in America, where religion is present in the public domain and "secularism is not an atheist philosophy but merely a set of procedural arrangements designed to safeguard the freedom of belief and thought." Islam, according to Ghanouchi, has known this separation between the religious and the political "since its inception and throughout its history," and this separation "is also clear in the thought of Islamic scholars and jurists," who have distinguished between "the system of transactions/dealings (*Mu'amalat*) and that of worship (*'Ibadat*)." For Ghanouchi, the critical objective "is to find a balance that would guarantee people's freedom and rights" while preserving religion's capacity to provide "spiritual and moral guidance," without which "things would get out of control and social harmony would be endangered," a very Tocquevillian concern.

We have come to a similar moment in the West, though for very different reasons. If Arab and other Muslim countries face the challenge of finding democracy while preserving traditional faith, in the West the challenge is to preserve democracy by rediscovering faith, which Havel has called "the only real alternative to extinction."[33] Far from there being a "clash of civilizations," which Samuel Huntington said would be the defining feature of global politics after the Cold War, the Muslim world and the West are ironically both seeking a way to integrate religion and democracy, the former in order to resolve a political and cultural crisis of modernity, and the latter to survive a moral and spiritual crisis of postmodernity. It is surely too much to hope that these processes will eventually meet on common ground, where the state is essentially secular, influenced but not controlled by religion, and society is strengthened by religious values that build character and sustain hope. But the fact that they are taking place at all is a testament to the enduring relevance of Tocqueville's two most deeply held beliefs—that the gradual development of democracy is "a providential fact," and that faith is "the only permanent state of mankind, . . . one of the constituent principles of human nature" that no democratic society dare abandon.[34]

In *Democracy on Trial,* Jean Elshtain wonders if democracy is "up to the task of satisfying the yearnings it unleashes for freedom and fairness and equality." The answer is that it is not up to that task if it is left entirely to its own devices, without a sustaining link to the belief in a transcendent being that is the source of these values. The answer is sobering, but it points the way forward for democracy and for humanity.

NOTES

1. Jonathan Sacks, "Reversing the Decay of London Undone," *Wall Street Journal,* August 20, 2011.

2. Ibid.

3. Jean Bethke Elshtain, "Religion and Democracy," *Journal of Democracy* 20, no. 2 (2009): 5–17.

4. Elshtain, "'In Common Together': Unity, Diversity, and Civic Virtue," in *Toward a Global Civil Society,* ed. Michael Walzer (New York: Berghahn, 1995), 84.

5. Václav Havel, *The Art of the Impossible: Politics as Morality in Practice* (New York: Alfred A. Knopf, 1997), 180.

6. Ibid.

7. Alexis de Tocqueville, *Democracy in America* (New York: Alfred A. Knopf, 1980), 1:308.

8. Ibid.

9. Ibid., 1:303.

10. Ibid., 1:307.

11. Ibid., 1:305.

12. Ibid.

13. Ibid., 1:303–5.

14. Tocqueville, *Democracy in America,* 2:22–23, 154.

15. Ibid., 2:154–55.

16. Ibid., 2:24.

17. Tocqueville, *Democracy in America*, 1:310–12.

18. Ibid., 1:314.

19. George Weigel, *The Cube and the Cathedral: Europe, America, and Politics without God* (New York: Basic Books, 2005), 117–18.

20. Ibid., 132–35.

21. Elshtain, "Religion and Democracy," 8.

22. Havel, *Art of the Impossible*, 179.

23. His Holiness the Dalai Lama, "Buddhism, Asian Values, and Democracy," *Journal of Democracy* 10, no. 1 (1999): 4.

24. Philip J. Costopoulos, introduction to *World Religions and Democracy*, ed. Larry Diamond, Marc F. Plattner, and Philip J. Costopoulos (Baltimore: Johns Hopkins University Press, 2005), 4.

25. Susilo Bambang Yudhoyono, "The Democratic Instinct in the 21st Century," *Journal of Democracy* 21, no. 3 (2010): 4.

26. Charles Kurzman and Ijlal Naqvi, "Do Muslims Vote Islamic?" *Journal of Democracy* 21, no. 2 (2010): 50–63.

27. David D. Kirkpatrick and Anthony Shadid, "Activists in Arab World Vie to Define Islamic State," *New York Times*, September 30, 2011.

28. Marc Lynch, "A Nobel Prize for the Yemeni People," *Foreign Policy*, October 7, 2011.

29. G. M. Tezcur et al., "Religious Participation among Muslims: Iranian Exceptionalism," *Critique: Critical Middle Eastern Studies* 15, no. 3 (2006): 222.

30. Taghi Azadarmaki and Mansoor Moaddel, "The Worldviews of the Islamic Publics: The Cases of Egypt, Iran, and Jordan," *Comparative Sociology* 1, nos. 3–4 (2011): 8.

31. Saeid Golkar, "Politics of Piety: The Basij and Moral Control of Iranian Society," *Journal of the Middle East and Africa* 2, no. 2 (2011): 207–19.

32. Wilson Lee, "Pakistan: A Tradition of Nonviolence," *Liberal Matters* (February 2009): 18–19.

33. Havel, *Art of the Impossible*, 172.

34. Tocqueville, *Democracy in America*, 1:6, 310.

CHAPTER EIGHTEEN

DEFENDING THE INDEFENSIBLE

The Tragedy of Jean Bethke Elshtain's Defense
of the Liberal Consensus

Patrick J. Deneen

The breadth and depth of the work of Jean Bethke Elshtain is quite astonishing to consider, and reacquaintance with that work is something of an education, or, in my case, a reacquaintance with my own education. Elshtain was one of those authors whom a good number of students in graduate school in the early and mid-1990s read as a model and an inspiration, I myself among them. Many of us hoped to fashion writing voices, to take positions in defense of a robust conception of human community and flourishing, and aspired to a level of public stature that Elshtain seemed so effortlessly and brilliantly to achieve.

Elshtain's work—and I will concentrate most of my comments on some of the themes in her short but trenchant best seller, *Democracy on Trial (DT)*, and on several essays from that same period spanning the early 1990s into the 2000s—strikes me in the first instance especially for its fierce *moderation*. In both tone and in that which she sought to defend, she aimed to carve out a middle position between what could be regarded as the extreme voices on both the Left and the Right that, in her view, posed a threat to the ongoing prospect of liberal democracy. Her pen waged mighty battle on behalf of, above all, *civility, citizenship,* and the realm of politics in which *compromise* can be understood to be an "adventure" (*DT*, 61). It was during this period especially that a perception arose that Elshtain had become something of a conservative, but her work consistently evinces a strong assertion of moderation on behalf of positions that encourage strengthening of a civic sphere and civic disposition that encourage speech, dialogue, and a "world of politics without end" (134). If her arguments could be considered to be "conservative," it was less because her views had changed than that her academic interlocutors and critics had become increasingly immoderate in their expectations of, and demands upon, politics, and especially had become impatient with the barriers and frustrations of liberal democratic politics.

What strikes me in the second instance about the work of this period—and, truth be told, most of Elshtain's work—is her keen sense of crisis and intimations of disintegration. In *Democracy on Trial* she wrote of the fragmentation of social webs, of pervasive consumerism (what she describes elsewhere in *Who Are We?* as a "nexus" of "consumerist-commodifiable" [*WAW*, 47]), of a "generous bounty of troubles," including cynicism, individualism, and a general waning of civility, that pushed her to join "the ranks of the nervous" (*DT*, 117, xvii). She generally describes democracy on the cusp of descending into either tribalism or even radical individualistic fragmentation, on the one hand, and a kind of bloodless, abstract, absorbing statism on the other, and instead urges a less visible and seemingly less viable "middle" position of citizenship and membership in civil society defined by "concrete moral obligations" and an array and web of particular memberships and commitments (19). In a significant number of works, Elshtain recommends *hope* as the proper disposition toward our condition—which she differentiates, like her dear friend Christopher Lasch—from *optimism*. Hope is a disposition of expectant awaiting without expectation of immediate or even earthly realization. Thus, Elshtain distinguishes a disposition of "democratic hope" from the urgent and impatient expectation of "political salvation," a species of *optimism* that leads to an impatience and even betrayal of politics, and hence democracy. Her analysis seems most often to imply that we are increasingly a *hopeless* people, a people who, in expecting too little, seek all; and in seeking all, we endanger everything.

Elshtain, then, reflects a curious and perhaps even singular combination of qualities: fearing and even anticipating crisis and social disintegration, while recommending moderation and chastening hope. She
points out that antidemocrats have historically used the fear of "disorder" to advance their critiques of democracy, in the face of pervasive fears of disorder, she urges fealty to the best traditions of liberal
democracy—thus seeking to invoke the specter of disorder precisely to
defend democracy as the last, best hope. She marshals rhetorically powerful descriptions of our "precarious present" not to urge a wholesale reex-
amination of the viability of liberal democracy, but rather to encourage
devotion to its "enduring promise." Even while invoking the possibility
that our children's children will someday poke "through the ashes of a
wrecked civilization," she predicts that they will not curse our memory,
a restraint that will acknowledge our shared efforts to defend democracy's prospects (*DT*, 138). In sum, Elshtain curses not the night—even
as she discerns the deepening dusk—but rather believes the modest and
moderate invocations of homely virtues of civility and citizenship can
produce sufficient light and heat to keep at bay the gathering shades.

In this study I will question the viability of Elshtain's project, and
more, suggest that all along, hers has been a tragic quest. For the dusk
is not in spite of the liberal democratic order she praises, but because
of its very trajectory toward a westward setting, a trajectory more self-
evident today than in the years when it seemed possible to hold together
a center that can no longer be held. And so, I come at once to praise and
to lament Elshtain's tragic project of defending the finally indefensible,
she among the last defenders of the liberal consensus.

THE LIBERAL CONSENSUS

In 1955, Louis Hartz of Harvard University published his classic study
The Liberal Tradition in America.[1] The title itself is a remarkable oxy-
moron: for, though liberalism on the one hand can be understood
to constitute a certain kind of peculiar tradition, it was a philosophy
that was born of reaction against not a tradition per se, but against
the very idea that tradition should be an authoritative guide to human

institutions—certainly public, and even private. In the most obvious first instance, the philosophical origins that informed the American founding —particularly those origins expressed in the thought of John Locke, and which undergirded the defenses of the American Revolution—sought to displace any residual remnant of political authority based upon the invocation of *authority* or evocations of the *ancestral*. The *First Treatise of Government* is entirely devoted to a demolition of the justification of authority based upon *paternalism* or *patriarchy*, a broadside launched specifically against the claims of the monarchist Robert Filmer. Locke effects a lawyerly dismantling of Filmer's position—and particularly Filmer's dubious claims to be able to trace back the British monarchy to the rule of Adam as established by God—but, more broadly still, Locke's is an attack upon any political claim that cannot be ultimately based upon the consent and voluntarism of rational self-calculators. All governments in all times and places are to be understood as the creation of individuals coming together for the sake of mutual convenience, in order to "secure" their natural rights that are retained from their natural condition (in the state of nature) even when they enter into civil society. All human political arrangements are thus the result of such voluntarist arrangements, and are thus always subject to revision and even outright dissolution when the natural rights of individuals are sufficiently compromised. We thus learn to evaluate all claims to *political* authority on the basis of their benefit or harm to our individual rights.

As Locke's initial effort to undermine *political* paternalism suggests, ultimately the logic of Locke's argument cannot be limited to merely political institutions. Locke explicitly addresses the problem of *actual* paternalism in the *Second Treatise*, and although he offers considerable latitude to the claims of parents—and, in particular, the duties of parents to raise children and the appropriateness of gratitude of adult children toward their parents—nevertheless, the relationship between parents and children, on the one hand, and husbands and wives, on the other, comes under the sway of Locke's voluntarist logic. The relationship between parent and child, Locke argues in chapter 6 of the *Second Treatise* (entitled "Of Paternal Power") begins with a traditional argument on behalf of the duties of parents to raise children and the corresponding duties of children to obey—a duty that springs, he argues, from the Mosaic

Law itself, and the commandment to "Honor thy father and mother."[2] However, Locke also insists that a child and parents' period of mutual obedience ends precisely when the law recognizes the end of the "age of nonage," or immaturity. At that point, the child will have "attained to a state of Freedom," which includes how the child will then view his or her relationship to his or her parents. "After that, the Father and Son are equally *free* as much as Tutor and Pupil after Nonage; equally subject to the same laws together."[3] Locke compares the relationship of parent and child to that of a teacher and student, with a specific term of beginning and conclusion. Locke does insist that the child owes to his parents "honour," but finally the act of honor becomes a matter of beneficial regard, not a disposition that tends to emphasize obedience or submission toward the claims of authority and the ancestral. Locke here tips the balance away from the default of the claims of tradition, and instead to the claims of the freedom of every child who reaches the end of nonage to evaluate any and all residual authoritative claims that arise as a matter of inheritance or gratitude toward a previous generation. Having disposed of Filmer's claims of monarchical power resembling that of a parent, Locke proceeds to argue that a parent's power is essentially comparable to monarchical power—that is, that it, too, is based upon an ultimately illegitimate claim to arbitrary authority, and must too be subjected to the logic of voluntarism and consent.

Every child must ultimately subject their inheritance to the logic of consent, and thus begin (evoking the origin of human society according to Locke) in a version of the state of nature in which we act as autonomous choosing individuals: "For every *Man's Children* being by Nature as *free* as himself, or any of his Ancestors ever were, may, whilst they are in that Freedom, choose what Society they will join themselves to, what Common-wealths they will put themselves under. But if they will enjoy the *Inheritance* of their Ancestors, they must take it on the same terms their Ancestors had it, and submit to all the Conditions annex'd to such a Possession."[4] In this extraordinary passage, Locke allows that effectively *all* inheritance—including one's patrimony, one's station, one's heritage, one's religion, even one's nation—are subject to the same logic as that which pertained to individuals in the state of nature. Every human moving from a condition of "nonage" to maturity effectively relives the decisions made in the state of nature, and with the same degree of radical freedom to completely make or remake their fundamental commitments. Moreover, even those who adopt the inheritance of their parents in every regard only do so equally through the logic of *consent*, even tacit consent. The default—even for those who adopt the traditions of the ancestral—becomes *choice*. All human relationships, commitments, and memberships are thus subject to the logic of voluntarism. Even marriage, Locke holds, is finally to be understood as a contract whose conditions are temporary and subject to revision, particularly once the duties of child-rearing are completed. If this logic applies to the most elemental and basic relationships of the family, then the looser ties that bind people to other institutions and associations are thus all the more subject to the withering logic of choice, in which continued membership is subject to constant monitoring and subject to assessment of whether it benefits or unduly burdens my individual rights.

In assessing that Americans were unconscious Lockeans in their rejection of any and all forms of a feudal past (indeed, that what made America unique was the complete absence of an experience with feudalism), Hartz appealed to an implicit understanding of Locke in which just such a rejection of all claims to the ancestral would become a way of life. Seeing in particular the legacy of several generations of immigrants who seemed equally to embrace the inheritance of philosophical and political Lockeanism in their rapid substitution of the "American Creed" for their respective cultural legacies, Hartz argued that the Lockean tradition was the *only* tradition in America—and thus, ironically, that America was a land that preternaturally distrusted *all* authoritative claims to tradition. As a result, Americans would come to hold "loose connections" to the constitutive associations that might have once been accorded a form of "default" membership.

Hartz's thesis seemed—and continues to seem—a powerful way of understanding certain aspects of American life, but it was always an incomplete and even willfully partial explanation. As long ago as the early nineteenth century, Alexis de Tocqueville had noted a similar aspect of American life, that modern democracy would tend men toward the shattering of bonds of the past and weaken democratic men's commitment to the ties that once bound men together in aristocratic ages. However, at the same time, he noted the widespread existence of the inheritance of the European aristocratic past—translated to the American shores by waves of immigrants—especially the profession of law (he might have mentioned the other guild professions also, such as medicine and the structure of the colleges and universities) and of religion. He also noted the capacity of democracy to generate new forms of connection and membership (though he linked their origin to a nonliberal, Puritan past), particularly civic associations that formed through a mutual willingness to come together to solve political problems, and through which men learned "the arts of association" and thus "the heart was enlarged." America was decisively a radical departure from the ethos of the aristocratic age, but it had received a rich if somewhat attenuated inheritance from an aristocratic past. Combined with its own resources, Tocqueville hoped (though he was not optimistic) that modern democracy in America (and eventually in Europe) would stave off its self-immolating tendencies toward atomism, civic apathy, and finally the willingness to substitute democratic self-governance for the soft despotism of statism.

Historians speak of a mid-twentieth-century period in which a "liberal consensus" reigned. The period of "liberal consensus" is often characterized as a willingness of disparate political persuasions to compromise around the existence of a then-nascent welfare system devised under the New Deal reforms of Franklin Delano Roosevelt alongside a robust form of state-friendly corporate capitalism, combined with a widely shared opposition toward the threat of communism. The "liberal consensus" was thus thought to comprise what historian Arthur Schlesinger characterized as "the vital center."[5] At the same time, less celebrated, but nevertheless a robust aspect of that "consensus," was the continued vitality of the wide variety of organizations and associations and memberships composing the fabric of civil society that existed alongside a political and economic system that philosophically foregrounded the voluntarism of Lockeanism. As revealed in the rich data collection of Robert Putnam's 2000 book *Bowling Alone*, Americans in mid-century were at a peak of belonging and membership: family and neighborhood life was robust; civic voluntarism was at a peak; and religious observance in the tradition of one's parents' and cultural inheritance remained high.

The "liberal consensus" seemed just as much to exist as the willing juxtaposition of a liberal politics and an "illiberal" way of life as it was a set of policy agreements.

It was into this world that Elshtain was born, one she describes so evocatively in a passage in *Democracy on Trial* about her civic education in the Colorado village of Timnath, where she grew up. It is this world to which Elshtain devoted her intellectual life and used a cascade of words to defend. It is this world that has proven—and that I fear and suspect was destined to be proven—to be finally unsustainable.

THE INCOHERENCE OF THE LIBERAL CONSENSUS

According to the telling of that education, Timnath Public School was a throwback—a single-classroom of seventh and eighth graders under the "eccentric tutelage" of Miss McCarthy. Most memorable about that tutelage was the recitation of the Civil War hymn "The Battle Hymn of the Republic" and the memorization of the Gettysburg Address. As she writes, she was raised "a lucky child, a lucky *democratic* child" (*DT*, 86). The argument of *Democracy on Trial* seeks above all to insist upon our shared recognition of a "democratic" belonging, and correspondingly the "presumption that none of us is stuck inside our own skins; our identities and ideas are not reducible to our membership in a race, an ethnic group, or a sex" (86). Though much of the argument of *Democracy on Trial* is a brief against the rise of "ascriptive identity" politics, Elshtain's response tends to stress our common membership as *democratic* citizens, and—as the evidence of her own education reveals—as members of the *national* democratic system. What holds us together ultimately is our relatively abstract membership as citizens of the American polity. Our identity as citizens is to trump all partial memberships, to call us out of our partial selves and instead be the common glue that is to serve as the basis of a shared identity, one that derives from a common allegiance to words such as those expressed in the Declaration of Independence (96). Facing what she perceived as a new threat of fragmentation through the late twentieth-century assertion of "identity" politics, Elshtain argues strenuously on behalf of the need for a deeper commitment to our identities as democratic citizens.

Elshtain was hardly alone in encouraging a devotion to a more abstract national identity in this response to the concerns over strong group identities of the sort she perceives in the assertion of "identity" politics. She echoes the response of the Progressives in the late nineteenth and early twentieth centuries in the face of the strong group identities of immigrant groups (especially the Irish urban machines), and again in the mid-twentieth century by the proponents of the "American consensus" who sought to forge a strong national response to the twin threats of fascism and communism. Elshtain's response to the rise of "identity politics" in the 1980s thus follows a long-standing pattern to the felt threat of national dissolution in the face of competing cultural identities, and so reflects a renewed effort to assert our fundamental and common national identity as the necessary response to the specter of "multiculturalism" in the 1980s and 1990s. This response was assertively stated by a number of defenders of the "liberal consensus" who are often categorized variously on the ideological scale, but all of these asserted the need for a recommitment to a national identity under the felt threat of the dissolution of partialities. On the liberal Left, Arthur M. Schlesinger, Jr., penned a short book defending the American liberal project that he had defended over the course of his life, *The Disuniting of America*. In the book's opening chapter, "The New Race?," Schlesinger describes the tortured efforts of Americans to settle upon an "American Creed," that—over time, and with the growing diversity of various cultural traditions entering the country—settled upon the liberal tradition itself as the form which that creed would take. All identities, thus, were to be seen and understood to be provisional and temporary, and Americanism, *qua* liberal doctrine, was to become the common and binding glue of the nation. Notably, among the figures singled out by Schlesinger as praising the American Creed is Jane Addams, subject of Elshtain's admiring intellectual biography and accompanying reader.[6]

A similar response was no less evident on the nominal Right. Allan Bloom published his best-selling jeremiad *The Closing of the American Mind* in 1987 to much criticism and even denunciation by liberals, but in spite of much of the book's rhetorical excess, it can and should be read today as fitting comfortably within the arguments of the American liberal consensus. In its opening pages Bloom decries the relativism that is reflected in multiculturalism, and instead appeals to the tried-and-true devotion to the American Creed:

> Above all, [the democratic citizen] was to know the rights doctrine; the Constitution, which embodied it; and American history, which presented and celebrated the founding of a nation "conceived in liberty and dedicated to the proposition that all men are created equal." A powerful attachment to the letter and the spirit of the Declaration of Independence gently conveyed, appealing to each man's reason, was the goal of education of democratic man. This called for something very different from the kinds of attachment required for traditional communities where myth and passion produced an instinctive, unqualified, even fanatic patriotism, unlike the reflected, rational, calm, even self-interested loyalty—not so much to the country but to the form of government and its rational principles—required in the United States.[7]

Bloom was never a "conservative" in any sense that stood by a defense of the "traditional" or ancestral"—like his teacher, Leo Strauss, he denounced the relativism represented by culture and tradition, and even denied explicitly that he was a "conservative."

Schlesinger and Bloom—and many like them, on the Left and the Right alike, from Todd Gitlin to Irving Kristol—invoked the American Creed as an antidote to the perceived threat of multicultural disintegration. Schlesinger, for instance, decried the rise of "hyphenated" American identity as a betrayal of the "amazing solvent power" of the American Creed, while Bloom defended an ideal of education as a force that "liberated" students from the cultural and traditional inheritances of their family and locality.[8] For each, the American Creed represented an ideational commitment that liberated individuals from the partiality of their particular inheritances, that set all Americans on an equal theoretical plane as rights-bearing citizens, and that offered in return for narrow, sectarian membership an open, capacious, and decultured form of identity. The commitments they called upon were to nation, and preeminently to its political system based upon the theory and anthropology first articulated in liberal philosophy, particularly that of John Locke.

Elshtain was suspicious of the absolutism of these claims even as she substantially made many of the same arguments. Unlike the work of so many contemporaries who argued against the specter of "multicultural" disintegration, Elshtain robustly defended the role of family, neighborhood, community, and religion as central features of human flourishing. She lamented their apparent decline in seemingly all spheres of life, and she worked assiduously to articulate the substantive goods of human and civic life cultivated and afforded by those various memberships, even as she willingly criticized what she rightly understood to be many of the forces of modern liberalism—both a liberationist and individualist orientation in both Left social policy and Right economic policy alike. Yet, at the same time, faced with the rise of the claims of "multiculturalism," like Schlesinger and Bloom, she asserted the need for a renewal of the liberal consensus.

Most tragic in Elshtain's efforts was her apparent willingness to accept on its face that what various feminist, ethnic, and racial defenders of "multiculturalism" were defending was actually a robust conception of culture. In fact, and more clearly in retrospect, what was at that time asserted as forms of "multiculturalism" was an intensified version of liberalism itself, and particularly, the efforts of members of self-identified disadvantaged groups to gain admission and recognition within the elite institutions of American society, particularly elite universities, where the multicultural agenda was most conspicuously and insistently pursued. If that admission was pursued through the strategy of group grievance, its practical ends was the effort to gain a foothold in the liberal system—in effect, logically and ultimately to supersede the identification of individuals with "culture." In most cases, what was being advanced and defended in the "multicultural" agenda was not even "culture" per se, but groups that could be marshaled by some form of ascriptive identity. The invocation of "multiculturalism" reflected the deeper liberal animus against culture *qua* tradition and inheritance.

This fact was well noted by the political theorist Wilson Carey McWilliams, who wrote as early as 1983,

Notably, the groups that [liberal reformers] recognize are all defined by *biology*. In liberal theory, where our "nature" means our bodies, these are "natural" groups opposed to "artificial" bonds like communities of work and culture. This does not mean that liberalism values these "natural" groups. Quite the contrary: since liberal political society reflects the effort to overcome or master nature, liberalism argues that "merely natural" differences ought not to be held against us. We ought not to be held back by qualities we did not choose and that do not reflect our individual efforts and abilities. [Reformers] recognize women, racial minorities, and the young only in order to free individuals from "suspect classifications."

Class and culture are different. People are part of ethnic communities or the working class because they chose not to pursue individual success and assimilation into the dominant, middle-class culture, or because they were unable to succeed. Liberal theory values individuals who go their own way, and by the same token, it esteems those who succeed in that quest more highly than individuals who do not. Ethnicity and class, consequently, are marks of shame in liberal theory, and whatever discrimination people suffer is, in some sense, their "own fault." We may feel compassion for the failures, but they have no just cause for equal representation, unlike individuals who suffer discrimination for "no fault of their own."[9]

All along, the claims of late twentieth-century multiculturalists were fundamentally shaped by deeper liberal presuppositions. Indeed, it was only at the point at which "culture"—above all as a social fact—had been so weakened in the American tradition that a faux form of culture could lay claim to its language. There was little fundamental commitment to culture per se, and rather a deeper commitment to entering the liberal narrative in which the inheritance of various cultures was ultimately evacuated by autonomous choosing individuals.[10]

Elshtain *could* have called out this faux multiculturalism for what it was. She might have articulated a defense of culture and community that resisted liberal theory *all the way down*, both in its "multicultural" manifestation and in its nationalist guise (these two being in fact only *apparently* in opposition). She was among the only authors during that period who had consistently defended a wide swath of cultural institutions, and understood more deeply than most the threat posed to such institutions by the realization of the liberal anthropology and political system. Instead, like Schlesinger and Bloom, she invoked and defended a shared membership within *democracy*—that is, liberal democracy—as the standard around which we could rally. At the same time, the liberal philosophy, politics, and economic system by which and to which the nation had been formed worked assiduously to weaken and even demolish the very forms of membership and belonging that Elshtain otherwise praised and defended as essential to the continued viability of liberal democracy. Liberalism was thus all along living off of a premodern, nonliberal inheritance that it could not replenish and even increasingly began hostilely to dismantle. Rather than consistently articulating a defense of human membership that robustly revealed the destructive tendencies of the liberal philosophy of the nation, she invoked our common membership in a "democratic culture" and even echoed Bloom's ideal of education that "liberated" students from their local partialities and inheritance.[11]

What's more, Elshtain gamely attempted to differentiate "good" from "bad" liberalism. In the 1994 essay "Catholic Social Thought, the City, and Liberal America," Elshtain differentiated her understanding of defensible liberalism from a corrosive and self-defeating alternative—what she calls "ultra-liberalism." By her telling, "ultra-liberalism" is based upon a particular definition of the "self." According to Elshtain, "ultra-liberalism's vision of self flows from seventeenth-century contractarian discourse, a doctrine linked to the names of Hobbes and Locke. . . . Contractarianism of an atomistic sort posits the self as a given prior to any social order—ahistorical, unsituated, a bearer of abstract rights, an untrammeled chooser in whose choices lie his freedom and autonomy."[12] Even in contrasting this understanding to a more defensible version of "liberalism," Elshtain never clarified what that alternative version of the "liberal" (vs. "ultra-liberal") self might be. When, in fact, she seeks to articulate an alternative to what she calls "ultra-liberalism," she resorts not to the liberal tradition that purports to serve as an alternative, but instead to Catholic social teaching, a tradition that rests on a pre-, non-, and even antiliberal conception of the human person.

Evoking the Catholic social teaching that begins in the nineteenth century with the encyclicals of Pope Leo XIII and continues through Pope Benedict XVI's *Caritas in veritate*, Elshtain states that human persons "are woven into a concept of community that envisions the person as a part, a sacred part, of the whole. Rights exist within and are relative to a historical and social context and are intelligible only in terms of the obligations of individuals to other persons. . . . [Catholic social teaching] begins from a fundamentally different ontology from that assumed and required by individualism, on the one hand, and statist collectivism on the other."[13] When resorting to an appeal to a distinct and competing ontology to that of "ultra-liberalism," Elshtain turns to the pre- and nonliberal tradition of Catholic social thought, and not its purported alternative of "liberalism." For, finally, liberalism of all varieties contains at its core some version of the autonomous choosing individual that stands in contradiction to the long Aristotelian and Catholic tradition that preceded it and that it explicitly rejected and sought to overturn. Elshtain clearly hopes to hold together a commitment to the political theory of liberalism with the preliberal inheritance of memberships and practices found in civil society, but gathering evidence suggests that this combination was temporary at best, and that today the logic of liberalism's emphasis upon individual liberation from all arbitrary bonds is finally evacuating the preliberal practices that Elshtain had long and correctly argued sustained liberalism itself.

By the time Elshtain was writing *Democracy on Trial* in the early to mid-1990s, it was increasingly evident that the memberships and commitments within family, community, church, and even nation were waning. State and market equally acted as a solvent upon all lasting human relationships and institutions of civil society. The trajectory and logic of liberalism's "liberation" of the individual from all nonchosen and arbitrary memberships was becoming increasingly evident. Few voices were raised in full-throated warning about the links between the logic of the liberal tradition and the accumulation of these dissolutions— certainly not "multiculturalists" and, in most cases, not those who urged a renewed devotion to the "American Creed." Among the very few was the historian and social critic Christopher Lasch, whose 1991 book, *The True and Only Heaven* (published shortly before *Democracy on Trial*), laid down a blanket condemnation of the liberal tradition and attempted to delineate an alternative American tradition based upon a populist and antiprogressive defense of political and economic localism that rejected liberal ontology.[14] Although Elshtain fiercely and loyally admired and defended Lasch's work, she was never able to fully endorse his more radical—and ultimately more coherent—critique. Rather, she sought to defend an unraveling and, what is all the more clear today, an indefensible American Consensus, tragically by invoking creedal allegiance to the underlying Lockean philosophy of that consensus that she believed could be reconciled to her defense of the remnant institutions of civil society. It was as if to put out the flames that she grabbed the nearest bucket—but its contents proved to be yet more flammables. Today, amid the ashes, one can admire Elshtain's valiant efforts, but not without some sadness and regret.

NOTES

1. Louis Hartz, *The Liberal Tradition in America: An Interpretation of American Political Thought since the Revolution* (New York: Harcourt, Brace, 1955).

2. Locke, *Two Treatises on Government*, ed. Peter Laslett (New York: Cambridge University Press, 1988), 303.

3. Ibid., 307 (Locke's emphasis).

4. Ibid., 315 (Locke's emphasis).

5. Arthur M. Schlesinger, Jr., *The Vital Center: The Politics of Freedom* (New Brunswick, NJ: Transaction, 1997).

6. Arthur M. Schlesinger, Jr., *The Disuniting of America: Reflections on a Multicultural Society* (New York: W. W. Norton, 1992), 39.

7. Allan Bloom, *The Closing of the American Mind* (New York: Simon & Schuster, 1987), 27.

8. Schlesinger, *Disuniting of America*, 45 (the phrase is originally that of James Bryce, cited approvingly by Schlesinger); Bloom, *Closing of the American Mind*, 42–43. See also Patrick Deneen, "Strange Bedfellows: Allan Bloom and John Dewey against Liberal Education, Rightly Understood," *The Good Society* 17, no. 2 (2008): 49–55. Schlesinger's fear of loss of national commitment was long-standing. Consider, for instance, the following passage first published in 1960: "At bottom, perhaps, we are seeking a new articulation of our national values in the belief that this will bring about a new effectiveness in our national

action. For national purpose is not something that is enshrined in monuments or preserved in historic documents. It acquires meaning as part of an ongoing process; its certification lies not in rhetoric but in performance. The values of the '50's have been, to a great degree, self-indulgent values. People have been largely absorbed in themselves—in their own careers, their own lives, their own interests. We tend to cover up our self-absorption by saying that what is good for our own interests is good for the country; but this is a gesture of piety"; Arthur M. Schlesinger, Jr., "A New Mood in Politics," in *The Politics of Hope* (New York: Houghton Mifflin, 1963), 82–83.

9. Carey McWilliams, "Politics," *American Quarterly* 35 (Spring/Summer 1983): 27.

10. I take this portion of an interview with the Georgetown University NAACP president, Carolyn Chambers, to be more frank and unguarded in its admissions than one typically hears from her elders:

Q: What do you think is the most prominent issue facing minority students in the United States of America?
A: Economic empowerment is the largest issue facing the people represented by the NAACP. For minorities, the issue of finding a job that pays enough income to support a family and suitable lifestyle has been a struggle not only decades in the making, but centuries, maybe even millennia. I feel like economic empowerment can manifest itself in different ways. It can be thought of in terms of the environment in which people grow up, such as the young children who grew up in weak neighborhoods that don't have good schools, or in terms of education, stretching from kindergarten all the way to college. *I feel [that] money and the lack of it, as well as the lack of opportunity to participate in our consumerist, capitalist society and economy, proves difficult* [my emphasis]. For many minorities, they find that they're not located on the same playing field as the rest of the nation. (Stephen Levy, "GU NAACP President Discusses Diversity Issues," *The Hoya*, October 19, 2010, http://www.thehoya.com/gu-naacp-president-discusses-diversity-issues/#)

11. See Elshtain, "Democracy's Middle Way," in *Real Politics*, 362–71. Elshtain approvingly cites Michael Oakeshott's following description of the aim of education: "School and university are places apart where a declared learner is emancipated from the limitations of his local circumstances and from the wants he may happen to have acquired, and is moved by intimations of what he has never yet dreamed. He finds himself invited to pursue satisfactions he has never yet imagined or wished for. They are, then, sheltered places where excellences may be heard because the din of local partialities is no more than a distant rumble" (*RP*, 366).

12. Elshtain, "Catholic Social Thought, the City, and Liberal America," in *Catholicism and Liberalism*, ed. R. Bruce Douglass and David Hollenbach (New York: Cambridge University Press, 1994), 154.

13. Ibid., 16.

14. Christopher Lasch, *The True and Only Heaven: Progress and Its Critics* (New York: W. W. Norton, 1991).

CHAPTER NINETEEN

THE LIMITS OF POLITICS AND THE INEVITABILITY OF ETHICS

Robin W. Lovin

Jean Elshtain explained politics by calling attention to its limits. In that, her way of thinking is biblical, even prophetic. Like the plumb line in the ancient vision of divine righteousness (Amos 7:7), Elshtain's writings measure policy against a standard that cannot be easily satisfied. Categories of gender, race, or ability that make political choices too easy are called into question by a higher standard of justice. So, too, are utopian schemes that promise more than politics or human nature can deliver.

But it is easy to confuse prophetic judgment with a stance that discerns limits by standing outside of politics, or beyond it. Biblical prophets understood all too well that they were also under the judgment they proclaimed, but there is a tendency today to see theology as an *antipolitics*, withdrawing legitimacy from political power, or withdrawing from society into a sectarian community that lives out of its own moral resources. Elshtain, by contrast, called attention to the limits of politics from within. She was as aware of what politics is *for* as of what it cannot do. She reminded us that politics is limited, but inevitable.

This, too, is biblical, though it belongs to a different tradition of Christian wisdom, one that was deeply influenced by Greek philosophy.

That influence began already with the use of Stoic and Neoplatonic ideas in Hellenistic Judaism, as in the eighth chapter of the book of Wisdom of Solomon, which praises the wisdom of Israel's God in terms that recall the Platonic virtues of courage, prudence, temperance, and justice.

For Elshtain, and for the rest of us, this way of thinking about the limits of politics is mediated through Augustine. On this point, the Christian bishop of Hippo remained a Platonist, as did almost every other educated person of his time. To be sure, Augustine saw the limits of politics differently from other philosophers, whose errors he catalogued in the *City of God*, because he had a different, more biblical view of human possibilities. But he organized his thinking about those possibilities in ways that were fundamentally Greek. For Plato, it is the limits of politics that make it intelligible. Politics has limits because it is a definite sphere of human action. Some things belong to it and others do not. Like anything else in this sublunary sphere of time and space, politics has a purpose that can be known when we recognize the limits that separate what it is from what it is not.

Because that way of thinking is now unfamiliar to us, many Christians find it hard to grasp Augustine's view of politics, and Elshtain's. What we remember from Augustine is his eschatological division of the world into the city of God, which loves God to the point of contempt for self, and the human city, which loves self to the point of contempt for God. We find it easier to grasp that sectarianism than a compromised, limited, and temporary peace, which is where Augustine's tale of two cities ends during the time of this earthly life.[1]

But it is our politics that is sectarian, not Augustine's. He may, in fact, have been the greatest Christian realist, as Reinhold Niebuhr saw him.[2] Augustine understood self-interest and power as only someone who has lived near the center of power in the waning days of a great empire can understand them. But he could not recoil from power, or simply withdraw from it, because it was integral to his idea of human nature. That is just the way his Platonic view of reality was organized. Power is potentiality. It aims at something, whether the one who possesses that power knows what that something is or not. Indeed, it may be that power is not something that can be possessed. To understand the realism of this Christian Platonist, we may have to think of power as something that possesses us.

Let us consider, then, the limits of politics from a point of view alien to us, but one that shaped Augustine's thought. Once we grasp what is different about this view, we will be in a better position to understand Elshtain's Augustinian politics and better able to see why she offers an alternative to the contemporary theological disillusionment with politics.

POLITICS AND THE GOOD

To understand Augustine, it helps to contrast him with Aristotle, who says, "Every art and every inquiry, and similarly every action and pursuit, is thought to aim at some good."[3] Despite the speculations of Clement of Alexandria, Plato and Aristotle probably had *not* read Moses or the Hebrew prophets, and the limits of their politics are not set by the eschatological judgment that is always on the horizon of Augustine's thought. Aristotle's politics emerges out of ethics. If it has limits, these lie in the intelligence and the virtue of the people making the decisions. For Aristotle, at least, those limits were fairly elastic, subject to almost infinite expansion by diligence and good training. We should not expect too much from the politics of young people, he warns us at the beginning of the *Ethics*, but when we get to the *megalopsychos*, the great-souled man of book 4, who takes an appropriate pride in himself, walks with a slow gait, and speaks in a deep voice, there is little we cannot expect from his thoughtful weighing of the public good.[4]

We may wonder about the elasticity of these limits to Aristotle's politics, and we may certainly question the confidence of class and gender that shaped his expectations. But it is important to get beyond Aristotle's estimate of human capabilities, which Augustine doubted, to see the purpose of Aristotelian politics, which Augustine largely shared. We will not understand Augustine's politics unless we see that the Greek idea of politics with which he began is through and through teleological. It aims at knowable goods that rational people can identify and set in order in relationship to one another. If they will think about it, people can determine which goods they ought to be pursuing now and how they are most likely to achieve them. The process of rational deliberation is a reliable way to get to those truths, though you are more likely to make the right choices if you have practiced them until they become habitual. Those habits we call virtues.

This teleology is the way the human mind naturally works, Aristotle believed. Everybody thinks about pursuing goods in this way in personal life. Politics is just the way they organize themselves to make good choices and develop virtues in groups. That was really what Aristotle meant when he said that human beings are political animals. It is not that we think like politicians, nor even that we live in cities, but that we are by nature designed to think teleologically, not only for our lives as individuals but also for our life together.

The development of this idea of politics marked a dramatic break with traditional societies in which the social order ensured customary ways of life and enforced existing patterns of authority. As Robert Bellah suggests, both the Hebrew prophets and the Greek philosophers introduced ways of critical thinking about traditional societies that marked an axial transformation in human social understanding.[5] So, too, did the Chinese sages and the Brahmin philosophers of ancient India. But each of these ways of making the axial transition was different, and the Western political world is largely a product of the way that Augustine and other early Christian thinkers reconciled the teleological politics of the Greeks and the prophetic politics of Israel.

Augustine probably did not read much Aristotle, and certainly not much of the *Politics*. He did not like reading Greek, and the parts of Aristotle's logic that reached him in Latin struck him, as they may strike us, as a bit pedantic.[6] But Augustine did not reject the teleological politics that we see in Aristotle. Indeed, it is hard to see how he could have done so, since the idea of an ordered system of goods provided the framework in which he understood divine creation. The intellectual process by which the human intellect identifies goods and orders them in relation to one another works because it mirrors God's ordering of creation. Everything that exists is good insofar as it is related to God the creator, and that goodness, however distant or diminished, displays the purpose through which the thing may be known as it truly is and be used as it ought to be used.

In this fundamental sense, then, persons were to Augustine's way of thinking as much political animals as Aristotle ever conceived them to be. In a way, indeed, they were more so; for the goods explicitly considered in Aristotle's politics were a rather narrow range of honors and virtues appropriate, as Aristotle himself recognized, only to a select group of free adult males who had the opportunity, resources, and leisure to pursue them. These were the goods appropriate to human beings as such, as Aristotle saw it, in contrast to the goods of trades, crafts, and domestic life, which were pursued for the most part unreflectively by ordinary people who could not expect to know the higher goods available to the man of action, or the man of contemplation.

Augustine's system of goods, by contrast, encompassed the whole of creation, and everything in the system was so dependent on the value that it had in relation to God that it could not easily be divided up into different kinds of goods for different kinds of people. The weakest, poorest, and most dependent person could nonetheless aspire to know and love God, and in order to do that, he or she had to learn how to use the things that were at hand for the purpose. What Aristotle would call politics is for Augustine inevitable whenever these goods, however simple, are shared by others and became common objects of love.[7]

In one important way, Augustine's politics was even less limited than Aristotle's, since for Augustine knowledge of the good could not be confined to a single group, social class, or place. Like the Stoics before him, Augustine conceived the political animal as a *cosmopolitan*, whose city— that is to say, whose politics—could be put into practice anywhere.

The limits were not in the access, but in the expectations. For although the ordered goods that we might seek together are present everywhere and available to everyone, we fail in our seeking them more often than Aristotle expected that we would. That is not because we are unlucky or unwise, but because we refuse the good we say we want. We love the things we ought to use and try to use the one thing that we ought to love. We reject the love of God because we fear that it will disrupt our love of self. We grasp for ourselves the things that we ought to love in common, preferring to hold onto them as though they were intended as good for me alone. Even in Aristotle's world, the tragedians and the Stoics thought that the kind of goodness Aristotle hoped to achieve was rather more fragile than he understood.[8] But for Augustine, the limits of politics appear not in the fragility of our achievements, but in our neglect of and contempt for the good we ought to be realizing in action. We recognize little of what we would need to know to seek the good together, and even when we see it, we often refuse it.[9]

ETHICS AND TIME

Augustine integrated this refusal, too, into his understanding of the ordered goodness of God's creation, identifying it with the willful rejection of God's commandment that ended the easy and natural relationship between persons and the human good and turned the good into an object of search and struggle (Gen. 3). I have always thought that having to do ethics is in some way part of the biblical curse that condemned Adam to get his bread by the sweat of his brow. There is a large body of theological literature that speculates on whether we would have had government, property, or marriage if Adam had not fallen. But it is pretty clear that ethics and politics, even Aristotle's teleological politics, are postlapsarian disciplines. If there had been ethics before the Fall, it would have been like the contemplative life in book 10 of Aristotle's *Ethics*. This business of using reason to figure out what the good is and then organizing ourselves and our society to realize it is just too much work to be part of anybody's idea of paradise, even when it turns out right.

And for Augustine, of course, the point is that it does not turn out right. It is in that failure that we can begin to identify the limits of politics in Augustine's thought in ways that may be relevant to thinking about theology and the limits of politics today. The clearest limit, and the one about which Augustine is most explicit in the *City of God*, is that politics has not delivered the true commonwealth.[10] If we take seriously the idea of a teleological politics and combine it with Augustine's notion of creation as an ordered system in which God is the highest good, we would expect politics eventually to produce a people united in worship of the one true God. It is probably the best evidence that Augustine's politics finally is teleological in the way described here that this is the definition that he offers of a "true" commonwealth, though of course he immediately says that politics as fallen human beings practice it has not yielded the expected result.

Indeed, it never will, within the limits of history and nature as we know it. We do not fail because we are unlucky enough to live in interesting times. We do not fail because there are some people who need watching lest they mess it up for the rest of us. We do not need to wait for a socialist revolution, enact a universal declaration of human rights, or set the markets free to allocate our resources with maximum efficiency. Next time will not be different. We will not get it right in such a way that it stays right, not in any place or any future that is recognizably part of the same world of time, and space, and history in which we are now living. That is the fundamental limit of politics, and it is the result of our fallen human nature, rather than of any particular shortcomings in ourselves or in other people.

It is for this reason that the question "who are we?" is a fundamental political question, at least in the way that Elshtain asks it in her book by that name (*Who Are We?*). Augustine tried to answer that question in the broadest possible terms. He was not interested in answers that separated Romans from barbarians, the rich from the poor, or the educated from the uneducated. He was not even particularly interested in answers that separated Christians from pagans, for though the distinction between the city of God and the earthly city is ultimately of great interest, we cannot be sure, in the time frame that is relevant to politics, who belongs to which city. Any answer that allows us to distinguish one group of people from another tempts us to think that we could solve the problems of politics by changing or eliminating somebody who is not us. We can discern the limits of the possible only by thinking about human nature in the broadest terms, so that whatever the problem is, we are always part of it. The limits of politics are written into our human nature. That is why Augustine does not expect the limits to go away. He warns us against expecting that we will be able to transform the earthly city into the city of God.

But neither does he say next what we might then expect him to say. He does not say, "The world of human society is a fragmented and violent place, where there are no goods worth having. You should turn away from it as quickly as possible to the true commonwealth of the Heavenly City, which is the only place where you may expect to enjoy any good." Instead, he says that there is a good to be sought in human society, and he even encourages Christians to seek it at some cost to themselves. That good is peace, which all people are united in wanting, even when they go to war, and even when their political talents extend no further than coordinating the efforts of a band of thieves.[11] In a true commonwealth, of course, peace would be lasting because love would be united on an object that would not change and could not be lost. That is not the kind of peace to which Augustine thinks the human society he sees about him can aspire. But our politics can produce a peace "for the time being," in which people are united in the sharing of limited goods, sustained by a shared effort that, for the moment, overcomes their skepticism about each other's motives.

It is a disputed point in the interpretation of Augustine's politics, but I do not think he believes that this peace for the time being has to be imposed by force. Given the level of coercion that characterized the Roman Empire, even at its most stable, and the level of violence that characterized Augustine's own turbulent times, it would hardly be surprising if he did believe that. But I think he believes nonetheless that people living together are capable of arriving at a minimal but sufficient agreement on the good out of their own knowledge and virtue, however inadequate these might be when measured against the requirements of a true commonwealth. An imposed peace is sometimes necessary, but it is important to see that in the framework of Augustine's thought as a whole, an imposed peace is a failure of politics. Contrary to what some later Christians have thought, coercion is not the essence of Augustine's politics, though it cannot be altogether dispensed with, either.

Rather, politics is what happens when people who know something of what the good is actually manage to achieve that limited good together. Such goods are always transitory. Changing conditions and changing coalitions eventually break the peace for the time being, and politics has to start over again, with no assurance that peace will be restored anytime soon. But the limited goods peace creates are real goods, and human beings are oriented by nature to pursue them.

TELEOLOGY IN THE MODERN WORLD

Such is Augustine's version of the possibilities and limits of the teleological politics that Greek philosophy bequeathed to the world of late antiquity and early Christianity. Augustine's place in that world was sufficiently important that it would be worthwhile to study his politics if only to understand how he influenced his contemporaries. But it is also worth asking whether Augustine's teleological politics can be of any use to us today. From the beginning of the modern period, the predominant answer to that question has been no. Augustine may have been a great theologian, or a great rhetorician, even a great statesman in the conflicts that beset the declining Roman Empire, but his ideas about politics have little application to the modern world. Modern political thought, in its various forms, seems united on the verdict that a teleological politics is impossible or unnecessary.

Hobbes began by proclaiming it impossible, for there is, he said, "no such *Finis ultimis* (utmost ayme [aim],) . . . as is spoken of in the Books of the old Morall Philosophers."[12] People with different interests and goals simply do not have enough in common in the ways that they use moral language for us to suppose that there are any real goods behind the words that they use. Those who hope for peace had better settle on a referee who will fix the meaning of the terms they use when they speak of what is good, right, and natural. Otherwise they will necessarily come to blows for want of any common measure by which to adjudicate the questions on which they are contending.

Of course, this referee is not qualified by any special moral knowledge, as there is none to be had. The referee is qualified only by the agreement that the parties will abide by his decision. Hobbes begins with what seems to be an analogy to two parties in a dispute over accounts, but the implications for political disputes on a larger scale are clear enough: those who expect to live in peace together need a sovereign over them, and the price of peace is the surrender of all their rights to that sovereign.

These terms may seem harsh. Others, notably Locke, tried to secure a space for rights and property in a state of nature, but the idea persisted that decisions that are meant to bind different individuals living together in society must rest on authority, rather than on truth. The convenient analogy to a personal sovereign who could decide between contending parties when they could not agree was elaborated into the idea of the sovereign state, which could establish a framework of law that would provide the only terms relevant to the settlement of disputes that came to the attention of the sovereign authority. People can argue all they want morally, or theologically, or aesthetically. They can declaim day and night about the requirements of nature and nature's God, but the legitimacy to enforce a resolution of the question lies with the sovereign authority that sets the terms on which the question will be decided. The other arguments may be interesting, but they are politically irrelevant.

Elshtain traced this Hobbesian transformation development in more detail than I can provide here in her *Sovereignty* (*S*, 104–17), but the main point for present purposes is that Hobbes finds it unbelievable that there is a common meaning to moral terms that people could know and use to guide their political decisions together. The problem is not only that human knowledge of the good is diminished by sin and by human unwillingness to do what the good requires. Christian moralists in the West had insisted on that since the time of Augustine. Hobbes's claim is that it is just impossible that moral terms could have any common meaning beyond that supplied by the shaky authority of unthinking repetition. In any real dispute, the meaning of the moral terms dissolves. Teleological politics becomes impossible.

Something further developed as market economics took on the role of making the social decisions that once were seen as moral choices. For it does not much matter that people want different goods if the sum of them can be maximized, and the differences between them become irrelevant as long as there is a common standard against which they can all be measured. Money will do nicely for the purpose, in fact. You do not have to decide which goods are important enough that we need to secure them in common, as long as we know what people are willing to pay to have them. The literature recognizes some problems around the edges with this approach—free riders, distributive justice, interpersonal comparisons of utility, and so forth—but the political salience of market economics as a solution to the problems of social choice is clear.

Teleological politics, which at the beginning of the modern era seemed impossible, now appears to be unnecessary.

There is a narrative that explains this displacement of teleological politics by the sovereign state and the rational market. It centers on the idea that the modern world began with the discovery of the risks involved in letting people argue about the good in public. In this narrative, the sovereign state and the rule of law, and also the separation of church and state, begin with Europe's recoil from the horrors of the wars of religion. Having seen the violence that claims to the good could do, philosophers set about to eliminate them, or at least eliminate them from public life. What we learned, as the age of Reformation gave way to the age of Enlightenment, is that teleological politics tends to enforce its views about the good on those who do not share them. Those who think they know the truth are apt to become violent. For Christopher Hitchens, this is one of the main ways that religion spoils everything.[13]

The problem with this narrative is that it seems to be a late arrival that says more about what modern, secular people think the wars of religion must have been about than what was really going on in the sixteenth and seventeenth centuries. Those who lived through them seem to have been pretty astute about the mixture of faith and interests that shaped events. Hobbes wanted to stop people from fighting about religion, but he may well have thought that the roots of the problem lay in epistemology rather than in religious commitments. Locke wanted to prevent conflict, too, but he thought that people were more likely to fight about property than about religion. Among the numerous causes of violence known in Europe and its growing empires at the time, few would have singled out pursuit of the good in politics as the root of all evils. And even if the prevailing narrative has it right about the origins of modern politics, it hardly accounts for the pursuit of unlimited politics by sovereign states or expanding markets.

Is Augustine's teleological politics at all relevant to our political problems? After all the attempts to make ethics impossible or unnecessary to politics, we may be rediscovering that we are indeed political animals in Aristotle's sense, with Augustine's qualifications: we seek the good in politics because we seek the good for ourselves, and we cannot secure what we seek, or even know for sure what it is we are seeking, without the cooperation of those who share this world with us. We are teleological by nature, but we are also reflective. Our pursuit of the good shows us how little we really know about it, and our chief commitments are to what Elshtain calls, in *Augustine and the Limits of Politics*, "our work in small ways and about small things," which "contributes to the overall harshness or decency of any social order" (*ALP*, 96). These achievements are the results of compromise and second thoughts and partial successes, and we know that the good we do depends on those compromises with the wills of other people and with our own ignorance. We learn in experience to be satisfied with that. Only those who have little or no experience of real politics feel what John Rawls called "zeal to embody the whole truth in politics."[14] We seek peace—limited goods of limited duration, achieved by compromises that only partly solve the problems, put in place by decisions that will have to be made over again, if not by us, then by those who come after us.

We undertake this difficult task because we know that the things we seek are genuine goods; not just interests or preferences, but constituents of a good life for ourselves and for anyone else who enjoys them with us. There is a place for this kind of politics, if we can reclaim that space from the sovereigns and the makers of markets. It is important that we do reclaim it, for though we hope to realize a larger good in more complete ways in the city of God, for the time of this life, it is this peace that makes us human.

NOTES

1. Augustine sharply distinguished the earthly city from the heavenly city, but he reminded his readers that in this life, the two are mixed up together, so that the people of God share the earthly city's interest in "the temporal peace which is shared for the time being by the good and the wicked alike"; Augustine, *The City of God against the Pagans*, trans. R. W. Dyson (Cambridge: Cambridge University Press, 1998), 962.

2. Reinhold Niebuhr, *Christian Realism and Political Problems* (New York: Charles Scribner's Sons, 1953), 145–46.

3. Aristotle, *Nicomachean Ethics*, trans. David Ross (Oxford: Oxford University Press, 2009), 3.

4. Ibid., 4–5, 67–70.

5. Robert Bellah, *Religion in Human Evolution: From the Paleolithic to the Axial Age* (Cambridge, MA: Harvard University Press, 2011), 265–398.

6. Augustine, *Confessions*, trans. Henry Chadwick (Oxford: Oxford University Press, 1998), 68.

7. Oliver O'Donovan, *Common Objects of Love: Moral Reflection and the Shaping of Community* (Grand Rapids, MI: Eerdmans, 2002).

8. Martha Nussbaum, *The Fragility of Goodness: Luck and Ethics in Greek Tragedy and Philosophy*, rev. ed. (Cambridge: Cambridge University Press, 2001).

9. Augustine, *Confessions*, 184.

10. Augustine, *City of God*, 950–61.

11. Ibid., 934.

12. Thomas Hobbes, *Leviathan* (Cambridge: Cambridge University Press, 1991), 70.

13. Christopher Hitchens, *God Is Not Great: How Religion Poisons Everything* (New York: Hachette, 2007), 15–36.

14. John Rawls, *Collected Papers*, ed. Samuel Freeman (Cambridge, MA: Harvard University Press, 1999), 574.

CONTRIBUTORS

Peter Berkowitz, Tad and Dianne Taube Senior Fellow, Hoover Institution at Stanford University.

Nigel Biggar, Regius Professor of Moral and Pastoral Theology; Director of the McDonald Centre for Theology, Ethics and Public Life, at the University of Oxford; and Canon of Christ Church, Oxford.

Chris Brown, Emeritus Professor of International Relations at the London School of Economics and Political Science.

Don Browning (January 13, 1934–June 3, 2010), Alexander Campbell Professor Emeritus of Ethics and the Social Sciences at the University of Chicago Divinity School.

Lisa Sowle Cahill, J. Donald Monan, S.J., Professor at Boston College.

John D. Carlson, Associate Professor of Religious Studies; and Associate Director of the Center for the Study of Religion and Conflict at Arizona State University.

Patrick J. Deneen, David A. Potenziani Memorial Associate Professor of Constitutional Studies at the University of Notre Dame.

Debra Erickson, Instructor of Philosophy at Bloomsburg University.

Francis Fukuyama, Olivier Nomellini Senior Fellow; the Mosbacher Director of the Center on Democracy, Development, and the Rule of Law at the Freeman Spogli Institute for International Studies; and Professor of Politics at Stanford University.

William A. Galston, Senior Fellow, Governance Studies and the Ezra K. Zilkha Chair in Governance Studies at the Brookings Institution; and College Park Professor at the University of Maryland.

Carl Gershman, President, National Endowment for Democracy.

Eric Gregory, Professor of Religion and Chair, Council of the Humanities, at Princeton University.

Nancy J. Hirschmann, Professor of Political Science; Director, Program on Gender, Sexuality, and Women's Studies; and Director, Alice Paul

Center for Research on Gender, Sexuality, and Women at the University of Pennsylvania.

James Turner Johnson, Distinguished Professor Emeritus of Religion at Rutgers University.

Michael Kessler, Managing Director, Berkley Center for Religion, Peace, and World Affairs; Associate Professor of the Practice of Moral and Political Theory, Department of Government at Georgetown University; and Adjunct Professor of Law at Georgetown University Law Center.

Michael Le Chevallier, Ph.D. Candidate at University of Chicago Divinity School.

Marc LiVecche, Scholar of Christian Ethics, War, and Peace; and Managing Editor, *Providence: A Journal of Christianity & American Foreign Policy*, at the Institute for Religion and Democracy.

Robin W. Lovin, Visiting Scholar in Theology at Loyola University Chicago; and Cary Maguire University Professor of Ethics Emeritus at Southern Methodist University.

Gilbert Meilaender, Professor Emeritus at Valparaiso University.

Erik Owens, Associate Director of the Boisi Center; and Associate Professor of the Practice in Theology and International Studies at Boston College.

Daniel Philpott, Professor of Political Science at the University of Notre Dame.

Nicholas Rengger, Professor of Political Theory and International Relations at the University of St. Andrews.

Arlene W. Saxonhouse, Caroline Robbins Collegiate Professor of Political Science and Women's Studies at the University of Michigan.

Michael Walzer, Professor Emeritus, School of Social Science at the Institute for Advanced Study.

INDEX

abortion, 133–34, 217
absolute sovereignty, Elshtain's antidote to, 191–92
ADA (Americans with Disabilities
  Act) and ADA Amendments Act
  (ADAAA), 115–17, 120–21
Addams, Jane
  American Creed and, 358
  Beautiful Soul trope and, 234, 246
  on disability, 119, 120
  ends of political life and, 314
  on "family claim" and "social
    claim," 237
  feminism and, 43, 108, 235
  Hull-House and, 3, 15
  influence on Elshtain, 11, 67
  *Jane Addams and the Dream of
    American Democracy* (Elshtain,
    2002), 15–16, 107–9, 358
  just war theory and, 286
  on power of human agency in
    shaping world, 118
  social feminism of Elshtain and,
    43
  urban associational life and, 318
Affordable Care Act, 105
Afghanistan, war in, 17, 156, 159, 201,
  232, 246, 247, 258, 259, 260
African American community,
  322–23

Aid to Families with Dependent
  Children program, 318
al-Qaeda, 17, 156, 246, 266, 267, 270,
  272, 273, 280
Althusius, 80
American Creed, 316, 355, 358–59,
  363
Americans with Disabilities Act
  (ADA), 115–17, 120–21
Anastasius (Roman emperor), letter
  of Gelasius to, 303–7
Antigone, Elshtain's reading of, 34, 44,
  45, 48–50
apathy and apathy theory, 54–57,
  106–7
Aquinas. *See* Thomas Aquinas and
  Thomism
Arab Spring, 343, 344
Arendt, Hannah, 17, 18, 20, 23, 152,
  180, 222, 314
  The Human Condition, 56, 58, 59
Argentinian "Mothers of the Disap-
    peared," 9–10, 17, 43, 44, 334
Aristotle and Aristotelianism, 47, 58,
  71, 75, 80, 198, 316, 363, 369–73,
  377
  History of Animals, 65
  Nicomachean Ethics, 369, 372
  Politics, 370
Arnhart, Larry, 80

on French Revolution and freedom, 87–90
on India, 86, 87–88, 90, 95–98, 99
on Ireland and Catholic Irish, 86,
87–88, 90, 94–95, 96, 98, 99
on moderation and liberty, 84–85,
98–102
*Reflections on the Revolution in
France*, 86, 87, 89, 99
on representation, liberty, and
reform, 90–98
"Speech at Guildhall," 94
"Speech on Conciliation with
America," 91
"Speech on Fox's East India Bill,"
95, 96, 97
Burke, Jane, 94
Burke, Richard, 94
Bush, George H. W., 254, 264n29
Bush, George W., 154, 201, 231–32,
254, 258, 267–69, 270, 282n2,
283n10
Butler, Joseph, 154

Cahill, Lisa Sowle, 22, 127
Callipolis, 58, 62–63
Calvin, John, 1, 143, 290, 295
Cameron, Euan, 195–96
Camus, Albert
ends of political life and, 314
on fact of human nature, 137
influence on Elshtain, 17, 18, 20,
23, 127, 152, 167, 180, 192, 205
just war theory and, 209
sovereignty and, 307
The Stranger, 20
caritas, Augustine on, 128, 179, 181,
287, 290, 301
Caritas in veritate (2009; papal encyclical), 363
Caritas Internationalis, 142
Carlson, John D., 15, 207–8

Cassiodorus, 167
Catherine of Siena, 198
Catholic Peacebuilding Network
(CPN), 142, 146n2
"Catholic Social Thought, the City,
and Liberal America" (Elshtain,
1994), 362
Catholics and Catholicism
Burke, on Ireland and Catholic
Irish, 86, 87–88, 90, 94–95, 96,
98, 99
Elshtain's conversion from
Lutheranism, 7–8, 114, 162–63,
192
global infrastructure of, 142
on just war, 287–88, 290, 292
liberal individualism versus, 316
Protestant Reformation and, 94,
133, 186, 194–95, 302, 307, 377
Protestant versus Catholic con-
science, 184, 186
social teaching, Catholic, 127, 132,
144–46, 362–63
See also papacy
Cavanaugh, William T., 196
The Myth of Religious Violence, 195
Centesimus annus (1991; papal
encyclical), 143
Central Intelligence Agency (CIA),
201, 273
Chambers, Carolyn, 365n10
Chapais, Bernard, 81
Charles, J. Daryl, 212n2
Charles V (Holy Roman Emperor),
195
"chastened patriot" trope, 248–49,
255–60, 286
Chesnut, Mary Boykin, 244, 258
Chilcot Inquiry, 267
children. *See* families, marriage, and
children
Chomsky, Noam, 179

in methodological approach to political philosophy and ethics, 74–75, 81

modernization process, Elshtain on strains of, 76, 78–79

mothers in U.S. military, 245–46, 253

in *Public Man, Private Woman*, 66

social feminism of Elshtain and, 42, 82n22

Tocqueville on democracy and religion stabilizing, 338–39

working women and, 110

"Families and Trust" (Elshtain, 2000), 105

Farley, Margaret, 134, 148n24

Federalist Papers, 100, 329

feminism, 4, 13–16, 28n7

Addams, Jane, and, 43, 108, 235

Augustine and, 180–81

Beautiful Soul trope and, 233–39, 245–49

critiques of feminist theory, 38–39, 45, 60–61, 65–67, 75–77

Democracy on Trial and, 17, 335

equality or equal regard, as common human value, 138–39

extremism of, 319

Jane Addams and the Dream of American Democracy (Elshtain, 2002), 15–16, 107–9, 358

liberal feminism, 75, 76–77

Marxist feminism, 75, 76, 77

methodological approach to political and social philosophy and, 70–71, 72, 75–76

modernization process, Elshtain on strains of, 76, 78–79

ontological egalitarianism, 78

patriarchy/paternalism, 72, 76, 237, 353–54

radical feminism, 75–76, 133–34

sovereignty and, 133–34, 147n7

working women and, 110

See also families, marriage, and children; gendered analysis of war; *Public Man, Private Woman;* social feminism in Elshtain's *Public Man, Private Woman; Women and War*

"Feminist Discourse and Its Discontents: Language, Power, and Meaning" (Elshtain, 1982), 52–54

Filmer, Robert, 353

Fiorina, Morris, 328

Firestone, Shulamith, 14, 38, 76

First World War, 132, 163, 274

Fishbane, Michael, *Biblical Interpretation in Ancient Israel*, 291

Five Eyes program, 277, 283n17

Fletcher, John, 73

Foreign Policy (journal), 277, 344–45

forgiveness, 157–59

Foucault, Michel, 263n23

Francis (pope), *Laudato si'* (2015), 143, 145

Franciscan versus Dominican Middle Ages, Milbank on, 224–25

Frankena, William, 78

freedom. *See* liberty/freedom

French Huguenots, 196

French Revolution, 87–90

French versus U.S. secularism, 347

Freud, Sigmund, 20

Fukuyama, Francis, 315

The Great Disruption, 317, 330n3

Trust, 317

Gadamer, Hans-Georg, 34, 71

Gallagher, Gary W., 299–300

Galston, William A., 34

game theory, 251, 263n15

Philpott, Daniel, 128–29, 194
    *God's Century: Resurgent Religion
    and Global Politics* (with Monica
    Duffy Toft and Timothy Samuel
    Shah), 201
Pickstock, Catherine, 229n19
Pieper, Josef, 167
Piestewa, Lori, 246
Plato and Platonism, 4, 71, 181, 182,
    198, 214, 368
    Neoplatonism, 227n2, 368
    Republic, 62–63
Platonic Academy, closure of, 167
plenitudo potestatis of papacy, 304–6
pluralism, political
    Elshtain's belief in, 41
    papacy, pluralistic society's need
        for, 163, 165
pluralist Christian realism, 223
polarization and incivility, political
    culture of, 16, 85, 108–9, 121,
    145, 320, 326, 328–29, 331n17,
    332
political decision-makers, pastoral
    empathy for, 159–60
Political Studies (journal), 55
politics, 26–28, 31–35
    Augustine of Hippo, politics of,
        127, 132, 139–42, 144, 145,
        178–81, 314, 369–70, 372–73,
        375–78
    conservatism, 85, 86, 89, 99–100
    ends of political life, 313–16
    just war as, 252–55
    religion and politics, 7–8, 18–22,
        27, 32–33, 125–29, 181–82,
        191–202
    religious actors in, 142
    theological genealogy of concepts
        of, 187–88, 190n17
    Thomas Aquinas, politics of, 127,
        132, 146

See also Burke, Edmund; civil
    society; democracy; international
    relations and war; liberalism;
    limits of politics, Augustin-
    ian view of; methodological
    approach to political philosophy
    and ethics; polarization and
    incivility, political culture of;
    Sovereignty: God, State, and Self,
    and concept of sovereignty
"Politics and Forgiveness" (Elshtain,
    1999), 157–58
polyarchy, 55
the poor and poverty
    global poverty statistics, 135
    preferential option for the poor, 143
Popenoe, David, 80
Porter, Jean, 184
positive law, relativization of, 154
Posner, Richard, 73
postcolonialism, 135
postmodernism, 135, 137, 348
Power, Samantha, 235
Powers, Johnny, 109
preferential option for the poor, 143
President's Council on Bioethics, 18,
    29n23
Prisoners' Dilemma, 153
progressives and progressivism, 86,
    89, 91, 219–22, 358
Protestant Reformation, 94, 133, 186,
    194–95, 302, 307, 377
Protestant versus Catholic con-
    science, 184, 186
Provisional IRA, 281
Public Man, Private Woman (Elshtain,
    1981), 12–14, 52–68
    Augustine influencing, 63–64, 66,
        68, 81, 181
    binary of title, moving beyond,
        67–68
    biographical elements in, 2, 6

.

www.ingramcontent.com/pod-product-compliance
Lightning Source LLC
Chambersburg PA
CBHW060323100426

42812CB00003B/864